NL ARMS

Netherlands Annual Review of Military Studies

Ministry of Defence

Series Information

The series aims to create an overview of scientific research in military sciences and it shows the extent to which researchers of the Faculty of Military Sciences (FMS) of the Netherlands Defence Academy contribute to this field of expertise.

Research at the Faculty is confined to military-relevant, multi-disciplinary areas and therefore deals with issues relating, among others, to:

- Command and control in military operations
- Leadership and ethics
- Military law and history
- Operational analysis
- Navigation
- Combat systems
- Military platforms
- Cyber warfare

The series is peer-reviewed and reflects the diversity and quality of the Faculty of Military Sciences at its best. With NL ARMS the FMS hopes to serve as a trigger for more international comparative research on military sciences.

Editorial Office

F.E.J. de Pee-Vencken MA
Faculty of Military Sciences
Netherlands Defence Academy
P.O. Box 90002
4800 PA Breda
The Netherlands

More information about this series at http://www.springer.com/series/13908

Robert Beeres · Gwendolyn Bakx · Erik de Waard
Sebastiaan Rietjens
Editors

NL ARMS Netherlands Annual Review of Military Studies 2016

Organizing for Safety and Security in Military Organizations

ASSER PRESS

Springer

Editors
Robert Beeres
Faculty of Military Sciences
Netherlands Defence Academy
Breda
The Netherlands

Erik de Waard
Faculty of Military Sciences
Netherlands Defence Academy
Breda
The Netherlands

Gwendolyn Bakx
Faculty of Military Sciences
Netherlands Defence Academy
Breda
The Netherlands

Sebastiaan Rietjens
Faculty of Military Sciences
Netherlands Defence Academy
Breda
The Netherlands

ISSN 1387-8050 ISSN 2452-235X (electronic)
NL ARMS
ISBN 978-94-6265-134-0 ISBN 978-94-6265-135-7 (eBook)
DOI 10.1007/978-94-6265-135-7

Library of Congress Control Number: 2016944166

Published by T.M.C. ASSER PRESS, The Hague, The Netherlands www.asserpress.nl
Produced and distributed for T.M.C. ASSER PRESS by Springer-Verlag Berlin Heidelberg

Printed on acid-free paper

This Springer imprint is published by Springer Nature
The registered company is Springer-Verlag GmbH Berlin Heidelberg

Foreword

"In this world nothing can be said to be certain, except death and taxes." With these poetic words, Benjamin Franklin in November 1789 explained in a letter to the French scientist Jean-Baptiste Leroy, that the recently signed Constitution of the United States of America might not be so certain and final as the delegates at the Constitutional Convention in Philadelphia, 2 years earlier, may have believed. When he wrote this letter, the first amendment to the constitution had already been submitted and he was convinced that the constitution would change over time. As a true polymath, Franklin realized that 100 % certainty is seldom achieved—except for death and taxes. Five months later, Benjamin Franklin died and 2 years later the first amendment was adopted—freedom of speech and free exercise of religion from now on being part of the United States Constitution.

Achieving a society in which safety and security are 100 % guaranteed is impossible. We have to decide what risks we deem acceptable, or, alternatively, which costs we are willing to pay to achieve the highest level of safety. Such costs can be of actual monetary value, but they may also refer to less tangible commodities, such as giving up individual freedom, freedom of movement and rights to privacy. An acceptable risk level for society as a whole may therefore be difficult to comprehend at the level of a single individual. Especially for individuals who have been subject to a disruptive event, there may be little consolation in knowing that chances of that event happening were very small. This constitutes an essential dilemma in risk management: lightning only strikes occasionally and although the chances that lightning will strike twice on the same spot are even lower, this can still happen.

This book is part of the so-called Netherlands Annual Review of Military Studies (NL ARMS) series of books on military relevant themes. NL ARMS 2016 offers several multi-disciplinary views, as provided by a number of researchers from the Faculty of Military Sciences of the Netherlands Defence Academy as well as from several universities, on the theme of organizing for safety and security, in which the military plays a pivotal role. We hope you enjoy this year's contributions and we are confident that the authors would be happy to give you further information. So, please do not hesitate to contact them directly.

Prof. dr. H. Rudolph
Dean of Faculty of Military Studies
Netherlands Defence Academy
The Netherlands Ministry of Defence
h.rudolph@mindef.nl

Prof. dr. ir. Patrick J. Oonincx
Research Director
Faculty of Military Sciences
Netherlands Defence Academy
The Netherlands Ministry of Defence
pj.oonincx@mindef.nl

Contents

Chapter 1
Introduction: Organizing for Safety and Security in Military Organizations

Robert Beeres, Myriame Bollen and Erik de Waard

Abstract The introductory chapter to NL ARMS 2016 provides an overview of the multidimensional and multiverse realms of safety and security. From the images, meanings, concepts and definitions aiming to capture safety and security the military relevance of organizing to prevent, detect and react to both *accidental* (i.e., safety) as well as *malicious* (i.e., security) risks becomes apparent. In its final section, this introduction navigates across the different contributions to this volume.

Keywords Military organizations · Safety · Security · Risk · Threat · Hazard · Organizing principles

Contents

R. Beeres (✉) · M. Bollen · E. de Waard
Faculty of Military Sciences, Netherlands Defence Academy, Breda, The Netherlands
e-mail: rjm.beeres@mindef.nl

M. Bollen
e-mail: mtib.bollen.01@mindef.nl

E. de Waard
e-mail: ej.d.waard.01@mindef.nl

R. Beeres et al. (eds.), *NL ARMS Netherlands Annual Review of Military Studies 2016*, NL ARMS, DOI 10.1007/978-94-6265-135-7_1

1.1 Introduction

Deeply rooted in the character of military organizations is their constant struggle to cope with intertwined safety and security issues. For example, from a political perspective a government may decide to fight terrorism in far-off places as part of its international security policy. Consequentially, however, the countries' citizens feelings of personal safety may be put at risk because of the growing threat of terrorist attacks at home. Moreover, when, in the light of national security, it has been decided to actually deploy the military, at a more down to earth level, a combat soldier, by definition, will put his own safety at risk to perform his operational task.[1]

From the 1990s, expeditionary missions have prompted thinking on security and safety. When tasked to undertake peace operations in Afghanistan, armed forces took to designing organizations to tackle security problems at hand, whilst, simultaneously, asking themselves how to conduct their jobs in the safest possible ways. During this era, also, it transpired, many veterans suffered from posttraumatic stress disorders (PTSD) which had to be coped with and preferably prevented, so as not to cause to much individual and societal harm. Questions have arisen as to whether PTSD can be prevented by safety measures or bolstered by psychological safeguards.[2]

Apart from such quite fundamental questions and dilemmas, the tension between safety and security also materializes in other organizing aspects. With their coming of age, Western armed forces have become increasingly dependent upon advanced technology (e.g., weapon systems, information systems, communication systems, as well as the interrelatedness between these systems). Being high-tech has offered many security and safety advantages. To mention one, the use of modern technology has enabled a faster pace of deployment, but also the ability to conduct surgical strikes, while, at the same time, less human lives have to be put at risk. Yet, relying on high-tech systems carries some inherent risks as well. The most obvious one being the potential malfunctioning of all technological assets, which in itself may be the cause of casualties amongst one's own personnel and innocent bystanders.

In this respect, another interesting trend is that military operations increasingly have developed into complex collaborative efforts, consisting of people, units, and assets from different countries, arms, services, branches, and even other government

[1] Soeters et al. 2010.

[2] Zohar et al. 2009.

agencies and private contractors. As to the latter, in Afghanistan, outsourcing to private firms of hitherto military activities, such as logistics, maintenance, food catering, but also the clearing of explosive ordnance has turned into daily practice.[3]

From a security perspective, mixing the contributions of these different actors into tailor-made organizational solutions has enabled the military to conduct a wide range of formerly unconventional tasks, such as nation-building and counter-insurgency operations. Despite such advantages, coordination requirements, needed for the safe and harmonious functioning of these complex organizational constellations, are massive. Friendly fire and other safety risks are constantly lurking.[4]

Safety and security are the heart of the matter of NL ARMS 2016, and, from the above, the military relevance of organizing for safety and security becomes apparent. Moreover, next to military experiences and insights, in NL ARMS 2016 we aim to broaden our scope to encompass the ways in which other institutions, organizations and individuals in the safety and security realms are attempting to resolve today's issues as well as finding ways to overcome tensions between the two.

Before presenting the outline of NL ARMS 2016, Sects. 1.2, 1.3 and 1.4, from an associative perspective, offer the background stage to safety and security by putting forward images, meanings, concepts and definitions and in Sect. 1.5 some principles underpinning organizing for safety and security are discussed. From these sections, a picture of the multidimensional, multilevel and multiverse world of safety and security emerges providing ample space for our contributors to add to as can be seen from Sect. 1.6 the outline of the book.

1.2 Images of Safety and Security

Thinking about the concepts of safety and security puts into mind philosophical queries into the meaning of truth or the essence of time. As to the latter, Augustine, while contemplating time, is presumed to have heaved a sigh when acclaiming that as long as nobody asked him, he knew, but when asked to elaborate, he couldn't explain his answer.[5] Compounding the intricacies concerning safety and security are more in-depth questions, such as, *what is the safest place on earth?* Or else, *what is the most insecure place to be?* And even more pertinent, *could the safest haven simultaneously be conceived of as the most unsafe one, and, is it possible to consider individual actors or institutions to produce both security and insecurity at the same time?* And, if so, *how do we measure safety and security, what should be measured* and, last but not least, *who should do the measuring?*

---

[3] Van Duren 2010.

[4] Snook 2000; Mair et al. 2012.

[5] Vennix 1998, p. 1.

The answers to such questions, to a certain extent, will be dependent on one's understanding of safety and security in a given context. Therefore, first, we attempt to take stock of some images safety and security provoke. When randomly asking some people it appears the images safety and security evoke are manifold. Having recently visited Madrid, one friend brought up Picasso's Guernica, while another, who barely escaped from an accident, offered rather eloquent thoughts on the detrimental effects to traffic safety caused by cyclists wearing headphones and continually checking their phones. The image that jumped to a midshipman's mind was that of a vessel protection detachment, protecting Dutch ships from pirate attacks. A colleague confessed losing sleep at the thought of his mortgage outnumbering the actual value of his house or his bank falling prone to a cyber-attack. In the Netherlands, as elsewhere, many people have doubts about food security. Will they contract mad cow's disease by consuming a rare T-bone steak or bone marrow, and, if they overcome these fears and do indulge in their feast, can they be sure they are being served beef that has not been fed on hormones? In an airplane, sitting next to a young man reading the Koran, some passengers do not feel at ease. Such feelings may be instigated by reports on young people on their way to Syria to join the fighting, by the ways in which airport authorities, ever since 9/11, have tightened security controls of all passengers and most certainly of Muslims, or else, may simply be due to some travellers feeling ill at ease when airborne or being of a superstitious nature altogether, but even so, the image appears to evoke some level of insecurity. Apparently, as our limited round of questioning above suggests, perceptions, images and allegations we hold on safety and security affect many aspects of our daily lives, ranging from wars and suffering—even bygone ones, economics, health, traffic, food, politics, livelihoods et cetera. So how do we keep on living our lives and minding our daily business amidst such turmoil in our minds?

Safety and security can be regarded as products or services delivered by private security firms, the police or the military. But at the same time, security and safety also have to do with feelings and perceptions about presumed risks, i.e., threats and hazards.[6] As a consequence, safety and security may lead to a paradox in which people, confronted by a decline of threat, as, for instance, was experienced after the fall of the Berlin Wall, November 9th, 1989, feel more secure and, therefore, will be inclined to spend far less on safety and security. On its turn, this behaviour may give rise to less actual safety and security, but it will generally take a novel major incident for people to let go of complacency and start to feel insecure and unsafe again. And then, of course, to start investing in safety and security all over, as became clear in the wake of the 9/11 attacks when the demands for security providers, both in the public and private sectors skyrocketed. The same is noticeable in the aftermath of the more recent unsuccessful attempt to attack the high speed train Thalys near the French city of Arras, August 21st, 2015.

Remarkably, when travelling by train in The Netherlands, many of us seem to take a certain level of safety and security for granted and we certainly don't devote much time to question any underlying assumptions. Boarding Thalys from

[6] Beeres and Bollen 2012, pp. 147–148; Kriaa et al. 2015, p. 158.

Amsterdam to Paris we routinely expect to arrive at Gare du Nord in 3 h and, to this end, we are prepared to pay our ticket fares. We may expect our train to depart late or be late on arrival in Paris, and, even though such prospect might cause some aggravation, again, it would still fit our expectations and would, therefore, be considered, to some extent, predictable. Even on August 21st, somewhat later in the day, passengers, according to their pre-set plan, boarded Thalys for Paris and when asked, claimed not to worry too much as to the chances of yet another attack. Apparently, our perceptions of safety and security also have to do with trust and confidence in routine systems and the display of routine behaviour, both of our own and of everybody else's. Routines, apparently, foster a sense of predictability and situational normality which, on its turn, serves to reduce our anxiety levels and reassures us about being in control of a situation, even if we're not. Perceived predictability and situational normality may well be the perfect antidote to feelings of insecurity and unsafety; paraphrasing the Rolling Stones, our "little helper to get us through the day". Meanwhile, on August 21st, as to railway authorities, governments and politicians in The Netherlands, Belgium and France, their awareness on possible gaps in routine safety and security was raised and some immediate courses of action were to install (in)visible control measures, such as keeping Thalys to its schedule as regularly as possible, patrolling railway police and to communicate along these lines, as soon as possible, to the public. In doing so, at least at face value, predictability and situational normality were reset and travellers by continuing their journey contributed to invoke the public perception that everything, once again, was back to business as usual.

Next, perceptions on safety and security may be grounded in cultural backgrounds, and, as it happens, various dimensions of perceived (in)security may appear to thwart each other. This could be witnessed in the tragic instance—at least from a Western point of view—when a father in Dubai restrained the beach patrol trying to rescue his daughter, out of fear they would harm her virtue. As a result, the girl drowned, her virtue uncompromised.[7]

From a linguistic angle, when looking at safety and security, some languages apply a single word to both safety and security (e.g., *säkerhet* (Swedish) *seguridad* (Spanish), *segurança* (Portuguese), *sikkerhed* (Danish) and *veiligheid* (Dutch), whereas both in English and in French (*sûreté* and *sécurité*)[8] two basic distinctions are made. Moreover, studying everyday language, Boholm et al. find safety and security are used in different application areas, "safety … often being conceptualized spatially, and associated with traffic, work and food, and *security* … being associated with domains of international relations and information technology".[9] Following Umberto Eco's novel, *The Island of the Previous Day*, where one of the main characters argues that inhabitants of the West Indies, in their language, do not distinguish a word for God, or, the exact opposite case of Inuit, whose language, to be able to communicate on the many distinctions in their weather

[7] Telegraaf 2015.

[8] Piètre-Cambacédès and Chaudet 2010, p. 56.

[9] Boholm et al. 2015, p. 12.

conditions, reportedly holds a wide variety of words for snow, the safest place on earth may very well be where there exist no words to phrase the concept. By the same token, the most insecure place might then be where people, in their language, draw the most distinctions within the domains of safety and security.

From the above, it appears safety and security invoke a gamut of images, and can be viewed from various perspectives. Moreover, as the concepts consist of multi-layered dimensions it is possible to operationalize safety and security in various ways. And, therefore, as to the questions asked before, whether it would be possible for the safest haven to simultaneously turn out to be the least secure place (e.g., a Dubai beach, in a particular context, regarding two differing dimensions) and whether a person, even a close and loving relative, could be an actor providing both security (regarding the dimension protecting one's virtue) as well as insecurity (regarding the dimension protecting one from drowning) the answers can only be affirmative.

1.3 Understanding Safety and Security

Before moving on, it seems indicated to devote some attention to how security and safety are being understood in literature.

Traditionally, security is linked to (inter)national security, as in internal security provided by the police and the ministries of justice and interior affairs and external security provided by the armed forces and ministries of defence and foreign affairs.[10] In 1993, regarding the concept of security, Mahncke holds, "It has become popular—as the military threat has declined and other problems such as raw material supply or migration have grown—to extend the concept beyond simply protecting against a violent threat from the outside".[11]

The author continues that whenever "raw material supply and mass-migration, but also for example, extended terrorist attacks from outside or cross-frontier ecological threats will increase, they can ultimately be part of a society's security". In saying so, Mahncke conceptualizes a threat to the security of a society or a community as "anything that ultimately and fundamentally threatens the autonomy (the freedom of one's own development) of that society or community". To this author, in other words, it is essential such threats are *vital*, instead of "such factors that for a society of community are burdensome, disadvantageous or even more than that, but not vital". To make his point as to what he considers to be non-vital factors, Mahncke mentions examples, such as "terrorist attacks", "pollution", "migration", "limited loss of raw materials and markets", and "certainly all threats to the welfare of a society that fall short of threatening the existence of that society".[12]

---

[10] Baldwin 1997.

[11] Mahncke 1993, pp. 7–8.

[12] Mahncke 1993, p. 8.

From the above, it would appear, Mahncke prefers to strictly limit the use of the concept of security and, particularly, security policy to situations in which military power can serve as a useful instrument. Although, for the sake of clarity, there may be something said in favour for such clear demarcation lines, there is little doubt that, to date, a number of factors, once considered non-vital by Mahncke, have become of paramount interest to the military domain. Back in 1993, hardly anyone would have thought cyber-attacks to constitute an issue on the national security agenda, nor would many people have foreseen the armed forces worldwide to be in the process of devising cyber commands, next to their Armies, Navies and Air Forces. (Inter) national (in)security and its ensuing policies prove to be highly dynamic concepts, valid during relatively short time spans. Factors, once considered vital may become obsolete, at least for the time being, whereas factors, not that long ago, considered non-vital may seem much better suited to the spirit of the day and age we live in, when it comes to perceived-threats to security.

Concerns for safety, on the other hand, stem from the industrial revolution, ranging from the 19th century until the first half of the 20th century, resulting, mainly, from undesirable effects caused by mechanization of production processes. As mechanization and rationalization to maximize profits increased, so did the numbers of occupational deaths amongst workers. As a result, researching (occupational) safety became an acknowledged field of professional expertise. Swuste, van Gulijk and Zwaard capture this era as follows, "Engineers are enclosing hazards and fencing heights, shaping up safety technique, and writing very practical publications on occupational safety. The publications predominantly published in the United States are leading to quite some safety related metaphors, with the iceberg and the domino's as the most famous ones. Sociologists, psychologists, and physicians are more concerned with questions related to accident causation, and these specialists are conducting research leading to two different safety theories. Causes of occupational accidents are found either in the workers' capacity to handle hazardous situations, or in external causes, like-very-long working hours, dangerous machines and the increased pressures of work and speed production".[13]

As a result, safety science has developed as a domain of evolving socio-technical perspectives on human factors and safety, e.g., Normal Accidents Theory (NAT),[14] High Reliability Theory (HRT),[15] Resilience Engineering[16] and the Systems-Theoretic Accident Model and Processes (STAMP).[17] Moreover, in practice, within organizations, safety management and safety management systems have being implemented as can be noticed in the armed forces.[18]

[13] Swuste et al. 2010, p. 1000.

[14] Perrow 1999.

[15] Roughlin et al. 1987.

[16] Hollnagel et al. 2008.

[17] Leveson 2004.

[18] MoD 2010.

From the above, it would appear that in attempting to understand and provide meaning to security and safety, an all-encompassing framework offering clarity is not available. Both concepts may be understood separately, for instance, based on their origins, underlying research domains or societal sectors, providers in the public and private realms, and within specific contexts, cultures and over particular periods of time. Also, both concepts appear layered, in the sense that they seem to consist of various dimensions that may react to and even counteract one another. Moreover, the concepts can be understood at several levels, varying from grand strategies (security) and corporate management strategies (safety) to the level at which individuals experience (in)security and (un)safety based on their awareness of perceived-threats and risks. It seems safe to say, that countries, organizations and people that are not aware of perceived-hazards or threats, cannot be expected to be aware of a lack of safety and security and, therefore, will not devote resources to invest in such assets. As recent history, however, is making abundantly clear, safety and security, increasingly, are becoming interrelated and therefore, may have to be understood interactively, as local Parisians experienced, when, in January 2014, they thought they went shopping for groceries in a familiar and safe kosher hypermarche, whereas, instead, in the aftermath of the attacks at Charlie Hebdo, they found themselves caught up in a violent (inter)national security situation.

In an altogether different realm, as yet lacking an acknowledged hegemon,[19] characterized by a multitude of threats and real harm, and compounded by frames considered suitable for electoral gains, from 2011, desperate people are fleeing insecurity in their home countries and travel to Europe by highly unsafe means along highly unsafe routes. Upon their arrival, often, they find themselves labelled as security risks under conditions dictated by security measures, albeit different ones than back home.

How do we study such inter-relatedness between safety and security? Is it possible that, by understanding the concepts more interactively, we may be able to anticipate or even prepare for such dire situations? Is it possible to organize for safety and security? Before elaborating on these questions, in the next section we will take a closer look into how security and safety may be related.

1.4 Relating Safety and Security

Although, based on the traditional dichotomy between safety and security, literature offers a variety of definitions, Piètre-Cambacédès and Chaudet argue, essentially, most definitions to be grounded in two paradigms.[20] The first paradigm distinguishes between systems and environment (S/E), holding that safety characterizes the inability of the system to have an undesired effect on its environment,

[19] Suhrke 1998.

[20] Piètre-Cambacédès and Chaudet 2010, p. 56, 59; Piètre-Cambacédès and Chaudet 2009, p. 156; also, Piètre-Cambacédès and Bouissou 2013, p. 12; Kriaa et al. 2015, p. 159.

Table 1.1 The SEMA referential framework

	Envt → Syst	Syst → Envt	Syst → Syst
Malicious	Defence	Safeguards	Self-protection
Accidental	Robustness	Containment ability	Reliability

Source Piètre-Cambacédès and Chaudet 2010

whereas, security denotes the inability of the environment to have an undesired effect on the system.[21] Within the second paradigm the distinction is made between malicious versus accidental harm (M/A), resulting in defining safety to designate the degree to which accidental harm is prevented, detected and reacted to, and security to designate the degree to which malicious harm is prevented, detected and reacted to.[22] Subsequently, the relations between both paradigms can be combined into the framework presented in Table 1.1.

The framework's horizontal axis depicts relations between both between environment and system, as well as relations within the system, resulting in three potential situations. First, the environment may impact the referent system to a detrimental effect; second, the referent system causes a detrimental effect to its environment, and third, the system is detrimental to its own functioning. On the vertical axis, the framework distinguishes whether the detrimental effect can be attributed to either malicious or accidental actions.

In doing so, six sub-quadrants, referring to potential scenarios to fit the situations are identified. First, in case of the environment maliciously impacting the system to its detriment, the scenario of defence is warranted. Defence aims at preventing, detecting and reacting to "external malevolent actions on the system". Second, whenever the environment accidentally impacts the system detrimentally, robustness is called for, as this means "dealing with external accidents consequences". Next, the system may maliciously cause detrimental effects to the environment, and to act upon this situation, safeguards are needed to prevent, detect and react to the impact of "malicious actions from the system on the environment". Fourth, counteracting the system to accidentally cause detrimental effects to the environment requires containment ability, "aiming at limiting the incidence of non-malicious system faults on the environment". In case the system is maliciously detrimental to its own functioning, self-protection is needed to prevent, detect and react "to internal malicious actions on the system" and, last, reliability enables the system to deal with "non-intentional internal faults with no harm to the environment".[23]

The authors explicitly state their framework is not intended to supplant the concepts of safety and security, "but rather to make their meanings and respective limits explicit in a given context, in order to avoid misunderstandings".[24] Furthermore,

[21] Piètre-Cambacédès and Chaudet 2009, p. 156; 2010, p. 58.

[22] Piètre-Cambacédès and Chaudet 2009, p. 156; 2010, p. 58; Firesmith 2003, p. 2.

[23] Piètre-Cambacédès and Chaudet 2009, p. 157; the names of the six sub-quadrants in Table 1.1 are based on Piètre-Cambacédès and Chaudet 2010, p. 60.

[24] Piètre-Cambacédès and Chaudet 2010, p. 60; Piètre-Cambacédès and Bouissou 2013, p. 111.

the authors note, that differing realms, such as, critical infrastructure protection, nuclear power generation, telecommunication and data networks, deal with safety and security issues in different ways. Both differences and similarities between these realms can be understood in the SEMA framework.

The SEMA framework can be regarded as a generic model to systematically study safety and security issues in various contexts, thus, providing more solid grounds to think on possible inter-relatedness and coherence when studying security and safety issues in the context of organizing for safety and security in military organizations. To do so, first, applying the SEMA framework in a meaningful way to the military security domain requires specific understanding. In a military sense, security encompasses the domain in which military capabilities and military power are produced to be used both defensively and offensively (e.g., to protect and advance the interests of a country's interests in the international arena).[25]

As to the sub-quadrant defence, in which the enemy in the environment aims for intentional-malicious-destruction of the referent system, this, also, implies explicit attention should be devoted to the situation in which the referent system uses malicious offensive measures (e.g., pre-emptive strikes or retaliation) aiming to destroy the enemy in the environment. The same holds with regard to the sub-quadrant safeguards, in which the environment by means of legal counteractions may act maliciously, as well as in the sub-quadrant self-protection, in which internal malicious sabotage is at the flipside.

Second, we note the terminology used in the three sub-quadrants dealing with safety appear better suited to safety literature. The use of resilience instead of robustness, for instance, fits in with resilience engineering, while the use of controllability instead of reliability appears in line with STAMP.

Third, in a military context, dealing with security and safety issues transgressing beyond demarcation lines and thereby interacting with one another, may make up for novel category on the SEMA framework's vertical axis, namely, an action that can be considered simultaneously malicious and accidental, such as, friendly fire. Friendly fire incidents can be regarded as combinations of the intention to kill an enemy in the environment (security) and (a series of) mistakes (safety). Friendly fire could therefore be considered a malicious accident or mistake.[26]

1.5 Organizing for Safety and Security

Pettersen and Bjørnskau, researching safety and security in a civil aviation context, argue the implementation of security measures in the wake of the 9/11 terrorist attacks have given rise to a novel set of challenges when organizing flight safety in civil aviation. Although their empirical research is limited to Norway, it is expected the same will go for most western civil aviation.

[25] Arvanitidis et al. 2014, p. 611.

[26] Mair et al. 2012, p. 77.

Table 1.2 Organizing principles of safety and security

	Safety organization	Security organization
Threats (goals)	Internal and regular	External and random
Outcome motivating measures/behaviour	Known/evidence- or experience based	Unknown
Organizational structure	Functional with local networks	Autocratic
Climate	Trust seeking	Suspicious
Power	Legitimate/expert	Coercive

Source Pettersen and Bjørnskau 2015

As aviation safety is firmly grounded in principles of anticipation, learning from failures and past experiences it is continuously directed towards both the discovery and correction of errors.[27] Paramount to organizing flight safety are both a functional organization structure, in which specialized roles follow standards and procedures as well as a capability to be flexible to learn from and cope with arising uncertainties. As a result, whenever necessary, and based on local and decentralized knowledge, it becomes feasible to switch from routine-oriented operating to novel problem-solving approaches.

However, from 9/11, a series of new security regulations and measures have been introduced in civil aviation, resulting in "a new and large interorganizational and cross-national structure within the European aviation system, with terrorism protection being a primary target".[28] The majority of these aviation security measures are based on the principle of anticipation, "focusing on preventing the entry of dangerous objects and hardening targets based on known problems and threats inferred from the most recent security incident". Although, according to Petterson en Bjørnskau, these may resemble former principles for organizing flight safety, major discrepancies are noted, such as, the novel measures "do not allow for aviation organizations to allow the degree of functional authority and flexibility that characterizes the organization of flight safety" or "the regulations allow only for standardized and detailed routine ways of achieving security".[29]

To make their point, the authors claim "organizational schizophrenia", underpinning this choice of words by discussing differences in organizational principles between flight safety versus aviation security, as illustrated in Table 1.2. In the remaining part of this section, differences in safety and security will be discussed, following Table 1.2. In doing so, we lay the grounds for our next section that will introduce the overarching theme of NL ARMS 2016.

[27] Pettersen and Bjørnskau 2015, p. 168.

[28] Pettersen and Bjørnskau 2015, p. 169.

[29] Pettersen and Bjørnskau 2015, p. 169.

1.5.1 Threats (Goals)

According to Pettersen and Bjørnskau, and caused by the nature of the problems, or threats, that have to be dealt with, the goals pursued in flight safety as opposed to aviation security fundamentally differ. Flight safety, primarily, is internally oriented at technological reliability and human performance. Any threats related to safety are "for the most part known". Essentially, flight safety aims to prevent risks from engine and systems failure, material and crew fatigue, and misunderstandings due to communications and information exchange. Security, on the other hand, is organized to protect from external remote dangers. Security risks, therefore, will primarily involve-potentially unknown-external actors and Petterson and Bjørnskau summarize: "whereas safety is organized to deal with *internal* threats, security's primary target is *external*".[30]

1.5.2 Outcome Motivating Measures/Behaviour

According to literature on leadership and motivation, human behaviour in organizations, to a certain extent, is directed by the ways in which workers feel stimulated and motivated to reach organizational goals. From a transactional leadership point of view, it appears people will respond to incentives or contingent rewards they expect upon delivering the desired performance. As safety and security organizations aim for different goals, both types of organizations will differ regarding the behaviour deemed desirable to pursue these goals. Moreover, as to safety, threats are considered internal. As a result, the effects of safety measures will become "knowns" that can be assessed according to yardsticks for efficiency and effectiveness and, hence, can be adjusted. To the workers, however complex their tasks may be, the internal goals and standards appear straightforward, and, moreover, it will also be clear what incentives or rewards will be obtained upon reaching these goals.

In case of organizing for security, however, Petterson and Bjørnskau argue the events for which security measures have been designed, may never take place and therefore, the possible effects will remain largely "unknowns".[31] For both managers and workers in security organizations, it may be less clear to assess whether an event has not taken place because the threat simply did not arise (a non-event, so to speak), or because the workers by displaying the desired organizational behaviour when applying the right security measures at the right time, prevented the event from occurring. And, compounding the latter case, often, the prevention of such an event will be little cause for celebrations within the organization or the public at large, nor will visible rewards and incentives be occurred, because of security reasons.

30 Pettersen and Bjørnskau 2015, p. 169.

31 Pettersen and Bjørnskau 2015, p. 170.

1.5.3 *Organizational Structure*

Pettersen and Bjørnskau hold "aviation safety is highly specialized with discretely designed and specialized roles (e.g., pilots, technicians, engineers)".[32] Typically, safety organizational structures will be both centralized as well as decentralized at the same time. On the one hand, there are actors holding central authority, such as the European Aviation Safety Authority, that, together with national authorities are entitled to keep aircrafts to the ground in case of suspected safety issues. On the other hand, the organization is aware even the most carefully designed process may harbour errors and for this reason, in flight safety organizations goes that "the flow of information between functional roles in order to optimize local performance as well as local processes of good judgment that allow sufficient adaptation to local constraints". However, in aviation security "the structure is centralized and depends on a few coordinated decision makers at the European level". According to Pettersen and Bjørnskau, another distinction between the two domains is the security domain offers "little opportunity for subordinates to offer feedback or suggestions", whereas this constitutes a paramount principle underpinning flight safety.[33]

1.5.4 *Climate*

From the above, it follows that in aiming for safety, the functional organization is built on trust. Every specialization, e.g. pilots, technicians and engineers, commands specialized knowledge and performs accordingly. Because these workers are all considered experts in their chosen fields, they will have to rely on one another to make sense of each other's actions. Aviation security, on the other hand, is "by and large fully based on macro-strategies through extensive access control and asset hardening". Workers in aviation security are described by Pettersen and Bjørnskau as suspicious minds.

1.5.5 *Power*

In organizations concerned with flight safety, power and authority gain legitimacy by being distributed across the pivotal organizational functions and specialisms. "In aviation, pilots and technicians are two groups of employees who are irreplaceable, giving the power due to their roles in the system". However, in aviation security things are different, as, for example, a security guard can prohibit a pilot

---

[32] Pettersen and Bjørnskau 2015, p. 170.

[33] Pettersen and Bjørnskau 2015, p. 170.

from accessing the aircraft. Such power and authority are meant to be "first and foremost coercive".[34] Instead of being grounded in evidence and experience based expert power, considered legitimate to the organization's expert workers, in aviation security organizations, power is vested in and enacted by centrally devised rules and regulations.

In conclusion, in their research, Petterson en Bjørnskau point to potentially clashing results when organizations involved with aviation safety, have to implement too many and overly strict security measures. One reason for the German Wings tragedy in France, 2015, originated from the implementation of a security measure that imposed the door to the cockpit not to be opened from outside, to prevent hijackers and terrorists from entering. As it turned out, this security measure blocked flight safety, leaving both the crew and their captain in a cramped galley just outside of the cockpit without any chance for problem solving, unable to prevent their depressed colleague from crashing the plane and everybody on board into the Alps.

Having discussed Petterson en Bjørnskau to some extent as to their insights into the differences between safety and security organizations in civil aviation, we feel some notes to be in place. For one, safety culture is often characterized by specialist staff scrutinizing manuals in search for the life span of specific nuts and bolts, a strong focus on procedures derived from schedules set in maintenance cycles, and, by their predominantly procedural outlook determining the organizational behaviour within all other departments, including the ones dealing directly with customers and suppliers.[35] As to organizations occupied in the security domain outside civil aviation, these encompass a whole gamut of institutions, international, supranational, local, private and publically funded or a mix between the two, some of them playing a major role on worldwide strategic agendas, besides being concerned with widely divergent goals to reach. Also, currently, it may be simply *en vogue* to label one's organization a security firm, when its core-business actually is to snoop on people cheating on their spouses. Fourth, a major challenge to us seems to do the job in contexts characterized by both security and safety issues requiring new interfaces for problem solving and dealing with ensuing conflicting interests.

Having said so, the question arises whether by attempting to organize for everything, despite contradictory threats and goals, unclear structures and power relations and unsupportive climates, we leave our clients, people and communities no choice but to adopt organizational choices made for them by outsiders, instead of falling back on their own resilience that may have been the best solution to begin with.

---

[34] Pettersen and Bjørnskau 2015, p. 170.

[35] Dekker 2014.

1.6 Outline of the Book

This year's theme 'Organizing for Safety and Security in military organizations' has been conceived of by the editors when developing a course on *Systems, Networks and Safety*, as part of the FMS degree programme on military management studies. As it turned out, there is quite an abundance of literature on either safety, security or managing military organizations. The same goes for studies on relations between security and military organizations, and, to a lesser extent, on the relation between safety and military organizations. As to research connecting all three concepts, however, there appears to be a void.

For this reason, we have chosen to provide the contributors to NL ARMS 2016 as much leeway as possible to think creatively and to add their expertise to this multifaceted field. We have actively scouted scholars we were convinced to be innovative thinkers and this turned out a great idea, even to the extent, some of them proceeded to do some scouting themselves, thereby greatly enhancing this volume. As editors, we want to thank all authors for delivering the goods, including everybody who has attempted to do so!

Despite our extending a free rein to all co-authors, in the end, of course, we had to come up with a way to meaningfully group all contributions. In NL ARMS 2016, four categories can be distinguished. The first category consists of research we consider *fundamental*, as these chapters, to us, are of a transcendental and conditional nature, thereby, preceding, in a sense, the trinity safety, security and organizing military organizations. In the second category, we have grouped all research in which organizational principles are attributed to military organizations' primary tasks regarding *organizing for security.* Third, we have clustered all studies that, from a safety perspective, investigate themes derived from the military's primary tasks and military ways of organizing, such as PTSS. Last, we distinguish chapters that apply knowledge from a specific domain, such as logistics, accounting and control or technology to organizing for safety and security in the military realm. Based on this categorization, NL ARMS 2016 will be divided into four parts as is presented in Table 1.3.

In Chap. 2, by combining three bodies of literature on organizing safety (NAT, HRT and RE), Eric Hans Kramer and Matthijs Moorkamp develop an analytical framework comprising the concepts of *organizational skeleton*, *normal work* and

Table 1.3 Overview contributions

Categories	Authors	Chapters
Fundamental	Kramer and Moorkamp	2
Organizing for security	Osinga; De Waard and Van As; Neuteboom; Wolbers	3–6
Organizing for safety	Bakx and Nyce; Wermser, Täuber, Essens and Molleman; Op den Buijs; Kalkman; De Jong	7–11
Applications	Moelker; Van Kampen, Van Fenema and Faber; Bijlsma and Broers; Heeren-Bogers and Soeters; Theunissen; De Jong	12–17

dynamic complexity. By means of this framework, the authors set out to study organizational vulnerabilities in military taskforces, and although they do not proclaim so, their framework can be put to use in both military security as well safety contexts. A truly *fundamental* contribution, therefore.

Laying the grounds for the part on *organizing for security*, in Chap. 3, Frans Osinga holds military combat units, in fact, are being organized for insecurity, rather than for security. In organizing for insecurity, according to the author, resilience theory and military theory are to be regarded natural partners. Drawing from modern and post-modern military theories, Osinga shows concepts, such as *mission command*, *swarming* and *network centric warfare* indeed to be underpinned by insights from resilience literature. This chapter concludes by offering some causes explaining the divergence in thinking on resilience in Western military organizations.

In Chap. 4, Erik de Waard and Henk van As agree with Osinga when putting forward, "The bare essential of military organizations is to overcome fear in a lethal environment; or in other words, making sure that soldiers and units keep fulfilling their designated roles under barrages of gunfire or other life-threatening circumstances". This chapter deals with a major problem faced by contemporary Western military organizations, that, although they can avail of a fair number of troops trained for conventional warfare (conventional forces), they command only a limited number of troops able to deploy for unconventional military tasks: Special Operation Forces. As a consequence, conventional forces are increasingly being used for unconventional tasks. In this respect, the authors argue that, "the misuse of conventional or unconventional forces may result in failing security strategies and, at the same time, may seriously jeopardize the lives of the soldiers actively involved in a mission". Using Lawrence's and Lorsch's classic *Organization and Environment, Managing Differentiation and Integration* De Waard and Van As conceptualize and visualize the issues at stake, identify the problems and provide organizational solutions.

Peter Neuteboom, in Chap. 5, subscribes to the case built by De Waard and Van As by arguing the lack of training of the Dutch Army conducting police tasks during stabilization operations in the Balkans, Iraq and Afghanistan, resulted in both jeopardizing the mission and safety problems to personnel. According to Neuteboom, police tasks still remain to be integrated in Army doctrines and the author strongly advocates to do so, as: "an adaptive professional standard and culture should be rooted in a clearly defined doctrine, ensuring the best possible organizational fit, tools, and mind-set for changing conditions on the ground".

In Chap. 6, Jeroen Wolbers, comparing *network centric operations* doctrine in both military operations and civil disaster management, critically adds to Chap. 3. In the military domain, the author argues, the concept of mission command relies upon commanders' intent and distributed decision-making to lower echelons by virtue of autonomy and self-synchronization. In civil disaster management, in an organizational network relying on goal consensus, a similar movement towards cooperation and coordination is noticeable. However, Wolbers observes an important discrepancy in the way in which both sectors organize and orchestrate the network. "Mission command in the military sector relies upon commanders' intent, thus having a clear commander in chief. In contrast, disaster management in the civil society requires acting in a network of autonomous organizations under conditions of goal consensus and, thus, is essentially a cooperative endeavor". Wolbers argues this requires a new approach to network centric operations. An approach that "does not only rely upon information sharing and self-synchronization, but also incorporates *negotiation*, *sense-making* and *network switching*". When involved in disaster management, the military will become part of this new approach.

Introducing part three *organizing for safety*, in Chap. 7, Gwendoline Bakx and James Nyce ask whether safety and security actually do differ. The authors imagine a scenario taking place during the Nuclear Summit, 24–25 March 2014, when world leaders are overrun by a crowd. Would this then have been considered a safety issue, a security breach, or both? From a practical point of view, the authors note, as security organizations, to a large extent, are confronted with the occurrence of intertwined security and safety problems, distinguishing between both concepts does not really seem to add to solving the problems. Analytically, however, distinctions can be made. Bakx en Nyce, discussing the consequences of such distinctions, put forward that safety oriented organizations will experience the introduction of security measures as disturbing the *normal work flow* (see also Pettersen and Bjørnskau in Sect. 1.5), whereas, in security oriented organizations, safety measures will be considered less important. According to the authors, both safety and security issues should matter equally to individuals, organizations and society.

In Chap. 8, against the background of political willpower to increase military cooperation across the European Union, Frederik Wermser, Suzanne Täuber, Peter Essens and Eric Molleman discuss *psychological safety during military integration*. Based on an extensive literature study, the authors offer insights into the psychological processes that should be considered when upholding both soldiers' psychological safety as well as the operational readiness of the integrated military organization. They suggest to encourage an explicit exchange on the fundamental meaning of being a soldier (i.e., the norms and behaviors that constitute a military identity) and, subsequently, to match these findings to the norms and behaviors forming other identities involved in military integration across the EU. According to Wermser et al., in doing so, "a development on incorrect expectations may be prevented and a more objective representation of cultural similarities and difference can be accomplished".

In Chap. 9, Tessa op den Buijs asks whether *post traumatic stress disorder* (PTSD) can be prevented. Based on a literature study, Op den Buijs presents a number of psychological and pharmacological approaches to prevent and reduce symptoms of PTSD. As to the question whether PTSD may be prevented altogether, the author remains reticent. Considered a crucial and practical next step in PTSD prevention, the author concludes by discussing the latest development, i.e. a clinical prediction algorithm to identify people in high risk of developing PTSD after combat trauma exposure.

In Chap. 10, Jori Kalkman explores the different roles of the armed forces in *Dutch Safety Regions*. Safety Regions, per region, pooling capabilities and skills of the fire brigade, medical services and municipalities, consist of relatively autonomous units developed to improve both management and operations of the emergency services. If necessary, assistance of other partners, including the military may be called upon. To improve civil military interaction, amongst others, lateral relations (liaisons) have been designed. Based on a typology of Dutch Safety Regions, and from a military perspective, Kalkman empirically investigates whether types of safety regions impact liaison roles. The author finds the type of safety region to be one explanatory factor to account for a variety in liaison roles, perceived interdependencies as well as the collaboration mechanisms in use.

From a perspective of organizational culture, Helena de Jong, in Chap. 11, elaborates on interorganizational collaboration to further safety and security. When starting collaboration, actors involved in crisis and disaster management will be confronted by organizational cultures, mandates, interests, often unfamiliar to their own. In literature, and dubbed by the author as the *culture-as-problem-focus*, such diverging organizational cultures will often be perceived a barrier to interorganizational collaboration. Striving to raise awareness on beneficial influences regarding cultural diversity and interorganizational efforts, De Jong links dimensions of interorganizational collaboration to organizational culture.

The final part of this volume, *applications*, consists of six contributions. René Moelker, in Chap. 12, relates a decline of inter- and intra states violence to governance. Using the concept of *government opportunity structure*, relations between state building and the organization of safety and security are discussed on four dimensions. First, *moral order* brings about societal cohesion from which a normative system, as manifested in *rule of law*, will be derived. Rule of law, on its turn, will be enforced by the state wielding the *monopoly of violence* and, last, by means of their *monopoly of taxation*, states will deliver collective goods, such as safety and security. Ample illustrations show positive correlations between governance and an increase of safety and security in society.

In Chap. 13, Ton van Kampen, Paul van Fenema and Nynke Faber note a lack of attention to security in both theory and practice of supply chain management. The authors aim to offer insight into managing *supply chain security risks* within defence organizations. To this end, two approaches to studying supply chain management in armed forces are identified. When applying a risk-based approach, typically, security risks and security risks levels will be mapped and mitigation strategies will be developed, or, else the focus may be on developing an adaptive capability within supply chain management. Drawing on both approaches, the authors come up with possibilities to manage supply chain security risks within defence organizations, and offer three pathways for future research.

Viewing *crew resource management* to be a combination of vision, methods and skills to work safer and, thus, enhancing the provision of security by the armed forces, in Chap. 14, Tom Bijlsma and Carla Broers illustrate the core of crew resource management at the level of competencies. The authors discuss the so-called seven skills (i.e., decision-making, assertiveness, mission analysis, communication, leadership, adaptability, and situational awareness) and show the effects of crew resource management in practice by means of three empirical case studies conducted in the safety region Noord-Holland Noord. The authors find crew resource management to enable professional cooperation between emergency services in case of incidents, disaster, or threat.

From a management accounting and control perspective, in Chap. 15 Jacqueline Heeren-Bogers and Joseph Soeters shed yet another light on the security-safety nexus by studying the ways in which the Netherlands armed forces deal with both financial and materiel resources. Defence organizations, as any other organization, are supposed to handle monetary means safely, and, moreover, defence organizations are accountable for safe weaponry management and control. Discussing empirical results of their investigation into both *hard* (formal) and *soft* (informal) *controls* applied within the Netherlands armed forces, the authors conclude improvements in hard controls predominantly result from modernizing control procedures. Improving soft controls regards raising organizational awareness on adages, such as, "devices or gear should not disappear; time is precious and nothing is for free". As to improving soft controls, across the armed forces, the authors encounter respondents stating it is not their job to pay attention to such issues, as, effectiveness in battle is paramount.

In Chap. 16 Erik Theunissen discusses how ever-increasing dependencies on information derived from the internet and the *Global Positioning System* (GPS) may impact safety and security in both military and civilian organizations. Due to *Distributed Denial of Service* (DDoS) attacks and GPS jamming information availability is affected, while *Man-in-the-Middle* attacks (MitM) disrupt information availability. Additionally, the author notes, when such attacks are not timely discovered, decision making will be based on unjust information. Theunissen offers suggestions to mitigate such problems, both on the short term (e.g., the use of existing dissimilar systems as a backup for applications that cannot afford a loss of position and timing information) and on the long-term (e.g., the use of encryption and authentication techniques).

In the final contribution to NL ARMS 2016, Michiel de Jong, over the period 1959–1992, analyzes changes in approaches deployed by the Spanish security forces during their counterterrorism operations against *Euskadi Ta Askatasuma* (ETA). In his historical case study, De Jong shows how the Spanish government and security forces, initially conceiving of ETA as an internal security issue with important external security dimensions, over time, transformed to view ETA as a transnational organization to be approached in a more comprehensive way if problems were to be solved. From that time, as the author describes in the case study, the approach of the Spanish authorities towards ETA became more effective.

We hope the insights put forward by De Jong may serve today's actors involved in approaches to terrorist attacks on Brussels and Paris, also.

Acknowledgments We are most grateful for the valuable comments of Robert J Smits and Bob de Graaff.

References

Arvanitidis P, Kollias C, Anastasopoulos K (2014) Is there an international convergence in defence burdens? Some initial findings. Peace Econ Peace Sci Public Policy 20:611–620

Baldwin DA (1997) The concept of security. Rev Int Stud 23:5–26

Beeres R, Bollen M (2012) An economic analysis of cyber attacks. In: Ducheine P, Osinga, F, Soeters, J (eds) Cyber warfare critical perspectives. T.M.C. Asser Press, The Hague, pp 147–164

Boholm M, Möller N, Hansson SO (2015) The concepts of risk, safety, and security: applications in everyday language. Risk Anal. doi:10.1111/risa.12464

Dekker SWA (2014) The bureaucratization of safety. Saf Sci 70:348–357

Firesmith DG (2003) Common concepts underlying safety security and survivability engineering. Carnegie Mellon University, Pittsburg

Hollnagel E, Woods DD, Leveson N (eds) (2008) Resilience engineering: concepts and precepts. Ashgate Publishing Company, Aldershot Hampshire

Kriaa S, Piètre-Cambacédès L, Bouissou M, Halgand Y (2015) A survey of approaches combining safety and security for industrial control systems. Reliab Eng Syst Saf 139:156–178

Leveson NG (2004) New accident model for engineering safer systems. Saf Sci 42:237–270

Mahncke D (1993) Parameters of European security. Institute for Security Studies Western European Union, Paris

Mair M, Watson PG, Elsey C, Smith PV (2012) War-making and sense-making: some technical reflections on an instance of 'friendly fire'. Brit J Sociol 63:75–96

MoD (2010) Veiligheidsmanagement bij Defensie. Een blauwdruk voor belegging en verankering. MoD, The Hague

Perrow C (1999) Normal accidents. Princeton University Press, Princeton NJ, Living with high-risk technologies

Pettersen KA, Bjørnskau T (2015) Organizational contradictions between safety and security—Perceived challenges and ways of integrating critical infrastructure protection in civil aviation. Saf Sci 71:167–177

Piètre-Cambacédès L, Bouissou M (2013) Cross-fertilization between safety and security engineering. Reliab Eng Syst Saf 110:110–126

Piètre-Cambacédès L, Chaudet C (2009) Disentangling the relations between safety and security. In: Proceedings of the 9th World Scientific and Engineering Academy and Society International Conference on Applied Informatics and Communications, pp 156–161

Piètre-Cambacédès L, Chaudet C (2010) The SEMA referential framework: Avoiding ambiguities in the terms "security" and "safety". Int J Crit Infrastruct Prot 3:55–66

Snook SA (2000) Friendly fire: the accidental shootdown of US Black Hawks over Northern Iraq. Princeton University Press, Princeton NJ

Soeters J, van Fenema PC, Beeres R (2010) Introducing military organizations. In: Soeters J, van Fenema PC, Beeres R (eds) Managing military organizations. Routledge, London and New York, pp 1–14

Suhrke A (1998) Burden-sharing during refugee emergencies: the logic of collective versus national action. J Refugee Stud 11:396–415

Swuste P, van Gulijk C, Zwaard W (2010) Safety metaphors and theories, a review of the occupational safety literature of the US, UK and The Netherlands, till the first part of the 20th century. Saf Sci 48:1000–1018

Telegraaf (2015) Man laat dochter verdrinken in Dubai, www.telegraaf.nl/buitenland/24360328/Man_laat_dochter_verdrinken___.html. Accessed 25 Nov 2015

Van Duren ECGJ (2010) Money is ammunition; don't put it in the wrong hands. A view on COIN contracting from Regional Command South. Militaire Spectator 179:564–578

Vennix A (1998) Wat is waarheid? De virtus quaestionis in het licht van Thomas van Aquino. Damon, Best

Zohar J, Sonnino R, Juven-Wetzler A, Cohen H (2009) Can posttraumatic stress disorder be prevented? CNS Spectr 14:44–51

Chapter 2
Understanding Organizational Vulnerabilities in Military Taskforces

Eric-Hans Kramer and Matthijs Moorkamp

Abstract In this chapter, the relevance of a perspective on organizational vulnerability for improving safety in military taskforces is outlined. Research of the Netherlands Defence Academy has shown that military taskforces are systems with typical organizational vulnerabilities. More specifically, this research has shown that military taskforces had difficulties in developing and maintaining functional integration. This chapter analyzes whether the safety management system of the Netherlands Defence organization is useful for understanding such organizational vulnerabilities. After the conclusion that this focus on organizational vulnerabilities is lacking in this safety management system, existing theories on safety in organizations are analyzed. Based on a combination of insights from these theories, a theoretical avenue for understanding such vulnerabilities is proposed.

Keywords Organizational vulnerability · Functional integration · Safety management · Organizational design · Normal work

Contents

E.-H. Kramer (✉)
Faculty of Military Sciences, Netherlands Defence Academy, Breda, The Netherlands
e-mail: fj.kramer@mindef.nl

M. Moorkamp
Saxion University of Applied Sciences, University of Twente, Enschede, The Netherlands
e-mail: m.moorkamp@saxion.nl

R. Beeres et al. (eds.), *NL ARMS Netherlands Annual Review of Military Studies 2016*, NL ARMS, DOI 10.1007/978-94-6265-135-7_2

2.1 Introduction

Approached as a problem of organizing, safety can be related to the issue of organizational vulnerability, which signifies "a reduced capability to maintain functional integration".[1] Maintaining functional integration refers here to the issue of how organizations manage to survive as coherent systems, and this approach understands safety problems such as accidents and incidents as particular manifestations of organizational vulnerability. By defining organizations as "social systems that conduct experiments with their survival", Achterbergh and Vriens place the issue of survival at the core of organization science.[2] Using this perspective, the organizational background of safety issues can be studied by taking into account the challenges to functional integration in a specific organization in a specific context. Organizational theories on safety specify a way to understand organizational vulnerability. Furthermore, debates between rival organizational theories on safety provide an interesting outlook on what is at stake when trying to conceptualize the dynamics of maintaining functional integration. Since many safety problems occur in organizational contexts, a focus on the organizational contributions to accidents and incidents is increasingly considered an important trend in safety science.[3]

Understanding organizational vulnerability is of the greatest relevance to the military organization because maintaining functional integration can be seen as a precondition to the ability of being effective in the first place. This seems particularly relevant as military task forces are operating in what Kramer calls dynamic complex environments in which operators are confronted with opponents that actively aim to undermine the operations of the task force.[4] As to the Dutch military organization, research within the Netherlands Defence Academy has shown that the expeditionary taskforces that the Netherlands Armed Forces have been deploying the last decades could be considered *vulnerable systems*. Being taskforces, they are a temporary system of units that did not exist as an integrated system before a particular mission.[5] Such a taskforce can be seen as a network of interconnecting units that are in contact with a dynamic environment at multiple

[1] Bijker 2006, p. 56.

[2] Achterbergh and Vriens 2010, p. 1; see Weick 1979 for another theorists that focuses on survival as a key issue.

[3] Dekker 2014.

[4] Kramer 2007.

[5] Snook 2000.

positions at the same time. Particularly in Western Europe, military organizations design expeditionary taskforces by mixing and matching existing units for the purposes of a specific mission.[6] The resulting collection of units has to be calibrated and re-calibrated extensively in order to develop an integrated taskforce that can deal with the specific demands of a complex operational environment.[7] Research has shown examples of cases in which operators within expeditionary military taskforces were continuously self-designing in order to establish some form of functional integration.[8] In particular, a case study of Task Force Uruzgan has shown that such efforts were seriously hindered by factors at the organizational level that could be associated with safety incidents.[9] The combination of challenging environments and—more or less—improvised organizational constructions are significant pre-conditions for organizational vulnerability in military taskforces. Subsequently, it is important to understand organizational influences and instruments, such as safety management, that can be employed to improve the ability to develop functional integration and reduce organizational vulnerability.

The goal of this chapter is therefore to show the relevance of an organizational vulnerability perspective for understanding safety within military task forces by outlining a particular approach to understanding and studying vulnerability of military taskforces. The next section starts by discussing how the topic of safety management is dealt with within the Dutch military and how it relates to the theme of organizational vulnerability. This discussion reveals a particular dilemma for an organization that is oriented on safety in dynamic environments. The subsequent section aims to outline frequently used organizational theories on safety and reconstructs the academic debate between them. After that, the approach that we developed to study safety from an organizational vulnerability perspective within military taskforces will be discussed. This approach has been developed at the Netherlands Defence Academy on the basis of existing theory on organizational safety in relation to the specific characteristics of expeditionary military taskforces.[10] The chapter will end by discussing why a relation between the topics of safety and organizational vulnerability is of more general relevance for organizations that operate in dynamic environments. All in all, this chapter not only contributes to the development of an understanding of the vulnerability of expeditionary military taskforces or network organizations more in general, but also to existing theoretical discussions on vulnerability in organizations.

---

6 De Waard and Kramer 2008; De Waard 2010.

7 Kramer 2007.

8 Kramer et al. 2012; Moorkamp et al. in press; Moorkamp and Kramer 2014.

9 Moorkamp and Kramer 2014.

10 Kramer 2007; Kramer et al. 2010, 2012, Moorkamp et al. 2014, in press.

2.2 Safety Management in the Dutch Military

Partly in response to demands made by the Dutch Safety Board,[11] a safety management system was implemented within the Netherlands Ministry of Defence.[12] The so-called *Veiligheidsmanagement Systeem Defensie* (VMSDef) complies with *International Organization for Standardization* (ISO) 9001, 14001 and *Occupational Health and Safety Management Systems* (OHSAS) 18001 norms. In safety science, safety management systems are criticized because they are considered to contribute to bureaucratization. They are criticized for focusing on how bureaucracy can work better and the assumption that safety will be the result of following procedures and rules.[13] If that is the case, the question is how the Dutch military deals with vulnerability against the background of a dynamically complex security environment on the one hand, and the demands of a typical safety management system on the other.

One of the most salient aspects of VMSDef is the precondition that it is not considered applicable for safety issues that involve the presence of hostile opponents. The VMSDef guideline states: "it involves all health and safety issues within the Defence organization that do not involve any dangers from hostile opponents".[14] This suggests that safety is not generally considered as a precondition for effectiveness, but in some conditions actually as an obstacle to effectiveness, that is, the very conditions the military is supposed to be effective. That means that VMSdef has incorporated a clause that formalizes under what conditions it can be put aside. "The minister of Defence and the Chief of Staff may deviate from existing safety rules and procedures under operational circumstances (…) and apply Operational Risk Management in order to identify and register risks". As such, Operational Risk Management (ORM) has a prominent place when it comes to developing safety under expeditionary operational circumstances. According to VMSDef: "Operational risk management is a systematic method, which is part of regular planning and executive processes, to make decisions on ways to control and minimize (unknown) risks during operations".[15] So it appears that under certain dynamic conditions VMSDef can be put aside in favour of a system that is better suited under those conditions.

The question is how this dynamic between VMSDef and ORM works out in taskforces and how this ORM procedure helps to understand vulnerability during operations in dynamic contexts. In a recent case study that was conducted within 107th Aerial Systems battery, a unit that operated Unmanned Aerial Vehicles (UAV's) within Task Force Uruzgan (TFU) it was learned that ORM was used to justify specific kinds of "safety rule-breaking".[16] On particular occasions, the commanding officer of TFU demanded that the UAV was deployed in conditions in which it was

[11] Onderzoeksraad Voor Veiligheid 2009.

[12] VMSDef; Ministry of Defence 2010.

[13] Dekker 2014, p. 349; Bieder and Bourrier 2013; Hale 2003; Moorkamp et al. 2014.

[14] Our translation; Ministry of Defence 2010, p. 1-1 (our translation).

[15] Ministry of Defence 2010, p. vii (our translation).

[16] Moorkamp and Kramer 2014.

forced beyond its known technological limitations. The UAV was, for example, deployed in a thunderstorm, in "icing-conditions" and in high temperatures in which it was feared that it would lack sufficient aerodynamic lift.[17] The commanding officer of TFU justified this by claiming that deploying the UAV was crucial for establishing "overview" when for example infantry platoons were confronted with a shooting. So indeed, safety rules for the deployment of the UAV were put aside in the interest of safety of infantry soldiers. In such occasions, a particular interpretation of ORM was employed to move responsibility for the UAV and liability for potential damages operations from the UAV unit to the Task Force commander by means of a written and signed document. Employed in this way, the ORM procedure provides formal protection for operators for deployment against their better judgment. It provides the formal justification—it needs to be signed by a commanding officer that has been allowed the formal right to do so—to put aside rules that are related to the safe deployment of assets. As such, ORM is a tool that is used in the interest of averting accountability from an operator that is responsible for the safe operating of a technical asset to a superior commander who considers it necessary to deploy this asset in light of operational necessity, even though this might challenge—for example—its technical limitations. This shows that ORM, interpreted and applied in a particular way, can function as a "get-out-of-the-safety-jail-for-free" card, because operational necessity is always something that is to be interpreted by a higher commander.

There are two issues here that are important to understand the relevance of the perspective of organizational vulnerability. In the first place, the example above shows that the way one understands the nature of a socio-technical system determines how one tries to establish safety. If an organization is considered a machine in which every small part needs to operate in a precisely specified way, then indeed the reliable and safe functioning of this machine necessitates a dense web of rules that guides how specific parts should operate.[18] As straightforward as this sounds to many people, this assumption quickly becomes problematic in dynamic environments. This is evident in the example above in the issue that the safety of one part (UAV) becomes opposed to the safety of another (a unit of infantry soldiers). The curious fact the VMSDef is not supposed to work in dynamic environments suddenly seems more straightforward.

Secondly, and related to the first argument, it is questionable whether the interpretation of ORM employed in the case helps military taskforces to understand challenges to functional integration. Although the phrasing suggests that ORM is a systematic method to minimize and control operational risks, VMSDef appears to lack an underlying theory and associated pragmatic tools that would enable the assessment of organizational vulnerability. One of the main examples that emerges in Moorkamp and Kramer's case study is that the Dutch UAVs experienced near misses with Dutch Apache helicopters because the UAV unit lacked integration into Task Force Uruzgan.[19] The point here is that in this way, ORM does not help oper-

[17] Moorkamp and Kramer 2011.

[18] Morgan 1997.

[19] Moorkamp and Kramer 2014; Moorkamp et al. 2014.

ators to develop or maintain functional integration, nor to understand threats to functional integration other than those resulting from breaking unequivocal rules.

The above-mentioned example and the research findings highlighted in the introduction showed that operators throughout TFU were concerned with issues of functional integration, which resulted in organizational vulnerability. To come up with a perspective that is sensitive to such issues, the next section will aim to relate frequently used theories on organizational safety to the perspective of organizational vulnerability.

2.3 Vulnerability and Organizing for Safety

In the previous section, it was claimed that the way one aims to organize for safety depends on how one understands the character of socio-technical systems.[20] Understanding and studying organizational vulnerability of military task forces therefore calls for explicating different paradigms that lie behind different frequently used organizational safety theories. Therefore, firstly, two different paradigms in organizational safety theory are discussed. Secondly, based on these paradigms a choice is made for frequently used organizational safety theories that enable understanding the issue of organizational vulnerability within organizations and military task forces in particular.

In connection to safety, Dekker distinguishes between two "models" that guide the way organizations think about making progress with safety.[21] The first model (*model 1*) perceives organizations as systems that are active in stable, or at least predictable environments. Following this assumption, the behaviour of organizations can be programmed by rules. Safety is seen as the result from people following procedures. Safety management is in this perspective "removing deviations" in order to improve predictability.[22] The last 20 years, safety scientists have become disenchanted with this model.[23] Rasmussen notes that this "classic command and control model" is inadequate in dynamic situations. Dekker calls it "(...) naive at best, and always misleading".[24]

This disenchantment has given rise to the development of a second model. According to the second model (*model 2*): "safety results from people being skillful at judging when and how (and when not) to adapt procedures to local circumstances".[25] Moorkamp et al. stress that according to this perspective organizations should be able to *cope with* uncertainty, rather than *remove* uncertainty, which is central in the first

[20] Zinck Pedersen 2013, p. 216.

[21] Dekker 2005, pp. 133–139.

[22] Moorkamp et al. 2014.

[23] Rasmussen 1997, p. 185.

[24] Dekker 2005, p. 137.

[25] Dekker 2005, p. 139.

model.[26] Defined in this way, safety is a *control-problem*—the problem of controlling an organization's central processes—indeed to maintain the organized coherence of an organizational system.[27] In the second model, procedures are seen as "resources for action", which cannot specify all circumstances in which they can be applied.[28] Nor can procedures dictate their own application. In fact, according to the second model, managing safety according to the first model can actually be counterproductive[29] and can encourage defensive behaviour in operators.[30]

It seems obvious that the second model fits the kind of environments in which military taskforces are deployed. As was sketched in the introduction, military taskforces operate in an environment with uncertainties they need to be able to cope with, rather than that they are able to remove uncertainty. That is, they are not able to shield an organization from environmental uncertainty. As such they are not able to create the conditions in which the assumptions of a stable environment apply, which was typical of the first model. In this chapter we, therefore, focus on theories that share *model 2* assumptions. Being concerned with the implications of operating in an environment with uncertainties, these theories all rely on a systems theoretical basis. However, they differ in the organizational characteristics and dynamics they focus on and the way they conceptualize these. The three theories that are discussed below are Normal Accidents Theory (NAT), High Reliability Theory (HRT), and Resilience Engineering (RE). The first two were developed within organization science and were initially hardly picked up in safety science. RE is a relatively recent development that can be understood as a response to Rasmussen's demand for modelling dynamic systems.

These theories and the academic debates between them will be discussed. One way to put the different organizational theories about safety into perspective is by relating them to the classic polemic in organization science between theories about *structure* and *process*. This polemic is essentially about a difference in studying organizations as solid entities and studying how these entities came into being in the first place,[31] and is related to the broader discussion in social science between structure and agency.[32] Weick refers to this dichotomy as a difference in studying the noun "organization" and the verb "organizing".[33] While structure refers to fixed—noun-like—characteristics of organizations, such as their structural design, process refers to the way activities—verbs—within systems are organized. From a safety perspective, this means a difference in focusing on organizational vulnerabilities that are related to the structural characteristics of systems versus a focus on vulnerabilities that are related to the way people act and coordinate to deal with disruptions.

---

26 Moorkamp et al. 2014, p. 3.

27 Leveson 2004, pp. 249–250.

28 Dekker 2005, p. 139.

29 Gilpin and Murphy 2008, p. 5.

30 Fucks and Dien 2013.

31 Tsoukas 2005, pp. 379–380.

32 Kramer 2007.

33 Weick 1979.

The next section will focus on developing a perspective in which elements of both a *structure* and *process* perspective are combined, which are both considered important in studying vulnerabilities in complex organizations.[34] In fact, Becker considers the issue of how to combine structure and agency to be essential for any social theory.[35]

2.3.1 Vulnerability and Structure

NAT is the organizational theory that mainly focuses on vulnerability from a *structure perspective*. Charles Perrow developed NAT in response to the high profile incidents in the Three Miles Island (TMI) nuclear reactor.[36] While previously safety science focused on either technical or human error,[37] NAT first identified *organization* as a decisive factor in safety. The idea is that in systems with certain organizational characteristics, accidents can be *normal*. That is, they can be considered as the predictable outcome of the organization's normal functioning. Basically, NAT is a theory about cascading failures. In systems with complex and partly unpredictable patterns of interacting parts (complex interaction), and in which these interactions are critically interdependent (tight coupling), small deviations, disruptions, technical glitches or mundane human errors can combine in a way that leads to a cascade of failures. Eventually such a cascade can lead to system accidents: the collapse of functional integration of a system. This was a disturbing argument at the time; systems with no significant technical malfunctions and in which no catastrophic blunders are made by operators still can collapse as a result of organization.

The essence of NAT's argument is that some organizations are more vulnerable to cascading failures than others. According to NAT, in dynamic environments disturbances are best absorbed locally—which demands decentralization—while in organizations in which crucial functions are tightly coupled, sufficient overview to make crucial decisions is only available at a centralized position. That is, systems that are characterized by complex interactions and tight couplings are confronted with conflicting demands: they should be centralized and decentralized at the same time. At the central positions there is too little understanding of local disturbances, which makes centralization an unfit control strategy. At the same time, because of a lack of overview of critical interdependencies between parts of a system, local disturbances with a potential to cause system-wide interference cannot be adequately controlled at the decentralized positions. Systems that are characterized by complex interactions and tight couplings are, according to NAT, therefore fundamentally vulnerable to cascading failures.

Focusing on interactions and couplings, like NAT does, is a way to analyze systems by taking stable, macro-level characteristics into account. Although Perrow emphasizes that NAT was an early formulation in which the systems theoretical

---

[34] Kramer 2007, pp. 87–88; also Hernes 2014, p. 67.

[35] Becker 2005.

[36] Perrow 1999.

[37] Reason 1997.

basis was not fully worked out,[38] it can, however, be related to a socio-technical theoretical perspective on organizations.[39] If systems possess a more or less solid hierarchical form (a layering of subsystems within systems[40]) and if this solid form is meant to interact in a specific way in order to handle certain tasks, this basic *production structure* can be called: "the grouping and coupling of operational activities in relation to order flows".[41] This particular interpretation of NAT leads to a view on safety in which the *production structure* is the object that is to be controlled by a *control structure*. The more complex the web of macro structural interdependencies and the more crucial the interrelations that make up a production structure is, the more a system is bound by rules, which subsequently limits its ability to handle disruption. Normal accidents are in this view situations in which the amount of potential mistakes produced by a production structure in relation to environmental disruptions exceeds the system's capabilities for control.[42]

2.3.2 Vulnerability and Process

At the end of the 1980s, HRT was initially formulated as a response to NAT. If one agrees that systems that are characterized by complex interactions and tight couplings are fundamentally uncontrollable, why aren't there more accidents? The idea that led to the development of HRT was that there are *sources of reliability* available in organizations that prevent a cascade into failure.[43] Organizations that maintain a high level of reliability, despite working with hazardous technology or in complex environments, are called High Reliability Organizations (HROs). The study of HROs was focused on finding these sources of reliability. The sources of reliability HRT was looking for were located in the abilities of operators to absorb disturbances, even within tightly coupled and centralized structures. This is for example illustrated by the study of flight decks by Weick and Roberts.[44] Besides aircraft carriers, the kinds of organizations studied by HRT theorists are submarines, air traffic control systems and nuclear facilities.[45]

Given this emphasis on organic organizing processes, HRT has sought theoretical underpinning in the organizational theory developed by Weick.[46] The attention for the dynamic process properties of systems is evident in Weick's claim that "streams,

---

38 Perrow 2004.

39 Kramer 2007, p. 122.

40 Simon 1962.

41 De Sitter 2000, p. 97 (our translation).

42 De Sitter 2000; De Sitter et al. 1997; Moorkamp et al. 2015.

43 La Porte and Rochlin 1994, p. 222.

44 Weick and Roberts 1993.

45 Bierly and Spender 1995; La Porte 1988; Perin 2006.

46 Weick et al. 1999.

flows, and changes are the essence of what managers manage".[47] In the perspective of Weick, "organizing" is an activity that "serves to narrow the range of possibilities, to reduce the number of 'might occurs'". "In this perspective, the activities of organizing are directed toward the establishment of a 'workable level of certainty'".[48] This fits with a particular view on organizations, "the image of organizations that we prefer is one that argues that organizations keep falling apart and they require "chronic rebuilding".[49] This view on organizations opposes the view of organizations as solid entities that every now and then are confronted with a threat. Also, Weick portrays an organization against the background of an uncertain, ambiguous, changeable or dynamically complex environment, although he specifically emphasizes that this environment is—partly—constructed by the organizing activities of a system.[50] The emphasis on the need for chronic rebuilding indicates that functional integration has to be continuously re-established. Therefore, notwithstanding the search for sources of reliability that keep systems with manifest design flaws safe, HRT in a sense portrays systems as even more vulnerable than NAT. Organizations are in this view fragile constructions held together by transient organizing processes. This has consequences for the view on safety: in an organization that needs constant rebuilding, safety cannot be established by enforcing pre-programmed behaviour, which follows from the definition of safety as a "dynamic non-event", "what produces the stable outcome is constant change rather than continuous repetition".[51]

Against the background of the organizing problem explained above, Weick considers sensemaking a crucial process in organizations. Sensemaking is about "the ongoing retrospective development of plausible images that rationalize what people are doing".[52] Sensemaking is certainly not straightforwardly portrayed as a "solution" to the problem of dealing with a dynamically complex environment. After all, if environmental signals are "really" uncertain, enactments cannot solely rely on existing knowledge. In dynamically complex environments sensemaking is equally about "sensediscrediting", that is, the challenging of existing ideas.[53] "Only with ambivalent use of previous knowledge are systems able to both benefit from lessons learned and to update either their actions or meanings in ways that adapt to changes in the system and its context".[54] Sensemaking is, in other words, the organization's confrontation with itself,[55] in which "doubt" is an essential ingredient. An important implication of this is that operators in dynamically complex contexts are in a

[47] Weick 1979, p. 42.

[48] Weick 1979, p. 3.

[49] Weick 1979, p. 44.

[50] Kramer 2007.

[51] Reason 1997, p. 37.

[52] Weick et al. 2009, p. 129.

[53] Weick 1979.

[54] Weick 2009 p. 139.

[55] Hutter and Power 2005, p. 25.

sense "beyond rules".[56] Operators might need to act, and to create, brake, bend and blend rules in order to keep a system from falling apart, which indicates that they occupy a meta-position in relation to the rules that govern their work.[57]

Since the early 1990s the academic debate on safety within organizations has been dominated by the polemic between NAT and HRT.[58] NAT criticized HRT for being overly optimistic,[59] for underestimating the influence of design on organic organizing processes, or for selecting case studies on the dependent variable (mainly relatively successful/highly reliable organizations were studied). HRT on its part criticized NAT for entertaining a too static view of organizations, and for confusing technical and social systems.[60] HRT argues that tight coupling and complex interactions are not static properties of systems.[61] Activities that appear loosely coupled can suddenly become tightly coupled as a result of certain unexpected developments. HRT furthermore claims that centralization and decentralization should not be seen as static opposites.[62] There are still publications emerging which try to develop a resolution to this debate,[63] or claim to have found a special case that cannot be explained by both theories and which requires a new form of explanation.[64] It is probably fair to say that most theorists would argue that some way of combining structure and process perspectives is necessary to understand organizational vulnerability. As such, NAT and HRT perhaps function as ideal-typical reference points in an academic debate on the interplay between structure and process, while few would adhere to one of the extremes while totally dismissing the other.

2.3.3 Vulnerability and the Interplay Between Structure and Process

The previous emphasized that NAT predominantly focuses on *structure* (i.e., the basic structural design of systems) while HRT focuses on *process* in organizations (i.e., the way people interact within an organization to coordinate their activities). As it emphasizes both structure and process, RE appears at face value as an approach that occupies a position between NAT and HRT. RE is not a theory that originates from organization science, but has been developed in response to Rasmussen's disenchantment explained above.

RE has developed a complicated account of structure in systems. Inspired by complexity science, Dekker has worked out a perspective on organizations in

56 Weick 1979; Kramer 2007.

57 Kramer and Van Bezooijen, in press.

58 Sagan 1993; Rijpma 1997.

59 Sagan 1993.

60 La Porte and Rochlin 1994.

61 Weick 2001.

62 La Porte and Rochlin 1994, p. 224.

63 Shrivastava et al. 2009.

64 Roe and Schulman 2008.

which the idea of *organized complexity* is central. "It is complex because there are a large number of components, and, as a result, a dense throng of mini-programs running and interacting, cross influencing each other". "But what it produces is not disorganized. Rather it is organized (...) as an amazing emergent product of the complex interactions between a multitude of simpler entities".[65] Although systems are organized and structured, they are according to this view not organized and structured as a result of design. The ant colony is the image of organization that is central here.[66] This image focuses on the complicated organized behaviour that is displayed by ant colonies, while no single ant has designed the colony, or understands it in its entire complexity. The organized behaviour of the colony is a macro-level phenomenon that emerges from the behaviour of interacting ants. The emphasis on emergence is meant to dismiss the idea of hierarchical layering or organization design. Structure is *organized complexity*, which refers to a complex web of interrelations between activities and is not designed.

Apart from a focus on structure, RE emphasizes process by emphasizing the role of operators in handling complexity. They are not considered as straightforward rule followers but as intelligent and mindful agents. An important issue for RE is that traditional *model 1* accounts lead to a biased understanding of the role of "human error" in accident causation.[67] The critique is that the context of errors is not taken into account.[68] RE has developed a view on "error" which emphasizes that they may be deeply ingrained practices that were developed to avoid "systems failures".[69] What looking back on an accident appears as a straightforward "human error" may have been a desperate attempt by operators to maintain functional integration. This leads to a different view on rules: "There is a deeper, more complex interplay whereby practice sometimes precedes and defines the rules rather than being defined by them".[70] Furthermore: "High reliability organizations (...) distinguish themselves by their constant investment in trying to monitor and understand the gap between procedures and practice. The common reflex is not to try to close the gap, but to understand why it exists".[71] Within safety science this has become known as a "normal work" perspective: it is the "normal work" of operators to handle complexity and studying "normal work" is seen as an important way to develop an understanding of safety dynamics.[72] Structure and process are interrelated in RE because the activities of operators in dealing with complexity can have counterproductive effects on a macro-level in the system of organized complexity.

65 Dekker 2011, p. 157.

66 Dekker 2011, p. 157.

67 Woods et al. 2010, p. 4.

68 Reiman and Rollenhagen 2011, p. 1272.

69 Dekker 2005.

70 Dekker 2005, p. 133.

71 Dekker 2005 p. 141.

72 Bourrier 2002.

The above makes clear that structure and process are very much intertwined in RE. Actually, what is called *organized complexity* seems to focus attention on the structured aspects of what was called process above: networks of acting and interacting operators, involved with the everyday business of maintaining functional integration. A focus on organizational design is not taken into account, and therefore it is apparently considered irrelevant. The attention is on *organized complexity* and Dekker considers complex systems both resilient and vulnerable by virtue of their complexity, which he deems a paradox. "Because they consist of complex webs of relationships, and because a lot of control is distributed rather than centralized, complex systems can adapt to a changing world". However, "Complexity opens up a way for a particular kind of brittleness. Their openness means unpredictable behaviour".[73] According to RE not just "organized complexity", but also accidents are the result of emergence.[74] Quite similar to NAT, accidents are according to RE the result of a cascade. "Failures, when they do occur, can cascade through these systems in ways that may confound the people managing them, making it difficult to stop a progression of failure".[75] The confusing aspect is that complexity science is about how higher-level *order* emerges out of local interactions, whereas system accidents are according to RE about how global *disorder* results out of local interactions.

Although RE emphasizes in a certain way both structure and process, its position is not really between NAT and HRT. For RE, *complexity* is a general condition of all organizations in all situations and an explanation for both resilience and accidents. Opposed to that, both NAT and HRT relate vulnerability to systems that are characterized by complex interactions and tight couplings.[76] By emphasizing a particular of idea of organized complexity that dismisses attention for design as a relic from mechanistic thinking, RE is insensitive to the way design shapes local interactions and to the way different designs may have differing influences on the ability of operators to deal with complexity.[77]

2.4 Studying Vulnerability in Military Taskforces

The organizational theories on safety summarize generic ideas about vulnerability in organizations. Despite differences in emphasis, all three basically adhere to a *model 2* perspective on organizations and rules. In this section we want to develop a conceptualization of vulnerability in organizations that uses ingredients from all three approaches, but differs in the way the interplay between *structure* and

[73] Dekker 2011 p. 153.

[74] Dekker et al. 2011, p. 942; Woods et al. 2010, p. 38.

[75] Dekker 2011, p. 128.

[76] Zinck Pedersen 2013.

[77] Moorkamp et al. 2014.

process is conceptualized. The basic idea is that in large socio-technical systems hierarchical layering of subsystems within systems—and therefore design—based on a particular "grouping and coupling" is a necessary and functional characteristic.[78] At the same time, any design is inevitably challenged and potentially outdated against the background of a confrontation with a dynamic complex environment that demands change and evolution. This outdated character of design is visible in process: operators that aim to maintain functional integration are essentially involved with this issue. For this reason, it is claimed here that systems need to organize their ability to continuously reflect on their organization: they need to "organize doubt" directed at their own organization.[79]

The approach we want to sketch takes up the idea of *normal work* from RE: the normal work of operators consists of dealing with dynamic complexity. Studying normal work offers therefore a particular lens on organizational vulnerability. However, because of the theoretical issues with the idea of *organized complexity* that were discussed in the previous paragraph, we want to propose a different conceptualization of normal work. This conceptualization is based upon a different idea about the interplay between structure and process, which is based upon a particular way of combining NAT and HRT. The idea of "the organizational skeleton", developed by Weick, is considered here as a particular useful way of combining NAT and HRT.[80] Weick uses a definition by Bate, Kahn and Pye who claim that: "design is a bare bones framework on which a more organic, emergent, social structure develops as people interact, argue, fall out, come together, and otherwise manage their day to day situation".[81] In this definition "the skeleton" refers to what was previously called a *production structure* (a division of labour), which has been related to NAT, while "the organic, emergent, social structure" refers to *process*, which was the object of study of HRT. The idea of the skeleton is applied by Weick to point out the value of underspecification in organization design. Weick's argument is that underspecification creates loosely coupled systems. Loose coupling is conducive of the development of an "organic, emergent, social structure", which is crucial because of adaptability. The idea of the *organizational skeleton* is different from the idea of *organized complexity* because of the role of organizational structure (the bones). On the one hand, organizational structure can be important for coherence in larger organizations. Division of labour and a resulting hierarchical nesting of subsystems within systems is according to Simon essential because it counters information overload.[82] On the other hand, an organizational structure can reduce the flexibility of the skeleton. If a structure establishes "the grouping and coupling of operational activities in relation to order

[78] Simon 1962.

[79] Kramer 2007.

[80] Weick 2004.

[81] Bate et al. 2000, p. 199.

[82] Simon 1962.

flows", critical specifications between subsystems will develop.[83] These critical specifications bind local emerging structures to specific rules, or to a need for a centralized command.

Given this focus on the *organizational skeleton*, *normal work* is not just about handling complexity, but about dealing with dynamic complexity in view of the possibilities and limitations that the skeleton allows. Normal work, in our view, needs therefore to be understood as being in its very essence about the interplay between structure and process, and as the very place in which organizational vulnerability manifests itself. Operators in dynamically complex environments are confronted with all kinds of disruptions. Indeed, the normal work of operators is to handle these disruptions. Studying normal work is informative because it provides insight into the everyday dealings within an organization that needs to deal with dynamic complexity. This handling of disruptions needs to be understood against the background of a *structure* that limits the degrees of freedom at the lower levels. If operators deal with a particular disruption, their options are limited by the flexibility that the organizational network allows. Furthermore, their particular perspective on their environment is influenced by the position they occupy in the organization.[84] Part of their creativity in handling disruptions is in finding solutions for operational problems in a way that does not break the functional integration of the skeleton. Ideally, the structural limitations that operators experience in handling dynamic complexity are used to reflect on the organizational structure of the organization (organizing doubt). In that case a relation is established between the struggles to deal with dynamic complexity and the nature of the organizational skeleton.

When this perspective on organizations is used it is obvious that they are considered inherently vulnerable. Their design is principally outdated against the background of a dynamically complex environment. In such environments, organizations are fundamentally unsettled. Functional integration needs to be established form moment to moment, and the resulting coherence is not a sort of system-wide symphonious harmony, but one that is good enough to survive to the next moment. In normal work, the conflict between on the one hand environmental disruptions and on the other hand the conflict with the existing structural design of an organization becomes visible. The solutions found by operators can potentially lead to vulnerability because they were unaware of certain dependencies between different processes, because they provoke a certain reaction from the environment and as such setting the stage for further environmental disruptions. Obviously, in order to understand the dynamics active in normal work, one needs to study more than just normal work. Insight in the organizational context of normal work is necessary, that is, insight in both the production structure and formal control structure, as well as the flow of the primary processes to which operators contribute, throughout the organization.

---

[83] De Sitter 2000, p. 97 (our translation).

[84] Kramer 2007.

2.5 Conclusion and Discussion

Studying normal work is according to the perspective in this chapter the royal road to understanding a particular kind of organizational vulnerability of a system. When this perspective is applied to military taskforces, specifically expeditionary taskforces that were deployed by the Netherlands Armed Forces, a couple of issues stand out. In the introduction, it was emphasized that expeditionary military taskforces are temporary constructions that are designed for a particular mission and that need to find a design that works in a particular environment. This is more than just the result of *underspecification*: the structure is *underdeveloped* because basic interactions within a system need to be organized. These taskforces are like a collection of bones that needs to find out what skeleton it needs to become and how to realize that.[85] Empirical studies into Dutch expeditionary taskforces consistently reveal that the internal structure needs to be (sometimes continuously) recalibrated in order to adapt to local conditions.[86] An implication of this can be that in some expeditionary taskforces operators essentially develop the organization or network design through normal work.[87] In trying to manage outside disruptions and internal hidden interactions, operators create structures that are meant to control (their own) future interactions.[88] In that case normal work almost equals designing.

If normal work is about dealing with dynamic complexity in view of the possibilities and limitations that the organizational skeleton allows, a particular vulnerability of typical expeditionary military taskforces deployed by the Netherlands Armed Forces becomes clear. Essentially, normal work proceeds against the background of a not fully worked out skeleton, and therefore with a limited view on structural constraints on normal work. In taskforces that are so large and complex that they escape the comprehension of those involved, this can lead to a threat of functional integration. If normal work contributes to creating structures this can lead to flawed skeletons. More specifically, this is the case if a structure mushrooms while it is unclear what the effects of local structuration efforts are on the integration of the whole. A structural design that mushrooms out of the control of those involved can lead to *tight coupling* between central processes with limited awareness of this at both the centralized and decentralized positions. Such an organization lacks the ability to reflect on its own design (organizing doubt). This

---

[85] This indicates a limitation of the modular design philosophy for designing military taskforces. This philosophy assumes an environment that is stable enough to be able to beforehand work out a basic design that can remain consistent, De Waard and Kramer 2010; Therefore, it is difficult to conceive of a design of a module that can remain consistent in the security contexts in which the Army is deployed. The modular design philosophy apparently lacks an idea of *organized doubt* that may be necessary to reflect on the design in the light of unpredicted dynamics.

[86] Kramer 2007; Kramer et al. 2012.

[87] Moorkamp et al. 2015.

[88] Moorkamp et al. 2015; Moorkamp and Kramer 2014.

particular vulnerability was indeed observed in an analysis of Task Force Uruzgan.[89] Basically, this situation sets the stage for normal accidents. This shows the importance of organizing the ability of a system to reflect on its own design (i.e., to organize doubt). It also shows the risks involved in portraying the ant colony as image of the ideal organization with supreme adaptability. One particular issue that makes the expeditionary taskforce vulnerable is that it resembles the ant colony, with ants that are unaware of the impact of their "normal work" on functional integration of the colony.

From this discussion, it is obvious that inherently vulnerable taskforces are in everyday reality polymorphously vulnerable systems. That is to say, from the perspective of maintaining functional integration, vulnerability can be witnessed at different organizational levels such the level of the local operational unit and the macro taskforce level. If a taskforce is seen as a network of interconnecting units that are in contact with a dynamic environment at multiple positions at the same time, different operators are trying to deal with the problems within their work domain on the basis of a limited understanding of critical interdependencies within this network. Furthermore, in developing the taskforces they are part of, operators may choose to solve local problems by inadvertently creating imbalances at the macro-level of the taskforces. The perspective developed in this chapter points to important limitations of safety management systems such as VMSDef that employ "model one" assumptions without consideration for organizational dynamics in complex security environments in which the defence organizations are deployed.

As a final remark, it can be stated that for two reasons the perspective outlined in this chapter is more generally relevant for organizations. Firstly, more and more organizations seem to employ a strategy of establishing temporary organizational forms in order to conduct operations in a challenging environment.[90] Some examples can be found in crisis management, project management literature and construction.[91] Comparable vulnerabilities may be found in such organizations. Further research however, needs to address these possibilities for generalization in more detail. Secondly, understanding safety problems by means of a vulnerability perspective that combines process and structure might be of added value in taking a more integrated perspective in understanding and tackling safety issues. As such, this chapter not only contributes to the development of an understanding of military taskforces or to temporary organizations, but to existing discussions on safety in organizations in general.

---

[89] Moorkamp et al. 2015; Moorkamp and Kramer 2014.

[90] De Waard and Kramer 2008; Modig 2007.

[91] Flyvbjerg et al. 2003.

References

Achterbergh J, Vriens D (2010) Organizations: social systems conducting experiments, 2nd edn. Springer, Heidelberg

Bate P, Khan R, Pye A (2000) Towards a culturally sensitive approach to organization structuring: where organization design meets organization development. Org Sci 1:197–211

Becker KH (2005) Luhmann's systems theory and theories of social practices. In: Seidl D, Becker KH (eds) Niklas luhmann and organizing studies. Liber & Copenhagen Business School Press, Copenhagen

Bieder C, Bourrier M (eds) (2013) Trapping safety into rules: how desirable or avoidable is proceduralization? Ashgate Publishing Company, Farnham

Bierly PE, Spender JC (1995) Culture and high reliability organizations: the case of the nuclear submarine. J Manag 21:639–656

Bijker WE (2006) The vulnerability of technological culture. In: Nowotny H (ed) Cultures of technology and the quest for innovation. Berghahn Books, New York

Bourrier M (2002) Bridging research and practice: the challenge of normal operations studies. J Cont Crisis Manag 10:173–180

De Sitter LU (2000) Synergetisch produceren: human resources mobilisation in de produktie een inleiding in structuurbouw. Uitgeverij Van Gorcum, Assen

De Sitter LU, Den Hertog JF, Dankbaar B (1997) From complex organizations with simple jobs to simple organizations with complex jobs. Human Relat. 50:497–534

De Waard EJ (2010) Engaging environmental turbulence. Organizational determinants for repetitive, quick and adequate responses. ERIM, Rotterdam

De Waard EJ, Kramer EH (2008) Tailored task forces: temporary organizations and modularity. Int J Project Manag 26:537–546

De Waard EJ, Kramer EH (2010) Expeditionary operations and modular organization design. In: Van Fenema SJ, Beeres PC (eds) Managing military organizations. Routledge, London

Dekker S (2005) Ten questions about human error: a new view of human factors and system safety. Lawrence Erlbaum Associates, Publishers, Mahwah, NJ

Dekker S (2011) Drift into failure. From hunting broken components to understanding complex systems. Ashgate Publishing Limited, Farnham

Dekker S (2014) The bureaucratization of safety. Saf Sci 70:348–357

Dekker S, Cilliers P, Hofmeyr JH (2011) The complexity of failure: implications of complexity theory for safety investigations. Saf Sci 49:939–945

Flyvbjerg B, Bruzelius N, Rothengatter W (2003) Megaprojects and risk: an anatomy of ambition. Cambridge University Press, Cambridge

Fucks I, Dien Y (2013) 'No Rule, No Use'? The effects of overproceduralization. In: Bieder C, Bourrier M (eds) Trapping safety into rules: how desirable or avoidable is proceduralization?. Ashgate Publishing Company, Farnham

Gilpin DR, Murphy PJ (2008) Crisis management in a complex world. Oxford University Press, New York

Hale A (2003) Safety management in production. Human Fact Ergon Manuf Service Ind 13:185–201

Hernes T (2014) A process theory of organizing. Oxford University Press, Oxford

Hutter B, Power M (2005) Organizational encounters with risk. Cambridge University Press, New York

Kramer EH (2007) Organizing doubt. Grounded theory, army units and dealing with dynamic complexity. Copenhagen Business University Press, Copenhagen

Kramer EH, Van Bezooijen B, Delahaij R (2010) Sensemaking during operations and incidents. In: Soeters J, Van Fenema PC, Beeres R (eds) Managing military organizations. Routledge, London

Kramer EH, De Waard E, De Graaff M (2012) Task Force Uruzgan and experimentation with organization design. In: Beeres R, van der Meulen L, Soeters J, Vogelaar A (eds) Mission Uruzgan. Amsterdam University Press, Amsterdam

La Porte TR (1988) The United States air traffic system: Increasing reliability in the midst of rapid growth. In: Mayntz R, Hughes T (eds) The development of large scale systems. Westview Press, Boulder

La Porte TR, Rochlin G (1994) A rejoinder to Perrow. J Cont Crisis Manag 2:221–227

Leveson N (2004) A new accident model for engineering safer systems. Saf Sci 42:237–270

Ministry of Defence (2010) Veiligheidsmanagement bij Defensie: een blauwdruk voor belegging en verankering. Vastgesteld Veiligheidsraad Defensie 14-06-2010; XPW-nr BS 2010014145

Modig N (2007) A continuum of organizations formed to carry out projects: temporary and stationary organization forms. Int J Project Manag 25:807–814

Moorkamp M, Kramer EH (2011) Ongevalsonderzoek als een organisatie-leerinstrument? Een systematische review van recente ongevalrapportages over incidenten met Unmanned Aerial Vehicles van het type Sagem-Sperwer. Internal report Ministry of Defence. Nederlandse Defensie Academie, Breda

Moorkamp M, Kramer EH (2014) Veiligheid van expeditionair organiseren binnen Task Force Uruzgan. Nederlandse Defensie Academie, Breda

Moorkamp M, Kramer EH, Van Gulijk C, Ale BJM (2014) Safety management theory and the expeditionary organization: a critical theoretical reflection. Saf Sci 69:71–81

Moorkamp M, Wybo JL, Kramer EH (2015) Pioneering with UAVs at the battlefield: the influence of organizational design on the emergence of safety. Saf Sci. doi:10.1016/j.ssci.2015.09.029

Morgan G (1997) Images of organization, new edn. Sage, Thousand Oaks

Onderzoeksraad Voor Veiligheid (2009) *Draadaanvaring Apache Helicopter. 12 December 2007.* Den-Haag: OVV

Perin C (2006) Shouldering risks: the culture of control in the nuclear power industry. Princeton University Press, Princeton

Perrow C (1999) Normal accidents. Living with high-risk technologies, 2nd edn. Princeton University Press, Princeton

Perrow C (2004) A personal note on normal accidents. Org Env 17:9–14

Rasmussen J (1997) Risk management in a dynamic society: a modelling problem. Saf Sci 27:183–213

Reason J (1997) Managing the risks of organizational accidents. Ashgate Publishing, Aldershot

Reiman T, Rollenhagen C (2011) Human and organizational biases affecting the management of safety. Reliab Eng Syst Saf 96:1263–1274

Rijpma J (1997) Complexity, tight-coupling and reliability: connecting normal accidents theory and high reliability theory. J Conting Crisismanag 5:15–23

Roe E, Schulman P (2008) High reliability management: operating on the edge. Stanford Business Books, Stanford

Sagan S (1993) The limits of safety. Organizations, accidents, and nuclear weapons. Princeton University Press, Princeton

Shrivastava S, Sonpar K, Pazzaglia F (2009) Normal accident theory versus high reliability theory: a resolution and call for an open systems view of accidents. Human Relat 62:1357–1390

Simon HA (1962) The architecture of complexity. Proc Am Philos Soc 106:467–482

Snook S (2000) Friendly fire. The accidental shootdown of U.S. Black Hawks over Northern Iraq. Princeton University Press, Princeton

Tsoukas H (2005) Complex knowledge. Studies in Organizational Epistemology. Oxford University Press, Oxford.

Weick KE (1979) The social psychology of organizing. McGraw-Hill, New York

Weick KE (1995) Sensemaking in Organizations. Sage, London

Weick KE (2004) Rethinking organizational design. In: Boland jr RJ and Collopy F (eds). Managing as Designing. Stanford University Press, Stanford, pp 36-53

Weick KE (2009) Making sense of the organization. The impermanent organization. Wiley & Sons, Chichester
Weick KE, Roberts K (1993) Collective mind in organizations: heedful interrelating on flight-decks. Admin Sci Quart 38:357–381
Weick K, Sutcliffe K, Obstfeld D (1999) Organizing for high reliability: processes of collective mindfulness. In: Sutton RS, Staw BM (eds) Research in organizational behavior. Stanford JAI Press, Stanford
Weick KE, Sutcliffe K, Obstfeld D (2009) Organizing and the process of sensemaking
Woods D, Dekker S, Cook R (2010) Behind human error, 2nd edn. Ashgate Publishing, Farnham
Weick KE, Making sense of the organization. The impermanent organization. Wiley, Chichester
Zinck Pedersen K (2013) Failsafe organizing? A pragmatic stance on patient safety. Copenhagen Business School, Frederiksberg

Part I
Organizing for Security

Chapter 3
Organizing for Insecurity and Chaos: Resilience and Modern Military Theory

Frans Osinga

Abstract This chapter addresses the remarkable disconnect between resilience literature and military theory. War puts high demands on the resilience of military organizations. Western militaries have adopted organizational and operational concepts to cope with the myriad challenges of violence, turbulence, uncertainty and an adaptive opponent that, when studied against the background of resilience literature, are quite sound. The maneuvrist approach and the idea of strategic paralysis both target the multiple nodes across various layers of an opponent's organization that allow it to display coherent and purposeful behaviour. Both aim to disrupt the resilience of the opponent. In turn, the concept of mission command and recent operational concepts such as network centric warfare and swarming are fully congruent with the literature about complex systems, adaptability and current insights on what produces organizational resilience in highly threatening and fluid environments: decentralization, formal and informal networks, solid feedback mechanisms, self-organization, mutual trust, and semi-autonomous units. This chapter suggests that, where resilience studies are still in the exploratory stage, without clear definition and coherent theory, there is benefit in studying military theory and military organizations, which are increasingly informed by the same literatures as resilience studies.

Keywords Mission command · Resilience · Counter-resilience · Military theory · Strategic paralysis · Complex adaptive systems · War · Boyd

---

F. Osinga (✉)
Faculty of Military Sciences, Netherlands Defence Academy, Breda, The Netherlands
e-mail: FPB.Osinga@mindef.nl

R. Beeres et al. (eds.), *NL ARMS Netherlands Annual Review of Military Studies 2016*, NL ARMS, DOI 10.1007/978-94-6265-135-7_3

Contents

3.1 Introduction

Military combat units organize for insecurity, not security. Theirs is by nature a very violent, highly dynamic and hostile environment filled with uncertainty, chaos and life threatening situations. Surviving and achieving organization success in such a turbulent environment requires very specific organizational characteristics. Military organizations, generally described as bureaucratic, traditional and hierarchical organizations, have attempted various models to deal with those challenges. Obviously, the capacity to absorb and bounce back from shock (i.e., resilience) is a key requirement and challenge.

Yet resilience literature has devoted little attention to military organizations, neither does disaster management literature. Military theory has likewise by and large not explicitly and deliberately incorporated insights from those literatures.[1] To be sure, Eliot Cohen and John Gooch long time ago already argued that many military misfortunes were due to the failure to anticipate, learn and adapt.[2] Moreover, military adaptation and innovation have recently gained prominence in strategic studies literature.[3] Nevertheless, it is still safe to say that military

[1] The exception here is perhaps the literature on Recognition Primed Decision making developed by Gary Klein, which is based on cases of first responders, which has found resonance in literature on military command and control.

[2] Cohen and Gooch 2006.

[3] Three recent publications are, Adamsky 2010; Farrell et al. 2013; Murray 2011.

theory—the body of knowledge concerning war, warfare, strategy and military command—and resilience literature are disconnected. That is remarkable for both literatures are natural partners, and indeed, as this chapter will suggest, the concept of resilience captures the aspiration of, as well as target for military organizations. It is central to contemporary strategic theory and military offensive doctrine as well as the dominant command philosophy of western armed forces.

To illustrate this, this chapter will introduce two dominant offensive concepts that have been adopted in doctrines of western militaries and applied in recent operations: John Warden's theory of strategic paralysis and the so called maneuvrist approach as pioneered by John Boyd. Another illustration is provided by discussing the command philosophy that most western militaries have adopted (in word or in deed) to cope with the challenges of the contemporary operational environment: mission command.[4] This excursion will demonstrate how integral the concept of resilience is to military organizations and military strategy, as well as suggest that intuitively or otherwise the solutions the military has developed show distinct parallels with the suggestions offered by resilience literature.

3.2 Resilience

Resilience has, in the past four decades, been a term increasingly employed throughout a number of sciences: psychology and ecology, most prominently. Increasingly one finds it in political science, business administration, sociology, history, disaster planning, urban planning, and international development. Recently it was explored in the context of counter-terrorism.[5] Resilience is, as a consequence, explored at different levels or scales: individual, familial, organizational, cultural, ecological, markets, and national and even global.[6] The shared use of the term does not, however, imply unified concepts of resilience nor the theories in which it is embedded. Different uses generate different methods, sometimes different methodologies.[7] The literature on organizational resilience is highly diverse and the empirical literature still remains on a conceptual and exploratory level. There is as yet no common agreement on how to measure organizational resilience.[8]

[4] Military command at all levels is the art of decision-making, motivating and directing to accomplish given missions.

[5] Canetti et al. 2014; Chasdi 2014; Gal 2014.

[6] Walklate et al. 2014.

[7] Martin-Breen and Anderies 2011, p. 5.

[8] Hillman 2013.

3.2.1 Resilience Defined

Nor is there much agreement on a single definition of resilience among scholars.[9] At the individual level resiliency has been described as "the process of coping with disruptive, stressful, or challenging life events in a way that provides the individual with additional protective and coping skills than prior to the disruption that results from the event",[10] or alternatively as the "capacity to bounce back, to withstand hardship, and to repair yourself".[11] In systems resilience can be defined as maintaining system function in the event of a disturbance. All can be subsumed in the following generic definition of resilience: the capacity of a system to absorb disturbance and reorganize while undergoing change so as to still retain the same function, structure and feedbacks, and therefore identity, that is, the capacity to change in order to maintain the same identity.[12]

This is a somewhat static perspective on resilience. It refers to the return to equilibrium. It does not include the creation of novel systems and structures as a response to shocks. It does not incorporate the notion of self-organization and evolution. As such the narrow definition of resilience excludes the way complex adaptive systems such as ecologies, cities and societies actually operate. The key feature of complex adaptive systems is adaptive capacity or adaptability and transformability. Resilience of socio-ecological systems requires the ability to adapt as well as to transform. This refers to the ability of systems—households, people, communities, ecosystems, nations—to generate new ways of operating, new systemic relationships. Adaptability captures the capacity of a system to learn, combine experience and knowledge, and adjust its responses to changing external drivers.[13]

But a perturbation can bring a system to a threshold after which it either incorporates change in its system and thus transform, or perish. Transformation is the capacity to create a fundamentally new system when ecological, economic, or social structures make the existing structure untenable. It follows that resilience includes the idea of self-organization, which is related to novelty and innovation: it generates inherently new ways of operating, ones that previously may not have been considered; certainly not predicted. Therefore, in complex adaptive systems, resilience is best defined as the ability to withstand, recover from, and reorganize in response to crises. Function is maintained, but system structure may not be.

---

9 Carle and Chassin 2004.

10 Richardson et al. 1990, p. 34.

11 Wolin and Wolin 1993, p. 5.

12 Walker et al. 2004; Folke et al. 2010.

13 Folke et al. 2010.

Table 3.1 Factors of organizational resilience

Before the event	Ability to anticipate
During the event	Ability to resist
	Ability to respond quickly
	Ability to act thoughtful
After the event	Ability to recover (fast)
	Ability of renewal/reinventing
	Ability to adapt
	Ability to learn

Source Hillman 2013

3.2.2 Preventing Accidents: Reading Perrow

The literature on organizational resilience draws from insights on organizational innovation, learning, flexibility, and networks. In addition, it draws in insight from accident theory and complexity theory. Theory on what exactly produces resilience is still scarce though. Hilman derived a number of factors facilitating resilience by looking at the various stages of a crisis (Table 3.1).[14] While this is useful for disaggregating the concept of resilience, it does not offer inroads for those who actually want to create resilient organization. For that it pays to start with accident and complexity theory (the theory explaining the behaviour of complex systems), the latter in particular as resilience originally was a reaction to the concept of stability in ecology.[15]

Perrow introduced the idea that organizations can be categorized as either simple or complex systems, and they consist of processes that are either linear or non-linear. Linear interactions are those in expected and familiar production or maintenance sequence, and those that are quite visible even if unplanned, whereas non-linear interactions are those of unfamiliar sequences, or unplanned and unexpected sequence, and either not visible or not immediately comprehensible. Complex as well as simple systems can have *tight* and/or *loose coupling* among subsystems and sub-processes. In a loosely coupled system there is slack or a buffer. Subsequently, what happens in the one item may not affect the other, until the buffer has been exceeded. Unexpected demands or lack of resources can be handled. In tightly coupled systems on the other hand there is no slack or buffer between two items. Quantities must be precise; resources cannot be substituted for one another.

Additionally, in tightly coupled systems, not only are the specific sequences invariant, but the overall design of the process and the number of specialized personnel and other essential, non-substitutionable production resources allow only one way to reach the production goal.[16] Generally, tightly coupled systems will

---

[14] Hillman 2013, p. 9.

[15] Martin-Breen and Anderies (2011), pp. 36–42; the following paragraphs are derived from Osinga 2006, Chapters 3 and 4.

[16] Perrow 1999, p. 90.

respond more quickly to perturbations. However, due to the rapid onset of non-foreseeable non-linear effects they may also react more violently and in more directions, with several layered effects, than loosely coupled systems.[17] Failure may not only be rapid, it may also manifest itself in various dimensions, at various moments and in various parts in the system and probably in totally unexpected places. The chance of incidents turning into accidents and system-wide catastrophe is larger in complex tightly coupled systems due to these factors, and the demands made on failure prevention and recovery measures are very high.

In contrast, loosely coupled systems can incorporate shocks and failures and pressures for change without destabilization. Loosely coupled systems tend to have ambiguous or perhaps flexible performance. Processes are not necessarily optimized for efficiency. It is possible to allow some parts latitude. In loosely coupled systems there is generally more time for recovery.[18] Concerning loosely coupled complex systems, Perrow argues that complexity requires that those at the point of disturbance are free to interpret the situation and take corrective measures, because that is where the incident is first noted. They should be allowed to diagnose the situation and take steps to contain the problem before the effects spread to other parts of the system. Because the interactions are loosely tight, there is time to develop a coherent picture and appropriate responses. Together with non-directive modes of synchronization and coordination, such as informal processes, shared culture, shared professional ethos, stable interaction patterns, slack and buffers, decentralization will allow a sufficient degree of control and sufficient failure recovery potential.

3.2.3 Learning from Complex Systems

Conceptually, Perrow's conclusions chime nicely with insights from complexity theory. Complexity theory examines emergent order in large, interactive, adaptive networks such as neural networks or ecosystems.[19] Robust ecosystems are characterized by interdependence, feedback (and cyclical flow of resources), cooperation, partnership, flexibility and diversity. The flexibility of an ecosystem is a consequence of its multiple feedback loops, which tend to bring the system back into balance whenever there is a deviation from the norm, due to changing environmental conditions. Disturbances are ever-present because things in the environment change all the time. The net-result is continual fluctuation. All the variables we can observe in an ecosystem—population densities, available nutrients, weather patterns, and so forth—always fluctuate. The more variables are kept

[17] For an in-depth account of the working of tightly coupled and non-linear effects see, Jervis 1997.

[18] Perrow 1999, pp. 93–94; Perrow 1972; Rijpma 1997.

[19] Richardson and Cilliers 2001; For studies that popularized this emerging scientific field, see Gleick 1987; Waldrop 1993.

fluctuating, the more dynamic is the system; the greater is its flexibility; and the greater is its ability to adapt to changing conditions. Lack of flexibility manifests itself as stress in the system. This will occur when one or more variables of the system are pushed to their extreme values, which induces increased rigidity throughout the system.

The role of diversity is closely connected with the network's structure. A diverse ecosystem will also be resilient, because it contains many species with overlapping ecological functions that can partially replace one another. A diverse community will be able to survive and reorganize itself because a damaged link in the network can at least partially be compensated for by other links. In other words, the more complex the network is, the more complex its pattern of interconnections, the more resilient it will be. Diversity means many different relationships, many different approaches to the same problem. The study of other complex adaptive systems suggests too that such systems co-evolve with the environment through self-organizing non-linear behaviour of agents navigating "the fitness landscapes". Under selective pressure they exhibit hierarchical self-organization.[20] Self-organization arises as the system reacts and adapts to its externally imposed environment.[21]

3.2.4 *From Complex Systems to Resilient Organizations*

Various authors argue that models of organization that are based on living systems are naturally organic and adaptive.[22] For organizations to survive, they need to co-evolve with their environment while maintaining internal stability. This requires variety, creativity and learning communities. An organization must embody enough diversity to provoke learning but not enough to overwhelm the legitimate system and cause anarchy. These studies maintain that, like ecosystems, organizations thrive when equipped with variety. Practically speaking, organizations (should) possess a range of coupling patterns, from tight to loose. Loosely coupled structures allow an organization to adjust to environmental drift, and when environmental shocks are particularly severe, loose structures react sluggishly, thus buying time to recover. Moderate and tightly coupled structures prevent an organization from over-responding to environmental perturbation. Coupling patterns, then, allow organizations to maintain relative stability in most environments and protect the system even against severe shocks.[23] Robust systems are characterized by "rich patterns of tight, moderate, and loosely coupled linkages; chains of interdependency branch in complicated patterns across nearly every actor in a broad

---

[20] van Uden et al. 2001; Lissack 1999, p. 112.

[21] The characteristics listed here are derived from Holland 1995; also Marion and Bacon 1999, p. 76.

[22] Lissack 1999.

[23] Marion and Bacon 1999, p. 76.

network of interaction. Such complex patterns of interaction protect the organization against environmental shock by providing multiple paths for action. If one pattern of interdependency in a network is disrupted, the dynamic performed by that subsystem can usually be rerouted to other areas of the network. Such robustness makes it difficult to damage or destroy the complex system, for complex interaction lends it amazing resilience".[24]

Structurally, the key theme is self-organization.[25] The optimal organizational form for adaptation in turbulent environments is seen as the *cellular form* operating in a network. Small teams operating relatively autonomously pursue entrepreneurial opportunities and share know-how among each other.[26] Cellular organizations tend to mirror the complexity of the environment with requisite variety, as individual cells sense new entrepreneurial opportunities. When environmental demands change, new cells can be formed and old ones disbanded as necessary. The freedom of activity is a key to enabling self-organizing behaviour. Control of such a networked organization is not provided by tight top-down controls. Instead, a combination of loose-tight controls is applied. The shared values of corporate culture in belief systems provide tight, but internal and perhaps even tacit control as a form of protocol. Loose control comes from interaction between supervisor and employees that encourages information sharing, trust and learning. The key to lose control is management's trust in employees to act according to the shared values, therefore setting them free to search for opportunities, learn, and apply accumulating knowledge to innovative efforts.[27] Successful leaders of complex organizations allow experimentation, mistakes, contradictions, uncertainty and paradox, so the organization can evolve. Managing an organization as a complex system means letting go of control and a focus instead on the power of the interconnected world of relationships and the feedback loops.[28]

Four key systems properties thus contribute to its resilience: (1) diversity and redundancy, (2) modular networks, and (3) responsive, regulatory feedbacks, loose-coupling and decentralized mode of command. The fourth has not fully been described yet: (4) learning. Resilience also requires, as noted, transformability and this revolves around the capacity to learn and translate novel insights into new organizational structures, entities and responses. Complex systems use mental models, or schemata, to make sense of the environment and take appropriate action in response to events. Learning involves validating the relevance of those schemata based on experience and adjusted them if necessary.

---

[24] Marion and Bacon 1999, p. 76.

[25] Kelly and Allison 1999, p. 5.

[26] Coleman 1999, p. 37.

[27] Coleman 1999, p. 40.

[28] The literature on complexity theory and its relevance for the humanities, social sciences and management theory is substantial, see Brown and Eisenhardt 1998; Merry 1995; Eve et al. 1997; Kiel and Elliott 1996; Eisenhardt and Sull 2001; Beinhocker 1999; Church 1999.

Indeed, as Mintzberg stated, the organizational capacity to learn is considered essential for professional-type organizations that operate in highly complex environments, where the knowledge required to create strategy is widely diffused, or that face truly novel situations, and/or that operate in dynamic and unpredictable environments.[29] Garwin, in similar vein, contends that adaptability and flexibility, for which learning is essential, is the defining parameter for organizational success (i.e., long-term survival).[30]

Various authors have observed that organizational learning is promoted by specific organizational characteristics. Argyris and Schon suggested that a loosely structured organization, unfettered by rigid internal hierarchies and overspecialization, would be more amenable to a free internal debate that would facilitate organizational learning and so facilitate change.[31] Facilitators for learning include a broad base of contributors and data sources; a process for sharing diverse perspectives and points of view and a willingness to embrace contradictory and unexpected findings; quick feedback; and forums for brainstorming in which new ideas are generated and creative thinking should be stimulated. When organizations interpret acquired information, they should adopt a dialectic mode in which various views are debated and tested. When information is transformed into action, new approaches must be tried, even when they result in some mistakes and failures.[32] There are echoes of insights from complexity theory indeed.[33]

3.3 The Nature of War: A Chaotic Clash of Complex Adaptive Systems

War can be construed as a clash between two or more complex adaptive systems, in fact, contemporary military literature has explored this notion and leading military doctrines are imbued with it.[34] And few environments put higher demands on the resilience of individuals and organizations than war and warfare. Few environments in civilian life are comparable to the horrific environment called war. It therefore is worthwhile to explore how military organizations have attempted to

---

29 Mintzberg et al. 1998, p. 229.

30 Garwin 2000, p. 9.

31 Argyris and Schon 1978, pp. 38–39, 143, 145.

32 Garwin 2000, pp. 28–43.

33 In recent popular management studies these same factors of resilience come to the fore, McKeown 2012 suggests that adaptability requires a modular structure, interoperability, swarming/clustering, tight feedback loops, de-coupling/de-intensify, Informal networks, strong communities bonded by values, beliefs, habits of mind, cooperation and trust, cognitive diversity and translational leaders; Similarly, Zolli and Healy 2012 suggest that resilience depends on innovation, learning, decentralization, critical thought, cooperation, swarming, and fostering change.

34 Davis and Czerwinski 1997; Beyerchen 1992; Atkinson and Moffat 2005; Mann 1992; Schmitt 1997; James 1995.

cope with such challenging conditions. Few organizations know more about the nature of war that the US Marine Corps (USMC) and few other military organizations have experimented so deliberately with organizational concepts to deal with the key challenges of war. The USMC has been at the forefront since the late 1970s in doctrinal developments that resulted in the widespread adoption of the mission command concept throughout western military organizations. It is therefore worthwhile to briefly summarize the USMC view on the key characteristics—the sources of violent turbulence—of the military operational environment called war.[35]

The starting point is that war is a violent clash of interests between or among organized groups characterized by the use of military force. The essence of war is a violent struggle between two hostile, independent, and irreconcilable wills, each trying to impose itself on the other. The opponent is not an inanimate object to be acted upon but an independent and animate force with its own objectives and plans. This dynamic introduces the key feature of friction, a concept from mechanics, and introduced into military strategic literature by Clausewitz. Friction refers to the force that makes the apparently easy so difficult. Friction is the force that resists all action and saps energy. In that latter context it also refers to the second law of thermodynamics in which all systems will grind to halt. Friction may be mental, as in indecision over a course of action. It may be physical, as in effective enemy fire or a terrain obstacle that must be overcome. Friction may be external, imposed by enemy action, the terrain, weather, or mere chance. Friction may be self-induced, caused by such factors as lack of a clearly defined goal, lack of coordination, unclear or complicated plans, complex task organizations or command relationships, or complicated technologies. Whatever form it takes, because war is a human enterprise, friction will always have a psychological as well as a physical impact.

Another attribute of war is uncertainty. All actions in war take place in an atmosphere of uncertainty, or the "fog of war." Uncertainty pervades battle in the form of unknowns about the enemy, about the environment, and even about the friendly situation. While we try to reduce these unknowns by gathering information, we must realize that we cannot eliminate them—or even come close. The very nature of war makes certainty impossible; all actions in war will be based on incomplete, inaccurate, or even contradictory information. Like friction and uncertainty, fluidity is an inherent attribute of war. Each episode in war is the temporary result of a unique combination of circumstances, presenting a unique set of problems and requiring an original solution. Nevertheless, no episode can be viewed in isolation. Rather, each episode merges with those that precede and follow it—shaped by the former and shaping the conditions of the latter—creating a continuous, fluctuating flow of activity replete with fleeting opportunities and unforeseen events.

War is also a complex phenomenon. Each belligerent is not a single, homogeneous will guided by a single intelligence. Instead, each belligerent is a complex system consisting of numerous individual parts. A division comprises regiments,

---

35 On purpose the following description is directly and almost verbatim derived from United States Marine Corps 1997, Chapter 1.

a regiment comprises battalions, and so on. Each element is part of a larger whole and must cooperate with other elements for the accomplishment of the common goal. At the same time, each has its own mission and must adapt to its own situation. Each must deal with friction, uncertainty, and disorder at its own level, and each may create friction, uncertainty, and disorder for others, friendly as well as enemy. As a result, war is not governed by the actions or decisions of a single individual in any one place but emerges from the collective behaviour of all the individual parts in the system interacting locally in response to local conditions and incomplete information. A military action is not the monolithic execution of a single decision by a single entity but necessarily involves near-countless independent but interrelated decisions and actions being taken simultaneously throughout the organization. Violence of course is integral to war; indeed, war is among the greatest horrors known to humanity. The means of war is force, applied in the form of organized violence. Violence is an essential element of war, and its immediate result is bloodshed, destruction, and suffering. While the magnitude of violence may vary with the object and means of war, the violent essence of war will never change. Since war is a violent enterprise, danger is ever present. Since war is a human phenomenon, fear, the human reaction to danger, has a significant impact on the conduct of war.

Even when military units are not engaged in high intensity combat, but instead conduct crisis response operation, as De Waard et al. contend, a military task force finds itself in a permanent state of flux. It needs to constantly react to changing local circumstances in order to keep or regain the initiative, it has to cope on an ongoing basis with intelligent actors actively trying to undermine its operations, and it needs to react at high speed all the time in order to stay ahead of the game.[36]

3.4 Destroying Organizational Cohesion; Counter-Resilience in Military Strategy

The features of war are not a natural phenomenon but due to deliberate and accidental human and organizational behaviour. Friction, violence, chaos, these are effects any party aims to create for the opponent. In fact, the core feature of western combat doctrines revolves around unhinging the opponent's system and causing organizational collapse. Indeed, two of the most discussed military concepts of the past three decades precisely focus on achieving organizational paralyzes by overloading the opponent's capacity to absorb and cope with systemic disruption. One focuses primarily on causing physical destruction while the other exploits physical and informational actions. The first one is associated with the concepts of Parallel Warfare and Effects Based Operations. The second one is associated with the maneuvrist approach. Both play with the organizational features that produce resilience.

[36] De Waard et al. 2012, p. 775; De Waard et al. 2013.

3.4.1 Inflicting Systemic Paralysis

Cold War military theory was largely defined by the potential of a massive clash between armoured forces in Germany. Inflicting attrition was key. In the background loomed the threat of even much larger destruction by nuclear weapons. However, during the mid-1980s new technologies suggested new possibilities for achieving victory with conventional weapons. The key theorist first to explore the potential of combining new targeting technologies such as precision weapons, cruise missiles, electronic warfare systems and stealth bombers was John Warden, a USAF colonel working at the time of the Iraqi invasion in Kuwait as a planner in the Pentagon.[37] Instead of adhering to traditional military doctrine, which saw air power mainly in a direct support role to the land campaign, Warden devised the targeting concept of parallel warfare, which in no small measure implied a rediscovery of conventional strategic attack. He had recognized that precision, stand-off and stealth capabilities offered new possibilities for strategic attacks against multiple target-categories—centres of gravity—of a nation state. This so-called five-ring model distinguished five subsystems that, combined, made up the 'enemy system': military units, population, organic essentials (e.g., energy, water, food supply), critical infrastructure and, centrally, leadership. Even if targets were in the vicinity of civilian objects, it was now possible to attack these near simultaneously in order to rapidly degrade the functioning of the entire enemy system. This became a key feature of the Desert Storm campaign plan.

Indeed, instead of the traditional model, in which a country's defeat required first a decisive victory over the armed forces, Desert Storm heralded the 'inside-out' model. The overwhelming air power capabilities offered the potential to strike at the heart of a country (the regime) from the first moment of a campaign and cripple the strategic command capabilities before attacking fielded forces, and thus potentially paralyze the entire system. Instead of focusing on armed forces exclusively, new options were now available, such as regime targeting and precise infrastructural disruption, which could have direct strategically-significant effects. It also held out the promise that several smaller-scale physical and non-physical attacks—with less destructive power—conducted simultaneously on vital and interdependent targets could achieve disproportionate strategic outcomes. With each bomb likely to strike within yards of a target, targeteers could now think in terms of specific first- and second-order effects that needed to be achieved instead of merely hoping targets would be destroyed. Effects Based Operations (EBO) as a targeting philosophy emerged.[38]

Applying his five-ring model on Iraqi political, military and economic systems, Warden and his planning team recognized seven core strategic target sets. The first, national leadership, and second, military and civil C2, should be attacked in

[37] Warden 1995; For an elaborate discussion of Warden's ideas, see Olson 2007.

[38] The EBO concept was developed by David Deptula, an assistant of John Warden, and key planner of the strategic part of the Desert Storm air campaign, see Deptula 1996.

order to put physical and psychological pressure on the regime, demonstrate its vulnerability to the Iraqi people, and reduce its capacity to command Iraqi forces, i.e., to isolate, incapacitate and paralyze it. In traditional fashion, electric power generation, oil refineries, distribution and storage were also listed ('organic essentials' in Warden's five-ring model), as well as transport infrastructure to isolate the Kuwaiti battle area (railroads and bridges). The final three targets sets pertained to military capabilities: nuclear, biological and chemical (NBC) weapons together with associated research and development (R&D) and production facilities; military support capabilities; and Scud ballistic missiles. The destruction of Iraqi air defences was added to the list as a prerequisite for any offensive air operation. The underlying idea of these concepts was that rapid, massive and continuous onslaught on key nodes in the enemy's system would either overwhelm the governmental and military command centres, or the destruction of their sensors and linkages—communication nodes, highway bridges, radar sites, intelligence centres—would leave them unable to keep up with the rapid pace of events and launch relevant actions to repair damages, create work-arounds, etc.

The end result of Operation Desert Storm was that, through this novel campaign design, informed and enabled by the combination of advances in targeting organization, targeting concept and air-power technologies, the coalition for all intents and purposes neutralized Iraq with decisive air attacks. Iraq's sophisticated air-defence system was defeated by stealth, large packages of EW aircraft, decoy drones, and attack aircraft using PGMs and gravity weapons, while key nodes in the electrical power system, air defences, C2 structure, and intelligence apparatus were attacked by stealth, by conventional aircraft using PGMs and by cruise missiles. As a consequence, Saddam Hussein and his military commanders were informationally isolated from the events occurring at the battlefield, logistically the battlefield was unreachable due to the interdiction of any traffic moving to Kuwait, Iraqi ground forces were pinned down and unable to move, and that tactical commanders too were isolated, confused and generally incapable of taking any meaningful action. The Iraqi military by and large had stopped operating as a coherent system.[39]

In 2003, a similar dynamic caused the rapid collapse of the Iraqi regime. Both operations benefited from the fact that the Iraqi political-military command system was highly centralized, marked by distrust between commanders and political leaders, intolerant towards low level initiative and repressive towards critical discussion. In Operation Iraqi Freedom these features were deliberately exploited by the US. Communication channels were physically cut, electronically disrupted and sometimes exploited by inserting disinformation and by sending text messages to key military commanders. Saddam Hussein, fearing for his personal survival, opted to move from safe house to safe house and to communicate through messengers in order to avoid detection by US aerial surveillance or signal intelligence

[39] This brief description of the operations draws from Osinga and Roorda 2016, pp. 42–50 and pp. 62–65; for an extensive analysis of Desert Storm, Hallion 1992; Cohen and Keaney 1995; for a balanced account of the strategic air offensive against Iraq, Davis 1998.

systems. Devoid of accurate information and communication facilities, this made effective command of his troops, who faced a persistent aerial onslaught and an extremely rapid ground assault, impossible.[40]

3.4.2 Attacking Complex Systems: Reading John Boyd

The maneuvrist approach, also developed in the mid-1980s, is the second military concept that aspires to inflict organizational collapse upon the opponent.[41] To properly understand the scope and intent of that approach one must be cognizant of its intellectual foundations. One of the key conceptual fathers of modern maneuver warfare, John Boyd, argued that, while attritionist mode of warfare might be suitable and effective for mass-armies, maneuver warfare was more suited to western militaries that could not afford to incur nor inflict massive casualties. And this approach was deeply informed by emerging insights concerning Complex Adaptive Systems. Armed forces are complex adaptive systems, or at least attempt to be. Units fill niches in the ecosystem and should operate with sufficient autonomy, yet interdependently with other systems. Doctrines, procedures, tactics, and organizational culture are like mental models that provide coherent behaviour. They are also like schemata that must evolve. Armed forces are like autopoietic systems, continually making efforts to maintain their distinctive character despite the turbulent environment. Defeat, demoralization, and a disorganized retreat can be seen as symptoms of a disintegrating system, unable to cope in the available time with the radical changes imposed on it by the environment, and unable to adjust its schemata or to speed up its rate of adjustment.

This reference to complexity theory is no coincidence. Apart from his reading of military history, Boyd was deeply informed by information theory, cognitive sciences (including works on individual and organizational learning), studies in epistemology which focused on the inherent subjectivity and uncertainty in any act of observation, and Neo-Darwinism which brought him the dynamics of adaptation with key features such as diversity, redundant layers of strong and weak interconnections and a variety of loose and tight coupling patterns, the variables affecting the strength of eco-systems and the functions of multiple feedback processes. Finally, he was deeply influenced by emerging studies on chaos theory and complex system which showed him the many non-linear phenomena that surround us, including was. That literature also cued him to the importance of open-systems and networks: only if organic, social or economic systems maintain an open relationship with their environment in terms of energy and information can they aspire to maintain the capability to adapt.

[40] For detailed analysis, see Mahnken and Keaney 2007; Murray and Scales 2003; Woodward 2004; Cordesman 2003; Gordon and Trainor 2006; Lambeth 2013.

[41] For a good historical study of the emergence of modern day maneuver warfare, Naveh 1997, Chapters 7 and 8.

Embedded in Boyd's work, and logically flowing from his conceptualization of armed forces as Complex Adaptive Systems, is the following set of generic strategic moves to influence an adversary system:

- Use multiple strategies/avenues;
- Affect the accuracy of the cognitive/feedback process;
- Overload his cognitive capacity;
- Eliminate (and/or threaten) particular crucial (real or imaginary) subsystems;
- Diminish the variety of subsystems;
- Disrupt moral, physical, and/or informational vertical and horizontal interdependencies;
- Close the enemy off from his physical/social environment;
- Introduce rapid and threatening change into the environment;
- Disrupt the information flow between the environment and the system;
- Ensure the irrelevance of the opponent's schemata;
- Disable the efforts to validate those schemata;
- Wage a form of warfare that does not correspond to the opponent's doctrine and strategic preference (schemata);
- Change the environment in terms of alliances, location, and/or stakes involved.

3.4.3 The Maneuvrist Approach

These ideas found their way into the maneuvrist approach as it was adopted by western militaries. This approach focuses on the moral and mental components of the opponent's system. It tries to erode organization cohesion through repetitive yet irregular physical and non-physical actions aimed at deception, threatening faints, disinformation, information overload, creating ambiguous situations, combined with lethal offensive actions that aim to destroy those connections that hold a system together such as command centres and communication nodes.

The overall objective is to induce organizational collapse by introducing massive threatening and confusing turbulence in the environment to such an extent that it overwhelms the opponent's capacity to adapt.[42] In various places in his work he tries to capture this dynamic. For instance, synthesizing the essence of guerrilla and Blitzkrieg warfare, Boyd deduced a plausible approach to induce what he calls "disintegration and collapse":

- Lethal effort: Tie-up, divert, or drain-away adversary attention and strength as well as (or thereby) overload critical vulnerabilities and generate weaknesses;
- Maneuver: Subvert, disorient, disrupt, overload, or seize those vulnerable yet critical connections, centres, and activities as basis to penetrate, splinter, and isolate remnants of adversary organism for mop-up or absorption;

---

[42] See Osinga 2006 for a detailed discussion of Boyd's work and his influence; for a recent concise summary of his legacy in strategic theory, Osinga 2013; for a more elaborate summary of Boyd's ideas, see Osinga 2015.

- Moral: Create an atmosphere of fear, anxiety, and alienation to sever human bonds that permit an organic whole to exist;
- Idea: Destroy adversary's moral-mental-physical harmony, produce paralysis, and collapse his will to resist;
- Aim: Render adversary powerless by denying him the opportunity to cope with unfolding circumstances.[43]

Or, as Boyd concluded in one of his many sometimes cryptic yet influential lectures in the mid-eighties of the 20th Century: 'the Strategic Aim [is to] Diminish adversary's capacity while improving our capacity to adapt as an organic whole, so that our adversary cannot cope while we can cope with events/efforts as they unfold'. The way to accomplish that was to 'penetrate moral-mental-physical being to dissolve his moral fiber, disorient his mental images, disrupt his operations, and overload his system, as well as subvert, shatter, seize or otherwise subdue those moral-mental-physical bastions, connections, or activities that he depends upon, in order to destroy internal harmony, produce paralysis, and collapse adversary's will to resist'. At the operational level one should 'get inside his mind-time-space, to create a tangle of threatening and/or non-threatening events/efforts as well as repeatedly generate mismatches between those events/efforts adversary observes, or anticipates, and those he must react to, to survive; thereby enmesh adversary in an amorphous, menacing, and unpredictable world of uncertainty, doubt, mistrust, confusion, disorder, fear, panic, chaos, and/or fold adversary back inside himself'.

These actions would, according to Boyd, 'Maneuver adversary beyond his moral-mental-physical capacity to adapt or endure so that he can neither divine our intentions nor focus his efforts to cope with the unfolding strategic design or related decisive strokes as they penetrate, splinter, isolate or envelop, and overwhelm him'. At the tactical level one should OODA [observe, orient, decide and act] more inconspicuously, more quickly and with more irregularity as basis to keep or gain initiative as well as shape or shift main effort; to repeatedly and unexpectedly penetrate vulnerabilities and weaknesses exposed by that effort or other effort(s) that tie up, divert, or drain-away adversary attention (and strength) elsewhere'.[44]

Boyd thus focuses on the factors that can impair an opponent's capability to adapt and those that preserve one's own capacity to do so. An armed force is by design a fairly robust system, structured to cause change within an opponent's system and resist external pressure to change itself. It equips itself with redundant connections, ample numbers of diverse units, good sensors, relevant schemata, and a supportive environment. It does anything necessary to ensure a modicum of coherence among its actions.

---

[43] John Boyd, slide 137 of unpublished briefing Patterns of Conflict, p. 137, these slides can be found in Osinga 2006.

[44] John Boyd, slide 134 of unpublished briefing Patterns of Conflict, p. 134, these slides can be found in Osinga 2006.

Military force, in Boyd's view, therefore aims to push an opposing system away from its ordered, disciplined state towards one where the several subsystems must self-organize because they lack higher direction, and then towards a state of randomness—but not necessarily in such a time-sequenced order. Randomness—the loss of cohesion—is the opposite of the capability to adapt. Thus, the units may still exist, but not as part of a higher order complex system. This mechanism of decreasing cohesion and degrading the capability to adapt can be applied to any system and subsystem, down to the lowest level that can be described as a system—in armed forces, the individual soldier. But the goal is not necessarily to make the system completely disintegrate in one massive blow. Because feedback loops will cause inappropriate or slow responses to magnify in impact over time, the force need only create an initial advantage and prevent the opponent from compensating for it. The nature of a system can change from less complex to complex, or, alternatively, to the point where almost no connections remain, where no information is shared, and where cohesion of action ceases to exist. At that point the different elements of a system act randomly and no longer constitute a part of a system.

Those ideas would find a place in the formulation of the maneuvrist approach of the US Marine Corps, and subsequently in the doctrines of various western militaries.[45] Maneuver warfare as defined by the USMC, is:

> a warfighting philosophy that seeks to shatter the enemy's cohesion through a variety of rapid, focused, and unexpected actions which create a turbulent and rapidly deteriorating situation with which the enemy cannot cope. Rather than wearing down an enemy's defenses, maneuver warfare attempts to bypass these defenses in order to penetrate the enemy system and tear it apart. The aim is to render the enemy incapable of resisting effectively by shattering his moral, mental, and physical cohesion—his ability to fight as an effective, coordinated whole—rather than to destroy him physically through the incremental attrition of each of his components, which is generally more costly and time-consuming. Ideally, the components of his physical strength that remain are irrelevant because we have disrupted his ability to use them effectively. Even if an outmanoeuvred enemy continues to fight as individuals or small units, we can destroy the remnants with relative ease because we have eliminated his ability to fight effectively as a force.

Clearly, this approach aims at the resilience of an opponent. For Boyd, and subsequently for the USMC, success in warfare relied on attacking the opponent's capability to adapt while guarding organizational integrity of the own units. The key was to magnify and exploit uncertainty—inherent in any mental effort to make sense of rapidly unfolding situations—while relying on an organization that could operate comfortably without much information or detailed top-down instructions.

NATO too has adopted the maneuvrist approach, including it in its capstone doctrine manual Joint Doctrine Publication 1. In Chap. 6 it explains that the manoeuvrist approach focuses on shattering the adversary's overall cohesion and will to fight, rather than his materiel. It is an indirect approach, which emphasizes targeting the adversary's moral component of fighting power rather than the physical.

---

[45] For the influence of Boyd on USMC doctrine, see Osinga 2006, Chapter 2.

The approach involves a combination of lethal and non-lethal means to create effects, which shape an adversary's understanding, undermine his will and shatter his cohesion. It aims to apply strength against identified vulnerabilities. Significant features are momentum, tempo and agility, which in combination lead to shock and surprise. It calls for an attitude of mind in which doing the unexpected, using initiative and seeking originality is combined with a relentless determination to succeed. It is applicable to all types of military activities across the spectrum of conflict. It:

a. Emphasizes defeat and disruption of the adversary rather than, for example, taking ground for its own sake and depends on the precise application of force against identified points of weakness.
b. Aims to defeat the adversary's will and desire to continue by seizing the initiative, and applying constant and unexpected pressure at times and places which the adversary least expects.

In combat, it continues, the Manoeuvrist Approach invariably includes elements of movement, firepower and positional defence. There will usually be a requirement to fix the adversary, to deny him access to routes and objectives, and secure vital ground and key points. However, any such defensive measures should only be seen as part of the means to the end, which is the adversary's defeat. The Manoeuvrist Approach is underpinned by centralized planning and decentralized execution that promotes freedom of action and initiative—Mission Command.[46] Indeed, resilience in war requires a very specific organizational structure and culture.

3.5 Thriving in Danger and Chaos: Military Command Approaches

Military history shows that military organizations have developed a variety of approaches for dealing with the challenges of war, and thus to ensure resilience. There is not a single best approach to (or philosophy of) command and control, as Hayes and Alberts have concluded a number of times.[47] The key finding from reviewing the evidence from that era is that the correct command and control (C2) approach depends on several factors. For instance, the demands upon a command organization are low in static warfare compared to maneuver warfare. It also matters whether communications can be relied upon to function continuously or intermittently. The volume and quality of information required for coordination versus the communications infrastructure is likewise a variable. The type of command philosophy a military can apply is also dependent on the professional competence of the officers at all levels of command. Finally, it matters whether subordinate commanders can be expected and relied upon to display initiative and creativity.

[46] NATO 2010.

[47] Alberts and Hayes 2003, pp. 18–27.

3.5.1 Six Philosophies

Six different philosophies were found in successful military organizations during the 20th century (rank ordered from most to least centralized) as: 1. Cyclic; 2. Interventionist; 3. Problem-Solving; 4. Problem-Bounding; 5. Selective Control; 6. Control Free.

Cyclic C2 approaches are detailed orders issued on the basis of a regular schedule from the central command. This usually occurs when communications bandwidth is severely limited in comparison with the amount of information that must be exchanged, the actions of the operating units are interdependent and must be coordinated in detail, and the subordinate commanders and their forces lack the ability to exercise independent creativity (which may be because they lack adequate information or the degree of professional expertise required), so they must be expected to follow the plan with great energy to overcome its lack of flexibility. Cyclic C2 systems are best suited for static warfare situations where there is time to gather all the information at the centre, make it available to senior commanders, have them make optimum decisions, and issue detailed directives and plans to the forces. Like cyclic C2, the *interventionist model* issues specific orders from the theatre level. However, they have a greater communications capacity that allows them to intervene and change their directives at irregular intervals, particularly if an opportunity or threat emerges. Both approaches apply centralized and detailed control. While this lowers the requirements of professional expertise at the lower levels, it conversely increases the demands put on the higher headquarters, which will also be substantial in size.

Neither of these two approaches are generally suitable for high paced maneuvre warfare. Alberts and Hayes discerned four variations of decentralized command concepts that do support high paced maneuver warfare. The first one—focused on problem solving—is still relatively centralized. Here the operational level headquarters concentrates on specifying the objectives for the elements of the force has been termed *problem-solving*. This approach does allow for innovation and flexibility by subordinate commanders, but does so within a set of constraints imposed by senior commanders. The objectives are stated clearly and are accompanied by a set of milestones that stress what is to be accomplished and when (either against a time schedule or in terms of a sequence). Higher headquarters also constrain the assets (force elements, lift assets, etc.) available to accomplish these missions. They also typically include specific guidance about boundaries (who has the use of which roads, who is responsible for which areas) that helps to define the objectives and constrain subordinate choices. In essence, this approach is a challenge to the subordinates to solve the problem of accomplishing their missions within the constraints established by the senior commanders. The second one is focused on *problem-bounding*. Here fewer milestones and constraints are provided to the subordinates. The mission(s) were offered to subordinates as problems, but much less detail was offered about how they would be solved.

The Israeli military applied a third variant—*selective control*. Here the theatre level headquarters is generally content to establish the initial conditions for success (providing very capable forces and assigning them general missions) and monitoring the situation to ensure no major threats or opportunities go undetected. This approach requires considerable capacity in the subordinate forces and trust in them by the higher headquarters. It also requires excellent information and awareness within the operating units. In essence, the approach relies on a series of "local optimums" as the elements of the force win engagements and battles that build toward the achievement of the overall mission. However, a selective control philosophy still assumes that circumstances may arise in which the theatre level will have to assert itself aggressively. It assumes therefore that the subordinates will, if and when the theatre commander decides to intervene, show the discipline needed to respond promptly and effectively to the new command intent.

In the final approach—*control free*—associated with the German Army during World War II, is the least centralized. Here the primary role of the theatre commander is to support the tactical units by creating the initial conditions that maximize the likelihood of mission accomplishment and providing the information and resources necessary for the force elements to succeed. The subordinate commanders subsequently enjoy a large degree of autonomy. Compared to the previous approaches, the selective and control free approaches require high levels of professional expertise of the commanders and a very specific organizational culture.

3.5.2 Coping with Uncertainty

Well before the Alberts and Hayes study, the historian Martin van Creveld similarly identified a variety of command concepts, and was very clear in his conclusions, which of those concepts was superior. Command, according to van Creveld was a function that has to be exercised, more or less continuously, if the armed forces are to exist and to operate. The need for command varied with size, complexity and differentiation. He observed an increasing complexity in military organizations due to the number of specialized troops made it more difficult to coordinate, the increasing mobility, speed and range of modern weapons, which provided little time to coordinate and control, and due to the dispersion of units across wide areas. While ICT and modern sensors offered help, this development in turn increased the complexity of command as now command centres saw an explosion of the amount of data that needed to be processed. Command centres subsequently grew in size which enhanced the risk that the command centre would focus inward on its own time-consuming organizational processes instead of the rapidly unfolding situation on the battlefield.

Increasing complexity therefore would hamper the commander in dealing with the inherent uncertainty of war. Indeed, van Creveld observed, the history of command in war consists of an endless quest for certainty, and demonstrates a race between the demand for information and the ability of command systems to meet it. The role of uncertainty to be expected on the battlefield therefore should be decisive for structuring a command system. This could be accomplished by increasing the information-processing capacity or, alternatively, design an organization, and the task itself, in such a way as to enable it to operate on the basis of less information. This implied a drastic simplification of the organization with the establishment of semi-autonomous forces. Based on military history, with Napoleon, the German Wehrmacht and the Israeli army as positive examples, van Creveld concluded that to be successful in warfare, commanders needed to accept that greater certainty at the top is only bought at the expense of less certainty at the bottom, and that would be counter-productive. Instead, he argued for the need for decision thresholds to be fixed as far down as possible, and for freedom of action at the bottom of the military structure. In addition, success required high levels of decentralization and self-contained units at fairly low levels in the organization. Reporting and information transmission should be both top-down and bottom-up, through formal as well as informal channels.[48]

3.5.3 Creating Resilient Organizations

Boyd agreed with that conclusion. The literature on military history, combined with management studies about total quality management and organizational learning informed his argument about the optimum command and control concept. History had showed him that Blitzkrieg (with its Auftragstaktik) and guerrilla forces worked in a decentralized manner with networks of semi-independent units that were not tightly controlled as in traditional hierarchical organizations. Instead of detailed control, these organizations were held together by shared doctrines and beliefs, shared experiences, cooperation between units, mutual trust between commanders and troops, between units, and between layers of command. Operational success relied upon low level initiative which was actually stimulated by higher level commanders.

Such a command concept could do without much formal and explicit communication which in turn fostered a high operational tempo which in turn introduced turbulence into the environment of the opponent. Authorized and expected to show initiative and exploit opportunities, guided by the overall mission stated by higher levels, it also allowed tactical units to deal with the level of uncertainty they encountered. The answer to uncertainty lies in a relatively large degree of autonomy of action at the tactical level of an organization.

In his presentation *Organic Design for Command and Control*, Boyd advocated creating adaptable, open, learning organizations consisting of people with varied backgrounds cooperating in informally networked teams that can comfortably operate in an insecure environment because they have relatively low information

[48] van Creveld 1988, Chapters 1 and 8.

requirements.[49] A high degree of mutual trust and shared orientation patterns created by common experience and training, combined with clear objectives and common doctrine, ensures that a minimum of communication suffices to maintain coherence among the actions of various units. In contrast to standard military hierarchical cultures with top-down control, each level and each unit must have the autonomy and repertoire of resources it needs to enable individual initiative and creativity. These, in turn, are driven by the need to deal with the degree of dynamism and uncertainty of the immediate organizational environment.

In such an organization, Boyd indicates that both command and control are inappropriate terms. Higher command levels must restrain their desire to know about everything that occurs at lower levels and to interfere. They must encourage cooperation and consultation among lower levels and remain open to suggestions, bottom-up initiatives, and critique. Thus, higher levels must exercise "leadership and appreciation" of activities and compare actions and events to their expectations. This approach to organization and leadership would allow a high tempo of operations and exploitation of opportunities. It would limit the need for time-consuming, detailed, top-down guidance and hence facilitate rapid adaptation to changing circumstances. This idea, also surfaces in another briefing—*The Conceptual Spiral*—where Boyd argues that successful organizations survive, and actually thrive, because of their ability to continually innovate and experiment to deal with uncertainty and to introduce novelty into their environment.[50]

3.5.4 Mission Command

The dominant contemporary military command philosophy fully embraces these insights. US, UK and NATO doctrines explicitly endorse and promote the virtues of mission command.[51] Uncertainty and initiative combined with adaptability as a response are key themes. As the USMC doctrine states, commanders can seldom predict with certainty how enemies or civilians will act and react or how events may develop. Commanders and subordinates must learn from experience, anticipate change, and develop adaptability so they can conduct operations more effectively than their opponents. Since war is a fluid phenomenon, its conduct requires flexibility of thought. Success depends in large part on the ability to adapt—to proactively shape changing events to our advantage as well as to react quickly to constantly changing conditions. Therefore, it continuous, efforts to fully centralize military operations and to exert complete control by a single decision maker are inconsistent with the intrinsically complex and distributed nature of war. Instead,

[49] Boyd 1987; see Osinga 2006, pp. 189–200 for a full-length treatment of this presentation.

[50] Boyd 1992, see Osinga 2006, pp. 219–222 for a full-length treatment of this presentation.

[51] For the United Kingdom, British Army Doctrine Publication (1995) or British Army Doctrine (2010), Chap. 6; The Netherlands armed forces also endorse mission command, see Ministerie van Defensie (not dated), Chapter 6.

in exercising mission command, and to cope with the challenges of violence, uncertainty and danger, commanders are guided by six principles— (1) Build cohesive teams through mutual trust; (2) Create shared understanding; (3) Provide a clear commander's intent; (4) Exercise disciplined initiative; (5) Use mission orders; (6) Accept prudent risk.

Indeed, the recent US Army doctrine notes, by enabling and fostering disciplined self initiative, mission command empowers agile and adaptive leaders, it helps commanders capitalize on the human ability to take action to develop the situation and integrate military operations to achieve the commander's intent and desired end state.

Uncertainty management is a key driver. As the US Army doctrine states, the nature of military operations requires responsibility and decision-making at the point of action. The mission command philosophy helps commanders counter the uncertainty of operations by reducing the amount of certainty needed to act. Commanders understand that some decisions must be made quickly and are better made at the point of action. Agile leaders are comfortable with uncertainty and understand that disciplined initiative is an important part of being adaptive. It is easy to see the resemblance of the suggestions offered by van Creveld and Boyd in these principles, as well the contours of the selective and control free approaches described by Alberts and Hayes.

3.6 Beyond Mission Command: Harnessing the Power of Networks

By the time of publication of the 1997 edition of USMC doctrine, other developments where well under way that aimed to extrapolate the tenets of mission command and the maneuvrist approach. All were geared towards enhancing internal flexibility, responsiveness and lethality, and all emphasized decentralization.

Desert Storm inspired concepts such as Command and Control Warfare (C2 W) and Information Warfare; indeed, Desert Storm was regarded by some as the first information war. Both focusing on the command functions of the opponent and both rode a wave of studies that explored the wider implications of the information revolution that swept throughout the commercial world and now had also reached the realm of warfare. Alvin and Heidi Toffler argued that the information age or 'third wave' economy would spawn 'third wave warfare' in which information would be the critical component.[52] The transition to the Information Age implied, and was manifested in, the awareness that information was becoming the driving factor in warfare. Information and communication technology improved the quality of sensor systems, it increased transparency of the battlefield, it enhanced precision of weapons systems and, finally, it enhanced speed of command and shortened the "sensor-to-shooter time".

[52] Toffler and Toffler 1993, p. 81.

The power of networks was a key element in these explorations. In 1993 Arquilla and Ronfeldt proclaimed that cyber war was coming, and emphasized that in the future those organizations would be successful on and off the battlefield that were able to harness the power of networks, not only in informational terms but also in its organizational consequences. Organizations would be forces to 'evolve from traditional hierarchical forms to new, flexible, network-like models of organization. Success will depend on learning to interlace hierarchical and network principles...Indeed, the information revolution favours the growth of such networks by making it possible for diverse, dispersed actors to communicate, consult, coordinate, and operate together across greater distances, and on the basis of more and better information than ever before.'[53]

3.6.1 Swarming

Several years later, Arquilla en Ronfeldt explored in more detail the possible optimal organizational concept for information age warfare. The idea that small units now had access to unprecedented levels of situational awareness, and could call in stand-off precision firepower offered new possibilities. They offered the "Swarming concept", taking their inspiration from Martin Libicki's chapter *The Small and the Many* that was included in *Athena's Camp.*[54] They saw swarming as the logical emerging paradigm in warfare, following three earlier paradigms in military history: the melee, massing, maneuver. The central idea is that information technology offers the potential for small networked units to operate as a swarm in a 'seemingly amorphous but deliberately structured, coordinated strategic way to strike from all direction, by means of a sustainable pulsing of force and/or fire, close in as well as form stand-off positions. It works best if it is designed mainly around the deployment of myriad, small, dispersed maneuver units that are tightly internetted and capable to communicate and coordinate with each other at will and are expected to do so'.[55]

A swarm force must not only engage in strike operations, but also form part of a "sensory organization", providing the surveillance and synoptic-level observations necessary to the creation and maintenance of "topsight".[56] The Marine Corps in similar vein explored a 'biological systems inspiration', asserting that, instead of the Newtonian, mechanical and ordered model of warfare, a more likely model is 'a complex system that is open ended, parallel and very sensitive to initial

[53] Arquilla and Ronfeldt 1993, p. 141; They elaborated on these ideas in an edited volume of studies on information war, see Arquilla and Ronfeldt 1997.

[54] Libicki 1997.

[55] Arquilla and Ronfeldt 2000, pp. 21–23; Edwards 2000.

[56] Arquilla and Ronfeldt 2000, pp. 21–23; Edwards 2000.

conditions and continued inputs'. To be successful in such an environment, structures and tactics should have the following operational characteristics: dispersed, autonomous, adaptable and small.[57]

3.6.2 Network Centric Warfare

From this momentum emerged the institutional initiative within the US military of Network Centric Warfare (NCW) that incorporated many of the concepts developed in various studies on the impact of the information age on warfare, including swarming and the network structure.[58] NCW, according to its advocates, was the emerging theory of war in the information age, a paradigm shift, and the military embodiment of Information Age concepts and technologies.[59] The essence of NCW is captured in the following description, "the US is poised to harness key information technologies—microelectronics, data networking, and software programming—to create a networked force, using weapons capable of pinpoint accuracy, launched from platforms beyond range of enemy weapons, utilizing the integrated data from all-seeing sensors, managed by intelligent command nodes. By distributing its forces, while still being able to concentrate fires, the US military is improving its mobility, speed, potency, and invulnerability to enemy attack".[60]

NCW, it was argued, derives its power from the strong networking of a well-informed but geographically dispersed force.[61] And networking does not only imply technological connectivity. NCW goes deeper in that it maintains that reaping the maximum benefit of information age tools, organization, command and control philosophy and doctrine, along with tactics and procedures, should also be radically adjusted.[62] In the "Physical domain", 'all elements of the force needed to be robustly networked which will enable 'achieving secure and seamless connectivity'. In the "Information domain" the force must have the 'capability to collect, share, access, and protect information', as well as 'the capability to collaborate in the information domain, which enables a force to improve its information position through processes of correlation, fusion, and analysis'. This would allow a force to 'achieve information advantage over an adversary in the information domain'. Importantly, in the "Cognitive domain" the force must have 'the capability to develop and share high quality situational awareness' and the 'capability to develop

[57] Cited in Coker 2004, p. 41.

[58] With the agreement by NATO in 2002 to create the NATO Response Force and embark on "military transformation", it has also entered the debates among European militaries, see Osinga 2010.

[59] Alberts 2002, p. 18.

[60] Gompert et al. 1997, p. 4.

[61] Alberts et al. 1999, p. 90.

[62] United States Department of Defense 2001, pp. 3-5 and 3-1.

a shared knowledge of commander's intent'.[63] This will enable 'the capability to self-synchronize its operations'. A force with these attributes and capabilities will be able to increase combat power by:

- Better synchronizing effects in the battle space;
- Achieving greater speed of command;
- Increasing lethality, survivability, and responsiveness.[64]

At the same time, alongside and in support of these conceptual developments, the US Department of Defense published a series of books highlighting the characteristics, benefit and need for agile innovative organizations. Agility referred to resilience and robustness. Agile—or "edge"—organizations were characterized by the ability to combine information in new ways, the ability to apply of a variety of perspectives and the ability to change the employment of assets commensurate with the changing situation.[65]

3.7 Conclusion: Military Theory and Resilience

This does not mean at all that the western militaries have developed the generic blueprint or gold standard for organizational resilience. Nor have these concepts been without criticism. Particularly NCW has received a wealth of critical comments and even downright dismissal. It relies too much on technology and instead of fostering decentralization and empowerment of the tactical level, the ability to monitor from hundreds of miles in real-time the actions by those units has spawned the '7000-mile screwdriver' effect when senior commanders interfered at the tactical level because they technology allowed them to.[66]

Mission command in turn has seen various levels of success in its implementation. Some organisations still adopt command by direct and detailed orders. There are a number of reasons for this. Some systems are too 'tightly coupled' and/or resource limited to allow for any degree of flexibility for individual initiative within the plan. Military organisations in totalitarian regimes tend not to favour decentralisation, in part owing to a generalised reluctance to delegate authority, but most prominently because of the size and standard of the armed forces concerned. The limited training and experience of personnel in such forces means that it is unreasonable to expect to be able to delegate authority owing to a lack of competence in more than a highly prescribed set of skills and procedures. Military

---

[63] Ibid, pp. 3-9 en 3-10.

[64] These tenets appear in several NCW publications, United States Department of Defense 2001, pp. i, v, 3-10.

[65] Alberts and Hayes 1995, 2003; Alberts et al. 2001; Atkinson and Moffat 2005.

[66] For a concise yet broad and balanced treatment of the debate concerning NCW and similar concepts under the rubric of the Revolution in Military Affairs, Shimko 2010.

operations for such organisations tend to involve the orchestration by the centre of a number of practiced tactical manoeuvres.[67]

Similarly, as recent studies have concluded, adaptation and innovation are necessary requirements but also significant challenges for large and politically constrained bureaucracies such as military organizations. Western militaries during the past two decades have readily acknowledge the need to continuously adjust to new types of missions, diverse geographical operational environments and different types of violent organizations. Murray concluded that real innovation required deliberate and critical study of experiences, an open debate, a broad base of contributors, acceptance of conclusions even they may constitute a threat to existing weapon systems and force structures, a willingness to experiment and accept failure and an absence of doctrinal rigidity. Amid constant real world operations, a diverse set of missions with different equipment requirements, budget cuts and stringent political oversights, such a climate has not always been forthcoming.[68]

Finally, not all organizational cultures are comfortable with delegation, trust and risk associated with mission command. As one author concluded in a comparison of the US, the UK and Israeli military, the implementation of Mission Command in all three militaries has been quite uneven, with the UK more comfortable with ambiguity than managerial leadership styles, detailed orders or dogmatic doctrines, than the US.[69] This is echoed in a much quoted article by a US Army colonel who challenged the US Army by commenting that, with mission command succeeding in a free-energy-dominated environment that values, promotes and demands innovation, creativity and initiative, will the Army default to its fixed-energy natural state imbued with rules, regulations and policies? When "bad" things happen under mission command, will we feel the need to control the outcomes better by increasing the approval level on a particular issue? For an organization that for generations has been conditioning its institutional commanders and leaders to respond to mandates, go by the book, and stick to the checklist, mission command does not come natural'.[70]

On the other hand, although initially not always consciously based on academic literature but more oriented on military history, western militaries have adopted organizational and operational concepts to cope with the myriad challenges of violence, turbulence, uncertainty and an adaptive opponent that, when studied against the background of resilience literature, are quite sound. The maneuvrist approach and the idea of strategic paralysis both target the multiple nodes across various layers of an opponent's organization that allow it to display coherent and purposeful behaviour. Both thus aim through various methods to disrupt the resilience of the opponent. Indeed, both explicitly state that their objective is to overwhelm the

---

[67] Stewart 2010.

[68] Murray and Millett 1996, Chap. 8; For similar conclusions concerning the need for and problems of adaptation and innovation, see Murray 2011; Farrell et al. 2013, 2010; Adamsky 2010.

[69] Shamir 2011.

[70] Guthrie 2012.

enemy's capability to adapt. In turn, the concept of mission command is fully congruent with the literature about complex systems, adaptability and current insights on what produces organizational resilience: decentralization, formal and informal networks, solid feedback mechanisms, self-organization, mutual trust, semi-autonomous units, etc. Subsequent concepts such as NCW and swarming aspire to extrapolate the positive tenets of mission command.

This chapter, to conclude, also suggests that, where resilience studies are still in the exploratory stage, without clear definition and coherent theory, there is benefit in studying military theory and military organizations, which are increasingly informed by the same literatures as resilience studies, and both of which are firmly grounded in centuries of warfare, those clashes of complex adaptive systems where resilience is key.

References

Adamsky D (2010) The culture of military innovation. Stanford University Press, Stanford

Alberts D (2002) Information age transformation, getting to a 21st century military. US Department of Defense, CCRP Publications, Washington DC

Alberts D, Hayes RE (1995) Command arrangements for peace operations. US Department of Defense, CCRP Publications, Washington DC

Alberts D, Hayes RE (2003) Power to the edge, command and control in the information age. U.S. Department of Defense, CCRP Publications, Washington DC

Alberts D, Gartska JJ, Hayes RE, Signori DT (2001) Understanding information age warfare. US Department of Defense, CCRP Publications, Washington DC

Alberts DS, Gartska JJ, Stein FP (1999) Network centric warfare. Department of Defense, CCRP Publications, Washington DC

Argyris D, Schon D (1978) Organizational learning: a theory of action perspective. Addison-Wesley, Reading

Arquilla J, Ronfeldt D (1993) Cyberwar is coming. Compar Strat 12:141–165

Arquilla J, Ronfeldt D (eds) (1997) In Athena's Camp, preparing for conflict in the information age. RAND, Santa Monica

Arquilla J, Ronfeldt D (2000) Swarming and the Future of Conflict. RAND, Santa Monica

Atkinson SR, Moffat J (2005) The agile organization, from informal networks to complex effects and agility. DoD CCRP, Washington DC

Beinhocker ED (1999) Robust adaptive strategies. Sloan Manag Rev 40:95–106

Beyerchen A (1992) Clausewitz, nonlinearity, and the unpredictability of war. Int Secur 17:55–90

Boyd J, Patterns of conflict, unpublished briefing. www.dnipogo.org/boyd/patterns_ppt.pdf. Accessed 10 March 2016

Boyd J, Organic design for command and control, unpublished briefing. www.dnipogo.org/boyd/patterns_ppt.pdf. Accessed 10 March 2016

Boyd J, The conceptual spiral, unpublished briefing. www.dnipogo.org/boyd/patterns_ppt.pdf. Accessed 10 March 2016

British Army Doctrine (2010) Manual operations. DCDC, MoD, Shrivenham

British Army Doctrine Publication (1995) ADP Command. MoD, Her Majesty's Stationary Office, London

Brown SL, Eisenhardt KM (1998) Competing on the edge, strategy as structured chaos. Harvard Business School Press, Boston

Canetti D, Waismel-Manor I, Cohen N, Rapaport C (2014) What does national resilience mean in a democracy? Evidence from the United States and Israel. Armed Forces Soc 40:504–520

Carle A, Chassin L (2004) Resilience in a community sample of children of alcoholics: its prevalence and relation to internalizing symptomatology and positive effect. Appl Dev Psychol 25:577–595

Chasdi R (2014) A continuum if national-state resiliency to watershed terrorist events. Armed Forces Soc 40:476–503

Church M (1999) Organizing simply for complexity: beyond metaphor towards theory. Long Range Plan 32:25–40

Cohen E, Gooch J (2006) Military misfortunes: the anatomy of failure in war. Simon and Schuster, New York

Cohen E, Keaney T (1995) A revolution in warfare? Air power in the Persian Gulf. Naval Institute Press, Annapolis

Coker C (2004) The future of war. Blackwell Publishing, Oxford

Coleman H (1999) What enables self-organizing behavior in businesses. Emergence 1:33–48

Cordesman A (2003) The Iraq War, strategy, tactics, and military lessons. Praeger, Westport

Davis P, Czerwinski T (1997) Complexity, global politics and national securit. NDU Press, Annapolis

Davis RG (1998) Strategic bombardment in the Gulf War. In: Hall RC (ed) Case studies in strategic bombardment. US Government Printing Office, Washington DC, pp 527–621

Deptula D (1996) Effects based operations, change in the nature of warfare. Aerospace Education Foundation, Arlington

De Waard EJ, Volberda HW, Soeters J (2012) How to support sensing capabilities in highly volatile situations. J Manag Organ 18:774–794

De Waard EJ, Volberda HW, Soeters J (2013) On drivers of organizational responsiveness experiences of a military crisis response organization. J Organ Des 2:1–14

Edwards S (2000) Swarming on the battlefield: past, present, and future. RAND, Santa Monica

Eisenhardt K, Sull DN (2001) Strategy as simple rules. Harvard Bus Rev 79:106–119

Eve RA, Horsfall S, Lee ME (1997) Chaos, complexity, and sociology. Sage, London

Farrell T, Terriff T, Osinga F (eds) (2010) A tranformation gap: American innovations and European military culture. Stanford University Press, Stanford

Farrell T, Osinga F, Russell J (2013) Military adaptation in Afghanistan. Stanford University Press, Stanford

Folke C, Carpenter SR, Walker B, Scheffer M, Chapin T, Rockström J (2010) Resilience thinking: integrating resilience, adaptability and transformability. Ecol Soc 15. http://www.ecologyandsociety.org/vol15/iss4/art20/

Gal R (2014) Social resilience in times of protracted crises: an Israeli Case Study. Armed Forces Soc 40:452–475

Garwin DA (2000) Learning in action. Harvard Business School Press, Boston

Gleick J (1987) Chaos: making a new science. Viking Penguin, New York

Gompert D, Kugler R, Libicki M (1997) Mind the Gap, Promoting a Transatlantic Revolution in Military Affairs. National Defense University Press, Washington DC

Gordon M, Trainor B (2006) Cobra II, The inside story of the invasion and occupation of Iraq. Pantheon Books, New York

Guthrie T (2012) Mission command: do we have the stomach for what is really required? Army Mag 26(June):26–27

Hallion RP (1992) Storm over Iraq, Air Power and the Gulf War. Smithsonian Institution Press, Washington DC

Hillman J (2013) Empirical research on organizational resilience: how far have we come?, Presentation at the autumn meeting of the section sustainability management of the German Academic Association for Business Research, 07.10.2013. http://sustainability.eu/pdf/vhb_nama_2013/presentations/Julia%20Hillmann_TrackC_Resilience.pdf. Accessed 11 March 2016

Holland J (1995) Hidden order, how adaptation builds complexity. Perseus Books, Reading

James GE (1995) Chaos theory: the essentials for military applications. Naval War College, Newport RI
Jervis R (1997) System effects, complexity in political and social life. Princeton University Press, Princeton
Kelly S, Allison MA (1999) The complexity advantage, how the sciences can help your business achieve peak performance. McGraw-Hill, New York
Kiel DL, Elliott E (1996) Chaos theory in the social sciences. University of Michigan Press, Ann Arbor
Lambeth B (2013) The unseen war, allied air power and the takedown of Saddam Hussein. Naval Institute Press, Annapolis
Libicki M (1997) The small and the many. In: Arquilla J, Ronfeldt D (eds) In Athena's Camp. RAND, Santa Monica, pp 191–216
Lissack M (1999) Complexity: the science, its vocabulary, and its relation to organizations. Emergence 1:110–126
Mahnken T, Keaney T (eds) (2007) War in Iraq, planning and execution. Routledge, Abingdon
Mann S (1992) Chaos theory and strategic thought. Parameters 22:54–68
Marion R, Bacon J (1999) Organizational extinction and complex systems. Emergence 1:71–96
Martin-Breen P, Anderies JM (2011) Resilience: A Literature Review. Bellagio Initiative, IDS, Brighton. http://opendocs.ids.ac.uk/opendocs/bitstream/handle/12345678/3692/Bellagio-Rockefeller%20bp.pdf?sequence=1. Accessed 4 July 2016
McKeown M (2012) Adaptability: the art of winning in an age of uncertainty. Kogan Page, New York
Merry U (1995) Coping with uncertainty, insights from the new sciences of chaos, self organization, and complexity. Praeger, Westport
Ministerie van Defensie (not dated), JDP 5 Command and Control, MoD, The Hague
Mintzberg H, Ahlstrand B, Lampel J (1998) Strategy Safari. The Free Press, New York
Murray M, Scales R (2003) The Iraqi war, a military history. Harvard University Press, Cambridge
Murray W (2011) Military adaptation, with fear of change. Cambridge University Press, Cambridge
Murray W, Millett A (1996) Military innovation in the interwar period. Cambridge University Press, Cambridge
NATO (not dated) Allied Joint Doctrine Publication AJP-3 Operations, Brussels
NATO (2010) Allied Joint Publication AJP-01. Allied Joint Doctrine, Brussels
Naveh S (1997) In Pursuit of Excellence, the evolution of operational theory. Frank Cass, London
Olson J (2007) John Warden and the renaissance of American air power. Potomac Books, Washington DC
Osinga F (2010) The rise of transformation. In: Farrell T, Osinga F, Terriff T (eds) A transformation gap? American innovations and European military change. Stanford University Press, Stanford, pp 14–34
Osinga F (2013) Getting a discourse on winning and losing: a primer on Boyd's 'Theory of intellectual evolution'. Contemp Secur Policy 34:603–624
Osinga F (2015) The enemy as a complex adaptive system. In: Olson J (ed) Airpower Reborn, the strategic concepts of John Warden and John Boyd. Naval Institute Press, Annapolis, pp 48–92
Osinga FPB (2006) Science, strategy and war. Routledge, Abingdon
Osinga FPB, Roorda M (2016) From Douhet to drones, air warfare and the evolution of targeting. In: Ducheine P, Schmitt M, Osinga F (eds) Targeting, the challenges of modern warfare. Asser Press, The Hague, pp 27–76
Perrow C (1972) Complex organizations; a critical essay. Scott, Foresman, Glenview, Ill
Perrow C (1999) Normal accidents. Princeton University Press, Princeton
Richardson GE, Neiger BL, Jensen S, Kumpfer KL (1990) The Resiliency Model. Health Education 21:33–39

Richardson K, Cilliers P (2001) What is complexity science? A view from different directions. Emergence 3:5–22
Rijpma JA (1997) Complexity, tight coupling and reliability: connecting normal accidents theory and high reliability theory. J Contingencies Crisis Manag 5:15–23
Schmitt J (1997) Command and (out of) control: the military implications of complexity theory. In: Alberts DS, Czerwinski TJ (eds) Complexity, global politics and national security. National Defense University, Washington DC, Washington, pp 219–246
Shamir E (2011) Transforming Command: The Pursuit of Mission Command in the U.S., British and Israeli Armies. Stanford University Press, Stanford
Shimko K (2010) The Iraqi wars and America's military revolution. Cambridge University Press, Cambridge
Stewart KG (2010) The evolution of command approach (Paper 192). http://www.dodccrp.org/events/15th_iccrts_2010/papers/192.pdf. Accessed 15 March 2016
Toffler A, Toffler H (1993) War and anti-war, survival at the dawn of the 21st century. Little Brown & Company, New York
United States Department of Defense (2001) Network centric warfare, report to congress, Washington DC. http://www.dodccrp.org/files/ncw_report/report/ncw_main.pdf. Accessed 10 March 2016
United States Marine Corps (1997) Doctrine Publication 1 Warfighting. Headquarters United States Marine Corps, Washington DC
Van Creveld M (1988) Command in war. The Free Press, New York
Van Uden J, Richardson K, Cilliers P (2001) Postmodernism revisited? Complexity science and the study of organizations. Tamara1 53–67
Waldrop M (1993) Complexity: the emerging science at the edge of order and chaos. Viking, London
Walker BH, Holling CS, Carpenter SR, Kinzig A (2004) Resilience, adaptability and transformability in social–ecological systems. Ecol Soc 9. http://www.ecologyandsociety.org/vol9/iss2/art5
Walklate S, McGarry R, Mythen G (2014) Searching for resilience: a conceptual excavation. Armed Forces Soc 40:408–427
Warden J (1995) The enemy as a system. Airpower J 9:40–55
Wolin SJ, Wolin S (1993) The resilient self: how survivors of troubled families arise above adversity. Villard, New York
Woodward B (2004) Plan of attack. Simon and Schuster, New York
Zolli A, Healy AM (2012) Resilience: why things bounce back. The Free Press, New York

Chapter 4
Organizing for Conventional and Unconventional Warfare

Erik de Waard and Henk van den As

Abstract Unconventional crises have gained the upper hand in today's international security environment. The numbers of Special Operations Forces (SOF) that most Western militaries have at their disposal do deal with these types of crises are limited; therefore regular troops are increasingly used to fill the gap. This article applies theory on differentiation and integration to offer an organizational perspective on the security and safety risks of the new reality of converging military task domains. History has shown that the misuse of conventional or unconventional forces may result in failing security strategies and, at the same time, may seriously jeopardize the lives of the soldiers actively involved in a mission. The article makes clear that establishing integrating units, taking a middle position between SOF and regular forces, could be beneficial. Yet, real progress depends on two additional measures. First, countries need to improve their strategic-political knowledge base on the ins and outs of unconventional warfare through liaison positions and standing committees, in order to task the proper military units for deployment. Second, specialized training programs and facilities have to be developed to serve as an organizational coordination mechanism to better incorporate basic unconventional warfare practices into the operational repertoire of a large proportion of regular forces.

E. de Waard (✉)
Faculty of Military Sciences, Netherlands Defence Academy, Breda, The Netherlands
e-mail: ej.d.waard.01@mindef.nl

H. van den As
Asymmetric Warfare, Joint Special Operations University, Tampa, FL, USA
e-mail: h.vandenas@home.nl

R. Beeres et al. (eds.), *NL ARMS Netherlands Annual Review of Military Studies 2016*, NL ARMS, DOI 10.1007/978-94-6265-135-7_4

Keywords Unconventional warfare · Special operations forces · Regular forces · Organization design · Differentiation · Integration

Contents

4.1 Introduction

The bare essential of military organizations is to overcome fear in a lethal environment; or in other words, making sure that soldiers and units keep fulfilling their designated roles under barrages of gunfire or other life-threatening circumstances. Throughout the ages and through bloodstained lessons a mechanistic way of organizing has emerged as the most appropriate military system to deal with the violent character of war. Well-drilled, individual soldiers form the smallest cogs of the machine; they have to be capable of meticulously executing their predefined tasks. Behaviour formalization has proven to be a reliable organizational mechanism to stimulate decisive action, while avoiding comprehensible, human contemplation and hesitation when at risk.[1] Functional tasks are departmentalized to streamline the complex machinery, meaning that different organizational elements can specialize and employ their expertise to the benefit of the entire organization. A hierarchical and centralized system of command has to control the composite machine, making sure that under threat everyone knows what to do next and who is in charge. Besides, staff elements serve as additional computation capacity to commanders at different organizational levels, to calculate risks and advise on courses of action. The rationale behind this distinct organizational system is that it tries to create a basic level of stability, predictability, survivability and sustainability within a combat environment that is known to become utterly chaotic when the bullets start flying.

Interestingly, however, this mechanistic approach to military deployment is not a one-size-fits-all organizational solution. In particular, conventional warfare, where two opposing sides, often nation states, deploy large armies to fight each other head-on, has thrived on the machine-like structure, culminating in the

[1] King 2013, p. 149.

massive NATO and Warsaw Pact armies of the Cold War. Yet, with the ending of the Cold-War era Western armed forces started focusing on all kinds of new security issues, such as ethnic and religious rivalry, territorial disputes, the dissolution of states, organized crime, and terrorism. These, what are known as, irregular threats, asked for an alternative and more unconventional approach to warfare, which has traditionally been the domain of Special Operations Forces (SOF). It is, therefore, not surprising that within a number of recent military endeavours, such as the wars in Iraq and Afghanistan, SOF have played a key role.[2] In Afghanistan a small number of SOF, in fact, took the lead role and, in a collaborative effort with the Afghan Northern alliance and U.S. aircraft flying overhead, toppled the Taliban regime in just a matter of weeks. Opposed to the machine-like organizational system of their conventional counterparts, SOF follow a more organic approach towards organizing, captured in adjectives like small, decentralized, self-organizing, peer-to-peer, creative, and versatile. Marquis explains that SOF are a special breed within the armed forces because they have to "conduct operations that are outside the realm and tactics of the conventional battlefield."[3] Refocusing on the Afghanistan case, a conventional approach was simply too slow and not suited for dealing with the Taliban's complex tribal structure and its ability to move quickly and blend in with the local community. Whereas, small SOF teams could be deployed straightaway, could offer an out-of-the-box solution, and were specially trained to communicate and collaborate with indigenous allies.

The growing dominance of unconventional security risks has turned into a major point of concern for contemporary Western militaries. Approximately 1 to 5 per cent of most Western armed forces can be categorized as SOF, but this proportion is far too small to properly deal with the number, size, and duration of most of today's irregular crises. Consequently, conventional forces are increasingly used for unconventional tasks or have to collaborate more intensively with SOF. That is why, in Afghanistan, soon after the Taliban regime had been overthrown by SOF, politicians in charge passed the ball on to regular forces, which started the ISAF mission. Robinson criticizes this transfer, arguing that ISAF's conventional commanders, who were not adequately trained in counterinsurgency operations, came up with a strategy of first and foremost helping the new indigenous government to start performing its basic functions, while the essential element of supporting the local population was strongly underestimated.[4] Robinson, furthermore, argues that if the initial game plan had been more thoroughly grounded in SOF knowledge and practices, the outcome of the nation-building effort could have been more advantageous.

Perceiving irregular crises, such as the Afghanistan case, exemplary for future military operations, effective cooperation between SOF and conventional forces seems to become a crucial prerequisite for mission success. Based on this assumption, the present article looks deeper into the structural divide between

---

[2] Robinson 2004

[3] Marquis 1997, p. 46.

[4] Robinson 2013, p. xviii.

conventional and unconventional forces from an organization and management perspective. To be more concrete, it will concentrate on the organizational trade-off between differentiation and integration. On one hand, differentiation offers organizational elements the possibility to specialize in a certain area or domain; yet, at the same time, each part develops its own typical identity, which makes fruitful collaboration not self-evident. On the other hand, a strategy of integration goes hand in hand with assimilation, which strengthens the common ground between collaborating organizational parts; but, simultaneously weakens the specialist character of these different parts. In the light of this trade-off, specific security and safety issues will be made explicit in the discussion on differentiation versus integration of SOF and conventional forces.

4.2 Differentiation and Integration

Organizations in general are no closed systems; they are in an ongoing open relationship with their environment. Organizations are also no homogeneous entities; they are mostly built up of different functional parts and subcultures. As a result, the influence that the environment exerts on an organization is always heterogeneous; it affects the separate functional parts differently. In a seminal study Lawrence and Lorsch have analyzed the rationale for differentiating an organization into distinct functional departments, such as R&D, sales, and production.[5] One of their key findings was that these different departments had diverging orientations toward time, inter-collegial relations, and structure. For example, production departments had a short-term focus, were mainly task-oriented, and had a very formalized structure. R&D departments, on the contrary, had a long-term perspective, were focused on inter-collegial interactions, and had a rather organic structure. Their findings make clear that there is no one best way to organize for the entire organization. The challenge is to smartly departmentalize and to organize the different parts in a way that suits the individual task environments best. Although this in not an easy task, Lawrence and Lorsch offer some intriguing thoughts on the principles of successful structuring.[6] In general, they explain (see Fig. 4.1) that the value of differentiation has to do with the relationship between an organization's managerial direction, materialized in its formal structure (straight line), and the dynamics of an organization's task environment (dotted line). Figure 4.1 shows two situations in which both variables largely correspond. Realizing that a perfect fit can hardly be achieved, Lawrence and Lorsch argue that a strong level of congruence between the two is sufficient to speak of appropriate differentiation.

[5] Lawrence and Lorsch 1967, p. 41.

[6] Lawrence and Lorsch 1967, p. 212.

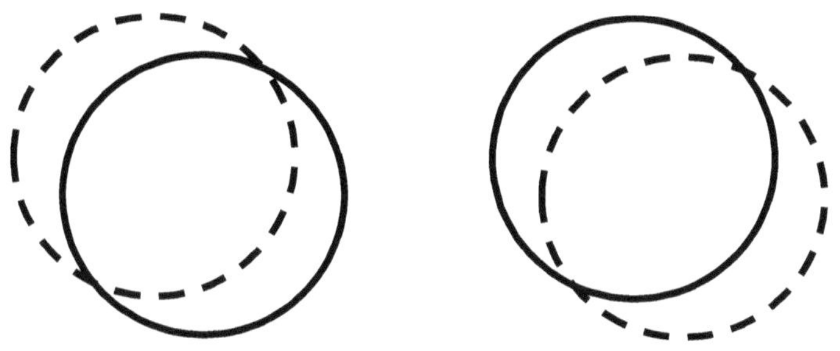

Fig. 4.1 Appropriate differentiation (Lawrence and Lorsch 1967, p. 214)

From a more practical perspective, it can be argued that Fig. 4.1 schematically represents the well-known business unit model, which was a very popular organizational structure in the 1980s and 1990s. During that period, the ruling assumption was that for large organizations, offering multiple products or services to various markets and customers, to properly deal with the wide range of market demands, they needed to diversify into a number of largely independent organizational elements—business units (straight circles)—that could completely focus on their own typical product-market combination (dotted circles). These business units needed to have full control over all necessary organizational functions to be really customer-centric. Interestingly, Fig. 4.1 seems to imply that the business unit structure, from a differentiation perspective, is doing quite well, evoking the question why it was abandoned? Well, it is important to realize that the business unit model primarily focuses its strategy on the task environments of the individual business units and not on the competitive environment of the organization as a whole. In this respect, a commonly accepted viewpoint among organization scholars is that a business unit structure is highly effective, because it is deliberately organized close to the customer; yet, due to the duplication of staff elements and functional departments it becomes quite expensive and, therefore, scores low on efficiency.[7] Moreover, self-supporting business units have the tendency to behave like kingdoms, seeking competition with the other business units to fight over resources, instead of sharing knowledge to stimulate innovation throughout the entire organization. All these downsides have become really dysfunctional in an increasingly hypercompetitive business environment, where the need to be effective, as well as efficient and innovative have to be combined.

As a result, the shared services model has emerged. The main goal of this model is to retain a high level of customer orientation, while at the same time saving costs and stimulating intra-organizational learning. The way to achieve this is for large multi-divisional firms to stick to the business unit structure, but also to withdraw certain support activities (e.g. ICT, logistics, transport, HRM) from their business units, and concentrate these activities in separate organizational

[7] Mintzberg 1983, p. 240.

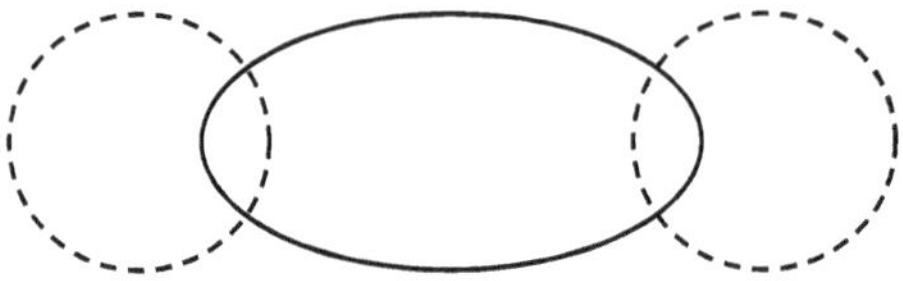

Fig. 4.2 Type 1 differentiation error (Lawrence and Lorsch 1967, p. 214)

departments—shared service centres. By this recombining effort, economies of scale as well as economies of skill could be regained within functional domains, from which the organization as a whole could benefit. So, what we see happening here, from a differentiation perspective, is that, for example, a logistics department, that had previously been a differentiated part of a business unit, was merged into one concentrated logistical centre together with other formerly decentralized logistical departments, offering services to the entire organization. Consequently, the level of differentiation declined, but the level of intra-organizational coordination increased. After all, the business units that had been largely independent before, now had to obtain support activities from a centralized shared service centre.

With the characteristics of the shared service centre model in mind, it becomes interesting to look at Fig. 4.2, in which a type 1 differentiation error is illustrated. Here two task environments can be seen (dotted circles) that are insufficiently being addressed by the organization's formal structure. Essentially, the case represented here is about an organizational department or unit that has been created to offer goods or services to two different markets. However, the dynamics of these markets are so diverse—literally far apart—that it becomes problematic for one organizational structure to satisfy both.

The situation sketched, resembles a risk that is typical for the shared service centre model, and therefore, the philosophy of the model is increasingly being brought up for debate. In short, a shared service centre has to offer similar services to a number of diverse business units and at the same time it is judged on cost-efficiency. Therefore, management of a shared service centre tends to act pragmatic and searches for a common service denominator for all business units. One can imagine that the generic service level offered does not adequately meet the more specific or extreme demands of the business units' separate task environments. That is shown in Fig. 4.2, where only a small proportion of the task environment is addressed. Another risk of the shared service centre model is that the intra-organizational coordination effort, within the shared service centre organization itself, but also between the business units and the shared service centre, becomes so intense that the focus on the customer or buyer is pushed to the back. In Fig. 4.2, this is represented by the large proportion of the formal organization that does not satisfy any need of both task environments at all. In a sense, most of the organization's energy is directed inwards and, commercially seen, generated in vain.

In discussing Figs. 4.1 and 4.2 a prevalent dilemma of organizational structuring surfaces. In the first situation of developing separate structures for distinct task environments, the main challenge is to create organizational synergy between the differentiated organizational elements. Too much differentiation leads to a sort of organizational archipelago, where the different organizational islands lose sight of each other, limiting their performance horizons. Metaphorically speaking, a parent organization deliberately has to invest in the building of bridges to cross the waters between the organizational islands for achieving overall connectedness. The second case makes clear that a strong focus on merging different organizational elements into one integrated whole, creates structures that can be used for multiple tasks, while avoiding too much redundancy. Yet, these structures will preferably focus on quick and dirty performance gains, whereas the more complex and extreme environmental demands are neglected or just unobtainable. Using another metaphor, a highly integrated structure can be compared with a massive bulk carrier that strictly follows its most advantageous course; and, in case a sudden change of course is needed, a lot of effort from the entire crew is required; or in organizational terms, a load of internal, vertical and horizontal coordination measures are necessary to properly align the internal processes in order to meet the demands of different task environments. Summarizing the dilemma, it could be argued that, on one hand, strongly differentiated organizations can exploit specialization advantages but can also easily become disconnected and evoke internal rivalry. On the other hand, highly integrated structures have a broad performance scope against low costs, but can never achieve the specialized and dedicated performance outcome of differentiated structures.

4.3 Differentiation Dynamics of Conventional and Unconventional Warfare

With this basic organizational dilemma in mind, let us take a closer look at the relationship between SOF and conventional forces. Although special units were used by armies before, they really developed into a professional, separate branch within the standing force structures during the Second World War.[8] The main reason for this was that conventional forces were unsuited to conduct certain special tasks. For example, the U.S. government founded the OSS (Office of Strategic Services) to gather strategic information and support resistance groups deep within enemy territory; the U.S. Navy established underwater demolition teams (UDTs), what later were to become the Navy SEALS, in support of the amphibious island hopping campaign in the Pacific, and the British Army created the SAS (Special Air Service) in 1941 to turn the tables in the desert war in North Africa, conducting commando raids behind enemy lines. All three examples comply with the basic lesson coming from organization and management theory, namely, to strive for a sufficient level of fit between the formal structure of an organizational element and the dynamics of the task environment it has to deal with. Because conventional forces were unable to meet emerging battlefield demands,

[8] Weale 1997, p. x.

a differentiation process took place to develop tailored units for the new task requirements.

Until the Cold War the status quo between conventional forces and SOF remained rather unchanged. Conventional forces were structured to fight a war of attrition, based on principles such as mass, firepower, and maneuver, whereas SOF were designed and trained to execute very specific, small-scale niche operations. At the same time, the Cold War has also been an era in which SOF has become an established part of the military toolkit. Earlier experiences had learned that SOF were an essential complementary asset for large-scale conventional warfare. For example, strategic intelligence gathering on troop numbers, troop positions, and logistical supply chains was vital to come up with viable battle plans for a main force. Moreover, direct action missions, such as raids on rear echelons or critical infrastructure were an important means to hamper an enemy's supply of follow-on forces. Consequently, SOF became a relevant part of both NATO's and Warsaw Pact's conventional strategy. However, apart from these considerations typically relevant for mass-mechanized warfare, the wider international security dynamics of the Cold-War era also contributed to the undisputed status of SOF. In reality, the latent threat of total nuclear destruction stimulated both the U.S. and Soviet Union to avoid a direct confrontation in Europe. As a result, the tensions between the two super powers surfaced in all kinds of proxy wars all over the globe, the most prominent ones being Vietnam and Afghanistan. Many of these wars were conflict situations in which indigenous factions took up arms to throw off the yoke of their colonial past. For American and Russian politicians alike, SOF became a valuable strategic instrument to train and professionalize such local warring factions in support of their own geo-political objectives. This is basically what occurred in Vietnam and Afghanistan, where respectively the Soviet Union supported the Viet Cong in fighting the Americans, and the U.S. helped the Mujahedin in their struggle against the Soviet Union.

As of the collapse of the Berlin Wall the predominance of conventional warfare rapidly evaporated. In the power vacuum that the Soviets had left behind all kinds of tensions surfaced that had been oppressed for years. Opposed to the conventional inter-state Cold-War security status quo, unconventional crisis situations have gained the upper hand ever since. Studying NATO's most recent Strategic Concept—Active Engagement, Modern Defence—makes clear that the alliance aims most of its arrows at countering irregular threats like the proliferation of nuclear weapons, terrorism at home and abroad, instability or conflict beyond NATO borders, and cyber attacks. Notwithstanding, the Strategic Concept also explicitly addresses the ever present risk of conventional warfare, stating: "Many regions and countries around the world are witnessing the acquisition of substantial, modern military capabilities with consequences for international stability and Euro-Atlantic security that are difficult to predict."[9] To cover the entire spectrum of security crises the alliance argues that it has to "develop and maintain robust,

[9] NATO 2010, para 8.

mobile and deployable conventional forces to carry out both our Article 5 responsibilities and the Alliance's expeditionary operations."[10] At the same time, it is emphasized that in order to improve effectiveness across the conflict spectrum there is a need to "further develop doctrine and military capabilities for expeditionary operations, including counterinsurgency, stabilization and reconstruction operations".[11] This seems to imply that the Alliance intends to increasingly use conventional forces for unconventional task-settings, while the knowledge and capabilities of these forces to successfully conduct these sorts of operations are not at the desired level yet. Interesting, moreover, is that within this strategic debate on the relationship between unconventional crises and military capabilities, the role or added value of SOF is acknowledged but also not seen as a panacea.

The reason for SOF not being the sole solution to deal with the reality of increasing irregular crises can be related to, Mintzberg's argument, that size effects structure. On this relationship he hypothesizes: "The larger the organization, the more elaborate its structure—that is, the more specialized its tasks, and the more differentiated its units."[12] The coming about of large-scale, conventional Cold-War military organizations largely fit this hypothesis. Although the overpowering Cold-War security context required SOF capabilities, the real organizational effort was directed at achieving battlefield supremacy through the combined arms philosophy of fire and maneuver. As a result, Western armed forces have evolved into a diverse collection of interrelated arms, services, and functional branches, of which SOF are only just one small part. Yet, the ending of the Cold War has rendered these massive organizational machines, tailored for conventional warfare, less useful for the new, largely unconventional task-setting. The balance between the size of the organization and the predominantly conventional security context has shifted towards a situation of mainly unconventional security challenges, for which only a small proportion of the organization is actually invented.

Building on Lawrence and Lorsch's earlier argumentation, Figs. 4.3 and 4.4 capture this development schematically. Figure 4.3 makes clear that during the Cold War a fit existed between the different task environments and organizational parts, in this specific case conventional forces and SOF. Figure 4.4 shows the differentiation imbalance that came into being after the Cold-War era. An unconventional task environment can be seen that has outgrown the SOF part that was originally developed to deal with these types of security risks. At the same time, it presents a dramatically decreased conventional task-setting, for which the intended regular military capacity has remained much of its original size.

Following Fig. 4.4, one could easily argue that increasing SOF whilst decreasing conventional capabilities would solve the matter, however on both fronts insurmountable problems would arise. First, significantly expanding SOF capacity is

[10] NATO 2010, para 19.

[11] NATO 2010, para 25.

[12] Mintzberg 1983, p. 124.

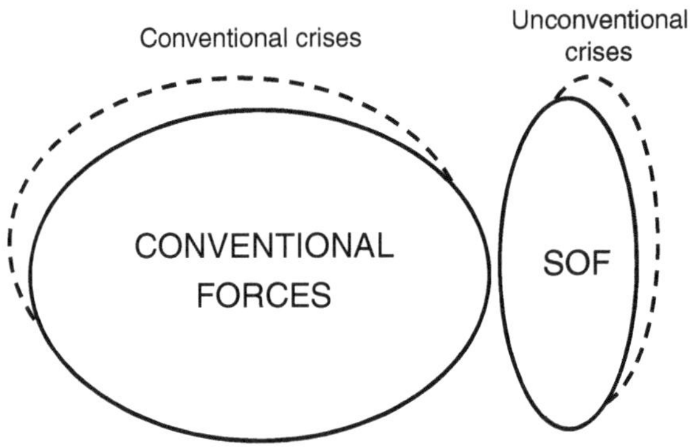

Fig. 4.3 Cold-war differentiation balance

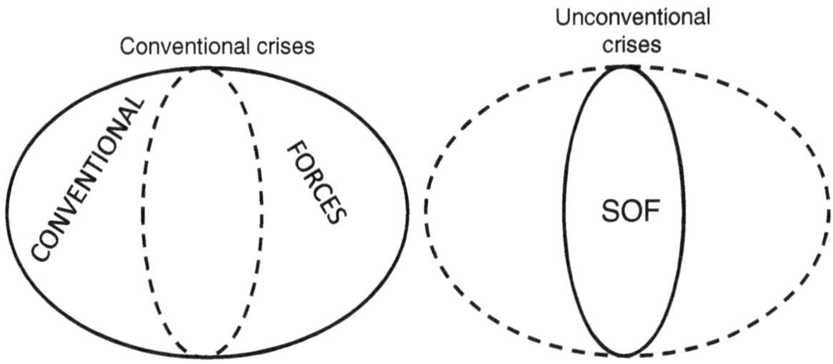

Fig. 4.4 Post-cold war differentiation imbalance

deemed largely impossible. Spulak offers a valuable account on the uniqueness and qualities of individual SOF operators.[13] He argues that only a maximum fraction of people can live up to the high standards of SOF's core values embodied in each of these elite warriors. Therefore, significantly expanding the SOF numbers to the desired level would undoubtedly lead to a loss of quality. Second, looking at the latter option, the contingency factor 'size' comes into play again. Mass is at the heart of fighting a conventional battle. In short, doctrine prescribes that a concentrated built-up of maneuver forces has to form a centre of gravity that, supported by direct and indirect fire, attacks an enemy's weak spot, breaks through the defensive line and advances further.[14] A rule of thumb is that the defence versus

[13] Spulak 2007, p. 11.

[14] Citino 2004, p. 264.

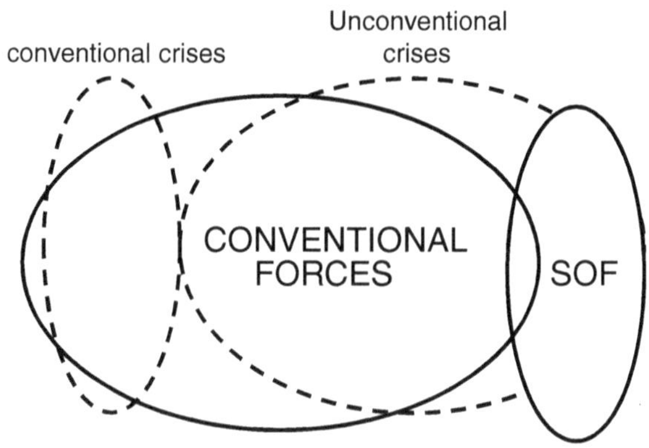

Fig. 4.5 Converging task settings

offense ratio should be at least 1:3. More concrete, to defeat a dug-in army corps, the opponent needs a minimum offensive force of three army corps. Therefore, when conventional numbers are considerably reduced, the numerical power needed to deter or take on a potential conventional foe is seriously put at risk.

Investing in multi-functional conventional forces has become the answer to this problem and is what NATO addresses in its Strategic Concept. The size of conventional forces remains intact, to keep the necessary mass for fighting a mechanized maneuver war, while at the same time these forces function as an overflow barrel for irregular crises, when the available SOF capacity reaches its limits. Although this solution seems quite logical, it has some inherent organizational disadvantages. Actually, Lawrence and Lorsch speak of a type 2 differentiation error, when two separate organizational parts concentrate their activities on the same task environment.[15] Competitive clashes, redundancy of effort, and poor coordination are typical malfunctions of these types of organizational arrangements. Figure 4.5 tries to capture the military differentiation approach schematically.

4.4 Security and Safety Consequences

Figure 4.5 illustrates that conventional forces are used for both conventional and unconventional crises. It also demonstrates that as a consequence conventional forces occasionally poach on SOF's territory. The organizational drawbacks, mentioned by Lawrence and Lorsch, are therefore lurking within the current military crisis response context as well. Earlier armed conflicts have made clear that especially competitive clashes between the two types of forces, on how to best deal with an unconventional crisis, are not uncommon. The size and historical-grounding of conventional forces has given them a key position in the decision-making

[15] Lawrence and Lorsch 1967, p. 215.

process. After all, most officers have made careers in the regular forces and, as a result, have more affinity with a conventional way of operating. Moreover, the specialist character and unique way of operating of SOF has isolated them from regular forces, causing a lack of appreciation or sometimes even disdain. Marquis has interviewed a former commander of the 75th Ranger Regiment, who states the following in this regard. "Of course we're all concerned with people who are different. We are uncomfortable with it…in particular [in] the military because it is so structured and when all of a sudden you have unstructured beings, people are not comfortable with them…We had some people who had tremendous capabilities, tremendous skills, but people didn't want to be around them… These free thinkers. These people who did things in an unconventional manner."[16]

Consequently, SOF representatives tend to be marginalized in the decision-making process on the conduct of operations. Bado offers a valuable account on the tensions between conventional and unconventional forces during the Vietnam War.[17] In the beginning of the war SOF were deployed under the umbrella of the CIA. A typical covert, unconventional approach was followed, aiming not to destroy the Viet Cong but rather to render them irrelevant through a pacification program in which SOF concentrated on winning the loyalty of the local population. Despite the program's success, conventional forces constantly tried to gain control over the Special Forces, arguing that these units were too statically and defensively used. Eventually, when in 1963 power over SOF was transferred to the conventional force; special units were no longer primarily used for pacification purposes. Border surveillance and control, offensive operations against infiltration routes, and direct action operations against Viet Cong war zones and bases became the new norm.[18] Bado argues that "the strategy and tactics used [by the regular army] matched exactly the theory of victory embodied in [conventional force] culture and the tactics that had been successful in two World wars and Korea."[19]

Other historical cases also clearly show that using conventional and unconventional military forces outside of their natural task domains may have serious security and safety implications. Regarding the former aspect, history provides some striking cases where the misuse of either special or conventional forces has resulted in disappointing or even dramatics security outcomes for the strategic decision-makers. Political loss of face or security crises spiralling out of control after misperceiving the conduct of operations are not uncommon. Regarding the latter, the military units involved have paid the ultimate price for the optimism bias or lack of knowledge of the strategic decision-makers responsible for their deployment. To be more specific, World War II, Korea, and Vietnam paint a picture in which SOF, in many cases, were used in a conventional way. As a result, the

[16] Marquis 1997, p. 6.

[17] Bado 1996, p. 106.

[18] Krepinevich 1986, p. 75.

[19] Bado 1996, p. 106.

attrition rates among these specialized units were high, while, generally speaking, the tactical gains were disappointing.[20]

Concentrating on the Vietnam War from a political-strategic angle, one could say that on the whole a conventional strategy was followed, relying on mainly conventional forces to overcome a typical unconventional warfare situation. We all know what the political and military outcome of this approach has been. Operation Desert One, the rescuing of Americans held hostage in the U.S. embassy in Teheran in 1980, is another good example to mention. The American soldiers killed in action unnecessarily and the ensuing political humiliation were ultimately blamed on the detrimental state of SOF in de U.S. military.[21] Being associated with much of the negative publicity on counterinsurgency operations in Vietnam, SOF received most of the blame, which resulted in their post-war neglect. Dramatic reductions in personnel, technological assets, but also in the training programs to maintain unique SOF skills went on for years. The conventional commanders in charge of the Army, Air Force and Navy believed that most SOF tasks could also be conducted by conventional forces, such as the 101st Airborne Division, the U.S. Marines, and regular pilots. However, the hostage situation in Iran was so complex that SOF participation was deemed essential. Therefore, the politicians and military officials in charge formed an ad hoc coalition of conventional and SOF elements to execute the mission together. Intra-organizational unfamiliarity, sub-optimal skill levels, and technological problems turned into a cocktail of organizational bad-fortune. A final interesting case to address is operation UNOSOM II in Somalia. Tucker and Lamb explain that SOF deployment in Somalia was in essence based on the political unwillingness to deploy a large conventional force to effectively deal with the fighting warlords, of which Aideed and his troops was the strongest.[22] SOF task force Ranger was tasked to apprehend Aideed and turn him over to the UN to be prosecuted. Aideed, who felt cornered by the international mandate but at the same time knew that his armed force outnumbered the SOF contingent, gradually slipped under the radar and increasingly challenged task force Ranger militarily. Critics, that as a result of these developments, suggested to either come to a political settlement with Aideed or to send additional armour to build a more potent military force, were not heard in the international political debate. The hunt for Aideed went on and so it could happen that during a daylight raid on the Bakara market, the place where Aideed and his forces were concentrated, the SOF units found themselves surrounded and outnumbered in a conventional urban battle, with an enemy who had the initiative and the capabilities to inflict serious damage.[23]

---

[20] Tucker and Lamb 2007, p. 79; Finlan 2008, p. 35.

[21] Marquis 1997, p. 72.

[22] Tucker and Lamb 2007, p. 116.

[23] Tucker and Lamb 2007, p. 126.

4.5 Organizational Solutions

Returning to the theoretical core of this study, structuring insights may be of value to mitigate problems, similar to the ones mentioned above, for future military deployment. Lawrence and Lorsch point to a "shared superior" as a means to effectively resolve conflicts between mildly differentiated organizational elements. However, when the parts are highly differentiated, they argue that alignment by a shared superior will not suffice. In such a case, the management hierarchy needs to be supported by creating an integrating organizational element.[24] Additionally, Mintzberg makes clear that investing in liaison devices and the standardization of skills is also crucial.[25] Interestingly, these rather generic organizational solutions seem to comply with both the actual measures taken by, for example, the U.S. military and the viewpoints brought forward in the current military scholarly debate on how to deal with the tensions of converging military task domains.

4.5.1 Establishing a Shared Superior

After the tragedy of Operation Desert One the US government started revitalizing its SOF capabilities. One of the most influential measures was the set-up of the U.S. Special Operations Command (USSOCOM). This new centralized command element "was responsible for selection and training of special operations forces and acquisition and development of equipment peculiar to special operations, as well as allocating resources to support these responsibilities."[26] SOF units from all services were hierarchically positioned under the umbrella of USSOCOM as a means to operationally bring the varied mixture of SOF elements closer together and control their deployment. Furthermore, at the political level a new Office was established, primarily focusing on unconventional crises: the Office of the Assistant Secretary of Defence, Special Operations and Low-Intensity Conflict (ASD-SOLIC). This latter action was initiated to better steer the strategic-political decision-making process to deploy SOF elements in compliance with their unique capabilities. In other words, incorporating a separate SOF entity within the strategic apex of the Department of Defence had to counter thc tendency of using these highly specialized forces for conventional tasks.

A perceptive reader may argue that these organizational measures strictly aim at improving SOF deployment by expanding differentiation between SOF and conventional units to the executive channels. Although this is true, the measures have also had an impact on dealing with the reality of converging task domains.

---

[24] Lawrence and Lorsch 1967, p. 220.

[25] Mintzberg 1983, p. 40.

[26] Marquis 1997, p. 149.

Important to realize, in this respect, is that the ASD-SOLIC can only fulfil its role adequately when there is clarity about the key tasks of special operations forces. So, together with the installation of this new Assistant Secretary position, the following typical special operations task settings have been formalized in law: direct action, strategic reconnaissance, unconventional warfare, foreign internal defence, civil affairs, psychological operations, counter terrorism, humanitarian assistance, theatre search and rescue, and such other activities as may be specified by the President or the Secretary of Defence.[27] With this step the boundaries between special operations and conventional warfare have been made explicit and by legal foundation made incontestable. As a result, when a crisis occurred, the first political reaction was to determine the type of emergency—conventional or unconventional, and next, to use this categorization as a transparent reference point for the allocation of actual units. From the moment USSOCOM and ASD-SOLIC were installed until the beginning of the 1990s, the process worked quite well. Yet, thereafter, when the number of unconventional crises dramatically increased, the decision-making process became less straightforward. This was not only the case for the U.S. military but for most Western armed forces. Since the number and size of the unconventional crises outgrew the available SOF capacity, strategic decision-makers were forced to consider deploying conventional forces for unconventional tasks. The Balkan war, Operation Iraqi freedom and, of course, the ISAF mission in Afghanistan, are recent examples of unconventional operations for which large numbers of conventional troops were used. These operations have shown that apart from a centralized command structure and a formalized domain consensus additional organizational mechanisms are needed to be more effective when using a mix of SOF and conventional forces. These mechanisms will be discussed in more detail below.

4.5.2 Creating an Integrating Organizational Element

The new reality of a heterogeneous security environment and highly distinctive organizational parts may push armed forces into a path of further differentiation. Following the logic of Lawrence and Lorsch, armed forces could consider to create specialized units that can fill the grey area between conventional and unconventional warfare. Important to emphasize is that such a choice may strongly depend upon the variable organizational size. Smaller militaries probably do not have the numerical luxury to diversify into too many organizational elements.

The U.S. Army, however, that possesses a wide variety of special units has plotted the use of these units on the spectrum of military operations (see Fig. 4.6). While certain units, such as Special Mission Units and the Green Berets are typically used for the left side of the spectrum, others, like Civil Affairs, PsyOps, and

[27] Marquis 1997, p. 146.

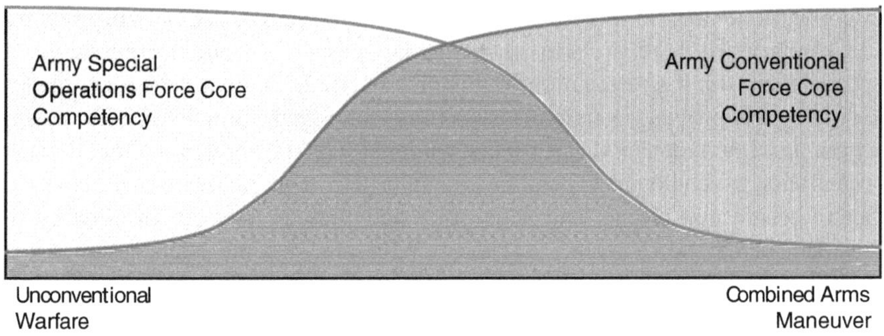

Fig. 4.6 The U.S. Army's Operational Spectrum (US Army Special Operations Command (2013), p. 16)

Army Rangers are assigned to the mid-section and right side. Within the much smaller Netherlands Armed Forces a similar approach is currently being studied.[28] Yet, in this specific case, SOF capacity is far too limited to further diversify, so the answer has to come from transforming a conventional air assault unit into a new SOF element comparable with the U.S. Rangers.

An interesting additional viewpoint Fitzsimmons brings forward is that because of the high demand for SOF in today's security environment, the current differentiation approach of the U.S. Army will not be enough.[29] Since most of today's crises belong to the middle part of the operational spectrum, the available SOF capacity reaches its limit quite fast. Consequently, the SOF units intended for the spectrum´s left wing will be called upon to increase overall numbers. This development carries the inherent risk that highly specialized units become occupied with conducting tasks that are too basic for them, diluting their specialized qualities. Fitzsimmons, therefore, suggests that the U.S. Army should, just like the Dutch, follow an alternative strategy of preparing a significant number of conventional units, especially light infantry, for unconventional deployment.

4.5.3 Incorporating Liaison Devices

The historical cases discussed earlier make clear that apart from these force structuring initiatives, policy-makers and senior commanders must more consciously task units for deployment, especially when a mission has conventional as well as unconventional characteristics. This requires extensive knowledge on the dynamics of unconventional warfare and on important, but sometimes subtle, differences between the operational capabilities of potential military units. Operations like

[28] Timmermans 2014, p. 173.

[29] Fitzsimmons 2003, p. 214.

Desert One, UNOSOM II, and ISAF show that incorporating this kind of knowledge into the decision-making process is not self-evident and that the process itself is quite often subject to political power play. Finlan therefore argues that knowledge of unconventional warfare and appropriate military responses has to improve by including more irregular warfare experts into the military-political establishment.[30] From an organization theory perspective he breaks a lance for investing in liaison positions. Mintzberg states the following on the nature of the liaison role, "because the incumbent serves at the crossroads of communication channels, he emerges as a nerve centre of the organization with considerable power. Note that this power is informal, deriving from knowledge not status. Some liaison positions serve between different line units. Other liaison positions join line and staff groups".[31] Tucker and Lamb add to this that also the use of standing committees should be more naturally accepted into the political decision-making process. They argue that such committees will strengthen the horizontal integration of the inter-departmental security bureaucracy and lead to better strategic decision-making regarding, hence organizational solutions for, contemporary security issues.[32]

4.5.4 *Standardization of Skills*

The increasing reality of SOF and conventional units collaborating or relieving one another also requires organizational measures to develop a common skill-set. First, De Waard and Kramer explain that standardized skills, drills and procedures are crucial to facilitate lateral coordination between different military units within modular task force structures.[33] Second, King makes clear that mastering basic and functional drills not only serves as leverage for effective inter-unit cooperation. He emphasizes that high levels of standardization enhance military professionalism, which positively affects the willingness and trust to conduct military operations together.[34] In this regard, theory on organizational networks refers to the added-value of achieving cultural compatibility.[35] Third, shared procedures safeguard uniformity, which is critical for military units that are mostly deployed within an organizational constellation of sequential rotations. In an unconventional crisis context, where the support of the local population is paramount, a lacking unity of action could easily jeopardize mission success. According to Krepinevich and Tucker and Lamb military training should be the focal point of this

[30] Finlan 2008, p. 116.

[31] Mintzberg 1983, p. 82.

[32] Tucker and Lamb 2007, p. 226.

[33] De Waard and Kramer 2008, p. 542.

[34] King 2013, p. 224.

[35] Sarkar et al. 2001, p. 361.

standardization effort.[36] He explains that currently training programs are still too much dominated by the traditional air-land battle doctrine of combined arms maneuver. Special training areas need to be developed where different types of forces can be trained in unconventional warfare scenarios, learning the basic skills and collaborative actions.

4.6 Conclusion

Recapitulating, this article has addressed today's intertwining of conventional and unconventional warfare and its consequences for force design. One of the main conclusions is that safety and security threats are lurking when the decision to either use regular troops for unconventional crises or SOF for conventional tasks is taken too lightly. Misjudgment on this issue may not only put the lives of soldiers at risk, it may also seriously endanger the intended outcome of a military operation. At the same time, the article has made clear that sticking to the traditional divide between conventional forces and special operations forces is becoming counter-productive. SOF's numerical capacity is simply too limited to cover the vast array of unconventional crises. Although, new integrating units, taking a middle position between SOF and regular forces, could offer some relief, the most viable solution, in terms of capacity, seems to be to better prepare conventional units for unconventional tasks. Yet, two additional organizational investments are required to make this shifting of tasks viable. First, the knowledge base of the strategic-political level needs improvement. Politicians have to learn the do's and don'ts of unconventional warfare through formalized SOF liaison positions in their committees. But also high-ranking military commanders of conventional units have to structurally incorporate irregular warfare expertise into their supporting staff elements. Second, tailor-made irregular warfare training facilities and programs are necessary to create a level playfield for all the forces involved. Elitism of SOF units will hamper inter-unit collaboration, as well as lacking unconventional warfare skill-sets of regular troops. Specialized training is a powerful tool to bring these strongly differentiated elements closer together, both professionally and culturally.

References

Bado CM (1996) Integration of special operations and conventional forces in unconventional warfare. Naval Postgraduate School, Monterey

Citino RM (2004) Blitzkrieg to Desert Storm; the evolution of operational warfare. Kansas University Press, Kansas

[36] Krepinevich 2002, p. 82; Tucker and Lamb 2007, p. 203.

De Waard EJ, Kramer FJ (2008) Tailored task forces: temporary organizations and modularity. Int J Project Manag 26:537–546
Finlan A (2008) Special forces, strategy and the war on terror. Routledge, London
Fitzsimmons M (2003) The importance of being special: planning for the future of US Special Operations Forces. Def Secur Anal 19:203–218
King A (2013) The combat soldier. Oxford University Press, Oxford
Krepinevich AF (1986) The army and Vietnam. The John Hopkins University Press, Baltimore
Krepinevich AF (2002) The army and land warfare: transforming the legions. Joint Force Quart 32:76–82
Lawrence PR, Lorsch JW (1967) Organization and environment: managing differentiation and integration. Harvard University Press, Boston
Marquis SL (1997) Unconventional warfare; rebuilding U.S. Special Operations Forces. Brookings Institution Press, Washington
Mintzberg H (1983) Structure in fives: designing effective organizations. Prentice-Hall, Englewood Cliffs
NATO (2010) Active engagement, modern defence. NATO Public Diplomacy Division, Brussels
Robinson L (2004) Masters of chaos; the secret history of the Special Forces. Public Affairs, New York
Robinson L (2013) One hundred victories; special operations and the future of American warfare. Public Affairs, New York
Sarkar MB, Echambadi R, Cavusgil ST, Aulakh PS (2001) The influence of complementarity, compatibility, and relationship characteristics on alliance outcomes. J Acad Market Sci 29:358–373
Spulak RG (2007) A theory of special operations; the origins, qualities, and use of SOF. Joint Spec Oper Univ 07:1–45
Timmermans MPP (2014) De Landmacht van Morgen. Militaire Spect 183:170–178
Tucker D, Lamb CJ (2007) United States Special Operations Forces. Columbia University Press, New York
US Army Special Operations Command (2013) ARSOF 2022. Spec Warfare 26:1–32
Weale A (1997) Secret warfare; Special Operations Forces from the great game to the SAS. Hodder and Stoughton, London

Chapter 5
Dealing with the Security Gap: The Netherlands Army's Doctrinal Struggle

Peter C.J. Neuteboom

Abstract Due to the absence or incapability of local police or lagging deployment of an international police force, to fill ensuing security gaps, military on international stability missions have been dealing with insecurity, criminality and insurgency. Although ensuring law and order exceeds the core tasks of the military, and meets with resistance, given the circumstances, (international) military acting as interim police-force has been considered the only option. This chapter explains how the Netherlands Royal Army has contributed to improving public security by providing some sort of interim policing during stability operations and concludes that it has not institutionalised these activities in its doctrines. It is argued that the NL Army must recognise the needs to engage in the restoring and maintaining of public security in case of a security gap. By clearly defining in the doctrines which policing tasks should be performed to establish public security, a better organizational fit for these tasks could be institutionalised and the necessary training, mind-set and culture developed.

Keywords Public security · Security gap · Interim policing · Stabilisation operation · Military doctrine · Institutional change · Netherlands Army

---

P.C.J. Neuteboom (✉)
Faculty of Military Sciences, Netherlands Defence Academy,
Breda, The Netherlands
e-mail: peter.neuteboom@ziggo.nl

R. Beeres et al. (eds.), *NL ARMS Netherlands Annual Review of Military Studies 2016*, NL ARMS, DOI 10.1007/978-94-6265-135-7_5

Contents

5.1 Introduction

War-torn societies often suffer from public disorder and lawlessness. International police often deploy late and local police forces have either ceased to function, are ineffective or have lost their legitimacy and impartiality. To close the security gap, there is often no other option but to engage international military forces to enforce the law and maintain public order.[1]

Security gaps occurred during the stabilisation operations of the Netherlands (NL) Army in the Balkans, Iraq and Afghanistan. Although it was never part of its initial mission, during these missions the NL Army executed a number of tasks that could be defined as policing. The NL Army's approach to these tasks has been rather ambiguous or implicit, however. With the exception of police reform in Iraq, the establishment of public security by providing some sort of interim policing never developed into a focal point of the initial planning and preparation. Because the doctrines defined these activities as military assistance to civilian authorities rather than as policing, Dutch Army battalions executed policing activities along military lines and according to military procedures. It could be argued that when operating in a civilian environment and in close interaction with the local population, the modes of operation should be adjusted and attuned to the activities that were *de facto* executed, for example by adopting relevant policing techniques, tactics, and principles.[2]

In addition, the Dutch government has shown reserves to a larger involvement of the Dutch military in establishing public security and providing interim policing. On various occasions, it favoured a strict interpretation of the respective mandates and focused on achieving the initial military or political objectives, such as

[1] Bayley, 2001, p. 53; Dobbins et al. 2007, p. 26; Dziedzic 1998, pp. 8–10; Hansen 2002a, p. 73; Hills 2009, p. 43; Hills 2014, p. 103; Jakobsen 2003, p. 139; Jones et al. 2005, p. 212; Holt and Durch 2006, p. 12; Kaspersen et al. 2004, p. 17; Cline 2003, p. 163; Oakley and Dziedzic 1998, p. 518; Schmidl 1998, p. 39; Voorhoeve 2007, p. 59.

[2] Neuteboom 2014, p. 309.

creating overall peace and stability, good governance, social and economic development and reconstruction, rather than to adjust to the demands of a security gap.

In terms of providing interim policing during stabilisation operations there seems to be a discrepancy between the tactical military efforts of the NL Army on the ground and the overarching doctrines, strategies and policies. In order to define the magnitude of this divergence, this chapter analyses and discusses current doctrines and observations of Army commanders regarding military involvement in public security and policing. The question addressed in this chapter is how the formal doctrine relates to the informal opinions of operational commanders of how to deal with security gaps during stabilisation operations and which lessons can be learned to adjust to public security demands on the ground.

To answer this question, this chapter first provides a definition of policing and lists policing activities that could be executed by military forces during a security gap of a stabilisation operation. Second, it defines the problem of the security gap and explains possible solutions identified by the international community. Third, it describes the extent to which the provision of interim policing is formalised in the latest Army capstone doctrine *Land Operations* followed by a discussion on and analyses of views and interpretations of senior officers about whether or not the NL Army should engage military forces in closing security gaps. Finally, this chapter discusses the option of incorporating interim policing in leading NL Army doctrines with a view to support the closure of a security gap.

5.2 Police Tasks During a Security Gap

A government can provide public security by enforcing the law and maintaining public security. Among police scholars there is a commonly shared view that enforcement of the law and the maintenance of public order define the main functions of the police.[3] Law enforcement mostly deals with the prevention, detection and investigation of crime. It involves collection and analysis of criminal information, forensic research, criminal investigations, and the arrest and interrogation of law-offenders. Public order maintenance basically refers to the handling and controlling of crowds in order to transform fragile, troublesome or violent situations into a normal and stable state. In addition, the police perform a large number of social activities that fall in a grey area between law enforcement and the maintenance of public order, such as keeping the peace, assisting the public, problem-solving and resolving small incidents, communicating and negotiating with the public, collecting information, and patrolling neighbourhoods.[4] Policing should therefore not be seen as only making arrests or controlling large crowds but rather

---

[3] Bittner 1970; Manning 1997; Midgal 1988; Ponsaers et al. 2006; Skolnick 1996.

[4] Bayley 2005, pp. 141–148; Bittner 2005, pp. 159–162; Ericson 2005, p. 217; Goldstein 2005, pp. 398–399; Rosenthal and van der Torre 2007, p. 288.

Table 5.1 Military policing tasks during a security gap

Order	Law Enforcement	Miscellaneous
Street and social patrolling	Crime prevention (e.g. looting, arson)	Providing on-call backup for civilian police
Public dispute resolution	Criminal intelligence and surveillance	Manning and running security checkpoints
Managing civil disturbances and demonstrations	Criminal investigations and evidence collection (including war crimes)	Protection of vital infrastructure, facilities and properties
Maintaining public order and security during elections	Cordon and search (e.g. search for criminal suspects, weapons, narcotics)	Protection of vulnerable persons and groups (e.g. refugees, endangered minority groups, witnesses of war crimes, personnel of international organizations)
Crowd and riot control	Identifying, arresting and detaining criminal offenders (e.g. war criminals, criminal groups, insurgents, arsonists, looters)	Regulation of freedom of movement of citizens, minorities and refugees (e.g. escorting civilians in violence-prone areas)
Monitoring compliance with curfews	Locate and safeguard key witnesses, documents, and other evidence related to on-going or potential criminal investigations and prosecutions	Security Sector Reform (deploy police trainers and advisors, support vetting, credentialing, and accounting for host-nation police forces)
Monitoring and assisting in disarming civilians	Secure facilities, records, storage equipment, and funds related to criminal justice and security institutions	Support for international organizations (e.g. war crimes tribunals, international police, UNHCR)

Based upon, Jakobsen 2003, p. 141; Ministry of Foreign Affairs (SE) 1997, p. 21; North Atlantic Treaty Organization 2010, pp. 3–5; North Atlantic Treaty Organization 2012, Chap. 4; United States Department of the Army—Headquarters 2008, pp. 3–6 and 3–7; United States Institute of Peace 2009, paras 7.6.1 and 7.6

as a social issue in which the police act as the *primus inter pares* in the provision of public security and where they address "all sorts of human problems when and insofar as their solutions do or may possibly require the use of force at the point of occurrence".[5]

During the first phase of a stabilisation operation, policing largely focuses on providing critical law and order functions aimed at re-establishing public stability and order, bringing lawlessness to a halt and breaking the cycle of impunity, for example by the arresting and detaining criminal offenders, insurgents and people who disrupt public order, protecting high-value facilities against looting, running security checkpoints and performing vehicle inspections, undertaking high-risk searches, and managing public order disturbances.

[5] Bittner 1970, p. 44.

However, policing in security gaps may also involve activities such as patrolling and keeping the peace in instable or vulnerable neighbourhoods, negotiating in public disputes, regulating public gatherings, guaranteeing the freedom of movement of civilians, minorities and refugees, and protecting high-value facilities and vulnerable groups and individuals. Table 5.1 displays a list of police tasks that can be executed by the military during a security gap.

5.3 Solutions to the Security Gap

Security gaps largely results from three major problems: a deployment gap, an enforcement gap and an institutional gap.[6] Deployment problems arise when international civilian police officers are unavailable for immediate deployment abroad, for example because police capacities are overstretched due to domestic demands.[7] This is often the case with in particular specialists, such as forensic investigators, police management and trainers.[8]

Although some countries, such as Canada, Germany and Norway, have introduced national rosters of police officers for immediate secondment abroad, and despite the establishment of a rapidly deployable United Nations (UN) Standing Police Capacity as a start-up capability for UN police missions,[9] donor countries are often reluctant or unable to recruit, train, and hold in reserve large numbers of police officers for immediate international deployment.[10] In addition, donor governments tend to carefully consider whether they could deploy their civilian police safely during the early volatile stages of a stability operation, and often wait until the security situation has stabilised before dispatching their police contingents.[11]

Enforcement problems arise when the international or local police are unable to cover the full spectrum of policing, notably lacking the ability to combat large-scale public disorder and organised crime.[12] To overcome these problems, the international community introduced rapidly deployable, formed police units (FPU), which in terms of training, equipment, weaponry and tactics fall between the police and the military. Early deployments took place in the late 1990s within the NATO framework of the SFOR mission in Bosnia and Herzegovina and that of KFOR in Kosovo. NATO's so-called Multinational Specialised Units (MSU) were composed of gendarmerie-like personnel and, with the exception of law enforcement duties,

[6] Dziedzic 1998, pp. 8–16.

[7] Call and Barnett 2000, pp. 50–51; Smith et al. 2006, p. 29.

[8] Benner et al. 2011, p. 83; Durch 2006, p. 591.

[9] Benner et al. 2011, pp. 90–91; Hills 2009, p. 79; United Nations, UNPOL, Standing Police Capacity www.un.org/en/peacekeeping/sites/police/capacity. Accessed October 21, 2015.

[10] Durch and Berkman 2006, p. 45.

[11] See for example: Call 2007, p. 11; Hansen 2002b, p. 49; Linden et al. 2007, p. 159.

[12] Dziedzic 1998.

they were generally tasked to promote public security, maintain public order including crowd control, and to gather information and intelligence for operational purposes.[13] Inspired by NATO's MSU concept, the UN also deployed FPUs, starting in 1999 in Kosovo and East Timor. The number of UN FPUs increased from two units in 2000 to over sixty in 2010.[14] They have become a standard feature in UN police missions to fill the gap between military and police capabilities.[15] Also the European Gendarmerie Force (EUROGENDFOR) could be seen as a FPU. Within the EU framework, it is as a robust and rapidly deployable police force with military status 'capable of covering the full spectrum of police missions, through substitution or strengthening, during all the phases of a crisis management operation,'[16] for example under the umbrella of an EU, UN, NATO or OSCE mission. The EUROGENDFOR was deployed as a FPU in Haiti and the Central African Republic.[17] FPUs have not solved the problem of the security gaps, however. Benner, Mergenthaler and Rotmann point out that the deployment of FPUs in recent peace or stabilisation operations faced various difficulties.[18] The deployment of the MSU in Bosnia and Herzegovina took nearly 8 months to be fully operational. The deployment of UN FPUs in Kosovo took even longer; the last FPU arrived in theatre 10 months after the start of the operation.[19] FPU deployments in Côte d'Ivoire and the Democratic Republic of Congo in 2005 were accomplished in 3–4 months.[20]

Furthermore, the resources of the EUROGENDFOR are limited. First, the donor organizations are often overstretched and are short of supply because resources have to be drawn from gendarmerie forces that have an institutionalised role within their respective domestic police systems.[21] Second, countries are not obliged to participate in a certain mission; they retain the right to decide whether or not to deploy units in a EUROGENDFOR operation. For example, taking into account national priorities, limited financial resources and the availability of personnel, countries may decide to deploy their gendarmerie capabilities initially pledged to the EUROGENDFOR to other stabilisation operations that are considered of higher

---

[13] Perito 2004, pp. 156–157 and 187.

[14] United Nations, UNPOL: Formed Police Units, www.un.org/en/peacekeeping/sites/police/units. Accessed October 21, 2015.

[15] Benner et al. 2011, p. 68.

[16] Treaty between the Kingdom of Spain, the French Republic, the Italian Republic, the Kingdom of the Netherlands and the Portuguese Republic establishing the European Gendarmerie Force, October 18, 2007, Article 4. Retrieved from www.eurogendfor.org/eurogendfor-library/download-area/official-texts/establishing-the-eurogendfor-treaty. Accessed October 21, 2015.

[17] European Gendarmerie Force, EUROGENDFOR Missions, www.eurogendfor.org/eurogendfor-missions. Accessed October 21, 2015.

[18] Benner et al. 2011, p. 75.

[19] Perito 2004, pp. 142 and 205.

[20] Holt and Durch 2006, p. 40.

[21] Hansen 2002a, p. 74.

political importance.[22] Finally, according to Benner, Mergenthaler and Rotmann, European countries rather deploy their units under NATO or EU command than to UN-led operations.[23]

Institutional problems, finally, can be solved by police reform, which involves, for example, Security Sector Reform (SSR) programmes to improve accountability of the police; increase public trust and professionalism; improve police training, professionalism, management, and practices; and to make police structures more efficient.[24] Police reform does not provide a solution to imminent public security problems, however. Based on experiences from recent stabilisation operations, there is a common agreement that reform programmes are time consuming and take 5–10 years to complete.[25] Dziedzic and Hawley therefore conclude that 'simple reconstruction programmes coupled with hasty exits will inevitably fail.'[26]

5.4 NL Army Doctrine and Policing

The next question is whether the provision of interim policing in case of a security gap has been incorporated in Dutch military doctrine. Military doctrines serve to codify the organization's institutional memory and institutionalise lessons learned.[27] Doctrinal adaptation is not always obvious, however. For example, as Nagl notes, 'the notion held by a dominant group of an organization as to what the main capabilities and primary mission of the organization should be' often determines the outcome and direction of institutional learning and codification of those lessons learned.[28] In other words, if the leadership of a military organization does not recognise the significance of recent experiences, it is unlikely that lessons learned will be recognised and codified in doctrines.

Box 5.1: Stabilisation Activities NL Army

The NL Army doctrine *Land Operations* discerns four stabilisation activities: "Security and Control", "Security Sector Reform", "Support to the initial restoration of services" and "Support to Initial Government". The first two are referred to as merely military activities while the latter are largely civilian.

22 Armitage and Moisan 2005, p. 5.

23 Benner et al. 2011, p. 75.

24 Oecd DAC 2007, p. 163.

25 See for example: Binnendijk and Johnson 2004, p. 7; Durch and Berkman 2006, p. 100; Jones et al. 2005, p. 22; Voorhoeve 2007, p. 174.

26 Dziedzic and Hawley 2005, p. 7.

27 Nagl 2005, p. 7.

28 Nagl 2005, p. 4.

During "Stability and Control" the military focuses on restoring and maintaining a safe and secure environment to establish the conditions for the normalisation of civic life and activity and the reinstatement of public services and governance. "Security and Control" involves a limited number of activities that could fit in the range of policing, such as patrolling, surveillance, observation, separation of groups and entities, and of escort of convoys,[29] but these are not further explained or refined in terms of fighting criminality or public disorder. "Support to Security Sector Reform" (SSR) focuses on the reorganization and reconstruction of local security agencies and capabilities that are essential to re-establishing the rule of law and providing public security. While the doctrine regards training and instructing local military forces as its priority, police reform is seen as a responsibility of international civilian institutions. However, stabilisation operations in Iraq and Afghanistan showed that there is often no international civilian police available for SSR purposes. As a result, military personnel were tasked to train and monitor the police. "Support to the initial restoration of services" relates to the reconstruction of infrastructure and the re-establishment of public services and utilities while "Support to Initial Government," involves the support to government, economic development and reconstruction. The doctrine stipulates that these stabilisation activities must be deployed in parallel to "Security and Control," which means that the military may have to perform interim governance tasks and provide basic public services, being the first representatives of the international community on the ground during or in the immediate aftermath of an armed conflict.[30] However, the doctrine refrains from addressing policing on an interim basis as a possible aspect of re-establishing governance in a war-torn society.

In terms of adaptation to experiences with interim policing during recent stabilisation operations, the Dutch Army doctrine could be perceived as ambiguous and implicit. Although some NL Army doctrines mention some policing tasks,[31] they do not define their character or provide guidance on how they should be executed. Notably, the Army capstone doctrine *Land Operations* (2014) does not specify the

---

[29] Koninklijke Landmacht 2014, para 7324.

[30] Koninklijke Landmacht 2014, paras 7321–7331. For an explanation of activities on the tactical level the doctrine *Land Operations* refers to the NATO doctrines *Allied Land Tactics* (ATP 3.2.1) and *Guidance for the Conduct of Tactical Stability Activities* (ATP 3.2.1.1). The NATO doctrine *Allied Land Tactics* does not further discuss a military role in interim policing during a security gap of a crisis management operation. This must be found in NATO's *Guidance for the Conduct of Tactical Stability Activities*, which explains various tactical stability activities including the provision of public security, North Atlantic Treaty Organization 2012, paras 0211, 0408, 04170 and 04172.

[31] See for example: Koninklijke Landmacht 1998, pp. 130–132; Koninklijke Landmacht 1999, pp. 292–298; Koninklijke Landmacht 2003, pp. 455–456, 476, 546, 615–616 and 666.

option of policing on a interim basis during the execution of a stabilisation operation (see Box 5.1), although it recognises that if the security situation is still vulnerable and civilian organizations are not (yet) available to or capable of executing their formal tasks, the international military may have to fill the void until civilian agencies are ready to fulfil their responsibilities.[32]

By not explicitly mentioning an option for establishment public security, the doctrine lacks a doctrinal peg or rationalisation to provide guidance to commanders to incorporate policing activities and tactics in their operational planning process when required.[33] It could be argued that the NL Army is hesitant to institutionalising interim policing in its doctrines and concepts of operations, although security gaps could be considered an integral part of the contemporary operational environment of militaries and military operations. In contrast, the US Army doctrine *FM 3-07 Stability Operations* of 2008 explicitly mentions interim policing as a stabilisation activity, noting that if local security forces fail to provide public security to its citizens, US troops can be assigned with policing duties, such as law enforcement, public order maintenance, crowd control, and the securing of critical infrastructure until the host nation is sufficiently capable of taking over its responsibilities.[34]

While the US doctrine *FM 3-07* reflects on lessons learned from Iraq, there is a gap in the Dutch Army doctrine between the Army's institutionalised memory and the realities it faced during operations in a security gap. Army officers who were involved in doctrinal planning explained that the exclusion of policing in the Army doctrine *Land Operations* is largely based on the views of the leadership of NL Army. They explained that the Army's leadership still regards kinetic operations against a military opponent as its core tasks and therefore of higher importance than engaging in soft power activities such as providing public security and that soldiers serve to deal with military matters and not with policing.[35] One doctrinal planner explained:

> We know that soldiers are confronted with tasks that are close to policing, but someone, preferably the Commander of the Army, has to make a statement on this subject to formalise them. Currently, such statement is still a step too far.[36]

It also seems that some aspects of the leading culture prevent operational commanders to expand their modes of operation to adapt effectively to civilian contingencies, as another doctrinal planner noted:

> Although there is some sense of urgency regarding the provision of public security, there is also resistance because commanders feel comfortable in executing operations and exercises that involve a military opponent. Although Dutch soldiers officially must be able to cover the full spectrum of stabilisation activities, including the provision of public security, it will take time to internalise this change at all levels of the organization, particularly due to a cultural blockade.[37]

---

[32] Koninklijke Landmacht 2014, paras 7321 and 7807.

[33] Neuteboom 2014, p. 298.

[34] United States Department of the Army—Headquarters 2008, pp. 3–6 and 3–7.

[35] Neuteboom 2014, p. 298.

[36] Interview by author with doctrinal planner, August 12, 2011.

[37] Interview by author with doctrinal planner, January 25, 2013.

As such, it could be concluded that the Army leadership seems to adhere to a more strict interpretation of the Army's mission, notably the execution of kinetic operations. The rationale of that interpretation could, for example, be based on risk reduction, markedly to prevent any form of mission creep by entering an operational field that distracts from initial tasks and mission planning, and exposing its troops to assignments alien to the basic military training. As such, the leadership could focus on some sort of risk reduction in order to protect the safety of troops against unknown and unpredictable situations and unfamiliar tasks or to prevent overstretch of the troops by avoiding the assignment of perceived non-military tasks.

5.5 Views on Filling the Security Gap

As explained above, in the Dutch Army doctrines marginal attention is paid to police activities in the early stages of security gap. This is at odds with the experiences of several NL Army battalions that were deployed in recent stabilisation operations. On a regular basis, troops executed activities during these operations that could be labelled as interim policing. These activities were executed beyond the scope of doctrines and training. Troops had to learn on the job when they were confronted with public security issues in theatre.

Forty commanding and staff officers who either served in stability operations such as IFOR/SFOR, KFOR, SFIR, and ISAF or were engaged in the development of Army doctrines were interviewed and were asked to reflect on the option of engaging the military to establish public security during a security gap of a stabilisation operation, for example by interim policing. To classify and interpret their views and observations, this article uses the categorisation provided by Jakobsen makes a distinction between "vacuum fillers" and "minimalists". Vacuum fillers regard military involvement in policing as an essential part of multi-functional stabilisation operations in which the military must be prepared to keep law and order if no one else can.[38] The minimalists, on the other hand, argue that the military can provide security but should not act as interim police force. From their point of view, the military involvement in public security should be as limited as possible and not go beyond of what can be expected from the military in terms of training and mandates.[39] To balance the dichotomy, this chapter introduces a third school, namely that of the "conditionalists." The conditionalists take the middle ground and are open to supporting the establishment of public security during a security gap under the condition that a number of critical preconditions are met, for example related to training, duration and activities.[40]

[38] Jakobsen 2003, p. 138.

[39] Jakobsen 2003, p. 137.

[40] Out of forty interviewees, twenty-eight can be categorized as vacuum-fillers, fourteen as conditionalists, and four as minimalists. Four interviewees took a neutral stand.

5.5.1 Vacuum Fillers

The vacuum fillers amongst the interviewed officers provided four main arguments to support their views on military engagement in a security gap. The argument mentioned the most was the inevitability of military support in this matter. These vacuum fillers concluded that in case of a security gap there is no other option than to provide some sort of interim policing. They argued that the closure of a security gap must be seen as a precondition for military success and is justified as long as it contributes to the execution of the formal military mission and to achieving the desired military end-state. One officer explained:

> Today, we cannot focus on our core tasks only. When I say core tasks, I mean our unique characteristic to deploy force on a large scale. No one else can do that, not even the police. If other structures fail to exist, we will have to plan for other contingencies to achieve the desired end-state. These contingencies include interagency cooperation, but if some of these agencies are unable to deliver because elements are missing, the armed forces will have to provide an alternative, including the provision of interim policing.[41]

Second, it was noted that an international military force is the most likely institution capable of providing public order and security in a failed state. Four vacuum fillers for example reasoned that in the early stages of a crisis management operation, the security situation often is too volatile and insecure to deploy (international) civilian police with a background in community policing. A Task Force Uruzgan (TFU) commander, for example, noted that:

> The military could be given a role in public security if there are no other alternatives available and if there is so much at stake that the international community needs to act. Under these circumstances there is a different level of public security compared to the situation in the Netherlands, and whereby the local institutions are unable to provide public security themselves. The security situation could be so severe that nobody dares to enter until the environment has been stabilised. Public security tasks could then be assigned to the military although, strictly spoken, these are no military tasks.[42]

The third reason provided by vacuum fillers was of a moral order. These vacuum fillers considered non-intervention to be ethically irresponsible. They argued that it would be hard to justify that the military stood aloof during a security gap if no one else could maintain law and order. One officer commented:

> Ultimately, the military organization will be held legally accountable when a situation escalated and does not intervene. Officially we are not officially responsible for public security, but if a situation turns chaotic you cannot stand aloof with your unit and say: 'Just let me know when it's over' while in the meantime there are casualties and houses are set on fire.[43]

Four and last, some vacuum fillers pointed at the legal responsibilities for the military, as defined in international humanitarian rights law and the law of armed

---

[41] Interview by author with senior staff officer KFOR, June 16, 2011.

[42] Interview by author with commander Task Force Uruzgan ISAF, June 27, 2011.

[43] Interview by author with senior staff officer ISAF, October 13, 2011.

conflict. In particular they pointed at Article 43 of the Hague Regulations, which compels an occupying power to restore and maintain public order and civil life, including public welfare, in an occupied territory.[44] The basic line of these vacuum fillers was that public security is always part of a stabilisation operation, as international human rights law defines the obligation of a military force towards the local community in terms of establishing public security. Sassòli supports this argument, although he does not agree that Article 43 applies to all stabilisation operations. Because Article 43 primarily focuses at occupying powers, he argues that it can only be applied to peace enforcing operations authorised or mandated by the UN Security Council that do not enjoy the consent of the State on the territory on which it is deployed.[45] Still, Sassòli backs the arguments of the vacuum fillers regarding the involvement of the military forces in public security in operations like KFOR and SFIR that (initially) did not enjoy the consent of the host nation.

5.5.2 *Conditionalists*

A number of the interviewed subscribed to the conditionalist views. They argued that the provision of interim policing by the military is possible but only provisionally. Training was seen as the first condition for military involvement in a security gap. Seven conditionalists considered the NL Army capable of delivering interim policing, provided that troops were properly prepared and trained. Their opinion was based on the assumption that the establishment of public security should not interfere with the existing and formal concept of military operations and competences. They argued that each mission is different and that the required skills and competences should be tailored to the individual mission. As such, the establishment of public security is seen as an additional task that could be trained for and that is not alien to the NL Army, as it has proven to be capable of executing various tasks during recent stabilisation operations. One officer reported, for example:

> I think that every soldier can be instructed and trained for all the work that may occur in a crisis management operation including crowd and riot control. It is not a soldier's job, but only a soldier can do it. As long as you are able to mentally prepare your troops on those situations that they might encounter and of you have time to train the necessary drills, you will be fine.[46]

Two officers were more cautious, however, and warned for the confined trainability of troops in relation to the magnitude of existing mission-oriented training

---

[44] Hague Convention (IV) concerning the Laws and Customs of War on Land, The Hague, October 18, 1907, Article 43.

[45] Sassòli 2004, p. 18.

[46] Interview by author with battalion commander IFOR/SFOR, October 5, 2011.

programmes and the limited time available for those programmes in advance of deployment. These training programmes, they noted, will always demand a compromise leading to a choice for the most likely and urgent tasks. Given the limited attention to public security in the doctrine, it was seen as unlikely to prioritise interim policing over other mission-oriented challenges during their pre-deployment training.

A second condition, mentioned by three conditionalists, was that the military could only provide public security for a restricted period of time after which policing responsibilities have to be transferred to the civilian police as soon as possible. One ISAF battle group commander, for example, emphasised that:

> Within a security gap, the military has a responsibility and a task and we might have to perform interim policing. However, it is not our primary task and is it not ideal. Therefore, we have to organise and train local resources in order to transfer these tasks as soon as possible. Military support [in public security] is always temporary of character.[47]

Other officers also made a reservation regarding the kind of police tasks that could be executed by the military during a security gap. They generally considered police activities, such as patrolling, public order maintenance and crime prevention, as suited to the operational concept of the Army, mainly because these activities were supposed to be based on mental rather than technical or physical skills. Specific law enforcement activities, such as crime-investigation and forensic policing were regarded at odds with the Army's operational concept, as these activities require specific expertise and skills unfamiliar to those of the Army. An officer deployed in KFOR, for example, underlined that skilled leadership enables troops to perform a large number of (basic) police tasks:

> You can ask the military to perform a large number of tasks that do not require specific training as long as you have people in the lead that are competent and are able to issue the right orders. For example, in the field of creating public order the military can be a valuable asset. On the other hand, in terms of specific police functions where you need specialist expertise such as taking fingerprints, these tasks go beyond the military competences and should be avoided.[48]

5.5.3 *Minimalists*

Four out of forty interviewees could be labelled as minimalists. Two officers had no principle or existential objections against a military role in policing. Their objections largely involved reasons of efficiency, underlining that during stabilisation operations the military is often over-stretched, which urges commanders to prioritise their activities and to exclude non-military tasks in order not to be

---

[47] Interview by author with battle group commander ISAF, June 20, 2011.

[48] Interview by author with senior staff officer KFOR, July 7, 2011.

distracted from performing their core mission. As such, these minimalist were no hard-line opponents, but related their choice to matters of prioritisation in relation to the scarcity of resources. One of them explained:

> Soldiers are capable of taking on a lot of activities. We have an aptitude to compensate where others fail to deliver. Temporarily you can go beyond your comfort zone and step into a vacuum. But you always have to ask yourself what the purpose of your existence is and what you are good at. Especially when your budget and resources are limited you need to prioritise. I don't believe in a Jack-of-All-Trades; ultimately that would lead to a Master-of-None. I rather execute a limited number of tasks perfectly than a larger number less well. As a soldier, my priority will be to achieve my military goals. Only if there is time for it, I can take on other assignments but they will never become my primary mission. We are no riot squad but a military organization capable of deploying force. (…) It is not our initial task to deliver interim policing. We have too many other things to do. We have to prioritise what can and cannot be done.[49]

Two other interviewees, however, had more fundamental and principled reservations. They considered interim policing to be a non-military task arguing that policing significantly differs from soldiering, for example in terms of mindset, skills and equipment. As such, they followed the general line of reasoning of many other opponents of military involvement in interim policing.[50] However, one of them addressed an additional argument to underpin his doubts regarding interim policing. He did not only consider the Army as unsuited to perform policing but also explained that any role of the military in policing would fundamentally affect the character of policing itself. Being responsible for maintaining public security, the execution of the police function would be approached from the military perspective of force dominance rather than from the police perspective of de-escalation of force.[51] Also Hills points at this risk, noting that militarisation of the police function is at odds with democratic policing values and the general objective of demilitarisation of policing.[52] Implicitly, Hills here points out that if the military wants to be successful in providing interim policing, it has to adapt to its (civilian) environment in order to execute these tasks in a police-like fashion to win the hearts and minds of the local population and maintain civil support for their operations.

5.6 Discussion

Security gaps during stabilisation operations will likely remain problematic for the foreseeable future, as the international community has not yet established sufficient and rapidly deployable civilian police capabilities. Deployment of military

[49] Interview by author with battalion commander IFOR/SFOR, June 10, 2011.

[50] Call and Barnett 2000, p. 49; Clark 2001, p. 462; Last 2000, p. 84; Smith 2005, pp. 9–10; West 2009, p. 8.

[51] Interview by author with SFIR police liaison, August 29, 2011.

[52] Hills 2009, p. 79.

forces to fill these gaps will therefore rather be the rule than the exception. To be effective in that role, military forces need to be open and adaptive and take into account the security and safety concerns of the civilian environments in which they operate.[53]

Despite significant experiences with security gaps in recent stabilisation operations, the NL Army refrained from incorporating the option of providing interim policing in its capstone doctrine *Land Operations*. This could leave Dutch troops vulnerable if security gaps will continue to characterise contemporary stabilisation operations.

There appears to be a discrepancy between recent operational experiences and views of operational commanders, and the formal doctrine. Although a majority of interviewees expressed support for a larger military involvement in closing the security gap, it seems that the NL Army as an institution prefers to adhere to a kinetic concept of operations instead of adapting to the shifting or unexpected contextual realities of security gaps. Public security appears to be viewed as a peripheral subject enjoying little recognition in the mainstream Army culture or of the leadership, which is largely focused on combat and kinetic operations. Without the commitment of the higher command, there will be little ground for an institutional debate on public security and policing during security gaps, although various international experts regard an imminent closure of a security gap as major condition for military success.[54] Without such debate, the NL Army may not be challenged to involve the subject in mission planning and preparation, which in turn will impede organizational internalisation required for an effective and efficient establishment of public security to support the closure of a security gap. The omission of public security can be partly explained by a supposed (cultural) reluctance to assuming tasks that are alien to the classical concepts of the Army and that are supposedly difficult to train for. As such, it looks as if the NL Army lacks a 'learning culture' in which organizations learn 'by means of on-going debate about constantly shifting discrepancies' to find new routines to cope with changing demands and environments.[55] This assumption leads to a fundamental challenge to the NL Army. By renouncing a learning culture and avoiding interim policing as a likely scenario during stabilisation operations, the NL Army may not only underrate the negative implications for both public security as public safety but may also jeopardise the final success of the mission.

To come to terms with the reality of security gaps on the ground, the NL Army has to recognise that military involvement in restoring and maintaining public security during stabilisation operations where there is a structural lack of sufficient police capacities is inevitable. To ensure effective execution of these tasks the doctrines should provide clarity about which public security tasks could or should be

---

[53] Burns and Stalker 1961 note that organizations that operate in dynamic environments need to be open and adaptive to these environments in order to be effective.

[54] Bayley 2001, p. 53; Hansen 2002a, p. 70; Oakley and Dziedzic 1998, p. 510; Smith et al. 2006, p. 12.

[55] Weick and Sutcliffe 2001, p. 136.

performed, under which circumstances and by establishing an organizational fit through ensuring the necessary training, mind-set and culture.

In addition, public security strongly correlates to public safety. Providing public security strengthens public safety and helps building a stable and secure society. In that sense, being open to adopt police tactics and techniques may help to further minimising the use of force and preventing accidental civilian casualties during the re-establishing of law and order. The prevention of civilian casualties is important if an international mission is to win the hearts and minds of the population and to maintain the popular support for the operation at home. Continuous media coverage of military operations may affect the public opinion negatively if public safety was violated due to the execution of inferior tactics to restore enforce the law or restore public order.

Commanders therefore have to be aware of public security and safety problems to understand the operational complexities of the environment in which they operate. If, for example, a significant part of the military's operational environment suffers from crime and disorder, commanders need to adjust to these singularities as these, undoubtedly, will define the characteristics of the military's operational environment, as Hills notes.[56] The mission and activities of the military in a given stabilisation operation should therefore be adjusted to the actual characteristics of the environment of that operation. This implies that the contextual reality of a stabilisation operation will define the course and content of military action. If the contextual reality of a given mission demands an intervention to restore public order and security, the military should refocus its efforts and provide interim policing since public order and security are conditions for stabilisation and socio-economic reform and therefore for the success of that mission. If the focus of a mission changes, this also needs to be translated into the operational concept of that mission. Ultimately, an adaptive professional standard and culture should be rooted in a clearly defined doctrine, ensuring the best possible organizational fit, tools, and mind-set for changing conditions on the ground.

References

Armitage D, Moisan A (2005) Constabulary forces and postconflict transition: the Euro-Atlantic dimension. Strateg Forum 218:1–8

Bayley D (2001) Democratizing the police abroad: what to do and how to do it. National Institute of Justice, Washington DC

Bayley DH (2005) What the police do? In: Newburn T (ed) Policing: key readings. Willan Publishing, Cullompton, pp 141–149

Benner T, Mergenthaler S, Rotmann P (2011) The new world of UN peace operations: learning to build peace? Oxford University Press, Oxford

Binnendijk H, Johnson S (2004) Transforming for stabilization and reconstruction operations. National Defense University Press, Washington DC

[56] Hills 1999, pp. 18–20; also Runia 2015, pp. 107–108.

Bittner E (1970) The functions of the police in modern society: a review of background factors, current practices, and possible role models. National Institute of Mental Health, Rockville
Bittner E (2005) Florence Nightingale in pursuit of Willy Sutton: a theory of the police. In: Newburn T (ed) Policing: key readings. Willan Publishing, Cullompton, pp 150–172
Burns T, Stalker G (1961) The management of innovation. Tavistock, London
Call C (2007) Introduction. In: Call Ch (ed) Constructing justice and security after war. United States Institute of Peace, Washington DC, pp 1–26
Call C, Barnett M (2000) Looking for a few good cops: peacekeeping, peacebuilding and CIVPOL. In: Holm T, Eide E (eds) Peacebuilding and police reform. Frank Cass, London, pp 43–68
Clark W (2001) Waging modern war: Bosnia, Kosovo and the future of combat. Public Affairs, Oxford
Cline L (2003) The new constabularies: planning US military stabilization missions. Small Wars Insurgencies 14:158–184
Dobbins J, Jones S, Crane K, Cole DeGrasse B (2007) The beginner's guide to nation building. RAND Cooperation, Santa Monica
Durch W (2006) Are We Learning Yet? In: Durch W (ed) Twenty-first century peace operations. United States Institute of Peace, Washington DC, pp 573–607
Durch W, Berkman T (2006) Restoring and maintaining peace: what we know so far. In: Durch W (ed) Twenty-first century peace operations. United States Institute of Peace, Washington DC, pp 1–48
Dziedzic M (1998) Introduction. In: Oakley R, Dziedzic M, Goldberg E (eds) Policing the New World Order: peace operations and public security. National Defense University Press, Washington DC, pp 3–18
Dziedzic M, Hawley L (2005) Introduction. In: Covey J, Dziedzic M, Hawley L (eds) The quest for viable peace: international intervention and strategies for conflict transformation. United States Institute of Peace Press, Washington DC, pp 3–22
Ericson R (2005) The police as reproducers of order. In: Newburn T (ed) Policing: key readings. Willan Publishing, Cullompton, pp 215–246
Goldstein H (2005) Improving policing: a problem-oriented approach. In: Newburn T (ed) Policing: key readings. Willan Publishing, Cullompton, pp 392–411
Hansen A (2002a) Civil-military cooperation: the military, paramilitaries and civilian police in executive policing. In: Dwan R (ed) Executive policing: enforcing the law in peace operations, SIPRI Research Report No. 16. Oxford University Press, New York, pp 67–84
Hansen A (2002b) From Congo to Kosovo: civilian police in peace operations. Adelphi Paper 343. Oxford University Press, New York
Hills A (1999) Criminality and policing in stability and support operations. Mil Rev November–December:18–22
Hills A (2009) Policing post-conflict cities. Zed Books, London
Hills A (2014) Insurgency, counterinsurgency and policing. In: Rich P, Duyvesteijn I (eds) The Routledge Handbook of Insurgency and Counterinsurgency. Routledge, London, pp 98–108
Holt V, Durch W (2006) Enhancing United Nations capacity for post-conflict police operations. The Henry L. Stimson Center, Washington DC
Jakobsen P (2003) Military forces and public security challenges. In: Pugh M, Pal Singh Sidhu W (eds) United Nations and regional security: Europe and beyond. Lynne Rienner Publishers, London, pp 137–154
Jones S, Wilson J, Rathmell A, Riley K (2005) Establishing law and order after conflict. RAND Corporation, Santa Monica
Kaspersen A, Eide E, Hansen A (2004) International policing and the rule of law in transitions from war to peace, NUPI Paper No. 4. Norwegian Institute of International Affairs, Oslo
Koninklijke Landmacht (1998) Gevechtsoperaties: Grondslagen. Landmacht Doctrinepublicatie II Deel A Landmachtstaf, Den Haag
Koninklijke Landmacht (1999) Vredesoperaties. Landmacht Doctrinepublicatie III. Landmachtstaf, Den Haag

Koninklijke Landmacht (2003) Gevechtsoperaties: gevechtsoperaties tegen een irregulier optredende tegenstander. Landmacht Doctrinepublicatie II Deel C. Landmachtstaf, Den Haag

Koninklijke Landmacht (2014) Landoperaties. Doctrine Publicatie 3.2. Land Warfare Centre, Utrecht

Last D (2000) Organizing for effective peacebuilding. Int Peacekeep 7:80–96

Linden R, Last D, Murphy C (2007) The role of civilian police in peacekeeping. In: Goldsmith A, J Sheptycki (eds) Crafting transnational policing: police capacity-building and global policing reform. Hart Publishing, Oxford, pp 149–175

Manning P (1997) Police work: the social organization of policing. Waveland Press, Prospect Heights

Midgal J (1988) Strong societies and weak states: state-society relations and state capabilities in the third world. Princeton University Press, Princeton

Ministry of Foreign Affairs (SE) (1997) Police in the service of peace: excerpts from the report by the Swedish Committee of Inquiry on Civilian Police in International Activities, SOU 1997: 104. Norstedts Tryckeri, Stockholm

Nagl J (2005) Learning to Eat Soup with a Knife: counterinsurgency lessons from Malaya and Vietnam. The University of Chicago Press, Chicago

Neuteboom P (2014) Beyond borders: the role of the Netherlands army in public security during crisis management operations. Wolf Legal Publishers, Oirschot

North Atlantic Treaty Organization (2010) Allied joint doctrine for peace support operations AJP-3.4.1. Ratification Draft. NATO, Brussels

North Atlantic Treaty Organization (2012) Guidance for the conduct of tactical stability activities and tasks ATP 3.2.1.1. Edition A Version 1, Ratification Draft 1. NATO, Brussels

Oakley R, Dziedzic M (1998) Conclusions. In: Oakley R, Dziedzic M, Goldberg E (eds) Policing the New World Order: peace operations and public security. National Defense University Press, Washington DC, pp 509–535

OECD DAC (2007) The OECD DAC Handbook on Security Sector Reform (SSR): supporting security and justice. OECD, Paris

Perito R (2004) Where is the Lone Ranger when we need him? America's search for a postconflict stability force. United States Institute of Peace Press, Washington DC

Ponsaers P, Devroe E, Meert D (2006) Het kerntakendebat: kiezen voor een democratische politie. Wat is dat? Orde van de dag 33:7–14

Rosenthal U, van der Torre E (2007) Het politiemanagement. In: Fijnaut C, Muller E, Rosenthal U, van der Torre E (eds) Politie: studies over haar werking en organisatie, 2nd edn. Kluwer, Deventer, pp 287–311

Runia E (2015) Het Srebrenica syndroom: hoe een historisch drama nagespeeld in plaats van opgehelderd werd. Amsterdam University Press, Amsterdam

Sassòli M (2004) Article 43 of The Hague Regulations and peace operations in the twenty-first century. Background Paper prepared for informal high-level expert meeting on current challenges to international humanitarian law. Harvard University, Cambridge. www.hpcrresearch.org/sites/default/files/publications/sassoli.pdf. Accessed 26 Sept 2015

Schmidl E (1998) Police functions in peace operations: a historical overview. In: Oakley R, Dziedzic M and Goldberg E (eds) Policing the New World Order: peace operations and public security. National Defense University Press, Washington DC, pp 19–40

Skolnick J (1996) Justice without trial: law enforcement in democratic society. Wiley, New York

Smith R (2005) The utility of force: the art of war in the modern world. Penguin Book, London

Smith J, Holt V, Durch W (2006) Enhancing United Nations capacity for post-conflict police operations. Working Paper. The Henry L. Stimson Center, Washington DC

United States Department of the Army—Headquarters (2008) Stability Operations. Field Manual No. 3-07. US Government Printing Office, Washington DC

United States Institute of Peace (2009) Guiding principles for stabilization and reconstruction. United Institute for Peace, Washington DC

Voorhoeve J (2007) From War to the Rule of Law: peacebuilding after violent conflicts. Amsterdam University Press, Amsterdam
Weick K, Sutcliffe K (2001) Managing the unexpected: assuring high performance in an age of complexity. Jossey-Bass, San Francisco
West F (2009) Counterinsurgency lessons from Iraq. Military Review March–April:2–12

Chapter 6
Enhancing Network Centric Operations Doctrine to Support Civil Military Cooperation in Disaster Management

Jeroen Wolbers

Abstract Network Centric Operations is a promising command doctrine in both military operations and during civil disaster management. As both sectors started intensifying their joint operational capacity through civil-military collaboration, it becomes increasingly relevant to address the different command doctrines underlying Network Centric Operations in both sectors. In this Chapter I explore the origins of network governance in both sectors and argue what steps need to be taken in order overcome the differences. I argue that governing the heterogeneous set of organizations that operate in disaster response networks requires a new approach for Network Centric Operations that does not only rely upon information sharing and self-synchronization. Instead, it requires negotiation, sensemaking, and network switching in order to overcome the different functional, normative and knowledge boundaries that come into play in heterogeneous disaster response networks.

Keywords Network Centric Operations · Civil-military collaboration · Coordination · Disaster management · Command and control

J. Wolbers (✉)
Faculty of Social Sciences, Vrije Universiteit Amsterdam, Amsterdam, The Netherlands
e-mail: j.j.wolbers@vu.nl

R. Beeres et al. (eds.), *NL ARMS Netherlands Annual Review of Military Studies 2016*, NL ARMS, DOI 10.1007/978-94-6265-135-7_6

Contents

6.1 Introduction: Organizing for Safety Through Disaster Response Networks

When disaster strikes numerous organizations are involved in the organization of safety response. The traditional blue light services of police, fire department and medical services make up the core set of organizations in the response network. In addition, the distress caused by the disaster often affects other organizations including the military, but also infrastructure companies, public transportation agencies, public utility companies, and waterboards. Organizing a coherent response operation becomes difficult when such a broad range of organizations are involved in the disaster response network. Each response organization has different responsibilities, goals and work practices, which triggers different jurisdictional and functional boundaries.[1] While there are clear interdependencies between the organizations, there exists little formal structure to guide the collaboration process.

Currently, several attempts are underway to formalize the collaboration in times of disaster. One of larger initiatives is to intensify civil-military collaboration. The aim is to arrange and formalize the requests for military support capacity at times of disaster. For example, the military can assist in search capacity, dike reinforcement, evacuation, CBRNe threats (Chemical, Biological, Radiological, Nuclear, and Explosives), and fire repression. In addition to operational support capacity, intensified civil-military collaboration also led to a cross-fertilization at the level of command doctrine based on the concept of *Network Centric Operations*. Network Centric Operations supports networked collaboration by improving the information exchange amongst response organizations. It is envisioned that Network Centric Operations will enable a shared understanding of the disaster situation by linking individuals and their distributed networks through a platform

[1] Comfort and Kapucu 2006.

that allows the rapid and timely sharing of information.[2] This development clearly shows that disaster management increasingly progresses towards disaster information management.

However, as the concept of Network Centric Operations was transferred from the military domain to the more heterogeneous civil disaster management sector, the process of information sharing needs to be problematized. The central tenet of Network Centric Operations is that information sharing leads to situational awareness and better-informed decisions. This idea of information superiority is problematic in disaster management operations, because multiple boundaries are at stake in a network where numerous civil safety stakeholders act under principles of autonomy and goal consensus.[3]

In this Chapter I will problematize the command doctrines underlying Network Centric Operations in both the military and civil disaster management domain, and show that they lead to very different ideas about how to coordinate civil-military operations. I will argue how the three central principles of Network Centric Operations in military doctrine—*self-synchronization*, *information superiority*, and *connectivity*—are problematic when transferred to network governance in civil disaster management. This has significant implications for the way in which civil-military collaboration can be improved in disaster response operations. To develop this argument I will first introduce the developments in civil-military collaboration of the previous decade that led to the implementation of Network Centric Operations.

6.2 The Changing Safety Landscape in the Netherlands

The physical safety landscape in the Netherland has changed drastically over the last decade. The change was marked by the rise of new institutions like the safety regions, and the regionalization of fire and medical services. The catalyst behind this change was a series of large disasters that took place around 2000, which had a severe societal impact. On 13 May 2000, a series of massive explosions in the storage facilities of SE Fireworks tore apart a whole neighbourhood in the city of Enschede.[4] About 8 months later, on New Year's Eve of 2000/2001 an intense fire in café 't Hemeltje in Volendam caused 14 causalities and left over 200 teenagers with severe burn traumas.[5] In the evaluation of both disaster response operations the investigation committees identified serious shortcomings in the coordination between disaster response organizations.

[2] Houghton et al. 2008.

[3] Comfort and Kapucu 2006.

[4] Committee Oosting 2001.

[5] Committee Alders 2001.

The investigation Committee Alders of the Volendam café fire concluded that during the response operation, "there was no structural multidisciplinary coordination. In each emergency response centre the same questions were repeated over and over ... There was no overview on the actions of other emergency responders".[6] In the same year the Committee Oosting, that investigated the SE Fireworks disaster, also concluded that there were serious coordination difficulties caused by a lack of clear responsibilities. "Immediately after the disaster, problems occurred on a number of points in the coordination and collaboration between the various units and services. In the initial hours, it was also not clear who was providing operational leadership during the combating of the disaster ... It took up to 6 h after the initial disaster to organize the first multidisciplinary coordination meeting".[7] As a result of these shortcomings, a trajectory was started to improve the official disaster response structure in the Netherlands. Numerous efforts to create new structures, define new roles and responsibilities, and prepare disaster plans rapidly succeeded each other, with the climax being the effectuation of the new 'Law of the Safety Regions' on October 1st, 2010.

These developments also affected the role of the Dutch military in disaster response. After the abolishment of the Civil Defence (Bescherming Bevolking) as far back in 1986, the military was deemed only a last resort in the years after.[8] It resulted in similar coordination issues, as the military only became involved when a disaster took place and the capacities of the civil disaster management organizations proved inadequate. In 2005, as a response to these problems, the Ministries of Internal Affairs, Justice, and Defence drafted the Civil Military governance agreements. A year later in 2006, the Dutch government decided to intensify Civil-Military Collaboration in the Netherlands to support disaster relief operations.[9]

To improve the operational collaboration between the military and emergency response organizations both sectors started mapping their capacity and demands in search for mutual dependencies. After 2006, the Ministry of Defence once again became a structural partner in national disaster management. In current disaster management practice, civil authorities make an appeal to use Defence capacities in terms of skills and hardware. To support this process Regional Military Command structures have been instated, and new liaison officers have been included in the different safety regions, which form the institutional landscape of disaster management in the Netherlands. At this moment the program has developed into a new phase: the Reinforcement of Civil Military Collaboration. This phase focuses on expanding the terrains in which civil military collaboration is effectuated.

This sets the stage for the role of Network Centric Operations. Network Centric Operations was introduced in both sectors as one of the new operational concepts that should enhance information exchange to support networked operations, and

---

[6] Committee Alders 2001, p. 215.

[7] Committee Oosting 2001, p. 162 and p. 270.

[8] Boom 2000.

[9] Remkes and Kamp 2006.

could potentially also support the intensified civil-military collaboration. Despite of the apparent integration of both the military and disaster management structures by creating new roles and information sharing platforms, the concept itself was implemented in different ways in different safety regions and organizations.[10] In roughly the last 5 years the concept of netcentric work, as it is called in the disaster management sector, has been implemented in the safety regions. Currently the Institute of Physical Safety manages its further development. Under their supervision the concept of netcentric work is also transferred towards other network partners, such as infrastructural agencies and waterboards.

Despite of the apparent integration of Network Centric Operations as an operational concept in both the civil and military domain, very different command doctrines lie behind the concept in both sectors. These different doctrines give rise to different ideas on how to govern the network of response organizations in times of disaster. In the following section I will explore these different command doctrines, and argue how they result in various network governance challenges.

6.3 Command Doctrines Underlying Network Centric Operations in the Civil and Military Domain

The concept of Network Centric Operations originates from two parallel developments in command and control doctrine in both the UK and US. In the United Kingdom ‘Network Enabled Capabilities’ (NEC) was developed as the new paradigm to help command and control through networked information sharing that enhanced situational awareness.[11] A similar development was underway in the US, but under the name of ‘Network Centric Warfare’ (NCW). NCW was defined as, “the conduct of military operations using networked information systems to generate a flexible and agile military force that acts under a common commander’s intent, independent of the geographic or organizational disposition of the individual elements, and in which the focus of the warfighter is broadened away from individual, unit or platform concerns to give primacy to the mission and responsibilities of the team, task group or coalition”.[12] Later the concept was renamed into Network Centric Operations, in order to encompass peacekeeping missions in addition to the focus on traditional warfare in collaboration between army, navy and air force.[13] As for this reason to encompass a broader network of actors, I will refer to Network Centric Operations in the remainder of this chapter.

In the Network Centric Operations doctrine a shared information platform allows individuals to connect and share information that results in a shared

---

[10] Boersma et al. 2012.

[11] Endsley 1995; Perry et al. 2002; Houghton et al. 2006.

[12] Fewell and Hazen 2003.

[13] Hayes 2007.

situated understanding of the situation, which in turn leads to better, more informed decisions.[14] Information superiority allows decentralized decision-making, as higher echelons are able to monitor the progress and intervene whenever necessary. In other words, situational awareness allows faster and more agile operations in more freedom, because the commander is able to monitor and guide the operation on overall progress, instead of getting lost in too many operational details.[15] Network Centric Operations focuses on enabling networked operations by creating a platform that allows units to share information with each other.[16] It offers units real time information on what is happening around them, so that they can make their own informed decisions based on their commander's intent. This enables units to act on the basis of self-synchronization.

Network Centric Operations builds upon a shift in command and control doctrine from 'befehlstaktik' towards 'auftragstaktik'.[17] *Befehlstaktik* represents an authoritarian form of top-down command in which subordinates receive rigid orders that leave little scope to exercise own initiative. It is suggested that befehlstaktik is appropriate in times of crisis as a one-way directional command approach, which increases the commanders feeling of control. However, this type of command proved inadequate, as it was not flexible enough to adapt to rapidly changing conditions on the battlefield.

A different doctrine proved necessary to increase the flexibility of military operations, which was found in *Auftragstaktik.* Auftragstaktik is based on a goal oriented approach, in which subordinate leaders understand the intent of the orders, are given proper guidance and training to act independently, and act according to their perception of the commander's intent.[18] Auftragstaktik finds it origin in Germany`s belief in the war or movement, which is based on the idea that war is fundamentally uncertain and thus can never be totally planned.[19] In this type of warfare authority was decentralized towards operational commanders who needed to act decisively and creatively to exploit changing battlefield conditions, which increased maneuverability. As such, auftragstaktik has been heralded as one of pillars of the Blitzkrieg concept. After the Second World War this type of warfare was incorporated through the concept of 'mission command', which became the leading command and control doctrine of modern Western armed forces.[20] The current development of Network Centric Operations builds upon this concept of mission command.[21]

---

14 Houghton et al. 2008.

15 Van Bezooijen and Kramer 2015.

16 Morris et al. 2007.

17 Van Creveld 1989.

18 Shamir 2010.

19 Von Clausewitz 1873.

20 Keithly and Ferris 1999.

21 Alberts and Hayes 2003.

One of the central elements of Network Centric Operations is the assumption that a *robustly networked force* increases the effectiveness of operations.[22] However, according to Hayes the term *force* is misleading, as it is most dominantly interpreted as a military force, which ignores that civil and military stakeholders develop their own separate networks.[23] This is precisely the challenge of civil military collaboration: acting in a network that includes a wide variety of disparate actors, such as military forces and blue light disaster response organizations, but also critical infrastructural organizations, water boards, international organizations, humanitarian non-governmental organizations and voluntary organizations. Therefore the network is rarely coherent and large differences in structures goals and processes remain.[24] This points to the fact that different governance dynamics are required to organize a coherent response between the civil and military domain.[25]

Partly based on this notion, also in the civil disaster management domain a movement can be witnessed between two different command doctrines: 'chaos, command and control' and 'continuity, coordination and cooperation'.[26] The Chaos, Command and Control doctrine starts with the notion of chaos, which adheres to the way disasters are perceived. It is assumed that a disaster causes 'Chaos' that needs to be put under 'Control' by constituting a 'Command' structure.[27] This idea prescribes how organizations and citizens affected by disasters need to be managed. Para-militaristic organizations are believed to be most capable of dealing with disaster response. The consequence of this notion is that non para-militaristic organizations are not capable of overcoming the chaos caused by the disaster. Moreover, also citizens are perceived as passive victims that cannot take care of themselves. Their spontaneous actions are seen as irrelevant or even disruptive to the command and control structure.[28] Therefore, these citizens need to be controlled, taken care of, and informed through official statements of authorities.

Similar to the move from befehlstaktik towards auftragstaktik in military doctrine, also in disaster management doctrine the Chaos, Command and Control doctrine proved to be inadequate. Recent studies into disaster situations have found this doctrine to be unrealistic or even having adverse outcomes.[29] A classic example is the failing intervention in the aftermath of Hurricane Katrina in New Orleans.[30] Several analyses of the disaster response operation in New Orleans

[22] Alberts and Hayes 2003.

[23] Hayes 2007.

[24] Comfort 2007.

[25] Provan and Kenis 2008; Moynihan 2009.

[26] Boersma et al. 2014.

[27] Quarantelli and Dynes 1977.

[28] Helsloot and Ruitenberg 2004.

[29] Solnit 2010.

[30] Tierney et al. 2006.

indicated that organizations operating on the basis of chaos, command and control dismissed the resilience that was present in society that helped to overcome the disaster effects.[31]

In response to these issues disaster sociologists started documenting new phenomena in disaster governance, which were encompassed in the 'Continuity, Coordination and Cooperation' doctrine.[32] This doctrine is rooted in research that shows that during disasters the society does not necessarily spiral into social chaos, but may actually be better characterized from the continuation of social and institutional structures, although these structures are under pressure.[33] This societal dynamic requires coordination between responding emergency response agencies in cooperation with existing organizations and groups that have expertise in the affected societal or infrastructural domains. The goal is not to control the chaos of the disaster, but the focus is put on joint collaboration to harness the expertise and resilience that is already present in society.

If we coalesce the doctrines in both military and civil disaster response, which feeds into the conceptualization of Network Centric Operations, we see a striking parallel. In the military domain the concept of mission command relies upon commanders' intent and distributed decision-making to lower echelons by virtue of autonomy and self-synchronization. In civil disaster management we see a similar movement towards cooperation and coordination in a network of organizations that relies on goal consensus. In both instances, directive control is not viable as an operational concept and there is a movement towards setting a common goal or mission.

However, there is an important difference in the organization of the network in both sectors. Mission command in the military sector relies upon commanders' intent, thus having a clear commander in chief. In contrast, disaster management in the civil society requires acting in a network of autonomous organizations under conditions of goal consensus and, thus, is essentially a cooperative endeavour.[34] Research into large-scale disaster situations revealed that disaster management inevitability requires inter-sectorial and cross-jurisdictional capacities, collaborative skills, and a decentralized flexibility to deal with the ambiguity and turbulence of disaster situations.[35] The issue is that in disaster response networks a diverse set of actors engages in emergent collaborations, while lines of authority remain separated by the different organizational responsibilities. This challenges command and control, as command lines in the network are bounded by the boundaries of the organizations themselves. A vibrant example is that in disaster situations in the Netherlands the command capacity of the supreme commander is severely limited,

---

[31] Comfort 2007; Tierney et al. 2006.

[32] Dynes 1994.

[33] Helsloot and Ruitenberg 2004.

[34] Hayes 2007; Moynihan 2009.

[35] Boin and 't Hart 2003; Dynes 1970; Tierney and Trainor 2004.

despite of the political authority to do so is positioned at the mayor's office.[36] Instead, command during disaster response relies upon network governance, in which goal consensus and trust are the central steering mechanisms that feed into coordination and collaboration.[37]

Therefore, it is important to revise some of the tenets of Network Centric Operations in order to incorporate the coordination dynamics present in the disaster response network. To understand civil-military collaboration in disaster relief operations more insight is required into the principles of cross-boundary coordination. I will address this by highlighting some of the cross-boundary coordination dynamics during disaster response, and by identifying three specific boundaries that appear during disaster response operations. The existence of these boundaries requires us to develop new coordination principles for Network Centric Operations.

6.4 Towards New Coordination Principles for Network Centric Operations in Disaster Management

The central tenets of Network Centric Operations can be categorized into three domains: cognitive, information and physical (Table 6.1). The promise in the cognitive domain is that, "the force has the capability to develop and share high quality situational awareness, develop a shared knowledge of commanders' intent, and has the capability to self-synchronize its operations".[38] In the information domain the promise is that, "the force has the capability to collect, share, access and protect information".[39] In the physical domain Network Centric Operations requires that, "all elements of the force are robustly networked achieving secure and seamless connectivity".[40] These tenets convey a very optimistic image to us, but are they realistic when used in civil-military collaboration, which encompasses a much broader and heterogeneous definition of a force?

The issue is that in the civil domain disaster managers need to coordinate their actions with partners from multiple organizations, which have different working practices, organizational values, expertise, and norms. This creates discrepancies during the coordination process and requires disaster managers to deal with these issues. In other words, *cross-boundary* coordination is required in order to effectuate Network Centric Operations. Cross-boundary coordination can be regarded as a temporally unfolding and contextualized process of managing interdependencies in response to the discontinuity of a boundary, in order to realize a collective

[36] Scholtens 2008.

[37] Provan and Kenis 2008.

[38] Fewel and Hazen 2003, p. 2.

[39] Fewel and Hazen 2003, p. 2.

[40] Fewel and Hazen 2003, p. 2.

Table 6.1 Tenets of Network Centric Operations translated towards civil disaster network governance

	Cognitive domain	Information domain	Physical domain
Tenets of Network Centric Operations	The force has the capability to self-synchronize its operations	The force has the capability to collect, share, access and protect information	All elements of the force are robustly networked achieving secure and seamless connectivity
Boundaries in civil-military collaboration	Normative boundary	Knowledge boundary	Functional boundary
Cross-boundary coordination process	Negotiation	Sensemaking	Network switching

performance.[41] In this definition boundaries take up an important role. Boundaries can be regarded as demarcations that mark the limits of a common set of practices. They can appear at multiple levels and at different locations simultaneously, and may include functional, hierarchical, knowledge, cultural, temporal, and spatial boundaries.[42] This is why disaster managers are often confronted with contradictory situations that make it hard to make a clear decision, as actors need to attend to competing demands simultaneously. Since coordination processes are constantly evolving during disaster management, boundaries are not fixed entities, but must be regarded as social objects that are shaped by spatial locations, temporality, personal interpretations, patterns of interactions, and formal and perceived accountabilities.[43] As obstructions to collaboration, boundaries create a temporal discontinuity that requires actors to negotiate the way in which interdependencies can be coordinated.[44] In the following sections I will argue that three specific boundaries impede the central tenets of Network Centric Operations when transferred from a context of military networked operations towards civil disaster network governance.

6.4.1 Facing a Normative Boundary: From Self-synchronization Towards Negotiations

The process self-synchronization is central in the tenets of Network Centric Operations, but it actually inhibits a tension between two competing processes. On the one hand, self-synchronization relies on predictability and anticipation embedded in the procedures and protocols of other stakeholders.[45] Self-synchronization rests on a certain degree of predictability in order to anticipate actions that follow the logical flow of work processes.[46] On the other hand, self-synchronization is meant to stimulate decentralized on-the-spot decision making, to increase flexibility for adapting to the continuously changing situation.[47] What creates the tension during the process of self-synchronization is that during disaster response such flexibility leads to mutual adaptation, improvisation, and ad hoc networking.[48] Once emergency responders arrive at the disaster scene predetermined plans need to be adapted to the dynamically unfolding situation at hand.[49] While such

[41] Wolbers 2016.

[42] Hsiao et al. 2012; Carlile 2002; Bechky 2003; Levina and Vaast 2005.

[43] Barley and Kunda 2001.

[44] Watson-Manheim et al. 2012.

[45] Rico et al. 2008.

[46] Okhuysen and Bechky 2009.

[47] Bigley and Roberts 2001; Moynihan 2009; Comfort 2007; Majchrzak et al. 2007.

[48] Kapucu 2006; Comfort 2007; Moynihan 2009.

[49] Bigley and Roberts 2001.

emergent adaptations enable flexibility, they also increase ambiguity that diminishes the predictability of the outcome of designed procedures.[50] This partly restricts coordination based on anticipation, because adaptation enforces a normative boundary between the expected and anticipated outcome.

Dealing with these unexpected deviations from plans and protocols in the heat of the disaster requires a different coordination approach: negotiation. Negotiation enables members of different backgrounds coordinate their actions temporarily and locally, navigating their differences in norms and interests only as needed.[51] It allows professionals to redefine how deviations from the protocols need to be enacted. During the negotiation process actors have to share their expertise to convince the other about the value of alternatives. In this way, actors exchange ideas, learn from one another and make sense of each other's position and professional background. This is useful in conditions of uncertainty, because such negotiation processes do not depend on shared ideas, interests, or norms.[52] By engaging in such a negotiation process the normative boundary between actors with a different professional background can be overcome.

6.4.2 Facing a Knowledge Boundary: From Information Sharing to Sensemaking

The second promise of Network Centric Operations doctrine is that it enables actors to collect, share, access and protect information, which leads to information superiority. Speed is an important element of information superiority, because if a commander is capable of going through the OODA loop (observe-orient-decide-act) faster than his opponent he obtains a superior information position.[53] For combat situations information superiority is a crucial variable to keep or regain the initiative. It is, however, debatable whether achieving information superiority is just as important for collaborative emergency response endeavours, when there is no clear opponent.

In disaster management operations the idea of information superiority is often rooted in an 'information warehousing logic', which implies information can be collected, sorted and exchanged in an accessible and univocal form.[54] The focus on information warehousing is problematic, as in disaster situations knowledge boundaries emerge when professionals from different organizations, having different expertise, interpret similar information differently. In the heat of the moment there is often only a limited understanding of what consequences information has for the actions and needs of other professionals.

[50] Okhuysen and Bechky 2009.

[51] Kellogg et al. 2006.

[52] Vaughan 1999.

[53] Alberts et al. 2001.

[54] Wolbers and Boersma 2013.

Therefore, it is important to recognize that disaster managers need to make sense of information.[55] Sensemaking implies that information is not univocal, but equivocal. Information is comprised of different voices that all have their own interpretation. As information incorporates different professional languages, it is often incomplete and changes when the situation it represents is in constant flux. In this dynamic environment sensemaking processes allow organizational members to (de/re)construct information influenced by their institutional background to find out what is going on in times of uncertainty.[56]

Sensemaking is a retrospective process, in the sense that it is influenced to a great extent by previous education, training, and past experiences.[57] The process of sensemaking takes place when actors react to different cues (or signals), based on their knowledge and expectations of a set of roles, scripts, and actions, which arise from the actors' different organizational backgrounds.[58] In dynamic environments these elements of sensemaking are enacted into collaborative time critical responses.[59] In order to do so, information must be made actionable to its different users. This requires professional judgment and skills that often remains embodied in the craftsmanship and proficiency of professionals.[60]

In that respect sensemaking is a crucial process underlying effective network centric operations in the disaster governance network. It is crucial to understand the role of sensemaking processes in order to understand the coordination dynamics that appear as a result of working with network centric platforms. As such, the tenet of information sharing is more focused on a homogenous network with professionals that are trained to interpret the information in specific ways, rather than being an effective tenet for more heterogeneous civil-military response networks.

6.4.3 *Facing a Functional Boundary: From Seamless Connectivity Towards Network Switching*

The promise of seamless connectivity by a robustly networked force is problematic when held against the nature of disaster management networks. An important coordination challenge in response networks is that as new organizations are included in the network membership fluctuates over time, and information sharing becomes increasingly complex.[61] In addition, information is transferred between different kinds of networks, from various positions, and at different times. This

[55] Weick et al. 2005; Maitlis and Sonenshein 2010.

[56] Weick et al. 2005.

[57] Taber et al. 2008.

[58] Weber and Glynn 2006.

[59] Faraj and Xiao 2006.

[60] Faraj and Sproull 2000.

[61] Topper and Carley 1999.

occurs because response organizations have operational field units at different levels, different functional command structures, and separate back-offices for information and resource management.[62]

As the network of disaster response agencies encompasses a wide variety of organizations, it requires effort to govern the interconnections between multiple networks, instead of focusing on increasing connectivity in one network. According to Castells, governing interconnections between different networks rests on two competing capabilities: programming and switching.[63] A network can be 'programmed' by assigning goals to the network. This corresponds closely with the idea of mission command, where an overarching goal is defined and monitored through command and control. However, this is not the only capability that is required for network governance. The other capability that needs to be addressed is 'network switching'. Switching is about creating the connection between different kinds of networks, by sharing common goals and combining resources, while fending off competition from other networks by setting up strategic cooperation.[64]

The emphasis on network switching shows that during disaster response there is often no clear commander, or possibilities for controlling the actions of heterogeneous network partners. In addition, disaster response networks are far from fully connected during the entire disaster response sequence.[65] The response network actually integrates and segments over time. Therefore it is important to recognize when moments of switching occur to bridge the different functional boundaries in the network.

6.5 Conclusion

I have addressed several different doctrines behind the concept of Network Centric Operations, underlying its implementation in both the military and the civil disaster management domain. As the process of intensified civil-military collaboration is fully underway in the Dutch safety landscape, the time has come to address these differences, as they give rise to very different network coordination principles. In order to improve and intensify civil-military collaboration in the safety domain, it is imperative to (re)develop the doctrine of Network Centric Operations by introducing new coordination principles.

From the military perspective Network Centric Operations relies upon the doctrine of 'mission command', but in civil domain it relies upon the doctrine of 'continuity, coordination & cooperation'. The difference lies in the nature of the network governance. A disaster brings together a heterogeneous set of organizations

[62] Comfort and Kapucu 2006.

[63] Castells 1996.

[64] Castells 1996.

[65] Wolbers et al. 2013.

that coordinate by constituting a loosely coupled network of emergent interactions. During this coordination process professionals from different organizations make sense of the situation based on deference to expertise, and negotiate the relevance of their perspectives to retain sensitivity to operations. In addition, they actively switch between different (parts of the) network(s) to overcome functional boundaries and retain speed of operations in a distributed environment. This requires a new approach for Network Centric Operations that does not only rely upon information sharing and self-synchronization, but also incorporates *negotiation*, *sensemaking* and *network switching* to overcome different functional, normative and knowledge boundaries that come into play.

References

Alberts DS, Garstka JJ, Hayes RE, Signori DA (2001) Understanding information age warfare. Assistant Secretary of Defense C3I Command and Control Research Program, Washington DC

Alberts DS, Hayes RE (2003) Power to the edge: command and control in the information age. Office of the Assistant Secretary of Defense Washington DC Command and Control Research Program (CCRP), Washington DC

Barley SR, Kunda G (2001) Bringing work back in. Organ Sci 12:76–95

Bechky BA (2003) Sharing meaning across occupational communities: the transformation of understanding on a production floor. Organ Sci 14:312–330

Bigley GA, Roberts KH (2001) The incident command system: high-reliability organizing for complex and volatile task environments. Acad Manag J 44:1281–1299

Boersma FK, Wagenaar P, Wolbers JJ (2012) Negotiating the trading zone. creating a shared information infrastructure in the Dutch safety sector. J Homel Secur Emerg Manage 9:1–26

Boersma FK, Ferguson J, Groenewegen P, Wolbers JJ (2014) Beyond the myth of control: toward network switching in disaster management. In: Hiltz SR, Pfaff MS, Plotnick L, Robinson AC (eds) Proceedings of the 11th International Conference on Information Systems for Crisis Response and Management ISCRAM 2014. University Park, Pennsylvania, pp 125–129

Boin A, 't Hart P (2003) Public Leadership in Times of Crisis: Mission Impossible. Public Adm Rev 63:544–553

Boom BE (2000) Atoomgevaar? dan zeker BB: de geschiedenis van de Bescherming Bevolking. Sdu Uitgevers, The Hague

Carlile PR (2002) A pragmatic view of knowledge and boundaries: boundary objects in new product development. Organ Sci 13:442–455

Castells M (1996) The rise of the network society. Blackwell, Malden

Comfort LK (2007) Crisis management in hindsight: cognition, communication, coordination, and control. Public Adm Rev, Special Issue:189–197

Comfort LK, Kapucu N (2006) Inter-organizational coordination in extreme events: the World Trade Center attacks, September 11, 2001. Nat Hazards 39:309–327

Committee Alders (2001) Cafebrand in Volendam. Rotterdam

Committee Oosting (2001) De Vuurwerkramp, Eindrapport. Enschede/The Hague

Dynes RR (1970) Organized behavior in disasters. Heath Lexington Books, Lexington, MA

Dynes RR (1994) Community emergency planning: false assumptions and inappropriate analogies. Int J Mass Emerg Disasters 12:141–158

Endsley MR (1995) Toward a theory of situation awareness in dynamic systems. Hum Factors J Hum Factors Ergon Soc 37:32–64

Faraj S, Sproull L (2000) Coordinating expertise in software development teams. Manage Sci 46:1554–1568
Faraj S, Xiao Y (2006) Coordination in fast-response organizations. Manage Sci 52:1155–1169
Fewell MP, Hazen MG (2003) Netcentric warfare, its nature and its modeling. Department of Defence Australia, DSTO Systems Sciences Laboratory
Hayes RE (2007) It's an Endeavor, not a Force. Int C2 J 1:145–176
Helsloot I, Ruitenberg A (2004) Citizen response to disasters: a survey of literature and some practical implications. J Contingencies Crisis Manage 12:98–111
Houghton RJ, Barber C, McMaster R, Stanton NA, Salmon P, Stewart R, Walker GH (2006) Command and control in emergency services operations; a social network analysis. Ergonomics 49:10–22
Houghton RJ, Barber C, Cowton M, Walker GH, Stanton NA (2008) WESTT (workload, error, situational awareness, time and teamwork): an analytical prototyping system for command and control. Cogn Technol Work 10:199–207
Hsiao RL, Tsai DH, Lee CF (2012) Collaborative knowing: the adaptive nature of cross-boundary spanning. J Manage Stud 49:463–491
Kapucu N (2006) Interagency communication networks during emergencies: boundary spanners in multiagency coordination. Am Rev Public Adm 36:207–225
Keithly DM, Ferri SP (1999) Auftragstaktik, or directive control, in joint and combined operations. Parameters 29:118–133
Kellogg KC, Orlikowski WJ, Yates J (2006) Life in the trading zone: structuring coordination across boundaries in postbureaucratic organizations. Organ Sci 17:22–44
Levina N, Vaast E (2005) The emergence of boundary spanning competence in practice: implications for implementation and use of information systems. MIS Q 29:335–363
Maitlis S, Sonenshein S (2010) Sensemaking in crisis and change: inspiration and insights from Weick (1988). J Manage Stud 47:551–580
Majchrzak A, Jarvenpaa SL, Hollingshead AB (2007) Coordinating expertise among emergent groups responding to disasters. Organ Sci 18:147–161
Morris JC, Morris ED, Jones DM (2007) Reaching for the Philosopher's Stone: Contingent Coordination and the Military Response to Hurricane Katrina. Public Adm Rev 67:94–106
Moynihan DP (2009) The network governance of crisis response: case studies of incident command systems. J Public Adm Res Theor 19:895–915
Okhuysen GA, Bechky BA (2009) Coordination in organizations: an integrative perspective. Acad Manage Ann 3:463–502
Perry W, Button RW, Bracken J, Sullivan T, Mitchell J (2002) Measures of effectiveness for the information-age navy: the effects of network-centric operations on combat outcomes. Report MR-1449-NAVY of the RAND Corporation, Santa Monica, California
Provan KG, Kenis P (2008) Modes of network governance: structure, management and effectiveness. J Public Adm Res Theor 18:229–252
Quarantelli EL, Dynes RR (1977) Response to social crisis and disaster. Annu Rev Sociol 3:23–49
Remkes J, Kamp H (2006) Rapportage Intensivering Civiel-militaire Samenwerking, letter to the Parliament about intensifying civil-military collaboration. Department of the Interior and Ministry of Defence, The Hague
Rico R, Sánchez-Manzanares M, Gil F, Gibson C (2008) Team implicit coordination processes: a team knowledge–based approach. Acad Manag Rev 33:163–184
Scholtens A (2008) Controlled collaboration in disaster and disaster management in the Netherlands, history and practice of an overestimated and underestimated concept. J Contingencies Disaster Manage 16:195–207
Shamir E (2010) The long and winding road: the US Army managerial approach to command and the adoption of Mission Command (Auftragstaktik). J Strateg Stud 33:645–672
Solnit R (2010) A paradise built in hell: the extraordinary communities that arise in disaster. Viking, New York

Taber N, Plumb D, Jolemore S (2008) Grey areas and organized chaos in emergency response. J Workplace Learn 20:272–285
Tierney KJ, Bevc C, Kuligowski E (2006) Metaphor matters: disaster myths, media frames, and their consequences in Hurricane Katrina. Ann Am Acad Polit Soc Sci 604:57–81
Tierney K, Trainor J (2004) Networks and Resilience in the World Trade Center Disaster. Research Progress and Accomplishments, vol. 6. Multidisciplinary Center for Earthquake Engineering Research, Buffalo, NY
Topper CM, Carley KM (1999) A structural perspective on the emergence of network organizations. J Math Sociol 24:67–96
Van Bezooijen B, Kramer EH (2015) Mission command in the information age: a normal accidents perspective on networked military operations. J Strateg Stud 38:445–466
Van Creveld ML (1989) Technology in war. The Free Press, New York
Vaughan D (1999) The role of organization in the production of techno-scientific knowledge. Soc Stud Sci 29:913–943
Von Clausewitz C (1873) On war. Trübner & Company, London
Watson-Manheim M, Chudoba B, Crowston K (2012) Perceived discontinuities and constructed continuities in virtual work. Inf Syst J 22:29–52
Weber K, Glynn MA (2006) Making sense with institutions: context, thought and action in Karl Weick's theory. Organ Stud 27:1639–1660
Weick KE, Sutcliffe KM, Obstfeld D (2005) Organizing and the process of sensemaking. Organ Sci 16:409–421
Wolbers JJ (2016) Drawing the line. Cross-boundary coordination processes in emergency management, Ph.D. Thesis VU Amsterdam. Ridderprint, Ridderkerk
Wolbers JJ, Boersma FK (2013) The common operational picture as collective sensemaking. J Contingencies Crisis Manag 21:186–199
Wolbers JJ, Groenewegen P, Molle J, Bim J (2013) Incorporating time dynamics in the analysis of social networks in emergency management. J Homel Secur Emerg Manage 10:1–31

Part II
Organizing for Safety

Chapter 7
Organizing Safety in Security Organizations

Gwendolyn Bakx and James Nyce

Abstract Safety and security are often regarded as two separate concepts, both scientifically and organizationally. Both are often seen as two fundamentally conflicting institutional demands and their agendas as being based on two profoundly different organizing principles. Because of this, safety may get less attention in security organizations than necessary as such a distinction would mean in the perception of people that funding for the one would go at the cost of the other. This chapter points out that organizing for security and for safety may not be so different after all as both safety and security seem to develop from the same social structures and institutional complexities. The differences between the two seem to be a matter of social construction, power and policy, rather than that these differences would inevitably follow from what one would regard as their intrinsic features.

Keywords Military · Safety · Security · System dynamics · Social-construction · Social science

G. Bakx (✉)
Faculty of Military Sciences, Netherlands Defence Academy, Breda, The Netherlands
e-mail: gch.bakx.02@mindef.nl

J. Nyce
Department of Anthropology, Ball State University, Muncie, IN, USA
e-mail: jnyce@bsu.edu

R. Beeres et al. (eds.), *NL ARMS Netherlands Annual Review of Military Studies 2016*, NL ARMS, DOI 10.1007/978-94-6265-135-7_7

Contents

7.1 Introduction

Despite the similarities that will be pointed out in this paper, a distinction is often made between safety and security in the literature. For example, it has long been argued that safety is concerned with accidental harm and that security addresses issues of malicious, intended harm, such as the 13 November 2015 Paris attacks.[1] In other words, safety deals in this perspective with accidents, while security deals with attacks. Making such an analytic distinction could be useful if this would allow us, for example, to excavate the underlying organizing principles for safety and security so as to determine if using one term or another would lead to different solution strategies. Making this distinction could then help to determine appropriate safety/security solution(s) and policy.

Some scholars, however, argue that safety and security agendas operate on and emerge from two profoundly different organizing principles and that they follow from two conflicting institutional demands.[2] Safety, according to these researchers, is directed toward internal (read psychological) threats for which, they assume, solutions are generally known or readily found, while security is directed towards external (objective) threats, to the unanticipated, and to the unknown. Indeed, safety is often associated both by experts and by lay people with known risks, and thus with rather bureaucratic (regulatory) procedures such as safety audits, standardization and certification, and risk identification and evaluation procedures. Also, we often tend to have folk or scientific models that explain accidents, while the rationales behind attacks are generally considered much less easy to understand or decipher.

One would expect that issues of safety would be a serious concern for any security organization (i.e., for organizations that have national and/or international security protection as their main task). On the other hand, if safety and security indeed follow from distinct institutional demands, as the literature suggests, then investments in one would of course go at the cost of the other. Taking into account, above all, that security, not safety, is core business of security organizations, then one would expect from this theoretical perspective, that it makes little

[1] Firesmith 2003, p. viii.

[2] Pettersen and Bjørnskau 2015, p. 170; also see Table 1.2 in Chap. 1.

organizational and budgetary sense for these organizations to emphasize safety issues except as some kind of fringe benefit that arises from their core enterprise. How this linkage between safety on the one hand and security organizations on the other could work will be explored in this paper, as well as what this would mean about how to organize for both safety and security in the context of today's society. We will specifically focus thereby on the Dutch armed forces. Let us first look, however, at how a security context would look like.

> On 24 and 25 March in 2014 the Nuclear Summit of 2014, an international summit aimed at preventing nuclear terrorism, took place in the Netherlands. Members from many nations' departments of foreign and national affairs, intelligence agencies, cyber and explosive experts, security agencies, and municipalities, all worked together to make certain that 58 world leaders[3] could meet safely in the Netherlands. They did this in collaboration with many Dutch non-governmental (and semi-governmental) entities, such as healthcare organizations, Schiphol and Rotterdam airport, the National Railway Association, and the Dutch Automobile Association. Others were also involved, like airlines, interpreters, catering companies and Information and Communication Technology (ICT) services. The armed forces alone had 8000 people involved,[4] among which there were the military police, air defence units, F-16's, helicopters, ground units, and AWACS airplanes (aircraft that are part of the airborne early warning system). Much of the traffic in the western part of the country was diverted, roads there partially or fully closed, recreational aviation had been forbidden to fly in certain areas, and maritime traffic was intensively monitored. The location of each individual police service unit involved was planned out thoroughly beforehand, and communicated throughout the Dutch police organization. One can only imagine the kind of logistic and informational challenges involved in this summit meeting.

What this Nuclear Summit example points out is that the environments in which security organizations operate today can clearly be very complex. Although individual security services are usually organized as single entities, they do need to collaborate with others prior to and especially when deployed to accomplish their tasks. It does not need much imagination to see that in these kinds of contexts flaws can develop without being noticed for a long period of time, until it is too late. In this particular case an example of a national scale has been described. These kinds of security contexts can be found, however, both inside and outside the Netherlands, where the Dutch armed forces can work, for example, not only with the North Atlantic Treaty Organization (NATO), United Nations (UN), and allied and other forces, but also with parties such as Non-Governmental Organisations (NGOs), local governments and other local authorities.

Nothing serious really went wrong at the Nuclear Summit of 2014. However, let's say a crowd had overrun a couple of world leaders during the summit. Then, would we have had a safety issue (i.e., an accident), a security breach (i.e., an attack), or both? When dealing with security organizations and their high-risk missions and contexts, this might not always be clear or useful because safety and security can be so intertwined in events like this world summit that any practical distinction

---

[3]NSS 2014.

[4]NOS 2014.

between the two can be hard to make. Still, as we have seen, the literature does make this distinction. Also, as the safety literature has pointed out several times, an organization's focus on particular core activities can sometimes severely hamper an institution's safety agenda, and thereby the protection of itself (e.g., Vaughan's elaboration on production pressures in the Challenger Space Shuttle accident).[5] Safety can thus be pushed aside by other priorities in organizations. We will argue in this paper, however, that the differences between safety and security that lie underneath this competitive thought are generally socially constructed, i.e. they seem to be the result of supposed rather than concrete intrinsic distinct features. Both safety and security, we will argue, reside in the same meaning, allocation and institutional structures. They seem to reside in the same socio-system dynamics. Also, what constitutes safety and security can only be distinguished from each other in an analytic sense. For this reason, there is some hope that safety issues can be addressed successfully by security organizations and that both safety and security can benefit the other as policy and solutions for both kinds of issues can be handled then in much the same ways.

7.2 Safety Lacks Sex-Appeal

One issue of concern for organizing safety in security organizations is that safety seems to lack sex appeal when compared to security, as safety is usually associated, boringly, with (enforcing and providing) certainty through rules, accountability, compliance and procedures like protocols. Safety advocates are, for instance, often seen as being much like the kinds of chaperones that we all used to try to avoid at high school dances. Even during the initial negotiations regarding this book, doubts had raised by the editorial board about whether the authors would be enthusiast enough to write about safety as opposed to security. Security issues, on the other hand, are linked, often, with the John le Carré (or James Bond) aspects of the social world. These include the more ambiguous and less predictable (and thereby more interesting) dimensions of social and institutional life. The fact that many security measures such as the Information Technology (IT) authentication protocols, aircraft boarding procedures, and the screening of Closed Circuit Television (CCTV) surveillance cameras can also be boring as hell also is often forgotten. Safety and security, however, often seem to be framed for the policy makers and the general public so that safety protects one from harm, but that security will protect you from evil, and guess which sells best?

From this, it is not surprising that safety and security issues and strategies are often strictly separated from each other, not just in the scientific literature but also organizationally. A couple of years ago, for example, the Dutch Air Force tallied up its ten top main risk activities. When this process was complete, the list did

[5] Vaughan 1997.

not include the Air Force's core security activity, flying. Still, the Dutch Air Force has a large and proactive flight safety organization in place, which would suggest that some safety risks could be associated with flying at least. However, even after having discussed (and acknowledged) these risks for many times during the inventory process, the Air Force management was reluctant to add flying to its list of top ten safety risks. Can we, and should we, however, separate safety and security, especially when organizations are concerned that operate in or protect high-risk environments?

7.3 Attention to Safety Does Seem to Pay Off

In complex and high-risk contexts such as with the Nuclear Summit case described here, one would think that safety and security would be so intertwined that any distinction between the two would be difficult to make, except perhaps in hindsight. Safety hazards, for instance, can obviously emerge from activities necessary to insure national and international security policy as these activities can involve the use of violence, the risk of injury and death, and potential long-term consequences such as Post Traumatic Stress Disorders (PTSD). Accidents (safety), on the other hand, can result in (or trigger) security breaches that can be turned into attacks or intrusions by one's opponents, which would then fall within the realm of security.[6] A couple of years ago, for example, the Dutch airspace's surveillance status was degraded for an hour or so because of a faulty upgrade of the air traffic controller software. This in turn led to both the primary and the secondary system to malfunction. It is often cascades such as this where the failure of one purpose in a system inadvertently leads to other kinds of failures in the same system (here both safety and surveillance were degraded). Safety efforts may therefore pay off, even when security is an institution's raison d'être. This may be more so in an organization such as the armed forces as they often operate abroad and in unpredictable environments in which casualties can, above all, lead to a decline in domestic support for the missions abroad.[7]

Studying the interconnectedness between security and safety would thus perhaps be more useful, analytically and pragmatically, than ignoring the commonalities between the two. The security literature, however, generally lacks the analytic models to evaluate both the commonalities and differences between what we define and practice as 'safety' and 'security' in the first place. The safety literature, on the other hand, does provide analytic models. Older models of safety, however, would have difficulty in handling the interconnectedness mentioned here. Contemporary approaches to safety, to the contrary, focus on the complexity of structures and on system dynamics and interconnections in real life settings

[6]Firesmith 2003, pp. 11–12.

[7]Larson and Savych 2005, p. 213.

specifically.[8] These 'New View' approaches, as they are often called in the safety literature, are thus able to gain a better understanding of why systems can thrive on 1 day and collapse on another; of why safety is taken into consideration in security organizations on 1 day, but not on the next. Understanding these kinds of mechanisms is important as generally it is very difficult to predict in advance whether or not a particular safety or security agenda, like those in place for the 2014 Dutch Nuclear Summit, will be successful. Perhaps, this New View focus on safety can give the field of safety therefore not just a bit of sex appeal but can it demonstrate also that safety and security may not differ so much after all, an issue which will be explored next.

7.4 Safety and Security Both Emerge from System Dynamics

For security organizations to perform their core business—providing protection—effectively, they often must have or participate in complex organizational, social structures. In the case of the 2014 Nuclear Summit, for instance, many different parties were involved to address the many different potential hazards such as cyber attacks, fires, car accidents, and protestor and terrorist attacks. One could say, given this, that taking complexity into account can be a virtue. The theory of complex adaptive systems, for instance, argues in this regard that organizations can be more effective when they are able to employ and thus handle a larger degree of variability.[9] However, the large number of parties involved in security operations can also make it more difficult, on the other hand, to coordinate the activities of all these parties together. It can make the system more vulnerable, for instance, both to security and safety breaches, as such complexity allows for more things to go wrong.

In the safety literature this is a well-known phenomenon.[10] The same complex structures that make a system work make it difficult, at the same time, to understand and control the system. Disaster can emerge from these complex systems, even though at the individual level all seems to be going well. In the Dutch armed forces this has once been the case also as can be illustrated by a study that was part of a series of studies on technological safety in the armed forces. In this one study the coordination between the two pilots of an Apache attack helicopter was investigated.[11]

---

[8]Dekker 2011, 2006; Marais et al. 2004.

[9]The theory of complex adaptive systems is based on complexity theory and cybernetics, e.g. Capra 1996; Wheatley 1992; Stacey 1995.

[10]Perrow 1999; Dekker 2012.

[11]Bakx and Nyce 2013.

> Over a long period of time changes in Dutch military missions had resulted in a large number of almost unnoticeable small changes in the unit's training and flying practices. The result of these changes was, among other things, that these pilots often flew either at a low level, or at a high altitude, and thus that they had not gotten much opportunity to build up the experience that was necessary for handling altitude changes smoothly during missions. These pilots, as a result, often lacked the skills and proficiency to identify troubles that could emerge during these altitude changes. Further, once such troubles had been identified in flight, they were not always able anymore to take over the controls from the other pilot effectively. Over years, these pilots had formed a large segment of the unit. The unit's management had, in the meantime, not realized or anticipated the consequences of these mission changes. This is in part because they themselves were from "before" this decade. They had thus been changing profiles many times during their initial training and in the years afterward. Consequently, a deficiency in skills with a large part of unit's population was not noticed for a very long time, until one day in 2007 one of the helicopter crews flew into a high-voltage line.

What can be learned from this Apache example and the Nuclear Summit case outlined before here is that security disasters can emerge from the very same social structures that play such a large role in accidents also. Both safety and security problems seem to emerge in often unpredictable ways from the complex, social and institutional structures that are necessary to get the system to work in the first place. This has much in common with what Giddens describes in his structuration theory, a theory that can be used to account for how structures, events and developments (such as the number of parties involved in a security task and the performance of this particular task) are all interconnected with each other.[12] Any distinction made between structure and agency in a social system is largely an arbitrary, analytic one according to Giddens—one that is more dependent on theoretical preference or bias than anything else. Giddens in fact argues that "the notion of human agency [in systems] cannot be adequately explicated without that of structure, and vice versa" because these social structures and the activities that reflect that structure, have both produced and reproduced these structures and activities to begin with. In other words, social structures, according to Giddens, enable and constrain, on the one hand, the actions in a system (because of which actions generally reflect a system's structures), but these actions can either reinforce or change, at the same time, the structures that produced these actions (reproduction).

Both the 2014 Nuclear Summit case and the Apache example seem to reflect the kinds of dynamics that Giddens writes about in his structuration theory as both situations emerged from their systems' usual complexity and social and institutional structures. Security disasters and accidents thus seem to emerge in much the same ways, which means that they may do not differ that much after all. One thing this means is that not only can security be perhaps linked with known threats more than this is often admitted, but also that safety science apparently deals just as much with the elusive—or the unpredictable—factors of the field of security. In other words, as we argued before, there seems to be no reason for safety and

---

[12]Giddens 1984.

security to rest on (and operate from) different underlying organizing principles. This is, however, not to say that safety and security cannot be analytically distinguished from each other. For example, organizations can be considered to be safe but not secure as in the case of denial-of-service computer attacks or when confidential documents have been stolen without individuals or other property being harmed. Likewise, the armed forces can be considered secure but not safe when one of their planes crashes without any confidential data being compromised. In real life, however, things are seldom so black and white as the social dynamics involved control how an incident is perceived and responded to. This is important because framing something as either a safety issue, a security issue, or both, can have a large impact on how the issue is handled, especially when safety and security are regarded by those involved as fundamentally conflicting demands, which itself is the outcome of some social process. The next section, building on elements from Giddens' structuration theory, will sketch out some of these social dynamics, especially those that may be relevant for how to organize for and handle safety in a security organization.

7.5 Organizing for Safety in a Security Organization

The (perceived) differences between safety and security are the result, apparently, of a series of complex social processes, which can either connect the two or set them apart. Seeing the safety agenda as being directed (only) towards known risks, for instance, ones that come with the job anyhow, does not help, obviously, to get safety issues high up the corporate or policy agenda. Nor does it encourage staff to advocate strongly for any safety agenda. Depicting security as being directed towards more malevolent and external threats on the other hand can make security issues seem that much more attractive. However, when safety and security are framed this way (i.e., in opposition to each other), it seems as if the characteristics associated with security organizations do not really go well with safety activities.

The system dynamics that Giddens identified in his structuration theory suggest that this is not necessarily so as safety and security issues may have a lot in common with each other. This is also the lesson that the Dutch Nuclear Summit and the Apache case seem to have taught us. Still, how efforts and resources for safety in security organizations are awarded depends on how both issues of safety and security are interpreted. This is congruent with Giddens' structuration theory, as well as with the social construction literature.[13] According to this literature, the allocation of meaning, and the actions that follow from this, represent a social process just as much, if not more, than that meaning might follow from the intrinsic features of things. People, in other words, may not act so much on the things themselves but rather on the representations and meanings that they attribute to these

[13]Berger and Luckmann 1966; Gergen and Gergen 2003.

things. These representations and meanings can be determined, in turn, by any number of factors, such as context and history, but also structure, hierarchy and power. From this perspective, it is thus the social construction of both safety and security, and of the relations between those two, which will determine how safety is understood and handled in any organization, and thus in security organizations also. What seems to be key in this is that, although safety and security may not necessarily represent fundamental conflicting institutional demands, they are generally perceived that way. Therefore, allocating resources to one or the other would automatically (and convincingly) rule out funding for the other.

Both safety and security thus seem to have no fixed, intrinsic features. On the contrary, how safety and security are defined and enacted in organizations, and thus in security organizations also, is often the result of organizational structural features as well as of other social dynamics which influence how these terms (and the acts and ideologies associated with them) are perceived within these organizations. Safety and security apparently are, in other words and perhaps more than anything else, socially constructed concepts, which can be distinguished from each other only in some analytic sense. The security realm could therefore benefit, probably, from some of the recent safety research, which links safety to complexity in general and to complex socio-technological system dynamics in particular.[14] These literatures cited here have done much to help us discover those mechanisms and processes that determine what safety means and can encompass in specific contexts, the latter one by connecting Giddens' structuration theory to the safety literature. In particular, these literatures help us understand how safety can emerge—or not—from the day-to-day complexities of ordinary life. With the addition of Giddens' structuration theory especially, it would be possible to look at how these literatures could help address not only how safety but security also is produced, reproduced and legitimatized institutionally within a particular society/social order, and also at how this order could influence the linkage between the two.[15] Dependent, for instance, on how both terms might be defined in a particular organization, safety can clearly benefit from being connected to security. Air Force and Navy organizations are exemplar in this, as these often have large safety organizations in place to prevent the accidental loss of the high-tech equipment that they usually have in only relatively small numbers in their inventory. What we see here is that the allocation of safety resources is often taken for granted, or even ignored, as long as resources are perceived as peripheral to an organization's core activities.[16]

Linking safety and security efforts together seems like something that requires little common sense, particularly as the mechanisms involved in both seem to have

[14]Dekker 2012; Dekker et al. 2011; Bakx and Nyce 2015.

[15]Giddens 1984.

[16]Although Vaughan's 1997 description of the NASA Challenger launch disaster suggests that this is not always necessarily so, that how production pressures are defined throughout an organization can put a tension on what is allocated for safety resources.

much in common. However, if safety and security can indeed emerge from the same institutional structures and if they differ indeed mainly by semantics as we have argued here, then linking safety and security efforts requires organizational innovation and cross (intra) organizational redesign more than anything else. What needs to be addressed here then is not so much issues of skill and competence but rather those of resource, power and policy.

7.6 Conclusion

The security context described in this paper has been used to point out that both safety and security can emerge from the same institutional complexities. Both safety and security, and their supposed similarities and distinctions, seem more socially, perhaps even ideologically, constructed than anything else. Security and safety need not represent, necessarily, fundamentally conflicting institutional demands. The favouring of security over safety agendas seems to reflect relative ignorance or prior institutional and policy commitments and agreements rather than anything else.

Indeed, security and safety, both as practice and thought, were seen to have much in common here, and knowledge from one domain could be well applied to the other. This could have considerable benefit for society because then much of the dynamics that have advanced the security agendas could perhaps be applied to safety issues as well. However, as for most things in society that are both valued and contested, power then becomes an issue. Power, after all, can determine the success or failure of any agenda, especially when one attempts to contest what beforehand has been seen as the natural order of things, such as in this case that a society's security is generally assumed more important than its safety.[17]

References

Bakx GCH, Nyce JM (2013) Is redundancy enough? A preliminary study of Apache crew behaviour. Theor Issues Ergon 14:531–545

Bakx GCH, Nyce JM (2015) Risk and safety in large-scale socio-technological (military) systems: a literature review. J Risk Res. doi:10.1080/13669877.2015.1071867

Berger PL, Luckmann T (1966) The social construction of reality: a treatise in the sociology of knowledge. Anchor Books, Chicago

Capra F (1996) The web of life. Doubleday, New York

Dekker SWA (2006) The Field Guide to Understanding Human Error. Ashgate, Hampshire

Dekker SWA (2011) Systems Thinking 1.0 and Systems Thinking 2.0: Complexity science and a new conception of "cause". Aviat Focus 2:21–39

Dekker SWA (2012) Drift into failure. From hunting broken components to understanding complex systems. Ashgate, Farnham

[17]For the role that power plays in the safety community, Dekker and Nyce 2014.

Dekker SWA, Nyce JM (2014) There is safety in power, or power in safety. Saf Sci 67:44–49
Dekker SWA, Cilliers P, Hofmeyr JH (2011) The complexity of failure: implication of complexity theory for safety investigations. Saf Sci 49:939–945
Firesmith DG (2003) Common concepts underlying safety, security, and survivability engineering. Technical Report CMU/SEI-2003-TN-033, Software Engineering Institute Carnegie Mellon University
Gergen KJ, Gergen M (2003) Social construction: a reader. SAGE Publications Ltd, London
Giddens A (1984) The constitution of society outline of the theory of structuration. University of California Press, Berkeley
Larson EV, Savych B (2005) American public support for US military operations from Mogadishu to Baghdad, RAND Arroyo Center report. RAND Corporation, Santa Monica
Marais K, Dulac N, Leveson N (2004) Beyond normal accidents and high reliability organizations: the need for an alternative approach to safety in complex systems. In: Presented at the Engineering Systems Division (ESD) Symposium, MIT, Cambridge, MA, March 29–31
NOS (2014) NSS is grootste klus voor Defensie, NOS, March 19, 2014
NSS (2014) http://ww.nss2014.com. Accessed 20 Aug 2015
Perrow C (1999) Normal accidents: living with high-risk systems. Princeton University Press, Princeton
Pettersen KA, Bjørnskau T (2015) Organizational contradictions between safety and security—perceived challenges and ways of integrating critical infrastructure protection in civil aviation. Saf Sci 71:167–177
Stacey RD (1995) The science of complexity: an alternative perspective for strategic change processes. Strat Manag J 16:477–495
Vaughan D (1997) The Challenger Launch Decision. Risky technology, culture, and deviance at NASA. The University of Chicago Press, Chicago
Wheatley M (1992) Leadership and the new science. Berrett-Koehler, San Francisco

Chapter 8
Psychological Safety During Military Integrations

Frederik Wermser, Susanne Täuber, Peter Essens and Eric Molleman

Abstract Increased military cooperation between member states of the European Union is a political given. The Netherlands and Germany form a spearhead in this process by integrating entire military units (i.e., brigades, battalions, companies) into higher-order units of the respective other nation (i.e., divisions, brigades, battalions). Researchers and decision makers emphasize that military integration is a long-term process for which the costs come before the benefits. In this chapter we will suggest that, in addition to the well-recognized financial, technical and procedural challenges resulting from military integrations, attention has to be paid to challenges revolving around soldiers' identities and cultural differences. Integrations are likely to disrupt soldiers' social environment and bear the risk of (intercultural) tensions at work—thereby impeding perceptions of psychological safety. By providing an understanding of the cultural and identity processes unfolding during a military integration this chapter aims to inform decision makers and encourage future research on how to overcome the initial psychological costs of military integrations.

F. Wermser (✉) · S. Täuber · P. Essens · E. Molleman
Faculty of Economics and Business, University of Groningen,
Groningen, The Netherlands
e-mail: f.l.wermser@rug.nl

S. Täuber
e-mail: s.tauber@rug.nl

P. Essens
Centre of Expertise Human Resource Management & Organizational Behaviour,
University of Groningen, Groningen, The Netherlands
e-mail: p.j.m.d.essens@rug.nl

E. Molleman
e-mail: h.b.m.molleman@rug.nl

R. Beeres et al. (eds.), *NL ARMS Netherlands Annual Review of Military Studies 2016*, NL ARMS, DOI 10.1007/978-94-6265-135-7_8

Keywords Military integrations · Organizational identification · Identity continuity · Cultural differences · Expectancy violation · Psychological safety

Contents

8.1 Introduction

> Military cooperation is no longer a choice, but a necessity! The German and Dutch armed forces are ready to take their cooperation to an unprecedented level of integration. It entails the harmonization of requirements, procedures, education and training. And yes, it will take time. But it is dogged that does it! As I said, it involves long-term commitment. At every level! It involves sincere determination to succeed. It involves commitment that reaches well beyond budgetary constraints and the push for efficiency. I am convinced that today's declaration will result in a deeper cooperation between our two countries … and that it will help to create and maintain the capabilities Europe needs.[1]

Since the minister's speech in 2013 the Dutch 11 Airmobile Brigade and 43 Mechanised Brigade have been put under the command of German divisions. This form of integration is unique in Europe and positions the Netherlands and Germany at the spearhead of bi-national military cooperation in Europe. Despite all due enthusiasm about the potential benefits of military integrations (e.g., retaining knowledge, maintaining and gaining capabilities), there is a general awareness that the costs come before the benefits and that therefore, as Hennis-Plasschaert notes, military integrations are a demanding long-term process.[2]

In this chapter we will explain why in addition to "the harmonization of requirements, procedures, education and training" a military integration also entails the harmonization of identities and culture.[3] To this end, we will describe

[1] Hennis-Plasschaert 2013.

[2] Bekkers et al. 2012.

[3] Hennis-Plasschaert 2013.

psychological processes revolving around identity and culture that are likely to unfold in soldiers involved in integrations. These processes are related to perceptions of psychological safety and can, if not taken care of, interfere with organizational processes, which ultimately may hamper military organizations' operational readiness. Moreover, we will outline how the psychological effects of integrations may influence involved military organizations at large. First, however, we will point out characteristics of military integrations that determine the context within which the processes of identification and culture develop.

8.2 Military Integrations - A Novel Type of Integration

The large majority of psychological research on organizational integrations is conducted in the context of different types of business integrations (i.e., mergers, joint ventures, alliances).[4] These different types represent how tightly organizations are coupled through integration: in a merger two companies fuse completely—two companies become one; in a joint venture two or more companies set up a new company together; and alliances represent a mere contractual commitment to close collaboration. However, none of these categories accurately represents the pattern of integration that has been applied to the recent integrations of Dutch and German army units - here, *complete* units are assigned to higher-order units of the other nation. For example, the integration of the Dutch 43 Mechanised Brigade and the German 1. Panzer division follows a novel pattern of integration sometimes compared with a 'Russian Matryoshka Doll': The 1. Panzer division (the biggest 'doll') gets command over the 43 Mechanised Brigade (the second biggest 'doll'). In turn, a German battalion is assigned to 43 Mechanised Brigade. Finally, a Dutch squadron is assigned to this German battalion. This unique integration pattern is pioneering and likely to become a blueprint for future bi-national military integrations in Europe. As we will illustrate below, this novel type of integration shares certain features with the types commonly researched in the organizational psychology literature. We will therefore translate insights from this literature to the military integrations (i.e., assigning complete units) discussed here.

8.2.1 Parent and Integrated Organization

In relation to considerations of national sovereignty (i.e., what if an integration partner takes another political stance?) the depth of bi-national military cooperation is often limited.[5] For example, the Dutch armed forces have only integrated

[4] De Man 2006.

[5] Bekkers et al. 2012; Van Outeren 2014.

two of their three army brigades with Germany and also cooperate with other nations (see e.g., UK/NL Landing Force of the Dutch navy). Additionally, substantial decisive power remains national. For instance, the allocation of resources to the Dutch army brigades under German command remains the task of the Dutch army command (CLAS) and the decision about deployment of soldiers of the brigades to missions requires approval of the Dutch government. Therefore, a distinction between the *integrated organization* (e.g., the 1. Panzer division and all its subunits) and the *parent organization* (e.g., the Dutch army) applies.[6] This distinction has, as will be outlined in Sect. 8.3, important consequences for soldiers' psychological group memberships.

8.2.2 Identity

From the literature on business integrations, such as mergers, joint ventures, alliances, it can be learned that when not managed well, such integrations may fail resulting in early termination, with reported failure rates ranging from 50 to 70 %.[7] Research over the past years has demonstrated that these failure rates can, to a large extend, be explained by dynamics of identification and culture as main factors for successful organizational integrations.[8] In particular, the harmonization of the unique identities, norms, and values that characterize each organization involved has been suggested as the main determinant of successful organizational integrations.[9]

Research on these processes in the military context is scarce. However, there are at least three noteworthy exceptions: First, Jetten and Hutchison conducted a study on the integration of military regiments in Scotland.[10] They showed that a perceived break with the historical past of regiments (that is a discontinuity of identities) was associated with a strong resistance against the integration. Second, Moelker and colleagues examined cultural differences in the bi-national military integration of the 1 (German/Netherlands) Corps.[11] In this context, they describe an incident surrounding the ISAF3 deployment in Kabul, Afghanistan, where "cultural frictions and differences in procedures and attitudes towards security" led to serious tensions between German and Dutch troops.[12] Third, Essens and Bekkers conducted research among (former) commanders of a Communication and Information Systems battalion in

---

[6] Li et al. 2002.

[7] Li et al. 2002; De Man 2006.

[8] Hogg and Terry 2000; Ullrich and Van Dick 2007; Stahl and Voigt 2008; Teerikangas and Very 2006.

[9] For an overview, see Giessner et al. 2016.

[10] Jetten and Hutchinson 2011.

[11] Moelker et al. 2007.

[12] Moelker et al. 2007, p. 497.

which Germans and Dutch work side by side.[13] They highlight the difficulties and advantages of this form of military cooperation and identify as one of their core points that social costs (i.e., the extra effort required to effectively interact with soldiers of another nation) of military integration is often underestimated. These studies conducted in the military context give important indications about identity and cultural processes that unfold in soldiers during integrations. However, they did not capture how these identity and cultural processes develop over time, which one needs to understand to be able to identify how well they develop and when to intervene if needed. In the following we will therefore combine insights from different literatures to develop theoretical ideas that can inform decision makers, and encourage future research on how to manage and foster the processes of harmonization of the unique identities, norms, and values. While the bi-national military integrations we discuss, as they result from political decisions and not business, are unlikely to fail, suboptimal performance would not be acceptable.

8.3 A Social Identity Approach to Integrations

A useful theoretical framework to better understand the identification processes at play during an organizational integration is the *social identity approach*.[14] The social identity approach combines the related theories of social identity and self-categorization theory.[15] The fundamental idea of social identity theory is that individuals derive a positive sense of self from the membership in groups that are positively distinct from relevant other groups.[16] Self-categorization theory contributes to this idea by identifying when and why individuals are more likely to act in terms of their social identity rather than as self-focused individuals.[17] Specifically, cues in the environment that make us-them distinctions salient will trigger thoughts, emotions, and behaviours based on individuals' social identity. For example, attending a soccer game between Germany and the Netherlands is likely to trigger Dutchmen to categorize themselves as Dutch (rather than as, for example, John Smith, an employee of firm X, a teacher or an European).

Applied to organizational contexts, this means that employees derive an important part of their self-concept from their belongingness to their specific organization. Van Dick and colleagues suggest that this psychological association with an organization—referred to in the literature as *organizational identification*—is a multi-level phenomenon.[18] Belongingness to an organization can influence employees' self-concepts at the

[13] Essens and Bekkers 2014.

[14] Haslam 2004.

[15] Tajfel and Turner 1979; Turner et al. 1987.

[16] Tajfel and Turner 1979.

[17] Turner et al. 1987.

[18] Van Dick et al. 2004.

superordinate level (i.e., identification with the organization as a whole) and the group level (i.e., identification with subunits within the organization). This section will focus on the superordinate level, which represents an identification with the parent and/or integrated organization. In Sect. 8.4 we will elaborate on the possible importance of identifications at the group level and their relations to identification at the superordinate level.

To the extent that employees identify with their organization, they will have integrated the corresponding norms, values, and goals and will feel loyal towards their organization.[19] The reason why organizational identification is considered so important in integration research is that it is highly relevant for organizational behaviour at the individual, group, and organization level.[20] Organizational identification positively affects performance, job satisfaction, and positive work behaviours such as taking charge, creative performance, and showing commitment to an organization beyond what is contractually required.[21] At the same time, organizational identification decreases negative work behaviours such as turnover and cynicism.[22] Importantly, organizational identification also fosters employees' perception of meaning, belonging, and control at the workplace, thereby contributing to employees' experience of their organization as psychologically safe.[23]

Motivated by the importance of organizational identification for work-related outcomes, research has focused on the development of a common identity among all employees that belong to an integrated organization. In the case of the integrations of both the 11 Airmobile Brigade and the 43 Mechanised Brigade with German divisions, those integrated organizations emerge as a new category of identification, while soldiers' parent organizations (i.e., the respective nation's army) persist as a category of identification. In such a setting, soldiers may solely identify with either their parent *or* the integrated organization or they may identify with *both* of them.[24]

Research indicates that it is undesirable if individuals solely identify with their parent organization, as in consequence they will pursue the parent but not the integrated organization's goals.[25] Moreover, it becomes more likely that frictions arise between employees from different parent organizations.[26] Such frictions have been related to negative outcomes such as lower job satisfaction and lower levels of cooperation, as well as increased conflict and discrimination. That individuals only identify with the integrated organization is unlikely.[27] Several factors have been

[19] Hogg and Terry 2000; Gleibs et al. 2013; Giessner 2011; Giessner et al. 2011; Li et al. 2002.

[20] Kreiner and Ashforth 2004.

[21] Kreiner and Ashforth 2004; Vadera et al. 2013.

[22] Kreiner and Ashforth 2004.

[23] Kreiner and Ahsforth 2004; Edmondson and Roloff 2009.

[24] Li et al. 2002.

[25] Li et al. 2002.

[26] Giessner et al. 2011.

[27] Giessner et al. 2011.

identified as impeding the development of a shared identification with the integrated organization, for example, status differences, perceptions of threatened group status and doubts about the legitimacy of the integration.[28] In terms of organizational outcomes it therefore seems most desirable that individuals identify with their parent *and* the integrated organization because than they are willing to pursue the goals of the parent as well as those of the integrated organization.

In Sect. 8.5 we will discuss psychological processes that may be able to facilitate identification with both organizations. First, however, we will discuss yet another factor, which is likely to impede the development of a common identification with the integrated organization in the next section: Diverging cultural norms and values of employees from different parent organizations and (incorrect) expectations about cultural similarity.

8.4 Cultural Differences and Expectations

A fundamental insight of psychological research on intergroup relations is that individuals hold particularly positive attitudes towards members of a group they identify with—the so called *ingroup*. However, research also indicates that ingroup membership is linked to norms and values. Ingroup members violating these norms and values are perceived as more negative than individuals violating the very same norms and values, who are not part of the ingroup.[29] Thus, when individuals categorize another individual as belonging to their ingroup (independent of the other individual's self-categorization) they will react more harshly to violations of (seemingly) shared ingroup norms.

Research suggests that soldiers from different nations identify with each other based on a shared professional identification—they all are soldiers.[30] Consequently, they should expect to share certain norms and values with other soldiers independent of national and parent organization affiliations. However, extensive anecdotal evidence suggests that norms and values which soldiers from different nations attach to being a soldier can differ. Due to this difference, certain behaviours may be evaluated as normative by some soldiers and as a transgression of norms by others. Thus, soldiers, who consider military personnel from many nations to be part of a common ingroup (based on the shared occupation), are likely to perceive soldiers who behave differently as transgressing shared norms—which results in particularly negative attitudes towards these transgressors. This idea finds further support in research on the role of cultural differences during organizational integrations, the expectancy violation theory, and a model of acculturation.

---

[28] Giessner et al. 2006.

[29] Abrams et al. 2003; Christensen et al. 2004.

[30] Farell 2001; Johansen et al. 2013.

Research on bi- and multinational integrations suggests that (expectations about) strong cultural differences can, somewhat paradoxically, contribute to a more successful integration of organizations. When low cultural closeness is assumed leaders and employees involved in an integration are more understanding of and attentive to culture differences.[31] Thus, expecting that an integration partner is similar (e.g., because both integrating organizations are military) can impede the integration process. This idea corresponds with the *expectancy violation theory*, which proposes that individuals make assumptions about what is typical or appropriate behaviour in a given situation.[32] When the other deviates from these expectations, the result is cognitive arousal and (mostly) negative evaluations of the behaviour in question (some violations reflect pro-norm deviance and are evaluated positively).[33] This suggests a greater potential for expectation violation and the resulting frustration for integrations of presumably similar organizations. The same dynamics also reflect in Hofstede and Hofstede's model of acculturation.[34] This model describes that after a first phase of curiosity and euphoria about an integration, which is usually characterized by very positive feelings towards each other, individuals may start to realize that cultural differences are bigger than previously expected, resulting in the so called culture shock and negative feelings towards the integration partner. Notably, experiencing another group as not predictable and their values as different from and incompatible with the norms of one's ingroup negatively affects feelings of trust towards the other.[35]

8.5 Psychological Safety, Disrupted Processes and Operational Readiness

In this section, we will outline in more detail how dynamics of organizational identification and culture in the context of military integrations can decrease individuals' sense of psychological safety—and how low psychological safety, in turn, can disrupt organizational processes which are relevant to accomplish operational readiness. Psychological safety describes people's perceptions of the consequences of taking interpersonal risks in a particular context such as a workplace.[36] Thus, work environments can be considered psychological safe when employees hold the shared belief that their team or subunit is safe for interpersonal risk-taking—they have "a sense of confidence that the team will not embarrass,

[31] Stahl and Voigt 2008.

[32] Burgoon 1993.

[33] Abrams et al. 2002.

[34] Hofstede and Hofstede 2005.

[35] Bijlsma-Frankema et al. 2015.

[36] Edmondson and Lei 2014.

reject or punish someone for speaking up".[37] In such a psychological safe work setting, employees can focus on the achievement of collective goals and the prevention of problems rather than on self-protection.[38]

Drawing on the above sections, we suggest that in the context of military integrations, soldiers' perceived psychological safety is likely to be impeded through at least two psychological effects. First, as indicated before, frictions can develop between soldiers from different nations if some soldiers identify only with their parent organization and not with the integrated organization.[39] Soldiers who do not identify with the integrated organization are more likely to focus primarily on goals of their national ingroup and to exclude and discriminate against soldiers from the other nation. Soldiers who become the target of such actions will have to defend themselves and perceive lower psychological safety at work. This relates to the notion of disengagement as related to psychological safety by Kahn.[40] Rather than commonly engaging in the solution of potential problems, employees disengage from interaction and focus on psychological self-protection.

Second, psychological safety is likely to be impeded due to expectancy violations. Above it was suggested that soldiers often expect other soldiers—independent of their nationality or parent organization—to be similar, because they share the same profession, and that this expectation is likely to be violated by someone from another nation. Such expectancy violations may have negative effects for the psychological safety of persons whose expectations were violated and persons who (unintentionally) violated the other persons' expectations. The violators may feel less free to speak up, as they (despite good intentions) received disapproval for previous behaviour (which unintentionally transgressed the other group's norms). Thus, lowered psychological safety is linked to uncertainty about the behavioural norms that apply in the work context. In turn, the persons whose expectations were violated may perceive lower psychological safety at work because they feel that the soldiers from the other nation are less trustworthy. After all, trust is commonly defined as being "based on positive expectations of the intentions of behaviour of another"[41] and a lack of trust is related to a reduced willingness to take risks.[42]

Research indicates that psychologically safety and, as a strongly related phenomenon, trust are related to smooth organizational processes when high and distortions of this processes when low. For example, high psychological safety has been related to better team learning and performance, high levels of job involvement and extortion of effort, as well as smoother collaboration.[43] In contrast, when

---

[37] Edmondson 1999, p. 354.

[38] Edmondson and Roloff 2009.

[39] Li et al. 2002.

[40] Kahn 1990.

[41] Rosseau et al. 1998, p. 395.

[42] Schoorman et al. 2007.

[43] Edmondson 1999; Baer and Frese 2003.

individuals feel psychological unsafe at their workplace they have been found to withdraw personally, cognitively and emotionally from their work.[44] Similarly, trust has been related to positive outcomes such as increased information sharing, group effectiveness and cooperation, whereas in settings of low trust individuals were found to invest considerable energy in monitoring others and interpret ambiguous information negatively.[45] Thus, psychological processes revolving around identity and culture that occur in the context of military integrations can potentially impede the psychological safety of soldiers, which in turn can disrupt important organizational processes (e.g., communication and collaboration). It therefore seems possible that the operational readiness of integrated military organizations is impeded when harmonization of identities and culture is not realized—and, as we will suggest in the next section, the effects of harmonizing identity and culture (or failing to do so) may even spread beyond the integrated organization.

8.6 Personnel Rotation and Transmission of Attitudes

Most military organizations apply an institutionalized three to five year rhythm in which higher-ranking soldiers rotate positions.[46] Therefore, independent of promotions or other career events, these soldiers change their position and often their unit within the armed forces on a regular base. This implies that new staff continuously enters the integrated organization (*incoming*) and that other staff continuously leaves the integrated organization and enters (back into) the respective parent organization (*outgoing*). This phenomenon adds substantial significance to two features of military integrations.

First, the rotation requires ways to uphold and transmit the newly developed identification with the integrated organization and the norms and values attached to it. In integrated units a challenge arises from the continuous flow of incoming military staff and constant effort has to be undertaken to socialize incoming soldiers to accept the integrated organization's identities and norms. In addition, the newcomers are in turn likely to constantly reshape the integrated organization's common identity.[47] One possibility to address this unique challenge for military integrations could be to couple identity, norms, and values with the respective functions and professional roles that are present in a team—because these functions and roles remain part of the team, thus are stable, and may therefore be suited for the transmission of core values and identity of the integrated organization.[48]

44 Kahn 1990.

45 Adams and Webb 2002.

46 Jans and Frazer-Jans 2004.

47 Nielsen and Miller 1997.

48 Bettencourt and Sheldon 2001.

Second, the rotation requires that attention be paid to 'contagion' effects, because soldiers are likely to share positive as well as negative experiences with other soldiers. However, psychological research indicates that negative information and attitudes spread faster and are more pervasive than positive experiences.[49] For instance, Bijlsma-Frankema et al. speculate that within-group convergence, the tendency of a group in conflict to "increasingly share negative perceptions of the other group", contributes to an increase in negative attributions and consequently distrust between groups.[50] Thus, soldiers who experienced the integration as negatively and rotate from an integrated organization into other units of their nation's military, are likely to spread and foster these negative attitudes in their new units. This can cause situations in which soldiers, without ever having had contact with another nation's military staff, develop negative attitudes towards members of this staff based on 'second-hand' information and what one might call 'contagion'. This will reduce the willingness among these members to join the integrated organization. On a more positive note, a similar (yet supposedly weaker) effect may contribute to the spreading of positive 'second hand' attitudes throughout the military organization. In sum, this underscores that management of identity and expectations is particularly important during military integrations—only soldiers who positively identify with the integrated organization and feel psychologically safe in this environment will spread positive intergroup attitudes, pro-actively collaborate with others, and be able to perform at their best.

8.7 How Can Identification and Cultural Processes Develop Positively?

The previous sections of this chapter discussed the importance of harmonizing identities and culture during the military integration process in order to foster psychological safety and, consequently, organizational effectiveness, and we described related psychological processes. In the following paragraphs, we will discuss the processes that support the development of identification with the integrated organization while simultaneously keeping the identification with the parent organization. Finally, we will outline how considerations about reciprocal expectations can lead to a reduction of tensions resulting from violated expectations and cultural differences in the context of military integrations.

[49] Skowronski and Carlston 1987, 1989.

[50] Bijlsma-Frankema et al. 2015, p. 4.

8.7.1 Common Identification and Perceived Identity Continuity

As has been outlined above, high identification with both the parent and the integrated organization is likely to result in positive organizational outcomes such as high psychological safety and job performance. However, identification with the integrated organization seldom reaches high-levels for all individuals involved in an integration, because factors such as pre-integration status differences and diverging expectations about the integration impede its development.[51] A possible solution to overcome the negative effects of these factors is the enhancement of individuals' perception of the continuity of their parent organization's identity. In the following we will elaborate on these psychological processes, which may facilitate soldiers' perception of being represented in both the parent and the integrated organization.

Research on *identity continuity* indicates how identification with both organizations could be realized.[52] The basic idea of identity continuity is that individuals have to feel and experience that elements of their self-concept linked to the parent organization are also represented in the integrated organization. For example, perceiving that one's conscientious manner of working, which was highly appreciated in the parent organization, is also valued in the integrated organization makes it more likely that soldiers identify with the integrated organization.

We propose that identity continuity derives largely from individuals' identification with multiple groups. Such identification goes beyond the distinction between the two organizations. For example, military organizations offer and actively signify (e.g., through badges) multiple group-level categories of identification (e.g., profession, rank, section, armed service branch). If identification with these groups is complemented with the awareness that the groups are nested in both organizations, a sense of identity continuity emerges.[53] For example, a Dutch army corporal with a background in mechanics who works for the logistic section has many potential categorizations that are more than the simple distinction of being a soldier of one nation or the other. A soldier embracing many of these possible categories simultaneously is more likely to recognize elements of identification significant to him- or herself in the integrated organization than a soldier focusing exclusively on one dimension. Haslam et al. describe such as "a situation in which employees define themselves in terms of a relatively complex superordinate identity (as members of the focal organizational unit), but are simultaneously aware of the subgroup memberships from which that identity has been forged".[54] This situation is likely to produce a range of positive organizational outcomes.

However, research indicates that adapting to an altered social environment at work will require additional (mental) resources.[55] This suggests that when persons

---

[51] Giessner et al. 2006; Gleibs et al. 2013.

[52] Lupina-Wegener et al. 2014; Van Leeuwen et al. 2003; Van Knippenberg and Van Leeuwen 2001.

[53] Amiot et al. 2015.

[54] Haslam et al. 2003, p. 95.

[55] Roccas and Brewer 2002.

experience negative emotions or are mentally exhausted, they are more likely to rely on less complex representations (e.g., focus on the group distinction most salient in a given situation). Therefore, during military integrations working time needs to be reserved and planned for soldiers to do 'identity work'.

8.7.2 Cultural Differences and Expectation Management

Emphasizing a shared professional identification of being a soldier may raise soldiers' expectations that their comrades from other nations embrace very similar values and norms. We argue that such expectations may result in negative affect between the groups, if proven wrong. Johansen et al., for example, propose that military identities revolve around aspects such as *idealism* (i.e., serving one's country), *professionalism* (i.e., instrumental focus on the ability to win combats), and *warriorism* (i.e., desire or attraction to be involved in combat).[56] Even though most soldiers will to some degree identify with these aspects of being a soldier, the concrete norms and values attached to these aspects may diverge substantially. This effect may be reinforced by a perception of a common military identity as 'holistic'—meaning that it is expected to provide shared behavioural norms for many, if not all, situations in a soldiers' life.[57]

However, a common military identity may provide a useful layer of identification during military integration, using the following strategy: If an explicit exchange about what it basically means to be a soldier—which norms and behaviour it prescribes—is encouraged, and such strategy is matched by comprehending potentially diverging norms and behaviours linked with other identities in the military context, then a development of incorrect expectations may be prevented and a more objective representation of cultural similarities and differences can be accomplished. Still, an initial culture shock may never be fully prevented and the development of mutual understanding requires time, as the research by Hofstede and Hofstede has convincingly shown.[58]

8.8 Conclusion

In this chapter some of the challenges revolving around soldiers' identities and cultural differences in the context of military integrations are being discussed. We argue, that, if these challenges are not being addressed, soldiers' psychological safety may be impeded which can result in disrupted organizational processes

56 Johansen et al. 2013.

57 Turner-Zwinkels et al. 2015.

58 Hofstede and Hofstede 2005.

and ultimately interferences with the operational readiness of the integrated military organization. Identification of soldiers with both the parent and the integrated organization is identified as a desirable state facilitated by perceptions of identity continuity derived from identification with multiple groups that are nested in both organizations. Expectations about cultural similarity and shared norms based on a common professional identification (i.e., being a solider) may be violated because of the stronger cultural differences, which may result in negative attitudes. We suggest that by explicitly addressing similarities of norms and values attached to a military identity and at the same time building understanding and appreciating the diverging norms and behaviours linked with the other identities negative experiences and attitudes may be prevented. This may also guard against a possible 'contagion' of the parent organization at large when soldiers rotate back to their parent organization. In sum, drawing on a broad scope of research literature, this chapter points out important psychological processes that should be considered in order to uphold soldiers' psychological safety during military integrations. Since there is limited research available on how precisely these processes unfold in the context of the bi-national military integrations discussed in this chapter, more extensive empirical research is needed. This will help to develop clearer guidance on how to address identity and cultural factors in the building of operationally ready, bi-nationally integrated units.

References

Abrams D, Marques J, Bown N, Dougill M (2002) Anti-norm and pro-norm deviance in the bank and on the campus: two experiments on subjective group dynamics. Group Process Intergroup Relat 5:163–182

Abrams D, Rutland A, Cameron L (2003) The development of subjective group dynamics: children's judgments of normative and deviant in-group and out-group individuals. Child Dev 74:1840–1856

Adams BD, Webb RDG (2002) Trust in small military teams. Presented at 7th International Command and Control Research and Technology Symposium, Québec

Amiot CE, de la Sablonniere R, Smith LE, Smith JR (2015) Capturing changes in social identities over time and how they become part of the self-concept. Soc Pers Psychol Compass 9:171–187

Baer M, Frese M (2003) Innovation is not enough: climates for initiative and psychological safety, process innovations, and firm performance. J Organ Behav 24:45–68

Bekkers F, De Boer M, Van Esch J, Korteweg R, Selleslaghs J, Wijninga P (2012) De waarde van defensie. The Hague Centre for Strategic Studies, The Hague

Bettencourt BA, Sheldon K (2001) Social roles as mechanism for psychological need satisfaction within social groups. J Pers Soc Psychol 81:1131–1143

Bijlsma-Frankema K, Sitkin SB, Weibel A (2015) Distrust in the balance: the emergence and development of intergroup distrust in a court of law. Organ Sci 26:1018–1039

Burgoon JK (1993) Interpersonal expectations, expectancy violations, and emotional communication. J Lang Soc Psychol 12:30–48

Christensen PN, Rothgerber H, Wood W, Matz DC (2004) Social norms and identity relevance: a motivational approach to normative behavior. Pers Soc Psychol Bull 30:1295–1309

De Man AP (2006) Alliantiebesturing: samenwerking als precisie-instrument. Koninklijke Van Gorcum, The Hague

Edmondson AC (1999) Psychological safety and learning behavior in work teams. Adm Sci Q 44:350–383
Edmondson AC, Lei Z (2014) Psychological safety: the history, renaissance, and future of an interpersonal construct. Annu Rev Organ Psychol Organ Behav 1:23–43
Edmondson AC, Roloff KS (2009) Overcoming barriers to collaboration: psychological safety and learning in diverse teams. In: Salas E, Goodwin GF, Burke CS (eds) Team effectiveness in complex organizations: cross-disciplinary perspectives and approaches. Routledge/Taylor & Francis Group, New York, pp 183–208
Farrell T (2001) Transnational norms and military development: constructing Ireland's professional army. Eur J Int Relat 7:63–102
Essens PJMD, Bekkers F (2014) Cost benefit analysis of strategic cooperation: case study deep integration. TNO, Soesterberg
Giessner SR, Horton KE, Humborstad SIW (2016) Identity management during organizational mergers: empirical insights and practical advice. Soc Issues Policy Rev 10:47–81
Giessner SR (2011) Identity management key to successful mergers. RSM Insight 2:7–9
Giessner SR, Viki GT, Otten S, Terry DJ, Täuber S (2006) The challenge of merging: merger patterns, premerger status, and merger support. Pers Soc Psychol Bull 32:339–352
Giessner SR, Ullrich J, Van Dick R (2011) Social identity and corporate mergers. Soc Pers Psychol Compass 5:333–345
Gleibs IH, Täuber S, Viki GT, Giessner SR (2013) When what we get is not what we want: the role of implemented versus desired merger patterns in support for mergers. Social Psychology 44:177–190
Haslam SA (2004) Psychology in organizations: the social identity approach, 2nd edn. Sage, London
Haslam SA, Eggins RA, Reynolds KJ (2003) The ASPIRe model: actualizing social and personal identity resources to enhance organizational outcomes. J Occup Organ Psychol 76:83–113
Hennis-Plasschaert JA (2013) Address by the Netherlands Minister of Defence on the occasion of the Berlin Strategy Conference. https://www.government.nl/government/contents/members-of-cabinet/jeanine-hennis-plasschaert/documents/speeches/2013/05/28/berlin-strategy-conference. Accessed 4 March 2016
Hofstede G, Hofstede GJ (2005) Cultures and organizations: software of the mind, 2nd edn. McGraw-Hill, New York, NY
Hogg MA, Terry DJ (2000) Social identity and self-categorization processes in organizational contexts. Acad Manag Rev 25:121–140
Jans N, Frazer-Jans J (2004) Career development, job rotation, and professional performance. Armed Forces Soc 30:255–277
Jetten J, Hutchison P (2011) When groups have a lot to lose: historical continuity enhances resistance to a merger. Eur J Soc Psychol 41:335–343
Johansen RB, Laberg JC, Martinussen M (2013) Measuring military identity: scale development and psychometric evaluations. Soc Behav Pers 41:861–880
Kahn WA (1990) Psychological conditions of personal engagement and disengagement at work. Acad Manag J 33:692–724
Kreiner GE, Ashforth BE (2004) Evidence toward an expanded model of organizational identification. J Organ Behav 25:1–27
Li J, Xin K, Pillutla M (2002) Multi-cultural leadership teams and organizational identification in international joint ventures. Int J Human Res Manag 13:320–337
Lupina-Wegener A, Drzensky F, Ullrich J, Van Dick R (2014) Focusing on the bright tomorrow? A longitudinal study of organizational identification and projected continuity in a corporate merger. Br J Soc Psychol 53:752–772
Moelker R, Soeters J, Vom Hagen U (2007) Sympathy, the cement of interoperability: findings on ten years of German-Netherlands military cooperation. Armed Forces Soc 33:496–517
Nielsen ME, Miller CE (1997) The transmission of norms regarding group decision rules. Pers Soc Psychol Bull 23:516–525

Roccas S, Brewer M (2002) Social identity complexity. Pers Soc Psychol Rev 6:88–106
Rousseau DM, Sitkin SB, Burt RS, Camerer C (1998) Not so different after all: a cross-discipline view of trust. Acad Manag Rev 23:393–404
Schoorman FD, Mayer RC, Davis JH (2007) An integrative model of organizational trust: past, present, and future. Acad Manag Rev 32:344–354
Skowronski JJ, Carlston DE (1987) Social judgment and social memory: the role of cue diagnosticity in negativity, positivity, and extremity biases. J Pers Soc Psychol 52:689–699
Skowronski JJ, Carlston DE (1989) Negativity and extremity biases in impression formation: a review of explanations. Psychol Bull 105:131–142
Stahl GK, Voigt A (2008) Do cultural differences matter in mergers and acquisitions? A tentative model and examination. Organ Sci 19:160–176
Tajfel H, Turner JC (1979) An integrative theory of intergroup conflict. In: Austin WG, Worchel S (eds) The social psychology of intergroup relations. Brooks Cole, Monterey, CA, pp 33–48
Teerikangas S, Very P (2006) The culture-performance relationship in M&A: from yes/no to how. Br J Manag 17:31–48
Turner JC, Hogg MA, Oakes PJ, Reicher SD, Wetherell MS (1987) Rediscovering the social group: a self-categorization theory. Blackwell, Oxford
Turner-Zwinkels FM, Postmes T, Van Zomeren M (2015) Achieving harmony among different social identities within the self-concept: the consequences of internalizing a group-based philosophy of life. PLoS ONE 10:e0137879
Ullrich J, Van Dick R (2007) The group psychology of mergers and acquisitions: lessons from the social identity approach. Adv Mergers Acquis 6:1–15
Vadera AK, Pratt MG, Mishra P (2013) Constructive deviance in organizations: integrating and moving forward. J Manag 39:1221–1276
Van Dick R, Wagner U, Stellmacher J, Christ O (2004) The utility of a broader conceptualization of organizational identification: which aspects really matter? J Occup Organ Psychol 77:171–191
Van Knippenberg D, Van Leeuwen E (2001) Organizational identity after a merger: sense of continuity as the key to postmerger identification. In: Hogg MA, Terry DJ (eds) Social identity processes in organizational contexts. Psychology Press, Sussex, pp 249–264
Van Leeuwen E, Van Knippenberg D, Ellemers N (2003) Continuing and changing group identities: the effects of merging on social identification and ingroup bias. Pers Soc Psychol Bull 29:679–690
Van Outeren E (2014) De orders komen nu van een Duitse generaal. http://www.nrc.nl/next/2014/06/11/de-orders-komen-nu-van-een-duitse-generaal-1388487. Accessed 15 January 2016

Chapter 9
Can Posttraumatic Stress Disorder Be Prevented?

Tessa op den Buijs

Abstract This chapter gives an insight in the possibilities and limitations of the prevention of Posttraumatic Stress Disorder (PTSD). An elaboration upon the diagnosis, criteria, onset and prevalence demonstrates the enormous impact of PTSD. Prevalence rates vary between countries and with the intensity of missions, but are lower in non-US Western countries. The risk factors for PTSD are well documented, as well as relationships between PTSD and an individual's psychological, biological, and social functioning. Less research is focused on protective factors for PTSD. Although resilience is an important protective factor for early prevention, current prevention strategies based on this concept are not very effective. The time frame after the trauma (*golden hours*) is important for applying psychological and pharmacological preventing strategies. It is not clear yet what kind of prevention will be effective in the future.

Keywords Posttraumatic stress disorder · Trauma · Combat exposure · Early secondary prevention · Risk factors

Contents

T. op den Buijs (✉)
Faculty of Military Sciences, Netherlands Defence Academy, Breda, The Netherlands
e-mail: tp.od.buijs@mindef.nl

R. Beeres et al. (eds.), *NL ARMS Netherlands Annual Review of Military Studies 2016*, NL ARMS, DOI 10.1007/978-94-6265-135-7_9

9.1 Introduction

Modern military missions impose unique demands and risks on soldiers not often seen with any type of civilian occupations. These demands affect their well-being and performance. Soldiers put their own safety at risk to perform their tasks during these high-risk and intense operational missions. Most of them are aware of the risks that go with the job, and hence the chance of physical and psychological injury.[1] The nature of military missions (e.g., Iraq, Afghanistan) makes exposure to horrible and life-threatening experiences a possibility for all deployed military personnel. These experiences can lead to severe stress and Posttraumatic Stress Disorder (PTSD). The use of new modern technology, new trends in organizing military operations (collaborative units of different countries, services, arms and branches) and the new high-tech systems that modern soldiers work with, offer many security and safety advantages. Among these advantages are a faster pace of deployment and less physical risks for military personnel. Drone operators for example often kill their targets from a continent away. However, this large distance cannot mitigate the war's devastating effects on mental health.[2] Actually, these modern developments also carry inherent risks for severe stress problems and PTSD.

This chapter reports on a literature research on PTSD, which demonstrates the current possibilities and limitations of preventing PTSD in the military. Since the war in Vietnam many scientific studies in military psychology and psychiatry have been conducted on the prevention and treatment of military stress and PTSD. Studies of Dutch soldiers deployed on missions show that 3–10 % of the veterans suffer from PTSD.[3] In the United Stated (US) these rates are significantly higher and vary between 11–20 % (Afghanistan and Iraq veterans). The rates vary with the intensity of the missions abroad. The symptoms of PTSD may include nightmares, flashbacks, severe anxiety and uncontrollable thoughts about the traumatic event.[4] PTSD causes much individual and societal harm and it also causes family stress as it can lead to alcohol abuse, violence and even suicidal behaviour.

---

1 Sookermany et al. 2015.

2 Whetham 2013.

3 Olff et al. 2004.

4 http//www.stress.org/military/. Accessed 2 March 2016.

In the last few years US researchers have noticed an increase in the PTSD prevalence rates and also in the rates of domestic violence, alcohol abuse and suicides among US veterans that returned from Iraq and Afghanistan. This increase of PTSD rates is a growing health concern in the US as they bring along direct medical costs and a loss in productivity (reduced employment and lower earnings). These kinds of PTSD issues generally receive a large amount of public and media attention.[5] For example, in 2015 there was much media attention concerning Dutch Lebanon veterans and the failing PTSD prevention system for these veterans.[6]

Most armed forces have developed (safety) procedures (e.g., Mental Health Care systems, clinical treatment and follow-up care for veterans and their families) to prevent and cure mental stress and PTSD. Current approaches to diminish PTSD generally consist of primary prevention strategies (before the traumatic event, including prevention of the event itself), secondary prevention strategies (between the traumatic event and the development of PTSD), and tertiary prevention and treatment strategies (after the first symptoms of PTSD have become apparent).[7] Primary prevention to prevent acute (combat) stress and PTSD is highly desirable but difficult because of the characteristics of the tasks in this high-risk military occupation and also because of the unpredictability of traumatic events. In addition, specific strategies for primary prevention are scarce. Prevention strategies for stress-related disorders therefore mostly concern secondary and tertiary strategies for the prevention and treatment of PTSD after trauma. These strategies use both psychosocial and pharmacological (multidisciplinary) approaches.[8] The development, implementation and effectiveness of preventing strategies and treatment are based on insights of scientific and clinical prevention studies in (military) psychology, psychiatry and neurology. Since the 1990s, scientific studies have demonstrated a growing interest in positive psychology with a focus on the mechanisms and processes of optimal functioning (such as increasing hardiness and resilience of soldiers in training programs).[9] Moreover, there are some new thoughts on pharmacological primary prevention. Also, new technologies that emerged from biological, biochemical, sleep physiological and brain imaging studies have been added to psychosocial approaches to treat veterans and help their families.[10]

---

[5] Weerts 2008.

[6] http://www.nltimes.nl/2015/12/14/court-netherlands-failed-its-veterans-needing-ptsd-treatment-after-lebanon/. Accessed 11 March 2016.

[7] https://www.iwh.on.ca/wrmb/primary-secondary-and-tertiary-prevention. Accessed 10 March 2016.

[8] https://www.iwh.on.ca/wrmb/primary-secondary-and-tertiary-prevention. Accessed 10 March 2016.

[9] Matthews 2008.

[10] https://www.ucsf.edu/news/2010/08/6001/post-traumatic-stress-disorder-ptsd-prevention-military. Accessed 10 March 2016.

In an attempt to provide in this chapter more insight in the opportunities and restraints in the prevention (and treatment) of PTSD, this chapter will start with a brief elaboration upon the diagnosis, criteria, onset and prevalence, which demonstrates the impact of PTSD. Thereafter, the chapter reviews the risk and protective factors and developments in current primary and secondary prevention approaches in the military. In doing so, the focus is at the most recent concepts and findings in military (positive) psychology and pharmacology for preventing PTSD. Finally, recommendations for preventing PTSD in future operations are discussed.

9.2 Posttraumatic Stress Disorder, Criteria and Onset

The long international military operations in Iraq and Afghanistan have been of a different nature in comparison to the UN peacekeeping missions during the years before. The US military, for example, is now challenged with how best to support the large numbers of the Iraq and Afghanistan veterans with posttraumatic stress symptoms or depression, and anxiety. The diagnosis of these symptoms is based on an official classification of PTSD. PTSD was first officially recognized as a stress disorder by the American Psychiatric Association in 1980 in the third edition of the Diagnostic and Statistical Manual of Mental Disorders (DSM-3). It was classified as an anxiety disorder in the DSM-IV. In 2013 PTSD was reclassified as a "trauma- and stressor-related disorder" in DSM-5 and this new label and formulation has gained widespread acceptance.[11] In the DSM-5, specific diagnostic criteria of PTSD are described. They consist of a history of exposure to a traumatic event that meets specific symptoms from four symptom clusters: 1. intrusion, 2. avoidance, 3. negative alterations in cognitions and mood, and 4. alterations in arousal and reactivity. The next criterion concerns the duration of the symptoms. Furthermore, the assessment of a person's functioning is important and the final criterion is that the symptoms may not be attributable to a substance or to a co-occuring medical condition. New in the DSM-5 are descriptions of delayed expression and a dissociative subtype of PTSD. Dissociation means that people feel disconnected from themselves and/or their surroundings, which can be caused, for example, by a disruption of the normal, subjective integration of one or more aspects of psychological functioning (including memory, identity consciousness, perception and motor control).[12]

PTSD is a unique psychiatric disorder in two ways. Firstly, there usually is a very clear point of onset after experiencing the traumatic event. In the first month

[11] Friedman 2013.

[12] http://www.dsm-5-nl.org/documenten/artikel/33/De-Posttraumatische-Stressstoornis-in-de-DSM-5 30 maart 2015. Accessed 2 March 2016.

after the experience of a trauma one cannot be diagnosed with PTSD. In this stage we speak of an *acute stress disorder*, or in military terms about *combat-related stress* or *combat stress reaction* (CSR). After this first month, people should normally return to normal functioning, which means that the symptom pattern for acute stress disorder must be resolved within 4 weeks of the trauma. If the symptom cluster lasts more than 1 month and up to 3 months, and the symptom pattern fits the characteristics of PTSD, then *acute PTSD* is diagnosed. If the symptoms last more than 3 months, people are diagnosed with *chronic PTSD*. They then do not seem to return to a normal state of functioning. Finally, if the symptoms start after 6 months after military operations soldiers are diagnosed with *delayed-onset PTSD*.[13] For military personnel in operations there are indications that timely frontline application of treatment for combat stress reaction may improve post-deployment mental health outcomes.[14] The second unique feature of PTSD refers to a failure of the normal response to resolve within the normal time frame. The expected response after the exposure to a traumatic event is to experience fear, shock, horror, grief, etcetera. These reactions are normal responses to an abnormal situation that only become diagnosed as a stress disorder or PTSD when these responses do not disappear within a certain time frame.[15] Only a few people do not return to normality. They get stuck in a state of constantly avoiding reminders of the trauma and they become sensitive to anything related to the traumatic event. They re-experience the traumatic event in dreams and flashbacks.[16]

9.3 Posttraumatic Stress Disorder Prevalence in the Military

PTSD is a mental health condition that is triggered by a terrifying event. PTSD is not only related to war or peacekeeping missions, but also to large events, such as the 9/11 event, and terrorist attacks (e.g., Paris 2015; Brussels 2016) and to serious illnesses (heart attacks). More common events such as car accidents for example and work-related accidents may also cause PTSD. About 50 % of the (Western) population would experience a traumatic event.[17] However, approximately 7 % of

[13] http://www.dsm-5-nl.org/documenten/artikel/33/De-Posttraumatische-Stressstoornis-in-de-DSM-5 30 maart 2015. Accessed 2 March 2016.

[14] http://www.dsm-5-nl.org/documenten/artikel/33/De-Posttraumatische-Stressstoornis-in-de-DSM-5 30 maart 2015. Accessed 2 March 2016.

[15] Zohar et al. 2011.

[16] Zohar et al. 2011; Tehrani 2011.

[17] Kessler et al. 2005.

this population will develop PTSD.[18] In Spain and Italy the prevalence of the general population is only 2 % and in North Ireland it is 8.8 %. Sweden and France are in between those rates.[19] In the Netherlands 61 % of the male population and 51 % of the female population will be exposed to a trauma in their life.[20] Women are to be at an increased risk of developing PTSD in comparison with men (10 % for women and 4 % for men) and they also tend to experience different traumas than men.[21] Women are more likely to experience sexual assault and they are more likely to blame themselves.

As described in the introduction, PTSD rates for the military also vary over missions and their intensity. In the US, for example, PTSD rates among veterans of the US Persian Gulf War and the recent conflict in the Middle East varied between 2 and 17 %.[22] Multiple studies of deployed military personnel indicate that 10–18 % of troops serving in Afghanistan and Iraq showed PTSD symptoms following deployment.[23] A 2008 review of available epidemiological studies showed that of the 1.64 million US military personnel who had returned home from Afghanistan and Iraq, approximately 75,000–225,000 (4.6–13.7 %) suffered from PTSD.[24] Burbiel referred in his study to a recent report of the US Department Veterans Affairs, which claims that between 2002 and 2012 approximately 257,000 veterans from Iraq and Afghanistan suffer from PTSD (out of 1.63 million veterans).[25] A Canadian study found similar PTSD prevalence rates for Iraq-deployed personnel (12.7 %) and Afghanistan-deployed personnel (7.1 %).[26]

In contrast, PTSD rates among British and Dutch veterans were generally lower and were less varied, about 3–6 % of returning Iraq War veterans from the United Kingdom (UK) and 3.5 % of returning Dutch Iraq War veterans in 2007.[27] Some Dutch survey studies, however, found higher numbers. This could be explained by differences between diagnostic interviews and the diagnostic accuracy of questionnaires in determining the prevalence of PTSD.[28] Questionnaires could therefore overestimate the rate of PTSD.[29]

18 Zohar et al. 2011.

19 Burbiel 2015.

20 De Jongh and Arts 2004.

21 De Vries and Olff 2009.

22 Richardson et al. 2010.

23 Hoge et al. 2004; Grieger et al. 2006.

24 http://www.rand.org/pubs/monographs/MG720.html. Accessed 2 March 2016.

25 Burbiel 2015.

26 Hines et al. 2014.

27 Jones et al. 2006; Engelhard et al. 2007.

28 McDonald and Calhoun 2010.

29 Engelhard et al. 2007.

In 2009, 2010 and 2012 a bibliographic study and two meta-analyses of longitudinal international studies investigating on the one hand mental health outcomes and on the other hand the prevalence of PTSD, reported different rates in military personnel from different military branches, units and populations.[30] These longitudinal studies all diagnosed PTSD in a similar way and used comparable questionnaires (self-reported PTSD-inventory). PTSD rates found in different UK studies were 2.5 % among a random sample of veterans from all branches deployed after 1999, 4.8 % for regular UK army personnel, and 4 % for regular soldiers and 6 % for army reservists deployed to Iraq in 2003.[31] Not surprisingly, in both meta-analyses a higher PTSD prevalence was found for combat-deployed personnel, army, navy or marines of Canada, UK and US compared to the other services. No clear differences between men and women were found. These longitudinal screening studies have also demonstrated that prevalence rates increase after a second deployment. Milliken collected data in the month before redeployment and also screened data from 4–10 months after the deployment.[32] He found that the prevalence of PTSD increased during this period from 11.8 to 16.7 % for active-duty soldiers. For Army reserve personnel and National Guard personnel the increase was even higher (from 12.7 to 24.5 %). Another study screened within 7 days of redeployment and also 120 days later and found an increase in PTSD from 3 to 8 %.[33]

In conclusion, the prevalence of PTSD seems to be lower in non-US Western countries and there is a lot of variation. Variability in prevalence rates is likely due to differences in countries, in sampling (sampling consisted mainly of convenience samples) and in measurement strategies. Differences were found in samples of military services, units and in the ways of diagnosing.[34] Some studies documented probably PTSD at time points more distal from the soldier's war-zone exposure. The generalization (external validity) of all these epidemiological studies also raises questions, because the respondents served in specific time periods and geographic areas in Iraq and Afghanistan.[35] Also, the symptoms are likely to be affected by overlap with other psychiatric disorders (e.g., anxiety, depression) and with cultural and socio-political factors (e.g., length of deployment) that may differ over time and countries.[36]

---

[30] Litz et al. 2009; Richardson et al. 2010; Pietrzak et al. 2012.

[31] Jones et al. 2006; Iversen et al. 2008; Hotopf et al. 2006.

[32] Milliken et al. 2007.

[33] Bliese et al. 2007.

[34] Pietrzak et al. 2012.

[35] Litz et al. 2009.

[36] Richardson et al. 2010.

9.4 Risk Factors

Risk factors may increase the chance to develop PTSD after being exposed to a traumatic event. These factors include the intensity and duration of the trauma; the experience of another trauma earlier in life; the suffering from anxiety or depression (emotional instability); a lack of a good social support system of family and friends; relatives with mental health problems (such as PTSD and depression); a high-risk job such as military personnel and first responders. The symptoms of PTSD may thus reflect the intensity or severity of the experience, a pre-existing individual trait, or the sensitization from prior trauma exposure of PTSD. Although little is known about the precise influence of predictive factors of PTSD and the immediate response to trauma, examples of specific events that were found to be associated with a higher number of PTSD casualties include combat exposure, childhood neglect and physical abuse, sexual assault, physical attack, and having been threatened with a weapon.[37]

Since the end of the Cold War, researchers have studied military stressors faced by soldiers during peacekeeping operations such as isolation, ambiguity, powerlessness, boredom, and danger/threat.[38] The focus of modern missions, however, such as those in Iraq and Afghanistan, has changed. Since 2000, therefore, studies in the military have focused on combat exposure and on the psychological and psychosomatic risk factors that influence the development of stress and PTSD. Exposure to combat-related stressors has been identified in these studies as a high risk factor for the development of PTSD. The results of a meta-study indicated that it is not so much deployment in general, but combat exposure specifically, which has an adverse effect on mental health.[39] Combat exposure has been defined in these studies by being personally exposed to witnessing: 1. violent death, 2. physical abuse (torture, beating, rape), 3. dead and/or decomposing bodies, 4. mutilated soldiers or civilians, and 5. prisoners of war or refugees.[40] An increase in exposure to these combat-related stressors relates to an increased prevalence of PTSD.[41]

Although PTSD is clearly precipitated by combat exposure, this does not fully determine the development of PTSD. Reported prevalence rates for PTSD indicate that there are many service members who are exposed to significant combat-related stressors and do not develop PTSS. This suggests that additional risk

[37] Other traumatic events can also lead to PTSD, such as fire, natural disaster, mugging, robbery, car accident, plane crash, torture, kidnapping, life-threatening medical diagnosis, terrorist attack, and other extreme or life-threatening events.

[38] Bartone et al. 1998.

[39] Pietrzak et al. 2012.

[40] Hoge et al. 2004; Pietrzak et al. 2012.

[41] Hoge et al. 2004.

factors, besides the exposure to combat-related stressors, that help determine whether PTSD will develop. Studies have identified important background factors. In the UK, for instance, higher risk of psychological distress was associated with female personnel.[42] Also, having a lower rank, being unmarried, and having a low educational background have all been associated with higher levels of PTSD.[43]

Military organizational factors should be considered as important factors in the relationship between combat-related stressors and higher rates of PTSD as well. For example, both the deployment length of the most recent deployment and the total time deployed to a war zone[44] are considered important factors. Studies indicate that deployments of 13 months or more over the previous 3 years are strongly related to higher rates of PTSD.[45]

Other military organizational factors that seem to affect PTSD rates are the type of military service (e.g., regular active-duty versus National Guard or Army reserve personnel), and the unit type (e.g., fight units versus support units). National guard and Army reserve personnel are at greater risk for developing PTSD, for instance, than regular active-duty soldiers, because they are less trained in comparison with regular active-duty soldiers.[46] The effect of the unit type is related to the unit's role in combat. Studies show that maneuver unit soldiers (e.g., infantry, cavalry, armour) have very different roles on the battlefield than support-unit soldiers (e.g., engineer, transportation, supply and logistics, maintenance, medical) and that these differences imply different levels of exposure to combat-related stressors.[47]

In recent years, there has been a growing interest in the identification of biological and clinical risk factors that may increase the likelihood that PTSD will develop following trauma exposure. The focus of these studies ranges from genetic to environmental factors and includes both characteristics of the traumatic event, and aspects of the post-trauma response. The intensity and immediate response to the trauma and reactions such as dissociative symptoms, panic-response, withdrawal, psychotic symptoms and suicidality are likely precursors of PTSD.[48] At the same time, studies demonstrate a growing interest in the role of neuroticism and perceived threat. Research, for instance, suggests that individuals who perceive a stressor as threatening their safety might be more likely to experience PTSD as a result. A meta-analysis of 12 studies made up of both civilian and military samples found a statistically significant relationship between perceived

---

[42] Mulligan et al. 2010.

[43] Iversen et al. 2008; Rona et al. 2009.

[44] Buckman et al. 2011; Rona et al. 2009.

[45] http://www.kcl.ac.uk/kcmhr/publications/assetfiles/2014/Rona-2014a.pdf. Accessed 10 March 2016.

[46] Vasterling et al. 2010; Milliken et al. 2007.

[47] Hoge 2004; Iversen et al. 2008; Leardman et al. 2009.

[48] Zohar et al. 2011.

threat and PTSD.[49] This indicates that those individuals who perceive that their lives are in danger during a stressful event (high perceived threat) will report more acute stress symptoms and larger rates of PTSD. A recent study demonstrates this influence of perceived threat. During a war-zone deployment higher levels of combat-related stressors and perceived threat were independently associated with larger numbers of PTSD.[50] Studies support that trait neuroticism and perceived threat during deployment are robust predictors of PTSD and depressive symptomatology in the initial years after deployment.[51]

9.5 Protective Factors

Prior research thus indicated many risk factors for PTSD among military populations. Well-documented links seem to exist between combat-related stressors and PTSD, as well as between PTSD and an individuals' psychological, biological, and social functioning in relation to risk factors. Less research has however focused on protective factors for PTSD. Identifying protective factors (which may also moderate the relationship between combat-related stressors and PTSD) has proven to be an important step in the creation of effective prevention efforts for those who have yet to deploy to a war zone. Multiple factors have been identified that may protect against the development of PTSD, such as coping, leadership and perceived social support. These factors moderate the relationship between combat-related stressors and the development of stress symptoms.

Coping research suggests, based on a wide range of military samples from different wars, that coping strategies can be both a risk factor and a protective factor for PTSD. In general, emotion-focused coping has been supported as a risk factor, while problem-focused coping has been supported as a protective factor. However, in contrast to previous studies a recent study suggests that higher emotion-focused coping, may buffer the effect of uncontrollable combat-related stressors on PTSD. Problem-focused coping has been found to be unrelated to PTSD.[52]

Leadership behaviour and leadership climate have been emphasized in the military psychology literature to ameliorate or buffer the effects of stressors experienced by soldiers.[53] For leaders it is important that they understand and recognize the signs and symptoms of PTSD among their soldiers, because it is a leader's

---

49 Ozer et al. 2003.

50 Bourque 2012.

51 James et al. 2013.

52 Roderigues and Renshaw 2010; Bourque 2012.

53 Britt et al. 2004.

duty to care for his/her personnel. In order for leaders to balance the demands and requirements of their unit with the mental health needs of the soldiers, leaders must have access to resources. A recent study has claimed, for example, that promoting supportive military leadership (of non-commissioned officers) and positive coping strategies such as posttraumatic growth or benefit finding, may reduce the risk of PTSD among soldiers exposed to combat.[54]

Social support has already been identified by Vietnam veterans as a potential protective factor against PTSD. Recent meta-analyses show that social support is indeed one of the strongest predictors for PTSD.[55] Research demonstrates that feeling prepared for deployment, positive feelings about the living and working environment during deployment, minimal concerns about family and relationship disruption, and a positive perception of social support all can reduce the chance of developing PTSD.[56] Indeed, very recent studies have demonstrated that social support is an important protective factor that could help to defend against significant mental health problems among veterans.[57] Social support not only has an impact on the relationship between stressors and the negative effects in mental and physical health, but also in relation with family concerns.[58] For example, a study confirmed that having fewer home-front concerns during deployment (e.g., missing important events at home) results in lower numbers of PTSD and this study also identified that having fewer stressful life-events (e.g., going through a divorce) right after the deployment relates to a decreased number of PTSD casualties.[59] Unit support, defined as assistance and encouragement obtained specifically from military unit leaders and other unit members, likewise has a negative relationship with PTSD and is suggested to protect against PTSD.[60]

In addition to the protective factors mentioned above, shorter deployment lengths and less total time deployed could also serve as protective factors.[61] Studies of Iraq and Afghanistan veterans have, above all, identified a wide range of potential protective factors, which include dispositional optimism, resilience; and cohesion.[62] A recent study indicates more precisely that higher vertical (non-commissioned officers) cohesion and vertical (officer) cohesion have a moderating effect on the relationship between with combat-related stressors and PTSD.[63]

---

[54] Posttraumatic growth or benefit finding is a cognitive process that involves finding purpose and meaning in one's suffering and thus refers to positive personal changes resulting from coping with a traumatic event, Wood et al. 2012.

[55] Brewin et al. 2000; Ozer et al. 2003.

[56] Vogt et al. 2008.

[57] Pietrzak et al. 2009; James et al. 2013; Han et al. 2014.

[58] Op den Buijs et al. 2010.

[59] Vasterling et al. 2010.

[60] Pietrzak et al. 2009; Dickstein et al. 2010; Han et al. 2014.

[61] Vasterling et al. 2010; Rona et al. 2006 and 2009.

[62] Thomas et al. 2011; Bartone 2006; Pietrzak et al. 2009; Siebold 2006.

[63] Bourque 2012.

9.5.1 Resilience and Hardiness

Since a few years a concept from a positive psychological perspective, resilience, has often been proposed and studied to lower the prevalence of PTSD.[64] Positive Psychology is a branch of psychology that uses scientific understanding and effective intervention to achieve a 'good life' and human development. The focus is on personal growth rather than on pathology and the treatment of mental health problems. Resilience has mostly been studied in relationship with hardiness, which also has been referred to as "dispositional resilience".[65] Psychological hardiness was first described by Kobasa as a personality variable that distinguished those who became ill under stress from those who remained healthy.[66] She identified three facets of hardiness: commitment, control, and challenge. Individuals with a high hardiness score have a strong awareness of life and work commitment and a greater feeling of control (internal locus of control). Also, they are more open to change and they see stressors as challenges that will make them stronger. Hardy and resilient persons tend to interpret stressful experiences as a normal aspect of existence.[67]

Studies showed that highly effective leaders can increase hardy, resilient responses to stressful situations within their units. Hardy leaders, for instance, can influence the entire group towards more resilient and hardy sense making.[68] A Norwegian study among military officer cadets found that military-specific hardiness is associated with a greater psychological well-being and with lower levels of stress.[69] Recent Dutch, Norwegian and Canadian studies support the importance of hardiness in psychological well-being. The concept is useful for the development of training programs so as to enhance readiness and recovery in the military context.[70] The research findings have led to the application of resilience in contexts of prevention (before exposure to stress) and treatment (when recovering from the harmful effects of stress).

In conclusion, a lot of protective factors that may reduce the risk of developing PTSD have been identified, including organizational factors (e.g., length of

---

[64] Bartone 2006; Pietrzak et al. 2009.

[65] https://www.ucsf.edu/news/2010/08/6001/post-traumatic-stress-disorder-ptsd-prevention-military. Accessed 10 March 2016.

[66] Kobasa 1979.

[67] Bartone 2006; Escolas et al. 2013.

[68] Bartone 2006; Escolas et al. 2013.

[69] Eid and Morgan 2006.

[70] Schok et al. 2010; Skomorovsky and Sudom 2011; Skomorovsky and Stevens 2013; Sudom et al. 2014.

mission), personal factors (e.g. coping, resilience), factors related to the unit (e.g., unit cohesion, leadership), and contextual factors such as social support. Stress models provide insight in the development of PTSD. They show the relationships between military stressors, influencing protective factors (organizational, personal, unit and contextual) and the outcome of the stress process, and can help to predict the adaptability and coping process in relation to the performance of soldiers under stress. The Soldiers Adaptation Model (SAM) is an example of such a meta-theory stress model, which can help to describe and predict stress and PTSD.[71] This model explains the impact of stressors on the performance of soldiers (from a psychological perspective) and depicts the influence of protective factors that decline or buffer the impact of the stressors during operational missions.

9.6 Prevention of Posttraumatic Stress Disorder in the Military

Strategies to prevent PTSD and reduce symptoms of PTSD in the military involve various psychological and pharmacological approaches. In World War and I and II the presumed best treatment to prevent PTSD in the long term was rest and the ventilation of feelings, followed by a return to one's duty and peer group. Frontline treatment in the war-zone was provided using a framework of *proximity*, *immediacy* and *expectancy*. Soldiers were treated near the battlefield, shortly after their problems were identified, and with the intent and expectation that they would return to duty. In theory, providing treatment close to a soldier's unit is important because it helps to maintain group support and cohesion, and also to lower the stigma. Today, clinicians still promote rest, but also prescribe pharmacological treatment to manage hyperarousal, along with psycho-education.

Modern prevention strategies have emerged since the 1990s. Most therapies in the military are designed to prevent the onset of PTSD and development of trauma-related stress symptoms after exposure to a traumatic event (secondary prevention). Most armed forces have embraced several strategies, such as Mental Health Care systems, special programs of (clinical) treatment, follow-up care for PTSD veterans and their families, pre-trauma training programs, but also the training of skills and drills (routine) and the development of a crisis management plan. Along with these strategies active-duty personnel and veterans have furthermore access to useful websites with information about PTSD and combat-related stress.[72]

---

[71] Bliese and Castro 2003.

[72] See for example the websites of the Department of Veterans Affairs, http://www.va.gov/. Accessed 5 July 2016.

Since a few years, there has been a shift in strategy from uniform PTSD prevention approaches (the delivery of one type of intervention (program) to all people exposed to trauma, regardless the specific symptoms or risk of developing of PTSD), to a more customized prevention. Based on evidence that debriefing interventions for all people exposed to particular traumas did not reduce PTSD and that most people exposed to traumatic events do not develop PTSD, a second generation of approaches has thus emerged, the so-called targeted prevention. This targeted prevention incorporates that people with a high risk for the development of PTSD are actively searched for, and that interventions are then provided to those people specifically.

Specific psychological interventions that have been studied for the prevention of PTSD include: battle mind training; trauma-focused cognitive behavioral therapy (CBT); cognitive processing therapy (CPT); cognitive therapy or cognitive restructuring; coping skills therapy, including stress inoculation therapy; debriefing interventions, including critical incident stress debriefing (CISD) and critical incident stress management (CISM); exposure-based therapies; eye-movement desensitization and reprocessing (EMDR); interpersonal therapy; psychoeducation and psychological first aid.[73] Interventions based on complementary and alternative medicine have also been studied. The scientific literature on the early (secondary) prevention strategies of PTSD demonstrates studies on psychological debriefing, pharmacology and psychosocial interventions.

Results of a meta-analysis of 19 studies on the effectiveness of PTSD prevention strategies show that most of these strategies were validated as low or insufficient effective.[74] Only a few studies scored moderate, for instance a cognitive behavior therapy study and two debriefing studies.[75] Specific and important methodological limitations (e.g., inadequate randomization procedures, inadequate statistical approaches for data analysis) may have influenced these findings. In the next sections the main primary (prevention) and secondary (early intervention) approaches in the military are described.

9.6.1 Cognitive Strategies: Resilience Training

Several studies demonstrate that psychological hardiness, which is a trainable resilience resource, leads people in stressful occupations to be more positive.[76] Thereby they negate some of the negative health effects of stress. For example, the

[73] https://effectivehealthcare.ahrq.gov/ehc/products/403/1444/PTSD-prevention-executive-130327.pdf. Accessed 10 March 2016.

[74] https://effectivehealthcare.ahrq.gov/ehc/products/403/1444/PTSD-prevention-executive-130327.pdf. Accessed 10 March 2016.

[75] Rose et al. 1999; Bryant et al. 2005; Sijbrandij et al. 2006.

[76] Bartone 2006; Escolas et al. 2013.

US Army currently uses a program called Comprehensive Soldier Fitness (CSF) to develop psychological resilience within five dimensions: physical, social, emotional, spiritual, and family.[77] The program combines principles of positive psychology and cognitive-behavioural therapy, with a particular emphasis on optimism, problem solving, self-efficacy, self-regulation, emotional awareness, flexibility, empathy, and strong relationships.[78] The training is customized according to a soldier's multidimensional score on the Global Assessment Tool, which is a self-report questionnaire that measures individual psychological fitness and resilience. This comprehensive soldiers fitness program has now widely been implemented in the US Army.[79] The program also includes the families of soldiers and army civilians. The goal of the program is threefold: 1. to increase the number of soldiers who derive meaning and personal growth from their combat experience, 2. to increase the number of soldiers who complete combat tours without pathology, and 3. to decrease the number of soldiers who develop stress pathologies.[80]

Although the CSF program seems to be useful to enhance resilience, there are scientific, ethical and pragmatic concerns (e.g., participant scoring methods, a lack of control groups, relevance in relation to PTSD) in relation to the effectiveness of the program.[81] Moreover, the protective effects of hardiness (as dispositional resilience) on PTSD symptoms have more been examined for their influence on time in the military, on the number of deployments, and on the total time spent on deployment, all variables that were positively related to PTSD symptoms. It turned out that hardiness only moderates the influence of time in the military on PTSD symptoms, which suggests that time in the military has no effect on PTSD for those who scored high on hardiness and resilience.[82] These findings would suggest a modification of current military resilience training programs to effectively enhance the benefits of resilience.

9.6.2 *Biological and Clinical Strategies*

Clinical researchers are mainly focused on biological and clinical risk factors. Clinical studies have shown that acute distress management, an early intervention, could help to control and reduce emotional reactions. They claim that preventing

[77] Taft et al. 2011.

[78] Reivich et al. 2011.

[79] Next to the CSF, the US launched the Mater Resilience Training (MRT) in 2009. The purpose of the MRT course is to teach NCO's a set of skills and techniques that build resilience and that they can, in turn, teach to other soldiers.

[80] Cornum et al. 2011; Griffith and West 2013.

[81] https://thewinnower.com/papers/49-a-critical-examination-of-the-u-s-army-s-comprehensive-soldier-fitness-program, Accessed 23 March (2016).

[82] Escolas et al. 2013.

the PTSD cycle from starting, and thus a reduction in psychiatric casualties, is feasible. Such acute distress management should help one to go through his or her emotional reactions. In this way it is believed to encourage one to return to full functioning and performance. In order to be helpful, the intervention should take place during *the golden hours*, a so-called time frame shortly after the exposure to a traumatic event.[83] Furthermore, the right intervention should be given in this critical time frame. Stress inoculation therapy and critical incident stress debriefing are described as examples of those kinds of treatments. The last few years, such psychological debriefing in an early phase has been increasingly used after psychological trauma.

Whilst psychological debriefing as intervention has become popular and its use has been spread to several settings, empirical evidence for its effectiveness as early intervention is lacking. A review study of a single session psychological "debriefing" in 2009 demonstrated that evidence was variable and that many studies suffered from methodological limitations.[84] The study does suggest though, that the effectiveness of brief psychological debriefing for the management of psychological distress after trauma, and the prevention of posttraumatic stress disorder is not necessarily beneficial.

Even more, a single-session debriefing is found to be associated with a less positive outcome as compared to non-intervention as studies suggest that amnesia (loss of memory) after the traumatic event (and this process takes place in the first critical hours) is associated with a decreased prevalence of PTSD.[85] In addition, studies on debriefing have demonstrated that an experimental design with an educational debriefing, an emotional debriefing and no intervention showed no significant differences.[86] Furthermore, debriefing may 'medicalise' normal distress as it could increase the expectation of the development of psychological symptoms in those who would otherwise not have done so. At the same time, from the prevalence rates of stress and PTSD it is clear that not everyone develops psychological distress. It is usually only a minority of people who will progress to a formal and long-term psychiatric disorder. By debriefing and by increasing the awareness of psychological symptoms, distress and disturbance of the amnesia process may be induced. Psychological debriefing could thus harm those participants that would have otherwise processed the trauma in a natural way (spontaneous remission). This would suggest that debriefing could thus, despite its aims, increase rather than decrease the chances to develop PTSD.[87]

83 Zohar et al. 2009.

84 Rose et al. 2002.

85 Klein et al. 2003.

86 Rose et al. 2002.

87 Klein et al. 2003; Rose et al. 2002.

In sum, the golden hours seem to be important for an early prevention approach. But it is not clear yet what kind of interventions could be really effective in these golden hours.[88] Debriefing could disturb the normal and important processing of the memory. Placebo-controlled psychological and pharmacological (experimental) studies are suggested to examine which interventions should and should not be made in these golden hours.

9.6.3 Pharmacological Interventions

The influence of stress on memory process is a central issue in both psychological and physiological studies. It is clear that pharmacological interventions could disrupt memory and therefore protect against the development of PTSD.[89] The rationale behind the use of substances is to block the formation of long-lasting memories of the traumatic event. These interventions should start early after the traumatic event.[90] In another study it is suggested to use benzodiazepines. It is quite common to use these, but there is support that early administration of benzodiazepines may interfere with the normal process in the memory, and thus to disrupt spontaneous recovery. The administration of cortisol, a stress hormone, has also been suggested as pharmacological treatment and is tested in animal studies. The present findings suggest that an early administration of corticosterone (in the first few hours after the exposure) could decrease the sensitivity, and increase someone's resistance to PTSD.[91]

Other research indicates that two promising medications that are often used for secondary prevention (morphine and ketamine), could be applied as primary prevention as well. However, these medications have undesirable side effects such as sedation, which could be very dangerous in operational situations.[92] Furthermore, so-called alpha and beta-blockers (e.g., propranolol, originally a heart drug) are suggested for primary prevention. These drugs seem to have the highest potential to be used as a primary preventing approach for PTSD. A French study showed that propranolol administered within 24 h of a traumatic event might help people to better manage their memories.[93]

Still, taking a drug to manage one's mental state has the potential to be stigmatizing. Also, there are many pharmacological obstacles in using these so-called 'memory blockers' in primary intervention. Propranolol, for instance blocks the

[88] Zohar et al. 2011.

[89] Klein et al. 2003.

[90] Zohar et al. 2009; Burbiel 2015.

[91] Zohar et al. 2011.

[92] Zohar et al. 2011.

[93] https://clinicaltrials.gov/ct2/show/NCT01713556, Accessed 23 March 2016.

action of stress neurotransmitters on the amygdala, a brain structure with a crucial role in fear conditioning and vigilance. Soldiers could then become fearless or numb, while during missions soldiers should stay alert and have an optimal performance. The idea of administering propranolol to soldiers in the field is thus not very attractive as there is evidence that these pharmacological substances either can cause medical harm or deteriorate mission critical performance.

9.7 Conclusion and Future Implications

This chapter has given an overview of the possibilities and limitations of PTSD prevention approaches. The title of the chapter is: Can PTSD be prevented? The answer is no. The exposure to traumatic events and the development of PTSD is inevitable in military operations. PTSD has an enormous impact and it causes much individual harm. In addition, PTSD is associated with high medical costs and high social costs, because PTSD is a strong risk factor for crime, poor work performance, and associated job losses and familial problems.

In scientific studies, PTSD is associated with differences in prevalence rates, most likely due to the intensity of mission and the exposure to combat-related traumatic events. Differences, however, also result from the ways in which the prevalence of PTSD was assessed (e.g., questionnaires versus medical diagnosis). It is recommended, therefore, that countries use a similar way of diagnosing, for example by a combination of questionnaires with diagnostic interviews, so as to distract more valid and comparable prevalence rates.

So far, PTSD prevention strategies have not proved to be very effective. The body of evidence is, however, highly limited because of sampling and other methodologically issues. Also, there is overlap with other pathology. These findings highlight the inherent limitations of conducting research on PTSD prevention interventions. These limitations are more challenging for mental-health-related research than for research on medical or other health-related issues and underscore a need for ongoing research efforts in the risk and protective factors and the underlying processes in the field of PTSD prevention. Developing a clinical prediction algorithm to identify those soldiers who are at high risk of developing PTSD after combat trauma exposure is perhaps a crucial and practical next step in PTSD prevention. This could be more effective than to continue to study which interventions are more effective than others. Policy and research efforts should therefore perhaps go to the identification of those soldiers primarily, and to the inventory of their opportunities and resources to prevent the onset and development of PTSD with these people.

References

Bartone PT (2006) Resilience under military operational stress: can leaders influence hardiness? Mil Psychol 18:131–148
Bartone PT, Adler AB, Vaitkus MA (1998) Dimensions of psychological stress in peacekeeping operations. Mil Med 163:587–593
Bliese PD, Castro CA (2003) The soldier adaptation model (SAM): Applications to peacekeeping research. In: Britt TW, Adler A (eds) Psychology of the peacekeeper: lessons from the field. Praeger Publishers/Greenwood Publishing Group, Westport, pp 185–203
Bliese PD, Wright KM, Adler AB, Thomas JL, Hoge CW (2007) Timing of postcombat mental health assessments. Psychol Serv 4:141–148
Bourque KP (2012) Combat-related stress, cohesion, coping, and perceived threat: predictors and moderators of posttraumatic symptomatology among deployed US Army soldiers. Thesis, USA, Boston College
Brewin CR, Andrews B, Valentine JD (2000) Meta-analysis of risk factors for posttraumatic stress disorder in trauma-exposed adults. J Consult Clin Psychol 68:748–766
Britt TW, Davison J, Bliese PD, Castro CA (2004) How leaders can influence the impact that stressors have on soldiers? Mil Med 169:541–545
Bryant RA, Ml Moulds, Guthrie R, Nixon RDV (2005) The additive benefit of hypnosis and cognitive-behavioral therapy in treating acute stress disorder. J Consult Clin Psychol 73:334–340
Buckman E, Sundin J, Greene T, Fear NT, Dandeker C, Greenberg N, Wessely S (2011) The impact of deployment length on the health and well-being of military personnel: a systematic review of the literature. Occup Environ Med 68:69–76
Burbiel JC (2015) Primary prevention of posttraumatic stress disorder: drugs and implications. Mil Med Res 2:24–31
Cornum R, Matthews MD, Seligman MEP (2011) Comprehensive soldier fitness: building resilience in a challenging institutional context. Am Psychol 66:4–9
De Jongh A, Arts B (2004) Eye movement desensitization and reprocessing bij PTSS. PatientCare. Neuropsychiatrie en Gedragsneurologie 3:61–65
De Vries GJ, Olff M (2009) The life-time prevalence of traumatic events and posttraumatic stress disorder in the Netherlands. J Trauma Stress 22:259–267
Dickstein BD, McLean CP, Mintz J, Conoscenti LM, Steenkamp MM, Benson TA, Litz BT (2010) Unit cohesion and PTSD symptom severity in Air Force medical personnel. Mil Med 175:482–486
Eid J, Morgan CA (2006) Dissociation, hardiness, and performance in military cadets participating in survival training. Mil Med 171:436–442
Engelhard IM, Van den Hout MA, Weerts J, Arntz A, Hox JJCM, McNally RJ (2007) Deployment-related stress and trauma in Dutch soldiers returning from Iraq. Prospective study. Br J Psychiatry 191:140–145
Escolas SM, Pitts BL, Safer MA, Bartone PT (2013) The main ideas behind the use of substances is to block the formation of long-lasting memories of the traumatic event. Mil Psychol 25:116–123
Friedman MJ (2013) Finalizing PTSD in DSM-5: getting here from there and where to go next. J Trauma Stress 26:548–556
Grieger TA, Cozza SJ, Ursano RJ, Hoge CW, Martinez PE, Engel CC, Wain HJ (2006) Posttraumatic stress disorder and depression in battle-injured soldiers. Am J Psychiatry 163:1777–1783
Griffith J, West C (2013) Master resilience training and its relationship to individual well-being and stress buffering among army National Guard soldiers. J Behav Health Serv Res 40:140–155
Han SC, Castro F, Lee LO, Charney MF, Marx BP, Brailey K, Proctora SP, Vasterling JJ (2014) Military unit support, postdeployment social support, and PTSD symptoms among active duty and National Guard soldiers deployed to Iraq. J Anxiety Disord 28:446–453

Hines LA, Sundin J, Rona RJ, Wessely S, Fear NT (2014) Posttraumatic stress disorder Iraq and Afghanistan: prevalence among military subgroups. Can J Psychiatry 59:468–479
Hoge CW, Castro CA, Messer SC, McGurk DM, Cotting DI, Koffman RL (2004) Combat duty in Iraq and Afghanistan, mental health problems, and barriers to care. N Engl J Med 351:13–22
Hotopf M, Hull L, Fear N, Bowne T, Horn O, Iversen A, Jones M, Murphy D, Bland D, Earnshaw M, Greenberg N, Hacker Hughes J, Tate AR, Dandeker C, Rona R, Wessely S (2006) The health of UK military personnel who deployed to the 2003 Iraq war: a cohort study. The Lancet 367:1731–1741
Iversen A, Fear N, Ehlers A, Hacker HJ, Earnshaw M, Greenberg N, Rona R, Wessely S, Hotopf M (2008) Risk factors for post-traumatic stress disorder among UK Armed Forces personnel. Psychol Med 38:511–522
James LM, Van Kampen E, Miller RD, Engdahl BE (2013) Risk and protective factors associated with symptoms of post-traumatic stress, depression, and alcohol misuse in OEF/OIF veterans. Mil Med 178:159–165
Jones M, Rona R, Hooper R, Wesseley S (2006) The burden of psychological symptoms in UK Armed Forces. Occup Med 56:322–328
Kessler RC, Chiu WT, Demler O, Walters EE (2005) Prevalence, severity, and comorbidity, of twelve-month DSM-IV disorders in the National Comorbidity Survey replication (NCR-R). Arch Gen Psychiatry 62:617–627
Klein E, Caspi Y, Gil S (2003) The relation between memory of the traumatic event and PTSD: evidence from studies of traumatic brain injury. Can J Psychiatry 48:28–33
Kobasa SC (1979) Stressful life events, personality, and health: an inquiry into hardiness. J Pers Soc Psychol 37:1–11
LeardMann CA, Smith TC, Smith B, Wells TS, Ryan MAK (2009) Baseline self-reported functional health and vulnerability to posttraumatic stress disorder after combat deployment: prospective US military cohort study. The BMJ 338:b1273
Litz BT, Stein N, Delaney E, Lebowitz L, Nash WP, Silva C, Maguen S (2009) Moral injury and moral repair in war veterans: a preliminary model and intervention strategy. Clinical Psychology Review 29:695–706
Matthews MD (2008) Toward a positive military psychology. Mil Psychol 20:289–298
McDonald SD, Calhoun PS (2010) The diagnostic accuracy of the PTSD Checklist: a critical review. Clin Psychol Rev 30:976–987
Milliken CS, Auchterlonie JL, Hoge CW (2007) Longitudinal assessment of mental health problems among active and reserve component soldiers returning from the Iraq war. J Am Med Assoc 298:2141–2148
Mulligan K, Jones N, Woodhead C, Davies M, Wessely S, Greenberg N (2010) Mental health of UK military personnel while on deployment in Iraq. Br J Psychiatry 197:405–410
Olff M, Langelanda W, Berthold PR, Gersons BPR (2004) The psychobiology of PTSD: coping with trauma. Psychoneuroendocrinology 30:974–982
Op den Buijs T, Andres MD, Bartone PT (2010) Managing the well-being of military personnel and their families. In: Soeters J, Van Fenema P, Beeres R (eds) Managing military organizations. Routledge, London and New York, pp 240–254
Ozer EJ, Best SR, Lipsey TL, Weiss DS (2003) Predictors of posttraumatic stress disorder and symptoms in adults: a meta-analysis. Psychol Bull 129:52–73
Pietrzak RH, Johnson DC, Goldstein MB, Malley JC, Southwick SM (2009) Psychological resilience and postdeployment social support protect against traumatic stress and depressive symptoms in soldiers returning from Operations Enduring Freedom and Iraqi Freedom. Depress Anxiety 26:745–751
Pietrzak E, Pullman S, Cotea C, Nasveld P (2012) Effects of deployment on mental health in modern military forces: a review of longitudinal studies. J Mil Veterans' Health 20:24–36
Reivich KJ, Seligman MEP, McBride S (2011) Master resilience training in the U.S. Army. Am. Psychol. 66:25–34
Richardson LK, Frueh BC, Acierno R (2010) Prevalence estimates of combat-related post-traumatic stress disorder: critical review. Aust N Z J Psychiatry 44:4–19

Rodrigues CS, Renshaw KD (2010) Associations of coping processes with posttraumatic stress disorder symptoms in National Guard/Reserve service members deployed during the OEF/OIF era. J Anxiety Disord 24:694–699

Rona JM, Hooper R, Wessely S (2006) The burden of psychological symptoms in UK Armed Forces. Occup Med 56:322–330

Rona RJ, Hooper R, Jones M, Iversen AC, Hull L, Murphy D, Wessely S (2009) The contribution of prior psychological symptoms and combat exposure to post Iraq deployment mental health in the UK military. J Trauma Stress 22:11–19

Rose S, Brewin C, Andrews A, Kirk M (1999) A randomized controlled trial of individual psychological debriefing for victims of violent crime. Psychol Med 29:793–799

Rose S, Bisson J, Churchill R, Wessely S (2002) Psychological debriefing for preventing posttraumatic stress disorders (PTSD). Cochrane Database of Systematic Reviews 2:No CD000560

Schok ML, Kleber RJ, Lensvelt-Mulders GJLM (2010) A model of resilience and meaning after military deployment: personal resources in making sense of war and peacekeeping experiences. Aging and Mental health 14:328–338

Siebold GL (2006) Military group cohesion. In: Castro C, Adler A, Britt T (eds) Military life: the psychology of serving in peace and combat. CT: Praeger Security International, Westport, pp 185–201

Sijbrandij M, Olff M, Reitsma JB, Carlier IVE, Gersons BPR (2006) Emotional or educational debriefing after psychological trauma. Randomised controlled trial. Br J Psychiatry 189:150–155

Skomorovsky A, Stevens S (2013) Testing a resilience model among Canadian forces recruits. Mil Med 178:829–837

Skomorovsky A, Sudom KA (2011) Psychological well-being of Canadian forces officer candidates: the unique roles of hardiness and personality. Mil Med 176:389–396

Sookermany A, Sand TS, Breivik G (2015) Risk-taking attitudes and behaviors among military personnel in dangerous contexts. A categorized research bibliography. Norwegian School of Sport Sciences Defence Institute & Norwegian Defence University College. Oslo

Sudom KA, Lee JEC, Zamorski MA (2014) A Longitudinal Pilot Study of Resilience in Canadian Military Personnel Stress and Health 30:377–385

Taft CT, Watkins LE, Stafford J, Street AE, Monson CM (2011) Posttraumatic stress disorder and intimate relationship functioning: A meta-analysis. J Consult Clin Psychol 79:22–33

Tehrani N (2011) Managing trauma in the workplace: supporting workers and organizations. Routledge, London and New York

Thomas JL, Britt TW, Odle-Dusseau H, Bliese PD (2011) Dispositional optimism buffers combat veterans from the negative effects of warzone stress on mental health symptoms and work impairment. J Clin Psychol 67:866–880

Vasterling JJ, Proctor SP, Friedman MJ, Hoge CW, Heeren T, King LA, King DW (2010) PTSD symptom increases in Iraq-deployed soldiers: Comparison with nondeployed soldiers and associations with baseline symptoms, deployment experiences, and postdeployment stress. J Trauma Stress 23:41–51

Vogt DS, Proctor SP, King DW, King LA, Vasterling JJ (2008) Validation of scales from the deployment risk and resilience inventory in a sample of Operation Iraqi Freedom veterans. Assessment 15:391–403

Weerts JMP (2008) Nederland en zijn veteranen: aantallen, achtergrond, onderzoek en beleid. Article via Springerlink 24:9–16

Whetham D (2013) Killer Drones. The moral ups and downs. RUSI J 158:22–32

Wood MD, Foran HM, Britt TW, Wright KM (2012) The impact of benefit finding and leadership on combat-related PTSD symptoms. Mil Psychol 24:529–541

Zohar J, Sannino R, Juven-Wetzler A, Cohen H (2009) Can posttraumatic stress disorder be prevented? CNS Spectrum 14:1

Zohar J, Juven-Wetzler AJ, Sonnino R, Cwikel-Hamzany S, Balaban E, Cohen H (2011) New insights into secondary prevention in post-traumatic stress disorder. Dialogues Clin Neurosci 13:301–309

Websites

Brown NJL (2016) A critical examination of the US Army's Comprehensive Soldier Fitness program. https://thewinnower.com/papers/49-a-critical-examination-of-the-u-s-army-s-comprehensive-soldier-fitness-program. Accessed 23 March 2016

Can post-traumatic stress disorder be stopped before it begins? 30 August 2010. https://www.ucsf.edu/news/2010/08/6001/post-traumatic-stress-disorder-ptsd-prevention-military. Accessed 10 March 2016

Center for Military Health Policy Research. Tanielian T, Jaycox LH (eds) (2008) Invisible wounds of war: psychological and cognitive injuries, their consequences, and services to assist recovery. RAND effective health care program, Santa Monica. http://www.rand.org/pubs/monographs/MG720.html. Accessed 2 March 2016

Institute of Care and Health. https://www.iwh.on.ca/wrmb/primary-secondary-and-tertiary-prevention. Accessed 10 March 2016

Jongedijk R (2015) De Posttraumatische Stressstoornis in de DSM-5. White paper. http://www.dsm-5-nl.org/documenten/artikel/33/De-Posttraumatische-Stressstoornis-in-de-DSM-5 30 maart 2015. Accessed 2 March 2016

National Center for PTSD. DSM-5 Criteria for PTSD. http://ptsd.va.gov/professional/PTSD-overview. Accessed 10 March 2016

NLtimes (2015) http://www.nltimes.nl/2015/12/14/court-netherlands-failed-its-veterans-needing-ptsd-treatment-after-lebanon/. Accessed 11 March 2016

Rona RJ, Jones M, Keeling M, Hull L, Wessely S, Fear NT (2014) Mental health consequences of overstretch in the UK Armed Forces 2007–09: a population-based cohort study. http://www.kcl.ac.uk/kcmhr/publications/assetfiles/2014/Rona-2014a.pdf. Accessed 10 March 2016

The American Institute of Stress. http://www.stress.org/military. https://effectivehealthcare.ahrq.gov/ehc/products/403/1444/PTSD-prevention-executive-130327.pdf. Accessed 10 March 2016

Treatment of PTSD by Reduction of Traumatic Memory Reconsolidation by Propranolol: A Multisite Trial (2016) https://clinicaltrials.gov/ct2/show/NCT01713556. Accessed 23 March 2016

Chapter 10
Explaining the Role of the Armed Forces in the Dutch Safety Regions

Jori Kalkman

Abstract This chapter explores the roles of the armed forces in the twenty-five Dutch Safety Regions. After distinguishing four types of Safety Regions based on the risks that they report, the rationale for the Safety Region is provided based on organization theory. Next, civil-military collaboration in Dutch emergency management is embedded within literature on interorganizational collaboration and expeditionary civil-military cooperation. Qualitative interviews with military liaisons suggest that the type of Safety Region influences the role that the liaisons play, the perceived dependency on the military as an emergency partner and the cooperation dynamics between the military and civilian response organizations in terms of the relative importance of trust and control measures. Avenues for further research, especially regarding the role of power in domestic civil-military interactions, are outlined.

Keywords Safety Regions · Civil-military collaboration · Trust · Control

J. Kalkman (✉)
Faculty of Military Sciences, Netherlands Defence Academy, Breda, The Netherlands;
Department of Organization Sciences, Vrije Universiteit, Amsterdam, The Netherlands;
Department of Defence, TNO, Soesterberg, The Netherlands
e-mail: jp.kalkman@mindef.nl

R. Beeres et al. (eds.), *NL ARMS Netherlands Annual Review of Military Studies 2016*, NL ARMS, DOI 10.1007/978-94-6265-135-7_10

Contents

10.1 Introduction

One of the three main tasks of the Dutch armed forces is the provision of assistance to civil authorities during crises and disasters.[1] The legal framework for military support to civil authorities ('national operations') is, amongst others, to be found in the Safety Regions Act, which entered into force in 2010. This Act prescribes the Dutch emergency management structure and specifies the roles of the central actors in the response to emergencies. Several civil-military frameworks and agreements have been drafted over the past decade to improve the military support to civilian actors during these emergencies. To guarantee the availability of certain military resources and to reinforce the cooperation in the preparation phase, the Ministry of Security and Justice, and the Ministry of Defence adopted the Civil-Military Governance Agreement (in 2005), the Intensification Civil-Military Collaboration agreement (in 2007) and the Strengthening Civil-Military Collaboration framework (in 2012).[2] Regardless of the fact that these agreements apply to all twenty-five Safety Regions that the Dutch Government set up, the role of the armed forces in the emergency response networks varies highly per region. In some of the response networks, the military is only called upon incidentally, whereas other Safety Regions have granted the military liaison a permanent position in the network in case the emergency transcends the ordinary response capacities of the public services in an area.[3] Thc goal of this chapter is to explore the different roles that the Netherlands armed forces play in the various Safety Regions.

To this end, the next section highlights the goals of the Safety Regions, the differences between them and the types of Safety Regions that can be distinguished. After this practical introduction, a theoretical perspective based on organizational

[1] Ministry of Defence 2015.

[2] Opstelten 2014.

[3] Audit Functie Defensie en Inspectie Veiligheid en Justitie 2013; Veiligheidsberaad 2014.

theory is used to explain the rationale behind the Safety Region as well as to position civil-military collaboration in the literature on interorganizational networks. Subsequently, the empirical part of this chapter discusses the findings of interviews with military liaisons and discusses how the theoretical insights apply to the practice of civil-military collaboration in the Safety Regions. Lastly, the chapter will conclude by briefly recapitulating the main findings and outlining possible future research.

10.2 Safety Regions: Raison d'être and a Typology

The Safety Regions have been established "to better protect citizens against risks; to offer better emergency services and after-care in the event of disasters and crises; to bring fire services, medical assistance, disaster and crisis management under one regional administrative authority when disaster strikes [and]; to reinforce administrative and operational effectiveness".[4] In order to improve the management and operations of emergency response in their regions of control, the Safety Regions pool the capabilities and skills of the fire brigade, medical services and municipalities in their region. If necessary, they may also ask for the assistance of other relevant partners, such as the police, vital infrastructural firms or the armed forces.[5] The management board of the Safety Region, consisting of the mayors whose municipalities are part of that specific region, is mainly operative on the policy-level in order to guarantee a well-functioning emergency management structure which is activated in times of crises. In this structure, representatives of the emergency response organizations as well as the Safety Region gather during crises in a temporary task force to discuss the operational and tactical approach until the emergency has been tackled.[6]

Regardless of their shared task and similar procedures, the twenty-five Safety Regions in the Netherlands are very diverse on many different fronts (e.g., size, population numbers, and infrastructure). The differences between the Safety Regions result in very diverse risk profiles. A risk profile, a four-year obligatory document for every Safety Region, outlines the Safety Region's risks, the probabilities of these risks and the potential consequences.[7] The risks can be measured along the two axes of a risk diagram. The *x*-axis shows the likelihood of a risk materializing as perceived by the Safety Region, while the *y*-axis shows the expected potential impact. Thus, four types of risks appear (Fig. 10.1). Firstly, there are risks which potentially have a low impact as well as a low probability (Type I), such as a temporary stop on the energy supply. Secondly, there are risks

[4] Ministry of Security and Justice 2010, p. 9.

[5] Ministry of Security and Justice 2010.

[6] Ibid.

[7] Ibid.

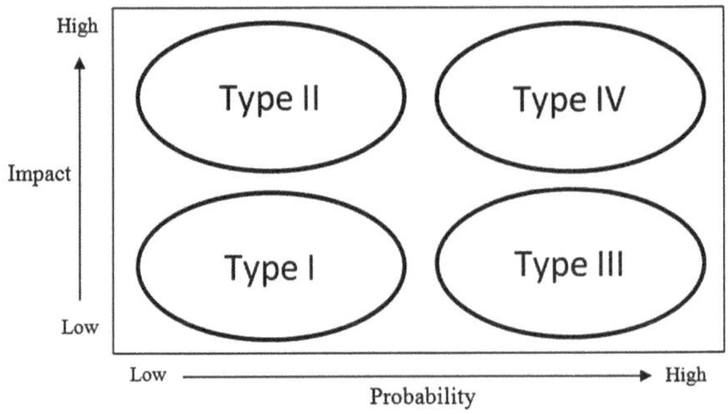

Fig. 10.1 Risk diagram

that are unlikely to materialize but would potentially have a large impact, (Type II), most prominently a nuclear meltdown but also the leakage of poisonous gases. The third type consists of risks with a low potential impact but a high probability (Type III), for instance storms. Lastly, a few risks can be classified as having both a high potential impact and a high probability (Type IV), such as the wide spread of a disease. The high-impact and/or high-probability risks (Type II, III and IV) are most relevant to the Safety Regions and are prepared for in their contingency plans.

The high-impact or high-probability risks can occur in different crisis spheres. Following a national risk profile guide, most Safety Regions discern seven spheres of crises in which a risk can materialize. These crisis spheres are: (1) the natural environment, (2) the built-up environment, (3) the technological environment, (4) vital infrastructure, (5) traffic and transportation, (6) health, and (7) the societal environment.[8] After allocating the high-impact and/or high-probability risks identified by the individual Safety Regions into these seven spheres of crises, it becomes clear that some regions face much more risks in one specific crisis sphere than other regions. A very urbanized Safety Region as Amsterdam-Amstelland, for instance, faces much more (type II, III and IV) risks in the societal sphere (e.g., societal unrest, panicking crowds during large events), whereas Safety Region Gelderland-Midden is more concerned with risks in the natural and health spheres (e.g., floods, epidemics, natural fires). While all Safety Regions face risks in all of the crisis spheres, they can be distinguished on the basis of the relative importance they attach to one or two specific crisis spheres. These diverging emphases of the regions allows for a typology of Safety Regions (Table 10.1).

Whereas some crisis spheres are helpful tools for dividing the Safety Regions in the four types, other crisis spheres are either similarly important for all regions or are generally perceived to be of little importance (i.e. low-impact and low-probability). For instance, the technological environment is absent in the typology. Although many Safety Regions mention a risk in the crisis sphere of the technical environment, this risk receives little attention since it is overwhelmed by more

[8] Treurniet 2014, pp. 29–30.

Table 10.1 A typology of Safety Regions on the basis of their risks

Natural environment and health	Traffic and transportation	Societal	Mixed
Brabant-Zuidoost	Kennemerland	Amsterdam-Amstelland	Brabant-Noord
Drenthe	Utrecht	Haaglanden	Fryslân
Flevoland	Zuid-Holland-Zuid		Groningen
Gelderland-Midden			Limburg-Zuid
Gelderland-Zuid			Midden- en West-Brabant
Gooi en Vechtstreek			Rotterdam-Rijnmond
Hollands Midden			Twente
IJsselland			Zeeland
Limburg-Noord			
Noord- en Oost-Gelderland			
Noord-Holland-Noord			
Zaanstreek-Waterland			

likely risks in other crises spheres. In addition, risks in the built environment and vital infrastructures are generally classified as unlikely to occur and of limited impact. This can be explained by the fact that, for instance, the collapse of a building is rare and geographically very confined whereas temporary stops on gas supply are not viewed as very impactful or probable either. Thus, as the Safety Regions' risk profiles show, most serious risks (risks of type II, III or IV) occur in the spheres of health and the natural environment, traffic and transportation, and the societal environment. These spheres can subsequently be used to identify four types of Safety Regions.

The first type of Safety Regions consists of mainly rural areas. These regions are characterized by large natural environments such as forests, heathland, agriculture, lakes or rivers. Although the number of inhabitants of a Safety Region may be high (e.g., Safety Region Noord- en Oost-Gelderland), this can be explained by the sheer size of the Safety Region in which many citizens live dispersed in villages. The main concerns in these regions include floods, natural fires and pandemics (i.e., risks in the spheres of the natural environment and health). The second type includes three Safety Regions which are important junctions for national and international transportation and traffic. Safety Region Kennemerland does not only host Schiphol airport, the biggest airport in the Netherlands, but is also responsible for a large number of highways in the area. Safety Region Utrecht, similarly, bears responsibility for some very busy highways, but also covers two of the main railway-stations in the Netherlands (Amersfoort and Utrecht), both of which are central links in the national railway system. Safety Region Zuid-Holland-Zuid, lastly, covers the busy seaways to Belgium and Germany as well as the largest rail yard of the country.

The third type comprises two of the largest cities in the Netherlands, consisting of more than 500,000 inhabitants. Next to being densely populated areas, the Hague (i.e., Safety Region Haaglanden) is tasked with the protection of many ministerial buildings, the parliament and several international institutions (e.g., International Criminal Court), whereas Amsterdam (i.e., Safety Region Amsterdam-Amstelland) has an international stature and hosts millions of tourists annually. Both urban areas, in short, are unique for the risks in the societal environment that they face. The fourth and final type consists of areas that have a very mixed nature. Although all Safety Regions combine risks in all seven crisis types, the characteristic of the Safety Regions in the 'mixed' type is that their risks are balanced over these crisis spheres. Practically, they often combine urbanized and industrial areas (e.g., Rotterdam-Rijnmond) or a significant city with an equally significant rural hinterland (e.g., Groningen).

10.3 An Organizational Interpretation of the Safety Region

Now the role and types of Safety Regions have been identified, the question may arise why the Safety Regions were established in the first place and why emergencies are not managed on the national or municipal level. In order to answer this question, it is important to realize that emergencies always come with a multitude of significant uncertainties.[9] Uncertainty can manifest itself in many different ways, for instance in the timing of an emergency and its nature, the nature of the tasks to be performed by an actor, the members in the response network and their reliability, the potential effects of the emergency and the availability or reliability of information.[10] Although some of these uncertainties can be reduced by thorough emergency planning, it is impossible to completely predict and prepare for an actual emergency.[11] In other words, when emergencies occur, the exact task of the emergency responders is bound to be uncertain (i.e., task uncertainty) since there are a variety of (potential) crises and disasters and a high number of unpredictable environmental factors of influence (e.g., victims, physical environment, weather). Galbraith argues that organizations are designed contingent upon the uncertainties in their environment.[12] He states that information is the key resource during task uncertainties, meaning that a rising level of task uncertainty requires a rising level of information exchange between decision-makers during task execution to enable on-the-spot adjustments in the allocation of resources, time

[9] Boin et al. 2005.

[10] Boin et al. 2005; Faraj and Xiao 2006; Majchrzak et al. 2007; Quarantelli 1996.

[11] Perrow 1994.

[12] Galbraith 1977, 1984.

schedules and the order of activities.[13] Under normal conditions, organizational units coordinate their activities through specific rules or programs for units, hierarchical relations and planned goals or targets.[14] When these can no longer make up for the uncertainty of the task, organizations either aim to reduce information flows or improve information processing. The former requires the creation of slack resources, the creation of self-contained tasks or management of the environment.[15] Information processing can be improved by investing in vertical information systems or by the creation of lateral relationships.[16]

Galbraith's theory provides some interesting insights for explaining the organization of emergency response in the Netherlands. It can, for instance, help to explain why Safety Regions were established in the first place. Due to the high level of task uncertainty in emergencies, the Dutch government reduced the need for information flows by the creation of relatively autonomous units (i.e., self-contained tasks): the Safety Region. While having the benefit of leading to economies of scale by pooling expertise and resources on a higher level,[17] the regional organization of emergency management avoids overburdening the hierarchy and a high number of exceptionalities which would have been a threat to even further centralized emergency management on the national level.

At the same time, to keep some homogeneity among the Safety Regions, the Dutch government improved the information processing capacities through investing in formalizing communication (i.e., vertical information systems).[18] An example of a vertical information system is the policy of 'upscaling' the response capacities by means of Coordinated Regional Incident Management Procedures (GRIPs). During an 'ordinary' emergency (e.g. fire, crime, accident), the public services implement their usual response. However, when a lead officer of one of the public services decides that the incident exceeds the usual response, the responding organization(s) can decide to 'scale up' based on the six scales of the GRIPs. GRIP 1 and 2 refer to the central, multi-disciplinary harmonization of operations, respectively on location or, when a larger area is hit, in a fixed place with higher ranking officers. GRIP 3 leads to the activation of governance support under the supervision of the mayor. In extra-municipal emergencies, the head of the Safety Region assumes supervision (GRIP 4). When multiple Safety Regions are hit, GRIP 5 provides for the coordination between the involved Safety Regions, whereas the final scale (GRIP Rijk) enables guidance by the national government during inter-sectoral crises threatening national safety.[19] Next to

---

13 Galbraith 1977, p. 36.

14 Galbraith 1977, pp. 42–49.

15 Galbraith 1977, pp. 49–55; Galbraith 1984, pp. 22–23, 26.

16 Galbraith 1984, pp. 23–26; Galbraith 1977, pp. 52–55.

17 Ministry of Security and Justice 2010.

18 Galbraith 1984, p. 24.

19 IFV 2014.

improving the information processing capacities of the Safety Regions, the GRIPs are also the clearest example of national-level attempts to create a consistent approach to emergencies across Safety Regions.

Another way to improve information processing is to invest in lateral relations. This is why, for crisis and disaster management in the Netherlands, a multitude of organizations are brought together under the umbrella of a Safety Region. Various liaison devices are being used to coordinate and harmonize the activities of these organizations.[20] In the emergency management structure, as activated by the GRIPs, the representatives of various emergency responders gather temporarily to coordinate their operations. This gathering of emergency response representatives can be viewed as a task force, since it has a specific task and disbands after this task is completed. Continuing this view, the management board of the Safety Region can be seen as a standing committee since a group of mayors, advised by emergency responders, "meet regularly to discuss issues of common interests".[21] The military is only in some cases part of the standing committee or task force and can hardly be seen as an equal partner of the structural emergency services. Instead, the military representative (OVR) fulfils a liaison role by communicating directly to the full members which capacities the armed forces can offer.[22]

Galbraith's and Mintzberg's theories focus specifically on task uncertainty reduction and liaison devices *within* an organization, characterized by a shared hierarchy, common decision-making processes and resources, and familiar partners. The Safety Regions, instead, are characterized by the presence of a large number of potential emergency response partners which face collaboration challenges. In order to explain the role of the armed forces in the Safety Regions, it is therefore essential to have a better understanding of which uncertainties organizations face in their dealings with partners and how these interorganizational uncertainties are resolved.

10.4 Interorganizational Uncertainties

Next to task uncertainties, the emergency responders in the Safety Regions often face uncertainties with regard to the exact composition of the emergency response task force. Interorganizational uncertainties in emergency response networks are a consequence of the fact that the traditional emergency responders (i.e. police, fire brigade, health services, and municipal services) can be supported by a variety of others (e.g. the armed forces, water management boards, companies in vital sectors).[23] One example of interorganizational uncertainty is that organizations may simply be

[20] Mintzberg 1983.

[21] Mintzberg 1983, p. 83.

[22] Mintzberg 1983.

[23] Ministry of Security and Justice 2010.

unaware of the other's existence or capabilities[24] and this unawareness may lead to one organization distrusting another organization's motives, use of resources or its very inclusion in the network.[25] Interorganizational uncertainties are also reflected in civil-military collaboration in the Safety Regions. For instance, many emergency responders mention their frustration about the difficult process for requesting military support, they distrust the military's way of operating and its motives, and they fear that the armed forces will take over after being asked for assistance.[26]

Theoretically, similar to civil-military partnerships in expeditionary environments, domestic civil-military collaborations can be viewed as interorganizational alliances that require four conditions to be met in order to be viable: interdependency to reach shared goals, awareness of this interdependency, mutual trust and control or domain-consensus.[27] Partner cooperation, then, requires the willingness "to pursue mutually compatible interests in the alliance rather than act opportunistically".[28] Noting the many civil-military agreements on Dutch emergency response, the national-level representatives of the military and civilian emergency services seem to be aware of their interdependencies, but the question arises whether a similar perception of mutual interdependency is present within the Safety Regions. Regardless of the perceived interdependencies, however, it is also important to look into the confidence of the actors in each other by highlighting trust and control measures.[29]

Trust "refers to the positive expectations about another's motives with respect to oneself in situations entailing risk".[30] Trust is needed throughout the collaboration. Firstly, it is a necessary condition for reliance on each other and for overcoming conflicting interests on the division of responsibilities and domains of cooperation. Secondly, trust is a requirement as there is no clear hierarchy in the collaboration, nor always time to build control mechanisms.[31] Distrust towards the military's operational approach and motives, however, was already mentioned by several emergency responders. The question, thus, arises how trust relations can be created. Trust can be built in various ways before becoming a sustainable source of mutual confidence over time.[32] Firstly, trust can result from taking initial risks as it signalizes some level of trust in the other partner which is likely to be reciprocated. Secondly, trust can be built by guaranteeing equity and fairness, meaning that higher investments must lead to higher benefits. Thirdly, trust is fostered by regular communication and the frequent exchange of information which improve coordination, credibility perceptions

[24] Treurniet et al. 2012.
[25] Bollen 2008.
[26] Veiligheidsberaad 2014.
[27] Bollen 2008.
[28] Das and Teng, 1998, p. 492.
[29] Das and Teng 1998.
[30] Rietjens and Bollen 2008, p. 242.
[31] Bollen 2008, p. 42.
[32] Das and Teng 1998.

and the continuation of interaction. Fourthly, a partner's adaptation to the collaboration's requirements, in terms of "flexibility and the willingness to accommodate deviations from the contract", is an essential trust-building activity.[33]

Control, then, can be defined as "a regulatory process by which elements of a system are made more predictable by establishing standards in the pursuit of some desired objective or state".[34] Control measures are complementary to trust, meaning that both confidence-enhancing strategies are needed for establishing a well-functioning alliance. Control measures may also lead to more trust between partners in the network over time, whereas a certain level of trust is a precondition for promising adherence to certain control measures.[35] Control can be built through multiple measures, which are reminiscent of Galbraith's means to coordinate tasks within an organization.[36] As a first control measure, organizations can set goals and ways to measure these goals in order to specify mutual expectations. Next, organizations may adopt structural arrangements to streamline the behaviour of partners by implementing rules, committing non-recoverable investments and monitoring. Lastly, organizations can exercise social control through their management of the alliance or partnership culture via blending the different organization cultures, which subsequently inspires predictable and cooperative behaviour.[37]

Das and Teng write specifically about interorganizational collaboration in the corporate sector, which may limit the applicability of some of their ideas to the study of civil-military collaboration since the main actors in this (mandated) alliance are public organizations.[38] Their ideas, however, are also applicable to the public sector. Provan and Kenis, in their study on network governance, focus on the public sector and validate the importance of trust and control in interorganizational collaboration.[39] They distinguish three governance forms, the appropriateness of which are, amongst others, determined by levels of trust and goal consensus (the latter representing control). First, the 'shared governance' network consists of few participants facing a low need for network-level competencies, but having a high goal consensus and high trust levels. In the Safety Regions, the operational collaboration in the field among public services bears many resemblances to this type of governance network. Second, the 'lead-organization' network faces moderate interdependency, a moderate number of participants, a moderately low goal consensus and a low level of trust which is concentrated around the lead organization. This type of network governance comes into existence when a crisis occurs within the sphere of influence of a Ministry.[40] Third, the 'network adminis-

33 Das and Teng 1998, p. 505.

34 Rietjens and Bollen 2008, p. 241.

35 Das and Teng 1998.

36 Das and Teng 1998, pp. 505–507.

37 Das and Teng 1998.

38 Ibid.

39 Provan and Kenis 2008.

40 Nationaal Coördinator Terrorismebestrijding en Veiligheid 2013.

Table 10.2 List of interviews

Interview	Type of Safety Region	Date	Rank
1	Natural environment/health	05-11-15	Major
2	Mixed	11-11-15	Major
3	Mixed	16-11-15	Major
4	Natural environment/health	17-11-15	Major
5	Societal	24-11-15	Major
6	Traffic/transportation	01-02-15	Major

trative organization' refers to an independent, administrative body that is established for governing a network. It is best used under conditions of moderate trust levels, several participants, moderately high goal consensus and a high interdependency. The head office of the Safety Region, as a network of mayors and emergency services, is a good example of this. The main focus of this study is on this latter type of network.

10.5 Methodology

In order to explore how the theories apply to the practice of civil-military collaboration in Dutch emergency response, a sample was taken which included Safety Regions from all four types in the typology. This sample comprised six military liaisons: one from the smaller types (i.e., traffic/transportation and societal) and two from the larger types (i.e., natural environment/health and mixed) (Table 10.2).

The sample size resulted from the exploratory nature of this research as the study aims to identify what role the armed forces have in the various Safety Regions, how the collaboration with partners is organized and which challenges come to the fore. The outcomes of this research will subsequently be an impetus for further research.

By conducting six semi-structured, in-depth interviews with the military liaisons in these Safety Regions, the military experiences of civil-military collaboration could be better understood. As the challenges to civil-military emergency network are primarily constructed in a social setting and individually perceived, conducting interviews with open-ended questions proved particularly suitable for this study.[41] The reason for interviewing military liaisons was twofold. Firstly, the aim of this study is to explore the roles of the armed forces in the Safety Regions. The military liaisons are best able to share relevant information on this topic as they are the prime representatives of the Ministry of Defence in the Safety Regions which means that the role of the armed forces is reflected in their

[41] Creswell 2003.

activities. To understand what role the armed forces play in a specific region, it is therefore essential to unveil the activities of the military liaison in that region. Secondly, since civilian network partners have to divide their attention over many emergencies and a multitude of emergency response actors, they are less likely to recall insightful experiences of civil-military collaborations than their military counterparts, providing another reason to interview military liaisons instead.

In the six interviews, military liaisons were first of all asked to provide information on the characteristics of their Safety Region in order to find out whether the Safety Region was correctly positioned in the typology. After confirming this, a number of questions were raised concerning the role of the military liaison in the specific region and on how actors (e.g. mayors, armed forces) aim to influence this role. Next, since the role of the military, as an organization, depends on its relations with emergency response partners, military liaisons were asked to share their insights on collaboration experiences with partners by specifically highlighting how they perceived the dependency awareness of partners as well as which trust and control measures were in place. The subsequent section presents the findings.

10.6 Findings

10.6.1 The Role of the Military Liaison

Although all military liaisons have the same mandate, their positions in the response networks and their daily activities vary significantly due to the relative autonomy of the Safety Regions. In the 'cold phase' (i.e., non-emergency phase), most liaisons are both representing the armed forces and they are involved in the daily activities of the Safety Region's head office, usually through helping drafting plans and preparing multi-disciplinary trainings (Interview 1 and 4). During an emergency (i.e., 'warm phase'), most liaisons join the inter-agency 'task force' to communicate to the other members what the armed forces could contribute, but they also give broader advice on crisis management as independent advisers (Interview 1, 2 and 6). It is beyond doubt that the military liaisons significantly improve the information processing capacities of the Safety Regions by providing better and faster communication with the armed forces.

In Safety Regions which are characterized by risks in the natural environment and the sphere of health, the military liaison is granted a rather large role since the armed forces are more likely to be called upon. Large natural fires and floods, for instance, can exceed the response capacities of the traditional emergency partners (Interview 1). Since these natural disasters tend to endure and thus exhaust the responders' resources, the military is seen as a relevant partner (Interview 4). In Safety Regions with many risks in the sphere of traffic and transportation, the military liaison used to be informed early on due to preparatory GRIP-2 notifications. Although new rules will change this procedure, the military liaison is still informed as soon as a GRIP-2 emergency is declared (Interview 6). In large cities, the risks in the societal sphere are usually tackled by the traditional emergency responders independently. These emergency response organizations have a sizeable pool of slack resources which they can employ if an emergency endures or worsens (Interview 5), rendering the military liaison a less central partner. The final type of Safety Regions (i.e. those with a mixed nature) take a middle position with regard to the position they grant to the military liaison. In general, however, there is a clear indication that the more urban and populous Safety Regions give a smaller role to the military liaison as defence representative than the more rural and sparsely populated regions (see Interview 2, 3 and 6).

As the relation between the armed forces and the other emergency management partners relies heavily on the military liaison, a distinction is to be made between inter-personal collaboration and interorganizational collaboration. Whereas the military liaisons report good working relationships with their direct colleagues, they also mention that partners sometimes take an ambiguous stance to collaboration with the armed forces as an organization. For instance, mayors, who have to issue the formal request for military assistance, simply want their population to be helped and emergencies to be tackled (Interview 2 and 4) but they may also have a (political) predisposition (as pacifists) against the support of the armed forces (Interview 1 and 6), which can partly be explained by the individual preferences of the mayor (Interview 1 and 5).

At the national level, the military leadership pursues a strategy of strongly enhancing the role of the armed forces and the military liaison in the Safety Regions, as exemplified by the various civil-military agreements and other official documents.[42] Aside from being able to offer specific useful resources, some liaisons argue that the military's interest in national emergency management also stems from the perceived need to justify its existence. They refer to the interest of the armed forces to regain a position in society after retreating from it with the end of conscription (Interview 3). Thus, in order to show the Dutch society that the armed forces have a right to exist, the military leadership aims at visible military assistance to domestic emergency management (Interview 2 and 4), which explains the appointment of twenty-five permanent military liaisons to the Safety Regions. The military liaison can only regain a societal position for Defence, however, when potential partners are open to collaboration with the military.

10.6.2 Interdependency Awareness

The openness of partners to collaborate with the armed forces differs significantly. This may partly be explained by the fact that the organizational culture and structure of the armed forces render collaboration with some partners easier than with others. For instance, just like the armed forces, the fire brigade is hierarchical and

[42] Ministerie van Defensie 2013, 2015.

uses similar terminology which facilitates good communication (Interview 3). The police, although preoccupied with a big reorganization, is increasingly making use of military capacities and, albeit less hierarchical, is similar in its mandate to use force (Interview 1 and 3). The health services, finally, are a networked organization and always need to seek agreement, rendering collaboration with this partner harder for the armed forces (Interview 4). Again, the typology provides useful insights. In large urban areas, the emergency partners are operating very independently and are less conducive to collaboration as a consequence (Interview 5), whereas in the other Safety Regions, emergency partners perceive higher mutual interdependencies (Interview 1 and 3).

Even when emergency partners are aware of interdependencies, they do not easily give up part of their operations or their positions in a response network. In emergency networks of larger cities, for instance, the fire brigade is disappointed when they need military assistance in one of their core tasks (Interview 5) and public managers may deem military support unwanted as it demonstrates their limitations (Interview 6). Thus, the provision of military assistance requires a careful and sensitive strategy. This may explain why military liaisons generally play a big role in multi-disciplinary training and exercising, which enhances the reputation and visibility of the armed forces (Interview 5) without antagonizing future partners.

From the side of the armed forces, collaboration can be negatively influenced. Firstly, the military itself is divided (Interview 2). The various branches do not always coordinate their activities in a region (Interview 5 and 6) and fail to show uniformity due to intra-organizational conflicts of interests (Interview 4). Secondly, the military liaisons tend to take a modest position, but some of their superiors do not necessarily do so as well. This may lead to frustrations as 'we can mean a lot, but we should not exaggerate, because it is not as much as we portray it ourselves' (Interview 2). Especially in combination with rejections of requests, this may lead to questions of reliability of the armed forces as a structural partner in the Safety Region (Interview 6). Adverse perceptions of the military may reduce the number of requests and thus negatively influence the perceived dependency on the armed forces.

10.6.3 Control and Trust

In order to improve the collaboration, various control measures are being used. Firstly, a covenant between the armed forces and the Safety Regions 'offers a legitimate basis during crises and disasters', and specifies mutual obligations and wishes (Interview 3), even though the covenant needs refinement in practice and is preceded by the wish to collaborate (Interview 1 and 2). Secondly, there are informal means of control, including work-floor agreements (Interview 2) and the military's guaranteed capacities.[43] Thirdly, some level of social control can be exercised via

[43] Ministerie van Defensie 2015.

the concentration of organizational cultures in the Safety Region, which is represented in the commitment to the Safety Regions that the military liaisons expressed. Lastly, the Safety Region has some direct control measures, such as certain influence over which candidate is appointed as the military liaison (Interview 2 and 4).

With regard to trust, it is again worthwhile distinguishing inter-personal and interorganizational trust. Initially, the military liaisons often encountered hesitance regarding the presence and use of the armed forces in the Safety Region since the military's mentality and image can be perceived as dominant and threatening (Interview 1 and 2). Trust in the liaisons simply increases over time due to positive social interactions, which normalizes the presence of the liaison in task forces. For instance, one liaison's membership of the emergency response task force 'has become so naturally over the last years that everyone considers it self-evident' (Interview 1). Liaisons are even asked to think along on personal title during emergencies about possible response strategies (Interview 1 and 6).

The armed forces, as an organization, can build trust through proving its worth. For example, the military contributions to the management of emergencies during a large event (Interview 4), a large wildfire (Interview 1) and an evacuation (Interview 5) are perceived to have had beneficial effects on the views of partners on the armed forces as a crisis partner. One liaison highlighted that if the armed forces would 'not have succeeded [to contribute during a large fire], trust would have really sank' (Interview 4). At the same time, the short terms of the military liaisons (Interview 4), rejections of requests (Interview 6) and unannounced military trainings (Interview 5) can tear down this newly built trust. Another liaison also argued that if the armed forces really want to be seen as a trustworthy partner, it needs to make some sacrifices in order to always have capacities available, but as of yet, the leadership seems unwilling to do so (Interview 6).

In general, there is a tendency to stronger rely on trust measures in Safety Regions with a large natural environment than in other Safety Regions. In these regions, the armed forces are more likely to provide military capabilities to tackle an emergency and the military liaisons have more social interactions with colleagues, which both lead to higher trust levels (see Interview 1). In areas with mixed risks or risks in the area of traffic and transportation, several control measures are being used in addition to trust mechanisms (see Interview 3 and 6), whereas in urban environments, there is a strong emphasis on control. At times, control measures can even be dictated by the other parties, for instance when the mayor provides the terms of engagement for military assistance (Interview 5).

10.7 Conclusion and Discussion

This research aimed to explore the different roles that the Dutch armed forces play in the various Safety Regions. As emergencies are inherently unpredictable, Galbraith's theory on organizational design under task uncertainty is particularly useful in explaining the rationale behind the Safety Region.[44] In his view, the Safety Regions are an outcome of the attempt to decrease information flows, whereas the appointment of a military liaison improves the information processing capacities. Since the role of the armed forces in the emergency networks comes with its own specific challenges, the work of Das and Teng, Bollen and Rietjens and Bollen is relevant as they highlight the importance of interdependency awareness, trust and control in interorganizational collaborations.[45]

The identification of four types of Safety Regions (e.g. natural environment and health, traffic and transportation, societal, and mixed) seems to be a useful way to elucidate the diversity of the Safety Regions and is helpful in explaining why roles, perceived interdependencies and collaboration mechanisms differ per Safety Region. Qualitative interviews suggest that military liaisons are granted a larger role in Safety Regions with large natural environments because emergency partners in these regions are more likely to face emergencies which exhaust their capabilities and are therefore more aware of the mutual interdependencies. In areas with many risks related to traffic and transportation, the military liaison is earlier informed when a threat is looming. Just like in the Safety Regions facing a mixture of risks, partners are aware of the value of military expertise and military contributions but tend to grant the military liaison a slightly smaller role. While in these three types of regions, trust is the dominant means for establishing good collaboration, control measures are more important in the final type of Safety Regions. The most urbanized regions, facing many societal risks, have large, independently operating emergency response organizations with significant slack resources, which perceive less dependency on military means and are less conducive to collaboration with the military as a consequence. In short, an organizational perspective on Dutch emergency management demonstrates that the role of the armed forces in Dutch emergency response networks can be largely explained by the characteristics of the Safety Regions.

Whereas this research suggests that the type of Safety Region is an explanatory factor for the different roles of the liaisons as well as for the perceived interdependencies and the collaboration mechanisms being used, the aspect of power is not addressed in theories on interorganizational civil-military collaboration, although being referred to frequently by military liaisons. Power is a relevant concept in interorganizational collaboration as organizational interests tend to clash and relative power positions in the collaboration are likely to be unequal, both of which can lead to sub-optimal collaboration if not managed appropriately.[46]

From a ‘power view’ on domestic civil-military collaboration, the military leadership’s wish to enhance the role of the armed forces and the calculated provision of assistance (including frequent rejections of requests) are logical consequences

[44] Galbraith 1977, 1984.

[45] Das and Teng 1998; Bollen 2008; Rietjens and Bollen 2008.

[46] Gray and Hay 1986; Hardy and Phillips 1998.

of the military's organizational interest in self-justification and reputation management.[47] Continuing this line of thought, the unwillingness of emergency partners to request support of the armed forces and the fear to lose control over domains of responsibility are indicators of interorganizational political tensions on the relative positions in the networks.[48] As power is an under-researched aspect both in the literature on emergency management and in the literature on civil-military collaboration, the study of civil-military collaboration in Dutch emergency response would benefit from further research on the applicability of this 'power view'.

References

Audit Functie Defensie en Inspectie Veiligheid en Justitie (2013) Civiel-militaire samenwerking: Eindmeting 2013. https://www.ivenj.nl/actueel/inspectierapporten/rapport-civiel-militaire-samenwerking-(2013).aspx. Accessed 9 Feb 2016

Benson JK (1975) The interorganizational network as a political economy. Adm Sci Q 20:229–249

Boin A, 't Hart P, Stern E, Sundelius B (2005) The politics of crisis management. Cambridge University Press, Cambridge

Bollen MTIB (2008) Refugees in Albania: a case of civil-military cooperation. In: Rietjens SJH, Bollen MTIB (eds) Managing civil-military cooperation: a 24/7 joint effort for stability. Ashgate, Hampshire, pp 51–65

Creswell JH (2003) Research design: qualitative, quantitative, and mixed methods approaches. Sage Publications Inc., Thousand Oaks

Das TK, Teng BS (1998) Between trust and control: developing confidence in partner cooperation in alliances. Acad Manag Rev 23:491–512

Faraj S, Xiao Y (2006) Coordination in fast-response organizations. Manage Sci 52:1155–1189

Galbraith JR (1977) Organization design. Addison-Wesley Publishing Company, Reading

Galbraith JR (1984) Organization design: an information processing view. Army Organ Eff J 8:21–26

Gray B, Hay TM (1986) Political limits to interorganizational consensus and change. J Appl Behav Sci 22:95–112

Hardy C, Phillips N (1998) Strategies of engagement: lessons from the critical examination of collaboration and conflict in an interorganizational domain. Organ Sci 9:217–230

IFV (2014) GRIP-regeling 1 t/m 5 en GRIP Rijk. Instituut voor Fysieke Veiligheid, Arnhem

Majchrzak A, Jarvenpaa SL, Hollingshead AB (2007) Coordinating expertise among emergent groups responding to disasters. Organ Sci 18:147–161

Ministerie van Defensie (2013) In het belang van Nederland. https://www.defensie.nl/documenten/beleidsnota-s/2013/09/17/in-het-belang-van-nederland. Accessed 10 Feb 2016

Ministerie van Defensie (2015) Catalogus Nationale Operaties. https://www.defensie.nl/onderwerpen/nationale-veiligheid/inhoud/catalogus-nationale-operaties. Accessed 10 Feb 2016

Ministry of Defence (2015) Tasks and Future. https://www.defensie.nl/english/topics/tasks-and-future. Accessed 10 Feb 2016

Ministry of Security and Justice (2010) Safety Regions Act. https://www.government.nl/documents/decrees/2010/12/17/dutch-security-regions-act-part-i. Accessed 10 Feb 2016

Mintzberg H (1983) Structure in fives: designing effective organizations. Prentice-Hall Incorporation, Englewood Cliffs

---

[47] Rodriguez et al. 2007.

[48] Benson 1975.

Nationaal Coördinator Terrorismebestrijding en Veiligheid (2013) Nationaal Handboek Crisisbesluitvorming. https://www.rijksoverheid.nl/documenten/brochures/2013/04/26/nationaal-handboek-crisisbesluitvorming. Accessed 10 Feb 2016

Opstelten I (2014) Toekomst van de krijgsmacht. Letter of the Minister of Security and Justice Nr. 39. https://zoek.officielebekendmakingen.nl/kst-33763-39.html. Accessed 10 Feb 2016

Perrow C (1994) The limits of safety: the enhancement of a theory of accidents. J Conting Crisis Manag 2:212–220

Provan KG, Kenis PN (2008) Modes of Network Governance: Structure, Management, and Effectiveness. J Public Adm Res Theor 18:229–252

Quarantelli (1996) Ten criteria for evaluating the management of community disasters. Disaster Research Center, Preliminary Paper #241

Rietjens SJH, Bollen MTIB (2008) Trends, dilemmas and future research on CIMIC. In: Rietjens SJH, Bollen MTIB (eds) Managing civil-military cooperation: a 24/7 joint effort for stability. Ashgate, Hampshire, pp 231–249

Rodriguez C, Langley A, Béland F, Denis JL (2007) Governance, power, and mandated collaboration in an interorganizational network. Adm Soc 39:150–193

Treurniet W (2014) Shaping comprehensive emergency response networks. In: Grant TJ, Janssen RHP, Monsuur H (eds) Network topology in command and control. IGI Global, Hershey, pp 26–47

Treurniet W, van Buul-Besseling K, Wolbers JJ (2012) Collaboration awareness—a necessity in crisis response coordination. In: Proceedings of the 9th International ISCRAM Conference

Veiligheidsberaad (2014) Een verkenning naar de samenwerking tussen veiligheidsregio's en Defensie. Veiligheidsberaad, Arnhem

Chapter 11
Interorganizational Collaboration in Crisis and Disaster Management: The Valuable Asset of Organizational Culture

Helena de Jong

Abstract Organizing for safety and security has become increasingly complex. A multitude of actors is involved trying to respond collaboratively to problems varying from terrorist attacks to natural or man-made disasters. Interorganizational collaborative crisis and disaster management has become an essential tool to deal with multifaceted extreme events. Despite the popularity of collaboration in theory, case research has shown that it is difficult to achieve in practice. The different organizational cultures involved in interorganizational collaboration are perceived as a severe challenge to effective collaboration. This chapter asserts that a culture-as-problem approach is an unhelpful perspective. Cultural differences provide the leverage that is to be gained from collaboration and, if managed, enhance the value of collaborative activities in the field of crisis and disaster management. Increased awareness of organizational culture as an important factor in interorganizational collaboration and a focus on culture as an asset could break an important barrier to effective interorganizational collaboration during crisis or disaster.

Keywords Organizational culture · Interorganizational collaboration · Crisis · Disaster · Crisis and disaster management

---

H. de Jong (✉)
Faculty of Military Sciences, Netherlands Defence Academy, Breda, The Netherlands
e-mail: h.d.jong.19@mindef.nl

R. Beeres et al. (eds.), *NL ARMS Netherlands Annual Review of Military Studies 2016*, NL ARMS, DOI 10.1007/978-94-6265-135-7_11

Contents

11.1 Introduction[1]

An important development in organizing for safety and security has been the forming of interorganizational collaborations. One of the fields in which interorganizational collaboration has become increasingly popular is crisis and disaster management.[2] Disaster and crisis operations, in particular large operations, involve a great amount of organizational and individual participants. The organizations involved in collaborative networks in this field are not just the traditional emergency services like the fire brigade, police and ambulance services but include a variety of actors, e.g.:

- Emergency services; fire, rescue, emergency medical services and law enforcement represent the first institutional response. They, and other emergency responders, might be involved in tackling the emergency on site, warning, evacuation, and communication;
- Authorities; public administrations play a prominent role at all levels during disaster and public servants or elected officials have the ultimate responsibility for making top-level decisions;

[1] The chapter has been written within the context of the Collaboration and Support Action project EDUCEN (European Disasters in Urban Centres: a Culture Expert Network) supported by the European Commission within the framework of Horizon 2020.

[2] Quarantelli 1998 and Perry and Quarantelli 2005 illustrate the existence of many definitions and understandings of disaster. This chapter follows the definition of Von Brainich Felth 2004. He perceives a crisis as a situation in which a vital interest is threatened and normal measures are inadequate to respond to the threat. In this understanding, a disaster is a crisis only on the terrain of the public or physical safety. This entails that disaster management is a part of crisis management, Scholtens 2008, p. 17.

- Other public services; utility companies in the field of electricity, water supply and communication are often involved in the response to restore services;
- Non-governmental organizations; local, national, and international NGOs may be involved in different aspects of disaster management. They may be engaged in disaster risk reduction and in the response phase they may provide e.g. emergency and transitional settlement, shelter, water, healthcare, sanitation;
- Armed forces; in some countries, response to disasters is managed by civil defence or civil protection departments dominated by armed forces personnel. Tasks of the armed forces often include operational and logistical support to civilian teams;[3]
- Communities; play a key role in the complete disaster management cycle.

As a consequence, the actors in crisis and disaster management are characterized by different organizational cultures, with different mandates, interests, assumptions, value commitments and structures influencing the quality of interorganizational collaboration. Despite its positive connotation, effective interorganizational collaboration between these actors has been difficult to achieve in practice.[4] In the context of crisis and disaster management, different organizational cultures have been perceived as an important barrier to interorganizational collaboration. While barriers are important to understand and remedy, a culture-as-problem focus is an unhelpful perspective as it may lead to ignoring important cultural assets in the process of collaboration that in fact provide the leverage that is to be gained from collaborating in the first place. This chapter argues that becoming aware of the different organizational cultures may unlock great potential and help the implementation of collaboration in disaster and crisis management.

An exploratory research approach is taken to highlight the significance of culture in interorganizational collaborations. The chapter first discusses the concept of collaboration, linking it to organizational culture. Second, experiences with interorganizational collaboration in crisis and disaster in practice are explored. Challenges to collaboration in practice are discussed and attempts to manage cultural differences between organizations are addressed. The fourth section looks at cultural aspects in interorganizational collaboration in crisis and disaster management in the Netherlands.

11.2 Collaboration: A Multidimensional Construct

Working collaboratively across organizational and sectoral barriers has become an important feature of organizational life. To improve the quality of disaster and crisis management, policies have been developed to tighten collaboration between emergency responders such as the fire brigade and police. In European context,

---

[3] Wisner et al. 2012.

[4] Scholtens 2007; Kapucu et al. 2010.

there is increasing attention to the role of the armed forces in disaster response within their own national territory. In many of these disasters, local civilian authorities are overwhelmed and call upon the armed forces to provide first aid and logistical support. In this section a definition of collaboration is provided and the influence of organizational culture on collaborative efforts is exemplified.

11.2.1 Defining Collaboration

In interorganizational collaboration, actors from different societal sectors are interacting, at least temporarily, to cope with problems at hand. The complexity of contemporary problems exceeds the capacity of a single organization to manage such issues and interorganizational collaboration has led to the adoption of new collaborative organizational structures.[5] The meaning of collaboration, however, is disputed and there is a lack of consensus among scholars and practitioners. The widespread and diverse usage of the term has for example been criticized by Scholtens who notes that collaboration has become an 'applause term'[6] with solutions to problems routinely being found in collaboration without questioning its necessity.[7] The more or less blind focus on interorganizational collaboration has been criticized by authors stating that there is little room left for the question of whether collaboration actually represents added value.[8] Based on a review of the theoretical literature and field research on collaboration experiences, Thomson et al. arrive at the following definition. "Collaboration is a process in which autonomous actors interact through formal and informal negotiation, jointly creating rules and structures governing their relationships and ways to act or decide on the issues that brought them together; it is a process involving shared norms and mutually beneficial interactions".[9]

Thomson and Perry are supportive of an integrative view on collaboration as a process.[10] Reference to interorganizational collaboration is made to describe, "a process that can emerge as organizations interact with one another to create new organizational and social structures".[11] As Thomson and Perry write, "a process framework for collaboration suggests that collaboration occurs over time as organizations interact formally and informally through repetitive sequences of negotiation, development of commitments, and execution of those commitments".[12] The above

5 Kapucu et al. 2010.

6 Van Twist 2000 uses this term to describe a word that has become so popular in policy debates that the use of it can count on uncritical acceptance among managers.

7 Scholtens 2007.

8 Scholtens 2008.

9 Thomson et al. 2009, p. 25.

10 See also Ring and van de Ven 1994; Gray 2000; Huxham and Vangen 2005.

11 Thomson et al. 2009, p. 23.

12 Thomson and Perry 2006, p. 21.

understandings of collaboration suggest collective action on a higher level than cooperation and coordination.[13] Both cooperation and coordination may occur in an early stage of collaboration but collaboration indicates a longer-term integrated process.[14] Thomson and Perry identify five key dimensions which together signify collaborative action: (1) governance; entailing the establishment of joint decision making structures and goals through shared power arrangement, (2) administration; the establishment of an effective operating system, stipulating the need for concrete achievable goals, communication-, coordination- and monitoring systems, (3) organizational autonomy; referring to the need for organizations in the collaboration to balance their own individual goals with the collaborative goals, (4) mutuality; which entails that collaborations must experience mutually beneficial interdependencies based either on differing or shared interests, and (5) norms; encompassing both reciprocity and trust.[15]

The dimensions illustrate that effective interorganizational collaborating relies not just on formal governance and administration structures, but just as much on mutuality and informal relationships and trust and reciprocity. This is particularly evident in crisis and disaster management, where interorganizational collaboration is often of a temporary, emergent nature.

11.2.2 Organizational Cultures in Collaboration: Challenge or Opportunity?

This chapter argues that interorganizational collaboration is influenced by culture. In the context of disaster and crisis management, fire departments, police, rescue services, civil authorities and others for example have to collaborate closely while working within different cultural frames, different system of values and with different priorities. *Culture* is an important concept across many disciplines used to refer to the characteristics of a particular group of people. This chapter focuses on organizational culture. Organizational culture refers to the shared climate, learned behaviour, and practices that organizations develop over time. It guides the way people work, the way they communicate, and the values they share.[16] Culture points to phenomena that are below the surface, but that are powerful influences on the organization in important ways. It instils shared values in organizational members

[13] The extensive literature on collaboration is without agreement on terms but there seems to be agreement that collaboration requires collective action on a higher level than cooperation or coordination (Thomson and Perry 2006; Alexander 1995) Most scholars agree that cooperation and collaboration are different in terms of their depth of interaction, integration, commitment, and complexity. In research and practice, coordination and collaboration have been used interchangeably.

[14] Thomson and Perry 2006.

[15] Thomson and Perry 2006; Thomson et al. 2009.

[16] Schein 2004.

and also guides their actions much like an individual's personality does. According to Schein, every organization is marked by its own distinct culture, encompassing artefacts (visible organizational structures and processes), espoused beliefs and values (strategies, goals, and philosophies), and underlying assumptions (unconscious, taken for granted beliefs, perceptions, thoughts, and feelings).[17] Organizations tend to develop traditions, symbols and language, ceremonies and customs, all setting them apart from other associations. Some organizations are highly disciplined, others are unsystematic. Some have sharp hierarchical structures, others are characterized by informal and egalitarian structures. Organizational culture can promote solidarity within groups, determine the organization's ability to move forward, to meet the needs of its stakeholders, and influence financial performance.[18] However, the distinctive cultural characteristics that develop within organizations might also strain interorganizational relationships.[19]

Huxham uses the term 'collaborative inertia' to describe situations in which "the apparent rate of work output from a collaboration is slowed down considerably compared to what a casual observer might expect it to be able to achieve".[20] There are several reasons why collaborations may reach such inertia. Among these are difficulties stemming from differences in aims, language, procedures, and culture.[21] Grounded in divergent root-organizations, organizations involved in interorganizational collaboration share only partly common aims. Whereas their diversity may provide the leverage that is to be gained from collaborating, diverging aims also mean that organizations' motives for engaging in collaboration will differ. Moreover, the collaborating organizations often come from different professional and societal sectors. Not only their aims differ, they also work with different professional languages which can make communication difficult. Difficulties in organizational culture result in straightforward tasks being carried out differently in different organizations. Difficulties arise because individuals make unwarranted assumptions about the way things are carried out in partner organizations, or because of the time it would take to make arrangements with all parties concerned. Moreover, real or perceived power differences serve to make some parties vulnerable and exacerbate the potential of misunderstandings.[22]

By definition, collaborative networks seek to bring disparate groups together so that they work effectively and synergistically together.[23] In short, it is collaboration "through which parties who see different aspects of a problem can constructively explore their differences and search for solutions that go beyond their own

[17] Ibid, p. 26.

[18] Barney 1986.

[19] Granot 1999.

[20] Huxham 1996, p. 4.

[21] Huxham 1996, p. 4.

[22] Huxham 1996, p. 4.

[23] Long et al. 2013.

limited vision of what is possible".[24] Many of the benefits of collaboration can be related to the fact that organizations with diverging cultures are involved. The collaboration of organizations with diverging cultures may for example not only result in the sharing of resources, but also in the facilitation of knowledge transfer. Moreover, exposure to alternative assumptions, values and artefacts may improve the quality of thinking about the issue at hand and may stimulate the formation of new knowledge and innovative solutions.[25]

This suggests that culture and cultural diversity can function as reservoirs of available assets that organizations and collaborations have available to them to prevent, mitigate, and respond to crises and disasters. As such, it is of crucial importance to take account of cultural differences between organizations while implementing and organizing collaboration. Moreover, in order to achieve the leverage inherent in the collaboration of organizations with different organizational cultures, it is important to recognize them as asset in the collaboration rather than as a challenge.

11.3 Interorganizational Collaboration in Practice: Managing Cultural Differences

Solutions to problems in crisis and disaster management are often considered routinely in a context of collaboration.[26] Despite the popular connotation of collaboration in disaster and crisis management, case research has shown severe difficulties for collaboration in practice. As Kapucu et al. aptly put it, "Large, complex, and seemingly unsolvable problems, such as catastrophic disasters, are best approached from a cooperative effort combining resources and preventing duplication; however, organizing the cooperative effort is almost as difficult as the problems they are created to address."[27] This section starts with an exploration of the challenges to collaboration in light of diverging organizational cultures. Second, efforts to manage interorganizational collaboration in practice are discussed.

11.3.1 Collaboration in Practice

Interorganizational collaboration in the field of crisis and disaster management is difficult not only because of the complexity of the nature of the incidents but also because of the diverse composition of people and agencies working together, all possessing different skills, knowledge, values, and assumptions. "As a result,

[24] Gray 1989, p. 5 in Thomson et al. 2009, p. 25.

[25] Jackson 1996.

[26] Scholtens 2007; Scholtens 2008.

[27] Kapucu et al. 2010, p. 19.

almost without exception, reports and reflections after disasters express concerns over the emergency agencies' abilities to collaborate".[28] Indeed, there is a lot of evidence suggesting that collaboration is not always happening successfully and that its potential value is therefore not realized.[29]

As an operation involving many players with various organizational backgrounds is not required frequently, the complex response to crisis or disaster is by no means routine. Nevertheless, high stakes are involved and the response must be quick and efficient. In particular at the operational level, collaboration between actors of diverse composition has, however, proved to be difficult. Research of Leukfeldt et al. reveals that collaboration between emergency services on everyday basis goes reasonably well but that shortcomings in the working relationships occur 'on the ground' because "in the heat of the moment employees temporarily lose sight of the interests of the other emergency services".[30] Something similar occurs in case of acute large-scale incidents that do not happen on an everyday basis.[31] Evaluations of large-scale incidents in the Netherlands for example revealed that the operational emergency services "generally function from a monodisciplinary perspective during the acute phase—this is based on their own findings".[32] Time and again, evaluations have shown that any coordination between the various services and organizations in this phase is completely lacking.[33] Interorganizational collaboration is left until later stages of the response. This phenomenon is related to divergence in organizational culture of the organizations. In the first hours of emergency relief, individuals organizations tend to rely on their organizational background and culture which defines the norms and different roles its members will act out intuitively.[34] Several authors point out that when individuals and individual units in crisis conditions have to decide in a split second what to do, they do what they would always do, and revert to the routines, skills and drills as dedicated by their core business: "no matter what the scale of the disaster is, firemen arriving on the scene will attempt to put out the first fires they come across and save the first people they see, medical personnel will concentrate on treating victims, while the police will focus on restoring order".[35] Whereas there has not been found evidence that this obstructs effective response to crisis and disaster,[36] in managing collaboration, cultural differences between the actors in disaster and crisis management are commonly perceived as a liability that needs to be surmounted.

28 Eide et al. 2012.

29 Huxham 1996.

30 Leukfeldt et al. 2007 in Scholtens 2008, p. 200.

31 Scholtens 2008.

32 Scholtens, p. 200.

33 Scholtens 2008 for an overview of evaluations.

34 Scholtens 2008.

35 Scholtens, p. 202.

36 Groenendaal et al. 2013.

11.3.2 Managing Cultural Differences

Managing interorganizational collaboration is complex. Stemming from different backgrounds, the organizations engaged in disaster and crisis management do not have a shared hierarchy or decision making structure. Temporary systems set up to respond to crisis or disaster differ from traditional, stable, systems in several ways. The tasks as well as the personnel are less well understood in a temporary crisis and disaster response, which means they cannot be assigned in ways traditionally relied on to achieve the most effective use of resources. Temporary systems furthermore differ from traditional stable systems because they include members who have never worked before and members who represent a diversity of functions or skills.[37]

To overcome the challenges inherent in diverging organizational cultures in crisis and disaster management, efforts have been made to align the governance and administrative structures of organizations. In managing interorganizational collaboration in crisis and disaster management it is commonly presumed that central coordination mechanisms are required to achieve effective collaboration.[38] Challenges to information sharing, coordination, and communication between the diverging organizations responding to a serious incident have been noted and a common approach to solve this is to align the coordination, information sharing and decision making structures of the collaborating organizations.[39]

In general, the efforts to manage collaboration in crisis and disaster management promote more hierarchical coordination and technological innovations as the solution for improved effectiveness of inter-organization collaboration. Whereas at first sight it might seem logical to coordinate and align the structures of organizations, this approach fails to consider the influence of organizational culture. A similar argument is made by Boersma and Wolbers who point to the importance of looking at cultural aspects in information sharing. During crisis and disaster response, each organization has operational field units at different levels, different command structures and separate back offices for information and resource management.[40] Adequate information sharing is therefore regarded as crucial to overcome problems with coordination and information sharing between the different organizational domains.[41] Wolbers and Boersma argue that the dominant approach of making information widely available is not enough for achieving effective crisis and disaster management.

The way in which information is interpreted and guides the operations of the emergency responders is just as important. Responding officers are confronted

---

[37] Meyerson et al. 1996.

[38] Waugh and Streib 2006; Moynihan 2008; Leonard and Howitt 2010; Groenendaal et al. 2013.

[39] Janssen et al. 2010; Comfort 2007; Netten and van Someren 2011; Kapucu and Garayev 2011.

[40] Wolbers and Boersma 2013.

[41] Wolbers and Boersma 2013.

with different professional languages, jargon, values, and assumptions. To achieve a shared goal, first responders need to coordinate their actions temporarily and locally across their organizational boundaries, in which they must navigate their differences in norms, meanings, and interests with members of other organizations. The research by Wolbers and Boersma shows that not only the information itself is important and points also to the importance of the way in which it is interpreted and subsequently guides the operations of emergency responders.[42] The above example reflects the vital importance of recognizing the influence of different organizational cultures in interorganizational collaborations. Managing these differences and using them as an asset to improve the collaborative effort would enhance the value and productivity of interorganizational collaboration during crises and disasters.

11.4 Taking Account of Cultural Differences in Interorganizational Collaboration in the Netherlands

The above sections have stipulated the necessity to consider organizational culture as an important factor in interorganizational collaboration in crisis and disaster management. So far, evaluations of interorganizational collaboration during incidents in the Netherlands have not been unequivocally positive. This section starts with an introduction on the organization interorganizational collaboration in crisis and disaster management in the Netherlands. Second, it illustrates how diverging organizational cultures are of influence on each of the collaboration dimensions identified by Thomson and Perry, stipulating how collaboration in the Netherlands may benefit from increased attention to the role of organizational culture. The section concludes with a framework providing an overview of the findings (Table 11.1). Table 11.1 provides an overview of the links found between the collaboration dimensions and the influence of organizational culture in crisis and disaster management.[43]

11.4.1 Introducing Collaboration in Disaster and Crisis Management in the Netherlands

The subject of multidisciplinary collaboration in the field of disaster management is very much in the spotlight in the Netherlands.[44] Since the 1980s, increased

[42] Wolbers and Boersma 2013 refer to this process as ‘collective sensemaking’.

[43] Thomson and Perry 2006.

[44] Scholtens 2008.

collaboration between emergency services and public bodies has received attention. In 1983 the *Reorganisatie Rampenbestrijding* (*Disaster Management Reorganization*) project was launched. Its objective was to create a new administrative and organizational structure for dealing with disasters. The idea was that the new disaster management organization consisted of a combination of independent organizations which would act as a single body during a disaster or crisis, stipulating a crucial role for collaboration between the organizations.[45] More recently, the 9/11 attacks in the United States, as well as large-scale national incidents such as the airplane crash in the Amsterdam suburb the Bijlmermeer in 1992, the explosion in the firework factory in May 2000 in the town of Enschede, and the fire in a Volendam café at New Year's Eve 2001 have put safety high on the political agenda and led to increased attention to the enhancement of interorganizational collaboration.[46]

Until 2010, the preparation of crises and disasters was the responsibility of local governments. With new types of disaster, such as the foot and mouth crisis of 2003, and the threat of terrorism, which easily exceed municipal boundaries—a different type of approach was needed, including different partners and a different strategy. As most municipalities are too small to be able to perform all tasks required for disaster and crisis management, uniform service levels were established within cooperation areas, or so called 'safety regions', to facilitate mutual assistance.[47] In 2010, with the establishment of 25 safety regions the responsibilities from the local level were therefore transferred to the regional level of government. With the safety regions, the Netherlands strives to achieve an efficient and high-quality interorganizational collaboration of the fire services, medical assistance and crisis management under one regional management board.[48]

11.4.2 Interorganizational Collaboration and Governance

Governance of the collaborative effort entails the establishment of joint decision making structures and the creation of structures for reaching agreement on collaborative activities. In the literature on collaboration governance is also described as participative decision making, shared power arrangements, and problem solving. Thomson and Perry note that each of these terms, amongst others, implies a lack of authoritative structure or hierarchical division of labor, a willingness to accept that partners in the collaboration have legitimate interests, and the chance of lengthy negotiations to reach agreement.[49] Despite this, a key presumption that

[45] Scholtens 2007.

[46] Boersma et al. 2009.

[47] Dutch Safety Regions Act 2010.

[48] Dutch Safety Regions Act 2010.

[49] Thomson 2001; Thomson and Perry 2006.

can be observed in the Netherlands is the belief that activities must be hierarchically governed to achieve smooth management of the emergency services and effective interorganizational collaboration.

As explained, the Netherlands is divided into 25 safety regions which can be seen as a form of extended local governance. Each municipality participates and has co-responsibility for the administrative and organizational management of the safety region.[50] Each safety region has a management board comprising all the mayors of the participating municipalities. The chairman of the management board is one of the mayors. The management board must be able to respond to a wide variety of disasters and crises and coordinate their actions with many partners. In the event of supra-local disasters, the chairman of the safety region takes over the relevant powers from the involved mayors. This entails that all authority is concentrated in one person. The decision to put one person in command is based on the presumption that clear hierarchical relationships are needed in the event of crises and disasters. In situations of crisis or disaster, the perspective is that without a clear command structure there is the risk of stagnation in decision making with regard to the measures to be taken and of miscommunication in the command lines to and from the organizations involved.[51] The disaster management coordination structure in the Netherlands is therefore also known as the command structure.

Cultural aspects

The understanding that collaboration implies a hierarchical command structure has serious consequences for collaboration between multiple actors with diverging organizational cultures in practice. Whereas a hierarchical approach works reasonably well in routine circumstances, it has been noted that under the dynamic conditions of crisis or disaster such procedures almost always fail.[52] A hierarchical form of governance furthermore assumes there is a need and possibility for controlling front-line units in the first hours of large-scale crises or disasters.[53] As demonstrated earlier, evaluations in the Netherlands have shown that coordination between the various services and organizations in the acute phase is completely lacking.[54] Research for example revealed that tactical and strategic commanders of the Amsterdam Amstelland Fire Service in the Netherlands have little control over their front-line units, despite their hierarchical position in the incident command system. There is no report of problems with this lack of control.[55] The priorities of the organizations are rightly aimed at fulfilling the tasks of one's own organization.[56] Hierarchical approach has been taken without much consideration of how

[50] Dutch Safety Regions Act 2010.

[51] Dutch Safety Regions Act 2010, p. 37.

[52] Comfort and Kapucu 2006; Janssen et al. 2010.

[53] Groenendaal et al. 2013.

[54] Scholtens 2008.

[55] Groenendaal et al. 2013.

[56] Scholtens 2008.

the individual, diverging organizational cultures could each contribute to the mutual goal of responding to crisis. It has even been noted that in some incidents, the professionalization of interorganizational collaborations have frustrated emergency responders in delivering their core business.[57] The important advantages of diverging organizational cultures, such as the transfer of knowledge, sharing of resources, and innovative solutions may easily be hindered by a hierarchical approach which poses constraints on innovation and the ability to shift resources and action to quickly meet new demands.

11.4.3 Interorganizational Collaboration and Administration

Organizations collaborate because they intend to achieve a particular goal. To achieve this goal, an administrative structure must exist that moves from governance to action. Such administrative structures require a central role for coordinating communication and organizing and disseminating information.[58] In the establishment of an effective operating system, both administrative coordination and operational coordination are considered crucial for the implementation of interorganizational collaboration in the Netherlands. Interorganizational collaboration in the acute phase of a disaster has been divided into three coordination levels: (1) administrative coordination (mayor in supreme command and in the case of large disaster on a greater than local scale); (2) operational leadership; and (3) presence and operations at the place of the disaster.[59]

The emergency management system consists of an emergent structure that can be scaled up after the emergency response center notifies the police, fire brigade, and/or medical assistance. Officers in command from the notified organizations are called to the incident scene, each responsible for their own operational units on the scene. An officer in command bears responsibility for the interorganizational coordination with other emergency services. A mobile field command center is established to support this duties.[60] Adequate information management is considered a crucial condition for effective functioning of crisis and disaster management.[61] The coordination structure as described above is however different from the day-to-day collaboration between the fire brigade, police, and other actors involved in disaster or crisis response.[62] In routine operations, the crisis management and incident room systems of the emergency services are often not connected with each organization using its own sources of information and its own systems. In the

[57] Helsloot 2015.

[58] Thomson and Perry 2006.

[59] Scholtens 2015.

[60] Wolbers and Boersma 2013.

[61] Wolbers et al. 2012.

[62] Scholtens 2008.

Netherlands, as in other countries, improvements regarding information management between different organizations are often sought in more advanced and better-equipped information systems that promise to support its users to reach shared situational awareness by creating a common operational picture.[63]

Cultural aspects

Despite clear differences between the assumptions, beliefs and values, and professional languages of disaster and crisis management organizations, current efforts to improve the quality of information sharing often do not take account of diverging organizational cultures. Rather, more advanced information systems and measures such as the creation of a common operational picture have been treated as a solution to the problem of incomplete information. This overlooks the cultural aspect that different organizations and actors give different meanings to information at different points in time. The research of Wolbers and Boersma on emergency response rooms in Amsterdam shows that information provided during disaster and crisis response incorporates different professional languages. If the aspects of organizational culture in information sharing are ignored, different interpretations of information do not become visible with potential misinterpretations or misunderstandings as a result. Overlooking the influence of organizational culture stands in the way of effective interorganizational collaboration. Rather they could be used as an asset to improve effective information sharing. Recognizing the influence of organizational cultures and their influence on, in this example, interpretations of information might enhance the value of information sharing and thereby contribute to the effectivity of interorganizational collaboration in crisis and disaster management.

11.4.4 Interorganizational Collaboration and Autonomy

The third collaboration dimension captures both the dynamism and frustration that is implicit in interorganizational collaboration.[64] In collaborative efforts, partners share a dual identity. Huxham refers to this tension as the autonomy-accountability dilemma: organizations maintain their own distinct organizational identities separate from the collaborative identity, thereby creating a tension between self-interest of achieving individual organizational missions and maintaining an organizational identity, and a collective interest.[65] When the collaboration's goals conflict with the goals of the individual partner organization, identities are at stake.[66] Considering the temporary nature of interorganizational collaboration during crises and

[63] Wolbers and Boersma 2013; Comfort 2007.

[64] Thomson and Perry 2006.

[65] Huxham 1996; Thomson and Perry 2006.

[66] Huxham 1996; Thomson and Perry 2006.

disasters, we can expect that representatives from collaborating organizations are pulled between feeling accountable to the demands of their root organization and the demands of their collaborative partners. Despite the fact that this may create tension in the collaborative effort, maintaining individual organizational cultures and identities is essential since partners need to justify their involvement in the collaboration in terms of its contribution to their own aims, or refrain from collaborating altogether.[67]

Cultural aspects

When a command and control system such as in the Netherlands is imposed on a highly collaborative context this could easily be seen as interference in organizations' individual approach.[68] As noted before in this chapter, evaluations of large-scale incidents in the Netherlands revealed that collaboration between the operational emergency services in the first response phase is lacking. Several authors have noted that this is not necessarily a problem and that on operational level, at least in the first response hours, 'working apart together'[69] does not obstruct effective crisis and disaster management.[70] Rather, the diverging organizational cultures of organizations bring important advantages and illustrate that the dual identity of organizations in collaboration does not necessarily obstruct effective crisis or disaster management. Individual organizational missions such as 'putting out a fire' justify organization's involvement in the collaboration in terms of its contribution to their own aims. Moreover, the increasing attempts of professionalization and top-down governance and administration of the collaborative effort might lead to frustration of representatives of the collaborating organizations which are then pulled between the requirements of their root organizations and the demands of the collaborative organizations. The autonomy of collaborating organizations might be hindered by command and control approaches, leaving little room for organizations' cultures and risking even to block the work of frontline responders, to an extent that they cannot do their jobs anymore.[71]

11.4.5 Interorganizational Collaboration and Mutuality

Mutuality has its roots in interdependence. Collaborating organizations must experience mutually beneficial interdependencies based on either differing interests (complementarities), or on shared interests which is usually based on similarity between organizations, or on a shared passion or moral imperative.[72] Given the current complex safety threats, in crises or disaster, organizations depend on each other's expertise to respond incidents. Indeed, crises such as Moerdijk, and the fire

[67] Huxham 1996.

[68] Scholtens 2007.

[69] See for example Bollen 2002; Helsloot 2008.

[70] Groenendaal et al. 2013; Scholtens 2008.

[71] Groenendaal et al. 2013; Helsloot 2015.

[72] Thomson and Perry 2006.

in a Schiphol detention center illustrates that during such incidents no single emergency responder in the Netherlands is capable of reaching its own goals without related activities, resources, and cooperative behavior of others.[73] Mutuality is manifest in partner organizations that combine and use each other's resources to everyone's benefit, share information to strengthen each other's operations and programs, feel respected by each other, and achieve their own goals better working together other than separate.[74] In short, "mutuality provides a foundation for forging common views out of differences".[75] It is about learning how to bring together each other's complementary skills, and about learning from the knowledge and experience of others. Awareness of each other's resources and goals is however not sufficient for effective interorganizational collaboration. Awareness about the organizational cultures of the collaborative partners is required as well.

Cultural aspects

Shared collaboration awareness entails knowledge about both the formal structures and the informal ways in which organizations work and achieve their goals. This chapter argues that to improve effectiveness of interorganizational collaboration in crisis and disaster management, the collaborating organizations must be aware of each other's organizational culture. Knowing the other actors during crisis and disaster management, and the artefacts, values, and underlying assumptions inherent in their diverging cultures, enhances the understanding of each other's individual assumptions and missions, thereby increasing the likelihood that mutual beneficial results can be reached.

An example of mutuality emerges from the increased involvement of the armed forces in national crisis and disaster management in the Netherlands. The 'traditional' actors in crisis and disaster management benefit from specialized technologies and resources of the Defence organization, such as specialized divers with high-tech equipment, helicopters, and manpower. The armed forces on the other hand benefit from collaboration as it legitimates their institutional existence and budgetary demands.[76] Providing insight into the capacities and resources of the armed forces and its added value in disaster and crisis management has been facilitated through the publication of the catalogue of national operations.

11.4.6 Interorganizational Collaboration and Reciprocity and Trust

Both trust and reciprocity are identified as key factors in successful collective action. Partners in collaboration are often only willing to interact collaboratively if

[73] Treurniet et al. 2012.

[74] Thomson et al. 2008.

[75] Thomson and Perry 2006, p. 27.

[76] Edmunds 2006.

other partners demonstrate the same willingness.[77] A reputation of trustworthiness has therefore proven critical in collaborative efforts.[78] Trust has been shown to have a beneficial impact on a range of individual, group, and organizational performance outcomes and high levels of trust are required to collaboratively respond to crisis and disaster. Both reciprocity and trust are seen as longer term processes that develop over time, and trust building in particular has been said to take a lot of time and nurturing.[79] Organizations that have previously been engaged in collaborative efforts have had the chance to build dialogue and trust and therefore tend to be more productive in collaborative decision-making.[80] The urgency and irregular incidence of crises and disasters however limits the opportunity for emergency responders to develop and rely on trust-based relationships during a crisis or disaster.[81] Collaborative training and exercises of organizations involved in crisis and disaster management could facilitate more structural forms of trust-building.

Cultural aspects

Issues relating to different organizational cultures pose serious challenges for building and sustaining reciprocity and trust in interorganizational collaboration. People from different organizational cultures often bring unfamiliar values and beliefs, distinctive behaviours, or even incompatible assumptions to the table. As Schein explains, we will be maximally comfortable with people and organizations who share the same set of values and assumptions and very uncomfortable and vulnerable in situations where different assumptions operate, because we either do not understand what is going on or the actions of others are misperceived and misinterpreted.[82] Developing and maintaining trust between different organizational cultures is a challenge. In order to improve familiarity and achieve situational normality with each other and reduce uncertainty about the intentions of the other actors, the safety regions in the Netherlands are obliged to organize training and exercises on an annual basis. The organization of exercises and trainings in the field of crisis and disaster management is however complex. Practicing the entire collaboration structure requires a huge logistical operation and the teams therefore hardly practice together. Despite its importance in interorganizational collaboration, interaction between the separate organizations almost never happens.[83]

Table 11.1 summarizes the findings of this section and provides an overview of the links found between the five collaboration dimensions and the influence of organizational culture in crisis and disaster management.

---

[77] Thomson and Perry 2006.

[78] Ostrom 1998; Thomson and Perry 2006.

[79] Huxham and Vangen 2005.

[80] Ansell and Gash 2008.

[81] Moynihan 2008.

[82] Schein 2004.

[83] Scholtens 2015.

Table 11.1 Collaboration dimensions and organizational culture

Collaboration dimension	Influence of organizational culture
Governance	The extent to which the advantages of diverging organizational cultures (e.g., the sharing of knowledge, adapting to new situations, and finding innovative solutions) are facilitated within the collaboration is dependent on the way the collaborative effort is governed. With a variety of organizational cultures involved in the collaboration, certain types of governance seem to be more suitable than others. A hierarchical command structure may pose constraints on the ability of first level emergency responders to shift resources and action to quickly meet new demands
Administration	The effectiveness of administrative structures and systems is influenced by organizational culture. Current solutions to improve administrative structures are frequently sought in technological systems which often do not take account of the impact of organizational cultures on the effectiveness of such systems. Information sharing systems may for example be prone to different interpretations of information by different organizations due to diverging professional languages and operational rules of behavior. The effectiveness of administrative structures and systems may increase when organizational cultures are taken into consideration
Organizational autonomy	Inherent in interorganizational collaboration is the tension between the autonomous goals of individual organizations, and those of the collaboration. Although this may create tension, maintaining individual organizational cultures and identities is essential since partners need to justify their involvement in the collaboration in terms of its contribution to their own aims. It is important that the increasing attempts to organize and lead the collaboration from above are sensitive to this issue, as individual missions often trump collaborative missions when challenged
Mutuality	Partners in collaboration need to experience mutually beneficial interdependencies to make the effort successful. This not only entails knowledge on each other's resources or a shared moral motive, it also implies knowing the other actors during crisis and disaster management, and the artefacts, values, and underlying assumptions inherent in their diverging cultures. This enhances the understanding of each other's individual assumptions and missions, thereby increasing the likelihood that mutual beneficial results can be reached
Norms: reciprocity and trust	The development of reciprocity and trust takes time. Organizational culture influences the openness and willingness of organizations to collaborate. People used to different organizational cultures have unfamiliar values and beliefs and other assumptions which might lead to misinterpretation or misunderstanding, or even release defensiveness. The organization of exercises and trainings including the entire collaboration might enhance trust-building in crisis and disaster management

Source Author's compilation based on the collaboration dimensions distinguished by Thomson and Perry 2006

11.5 Conclusion

In organizing for safety, an important quest can be seen in working collaboratively across organizational and sectoral boundaries to solve complex contemporary problems. Crisis and disaster management has been one of the fields in which interorganizational collaboration between authorities, emergency responders, the armed forces and others has risen as an important means to respond to new types of threats crossing local, regional, or even national boundaries. The aspect of organizational culture has so far received limited attention in such interorganizational collaborations. This is despite the fact that case research has demonstrated that diverging organizational cultures influence the collaborative effort.

The chapter has argued that the inclusion of organizations with diverging organizational cultures provides important leverage to interorganizational collaboration in crisis and disaster management. Organizational diversity for example allows organizations to learn from each other and to search for innovative solutions that go beyond their own views.

It has been illustrated in this chapter that organizational culture is of influence on each of the five collaboration dimensions distinguished by Thomson and Perry. This has been largely disregarded in current efforts to implement collaboration in crisis and disaster management, leaving little room for the advantages diverging organizational cultures might bring to the collaboration. Rather, efforts to manage collaboration have largely taken a culture-as-problem approach that can be solved through hierarchical leadership and more advanced technological systems. Moreover, limited attention has been given to the facilitation of knowledge on what each other's organizational cultures can bring to the collaborative effort, and to the building of reciprocity and trust through combined exercises and trainings. It can be concluded that a culture-as-problem focus is unhelpful in facilitating effective interorganizational collaboration. To enhance the value of collaboration in crisis and disaster management, an increased awareness of the role of organizational culture as an asset is essential. Further research is required on how to integrate organizational culture not only into research but also in policy and practice of crisis and disaster management.

References

Alexander ER (1995) How organizations act together: interorganizational coordination in theory and practice. Gordon and Breach Publishers, Luxembourg

Ansell C, Gash A (2008) Collaborative governance in theory and practice. J Public Adm Res Theor 18:543–571

Barney JB (1986) Organizational culture: can it be a source of sustained competitive advantage? Acad Manag Rev 11:656–665

Boersma K, Groenewegen P, Wagenaar P (2009) Emergency response rooms in action: an ethnographic case-study in Amsterdam. Proceedings of the 6th International Conference on Information Systems for Crisis Response and Management ISCRAM. Gothenburg, Sweden, pp 1–8

Bollen M (2002) Working apart together. Civiel-militaire samenwerking tijdens humanitaire operaties. Ph.D. dissertation Wageningen University, HAVEKA BV, Alblasserdam

Comfort LK (2007) Crisis management in hindsight: cognition, communication, coordination, and control. Public Adm Rev 67:189–197

Comfort LK, Kapucu N (2006) Inter-organizational coordination in extreme events: the World Trade Center attacks, September 11, 2001. Nat Hazards 39:309–327

Dutch Safety Regions Act (2010) https://www.government.nl/documents/decrees/2010/12/17/dutch-security-regions-act-part-i Accessed 15 March 2016

Edmunds T (2006) What are armed forces for? The changing nature of military roles in Europe. Int Aff 82:1059–1075

Eide AW, Halvorsrud R, Haugstveit IM, Skjetne JH, Stiso M (2012) Key challenges in multi-agency collaboration during large-scale emergency management. In: AmI for crisis management, international joint conference on ambient intelligence, Pisa, Italy

Granot H (1999) Emergency inter-organizational relationships. Disaster Prev Manag 8:21–26

Gray B (1989) Collaborating: finding common ground for multiparty problems. Jossey-Bass, San Francisco, CA

Gray B (2000) Assessing inter-organizational collaboration: multiple conceptions and multiple methods. In: Faulkner D, de Rond M (eds) Cooperative strategy: economic, business, and organizational issues. Oxford University Press, New York, pp 243–260

Groenendaal J, Helsloot I, Scholtens A (2013) A critical examination of the assumptions regarding centralized coordination in large-scale emergency situations. J Homel Secur Emerg Manage 10:113–135

Helsloot I (2008) Coordination is a prerequisite for good collaboration, isn't it? J Contingencies Crisis Manag 16:173–176

Helsloot I (2015) De magere opbrengst van 30 jaar continue professionalisering in de rampenbestrijding in Nederland. In: Devroe E, Duchatelet A, Ponsaers P, Easton M, Moor LG, Wondergem L (eds) Zicht op first responders: Handboek bij het beheer van evenementen en noodsituaties in Nederland en België. Maklu, Antwerpen/Apeldoorn, pp 323–337

Huxham C (1996) Collaboration and collaborative advantage. In: Huxham C (ed) Creating collaborative advantage. SAGE, Thousand Oaks, pp 1–18

Huxham C, Vangen S (2005) Managing to collaborate: the theory and practice of collaborative advantage. Routledge, London

Jackson SE (1996) The consequences of diversity in multidisciplinary work teams. In: West MA (ed) Handbook of work group psychology. Wiley, New York, pp 53–76

Janssen M, Lee J, Bharosa N, Cresswell A (2010) Advances in multi-agency disaster management: key elements in disaster research. Inf Syst Front 12:1–7

Kapucu N, Garayev V (2011) Collaborative decision-making in emergency and disaster management. Int J Public Adm 34:366–375

Kapucu N, Arslan T, Collins ML (2010) Examining intergovernmental and interorganizational response to catastrophic disasters: toward a network-centered approach. Adm Soc 42:222–247

Meyerson D, Weick KE, Kramer RM (1996) Swift trust and temporary groups. In: Kramer RM, TR Tyler (eds) Trust in organizations: frontiers of theory and research. Sage, Thousand Oaks, pp 166–195

Leonard HB, Howitt AM (2010) Organizing responses to extreme emergencies: the Victorian bushfires of 2009. Aust J Public Adm 69:372–386

Leukfeldt ER, van der Straten KWC, Stol W (2007) Ter plaatse. Alledaagse samenwerking tussen de primaire hulpverleningsdiensten. Boom Juridische Uitgevers, The Hague

Long JC, Cunningham FC, Braithwaite J (2013) Bridges, brokers and boundary spanners in collaborative networks: a systematic review. BMC Health Services Research 13:158

Moynihan DP (2008) Learning under uncertainty: networks in crisis management. Public Adm Rev 68:350–365

Netten N, van Someren M (2011) Improving communication in crisis management by evaluating the relevance of messages. J Contingencies Crisis Manag 19:75–85

Ostrom E (1998) A behavioral approach to the rational choice theory of collective action. Am Polit Sci Rev 92:1–22

Perry RW, Quarantelli EL (eds) (2005) What is a disaster? New answers to old questions. Xlibris Corporation, USA

Quarantelli EL (1998) What is a disaster? Perspectives on the Question. Routledge, London

Ring PS, van de Ven AH (1994) Development processes of cooperative inter-organizational relationships. Acad Manag Rev 19:90–118

Schein EH (2004) Organizational culture and leadership. Wiley

Scholtens A (2007) Samenwerking in crisisbeheersing. Overschat en onderschat. Lectorale rede. http://www.nifv.nl/upload/117924_668_1197380114765-Lectorale_rede.pdf Accessed 14 Mar 2016

Scholtens A (2008) Controlled Collaboration in Disaster and Crisis Management in the Netherlands, History and Practice of an Overestimated and Underestimated Concept. J Contingencies Crisis Manag 16:195–207

Scholtens A (2015) Samenwerkingsstructuren bij beheer van rampen in Nederland. In: Devroe E, Duchatelet A, Ponsaers P, Easton M, Gunther Moor L, Wondergem L (eds) Zicht op first responders: Handboek bij het beheer van evenementen en noodsituaties in Nederland en België. Maklu, Antwerpen/ Apeldoorn, pp 103–117

Thomson, AM (2001) Collaboration: meaning and measurement. Ph.D. dissertation, Indiana University, Bloomington

Thomson AM, Perry JL (2006) Collaboration processes: inside the black box. Public Adm Rev 66:20–32

Thomson AM, Perry JL, Miller TK (2008) Linking collaboration processes and outcomes: foundations for advancing empirical theory. In: Bingham LB, O'Leary R (eds) Big ideas in collaborative public management. ME Sharpe Publishers, Armonk, New York, pp 97–120

Thomson AM, Perry JL, Miller TK (2009) Conceptualizing and measuring collaboration. J Public Adm Res Theor 19:23–56

Treurniet W, van Buul-Besseling K, Wolbers J (2012) Collaboration awareness—a necessity in crisis response coordination. Simon Fraser University, Vancouver Canada

Van Twist M (2001) De corrosie van het begrip corridor. Producten, projecten en processen. Berenschot Procesmanagement, Den Haag, pp 47–49

Von Brainich Felth ET (2004) Het systeem van crisisbeheersing. Boom Juridische Uitgevers, Den Haag

Waugh WL, Streib G (2006) Collaboration and leadership for effective emergency management. Public Adm Rev 66:131–140

Wisner B, Gaillard JC, Kelman I (eds) (2012) Handbook of hazards and disaster risk reduction and management. Routledge, New York, London

Wolbers JJ, Boersma K, de Heer J (2012) Netcentrisch werken in ontwikkeling. Een cultuuronderzoek naar multidisciplinaire samenwerking en gezamenlijke operationele beelden in de Veiligheidsregio's. http://keesboersma.com/wp-content/uploads/2012/05/Netcentrisch_Werken_inontwikkeling_def.pdf. Accessed 14 Mar 2016

Wolbers JJ, Boersma FK (2013) The common operational picture as collective sensemaking. J Contingencies Crisis Manag 21:186–199

Part III
Applications

Chapter 12
Governance and the Decline of Violence

René Moelker

Abstract Historians and political scientists alike have confirmed a decline in inter and intra state violence. There is broad consensus regarding this decline. The world never will be perfectly safe, but many correlates of violence are known and therefore it is possible to manage safety and security. War, is neither a fate of nature nor a whim of Gods. In this chapter the relation of governance and safety and security is studied. Therefore, we look at the interplay of agency and the opportunity structure, or the interplay between the governance triad and the governance opportunity structure. In more plain words, one should study the tensions between actors within the context of the historically grown structure. This structure restricts action and the degrees of freedom to human action but it is also an enabler. It enables actors to realize their objectives within the limits of political feasibility and these limits are in fact a balancing act. Governance develops from the tensions between actors and the interplay of these tensions with the dimensions of the opportunity structure and governance in its turn is correlated with a decline of violence. To understand the mechanism at work better we should look more closely into the dimensions of this opportunity structure and study how the monopoly of violence and taxation, the rule of law and the moral order contributes to safety and security. The chapter concludes that although in general governance is on the rise, and violence is declining, serious challenges will have to be dealt with.

Keywords State · Violence · Safety and security · Governance triad · Governance opportunity structure · Rule of law · Monopoly of violence · Monopoly of taxation · Moral order

---

R. Moelker (✉)
Faculty of Military Sciences, Netherlands Defence Academy, Breda, The Netherlands
e-mail: r.moelker.01@mindef.nl

R. Beeres et al. (eds.), *NL ARMS Netherlands Annual Review of Military Studies 2016*, NL ARMS, DOI 10.1007/978-94-6265-135-7_12

Contents

12.1 Governance and the State

Life in the Middle Ages was gruesome, hard, grim and fierce … and also some kind of beautiful, joyful and in a way abundant. That much we understand from Huizinga's *Autumn of the Middle Ages*.[1] Huizinga is difficult to translate, and even the latest translation poorly reflects his beautiful prose. For starters, the title of the opening chapter *'s levens felheid* is semantically a complex construct. 'Felheid' actually refers to the emotional life during feudal times, which was certainly more spiked with ups and downs than dulled life in modern times. Perhaps Huizinga was not the first chronicler of emotions but he certainly ranks among the best. In English the chapter is translated *The Passionate Intensity of Life* which only captures the meaning of 'felheid' by proximity.

Punishments were harsh and without the penal system followed the whims of the ruler. Corporal punishment, interrogation systems, torture, and hanging from the gallows (and worse) where not only tools of inquiry or execution but foremost they publicly reaffirmed the order of things. And the executions attracted large crowds who were thirsty for some rough kind of justice and thirsty for blood. The governmental display of violence was greeted with public enthusiasm. One at least gets the impression that the populace enjoyed the public display of horror in the same manner that we nowadays applaud celluloid representations of atrocities by actors re-enacted. Disease and disaster made people realize they still were close to nature and thus they turned to some deity that provided a theodicy, an explanation for suffering.

For sure there was a governance system, but it deviated in many respects from the characteristics of good governance formulated by the United Nations: consensus oriented; participatory; following the rule of law; effective and efficient; accountable; transparent; responsive; equitable and inclusive.[2] The governance

[1] Huizinga 1997.

[2] Bovens et al. 2012, pp. 24–35; these characteristics of good governance are well described, well documented, and widely accepted. Many sources refer to these characteristics. Moreover, many data banks have been compiled that present a clear overview. One of the most comprehensive is the data bank from the World Bank that gives specifics for all characteristics (indicators) of good governance, http://info.worldbank.org/governance/wgi/index.aspx#reports.

that Huizinga described was by comparison rude and primitive, in transparent, unjust, not really participatory, nor accountable or responsive. Rule of law was subordinate to the rule of the duke, count, or other noble man. And efficient or effective? Well, that is a matter of definition. After all the moral order, installed and condoned by God himself, was perpetual and defended by honourable knights who were portrayed to be living by their code of chivalry but who in reality abused the servant class and forced them into bondage. Servitude in an agricultural system, based on land ownership, defined the foundations of the socio-economic and socio-political system. Life was not safe and not secure, but it was intense, and it flamed whenever allowed to flame, and also it was short.

Huizinga's vivid description of war is even more enlightening. And the narrative is quite in line with works of other historians. The Middle Ages have seen many wars. War really was an accepted continuation of politics. The astonishing word in this last sentence is 'accepted'. Politicians nowadays ponder and hesitate before they rally the nation.[3] But prominent scholars on the brink of the renaissance could imagine a state even worse, the state of nature. Thomas Hobbes hypothesised a state without any form of government and paraphrasing Plautus he stated men in the state of nature to be *homo homini lupus*. Men are in a state of wolves amongst wolves pursuing their self-interest, which would result *in bellum omnium contra omnes*, a war of all against all. Life scientists object to this egoistic image of men, because the human kind as species is social and in need of affiliation. Additionally, life scientists jokingly object because Hobbes' premise does not do justice to wolves! But Hobbes does make sense to a certain degree. Anthropologists no longer unconditionally view hunter-gathering societies as peaceful and they have the evidence to substantiate their findings. Modern warlord politics is very much reminiscent of feudal strife and seems to operate by similar mechanics. In 'nature' people are not restraining from violence by default, but by some kind of rule of law.

Because of the rather cruel state of nature, rational actors agree to a covenant with the state *in casu* the king who is granted sovereignty. The idea is that it is preferred to have a single authority above the population instead of anarchy. Hobbes distinguishes monarchy, aristocracy and democracy as possible ways to organize governance. But even autocratic forms of governance have merits. People would rather consent to an autocratic and even despotic leader, than be subjected to chaos, anarchy and the war of all against all. Thus the social contract implies a trade off between autonomy of the individual against collective security. Hobbes describes the range of power of the ruler to be almost absolute, hence he nicknames the state 'Leviathan', which refers to a biblical sea monster.[4] The power of

---

[3] Sheehan 2006.

[4] In Melville's Moby Dick the sperm whale is respectfully referred to as the 'Leviathan'. Some translations of the bible mention the Leviathan to be a gigantic sea crocodile. The metaphor of the state being a monstrous construction is evident.

the state is omnipotent, omnipresent and absolute because "covenants without the sword, are but words, and of no strength to secure a man at all".[5]

Hobbes is criticized for both his rational actor model, his negative view of human nature and his social contract exchange solution, but Hobbes' contribution regarding the primary function of the state is still standing, and this function regards the provision of safety and security. A Janusian face thus characterizes the state: on the one hand states are power containers, on the other they are safety and security containers.[6] *Security* often refers to protection from other people, such as thieves, terrorists, adversaries in conflict and war, whereas *safety* etymologically stems from the latin *salvas*, meaning *healthy*. Sometimes the latter means 'firmly fixed'. Hence organizing for security is externally oriented, whereas organizing for safety is internally oriented.[7]

In this chapter the relationship between governance and the organization of safety and security will be explored. Due to its exploratory character the method applied is based on an eclectic perusal of literature that will offer a theoretical framework as well as examples. First, the governance triad will be defined and illustrated by amongst others an Afghan example. This example is given to illustrate the action logic of the stakeholders in a particular given situation. Then four dimensions of the governance opportunity structure are introduced. These dimensions are then elaborated in sections on the monopoly of violence, the monopoly of taxation, rule of law, and the moral order. The conclusion ends the chapter.

12.2 The Governance Triad

People in real life don't always act rationally but our models of human agency are rational, to quote Max Weber "Soziales Handeln aber soll ein solches Handeln heißen, welches seinem von dem oder den Handelnden gemeinten Sinn nach auf das Verhalten anderer bezogen wird und daran in seinem Ablauf orientiert ist".[8] Thus, "Action is social insofar as its subjective meaning takes account of the behaviour of others and is thereby oriented in its course".[9]

If we would only have two actors, one can take into account the ambitions and desires of the other and when there is an irreconcilable conflict of interest there

[5] Hobbes 1996, Chap. 17; the power of the state is absolute, and in Hobbes view the individual must obey except when his life is threatened by the state. So in life threatening situations Hobbes sets the limits to the power of the state. This actually still is a modern thought, because nowadays we would emphasize the integrity of the human body and human mind..

[6] Giddens 1985.

[7] Petterson and Bjornskau 2015, p. 167.

[8] Weber 1968 [1920], p. 542. The note refers to the German version. The English reference is Weber 1979.

[9] Weber 1979.

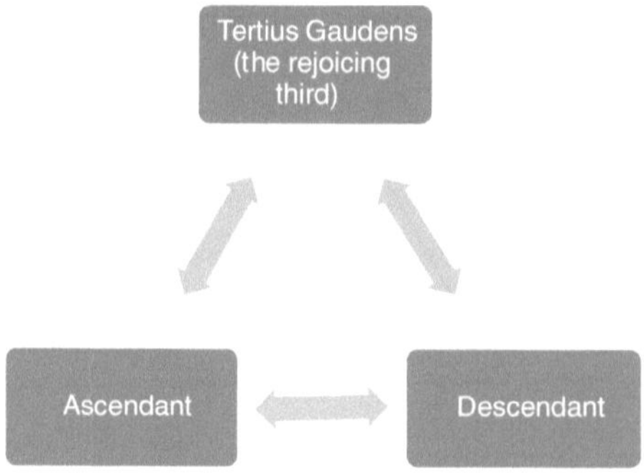

Fig. 12.1 The governance triad

would probably be a strife or even fight. A conflict model like this would allow for development in a dialectic fashion like Marx proposes. But this is a rough model of only two stakeholders. When going beyond the overly simple Marxian schema of 'haves versus have-nots' we would bring in three parties[10] that form the governance triad: one aspiring party that is on the ascendant, one defending party that perhaps is socially descending and one party that balances out the former parties and is hence the *rejoicing third* or Simmel's Tertius Gaudens (Fig. 12.1).[11] This sophisticated model suffices to define the action logic of governance and can be applied to macro, meso or micro interactions between people because the actual interactions form a dynamic "latticework of tensions".[12] In this latticework, or in other words in this figuration, the rejoicing third is the actor who can play the game of divide and rule, meaning that he can favour the descendant to counterbalance the ascendant. So, in history kings often threw their weight on the side of the second most powerful group to counterbalance the most powerful. Elias coined this form of agency the royal mechanism. If the rejoicing third does not play the game well, he probably will at some moment in the future be toppled from his position by the ascendant.

The three party figuration is basic to the Elias' analysis of the *The Court Society* and *The Civilizing Process* and serves as a model for world history where governance triads develops from: (1) the tensions between king, nobility and commoners, (2) to tensions between parliament, middle class and working class and (3) welfare state, established, outsiders (Fig. 12.2). In particular, the concept of *an axis of tensions* (this refers to the tension between ascendant and descendant) illustrates this approach to tensions.[13] The main axis of tensions shifted more definitely to the commercial and indus-trial section of the population, dividing it into two camps, the working classes and the middle classes.[14] Development and change

[10] Bröckling 2010.

[11] Simmel 1908.

[12] Elias 2012, pp. 123–128.

[13] Elias 2000.

[14] Elias 2007, p. 40.

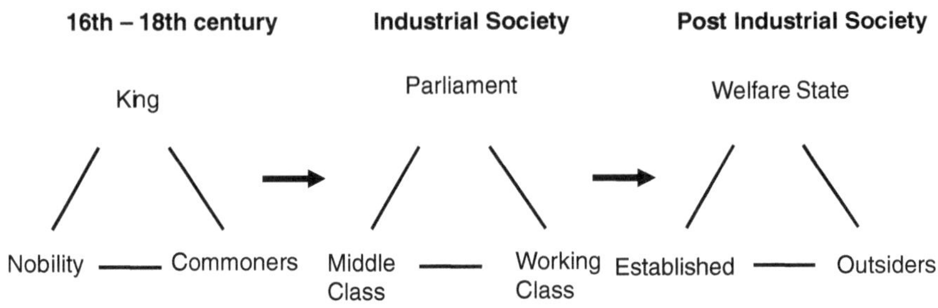

Fig. 12.2 Developments in governance triads

and thus progress in governance also stems from the tensions between the stakeholders in this model, that is not a two party dialectic, but a dynamic agency model involving at least three groups of stakeholders.

If we would like to analyse tensions of the present day we would have to look into the relationship between those who rightfully claim their share of the welfare provisions, and those who are excluded from those goods (i.e., the established versus the outsiders). The theory is thus instrumental in describing the genesis of parliamentary democracy as the form of governance that is the mainstream in the western world and the model that often (but not always wisely) is projected as a normative model for nations worldwide.

Governance implies a balancing of stakeholders, but the relationship between the stakeholders always is dynamic. The balance develops gradually and slowly, but sometimes the triad can tilt suddenly. Thus for the Netherlands the axis of tensions in the seventeenth century has seen clashes between Stadholders and Statesmen (we would nowadays describe the former as the supreme military commanders and the latter as prime ministers) that on several occasions led to tragic and brutal executions of the statesmen. But none withstanding the clashes, the merchant elite was in actual power during the seventeenth century. The first constitution from 1813 tilted the governance triad and as a result the merchant elite had to step down in favour of merchant king William I. The stadholders dynasty finally succeeded in its aspirations and the monarchy was established. But the Oranges were only the rejoicing third for a short while, because the constitution was rewritten in 1848 when statesman Thorbecke introduced ministerial responsibility that rendered the king inviolable but also reduced him to a ceremonial functionary. Thus Thorbecke tilted the triad resulting in the government taking over the top position in the triad. Over time universal suffrage developed into the system that underpinned the safety and security system of the state. The deal remains simply Hobbesian in nature: safety and security arises from the exchange of people serving as conscript in the armed forces and from the taxes that people pay for which they get in return the right to regularly vote their representatives in parliament, they obtain active and passive voting rights, civil, political, social and economic rights, i.e. the welfare state.[15] It took the

[15] Moelker et al. 2009, pp. 15–40.

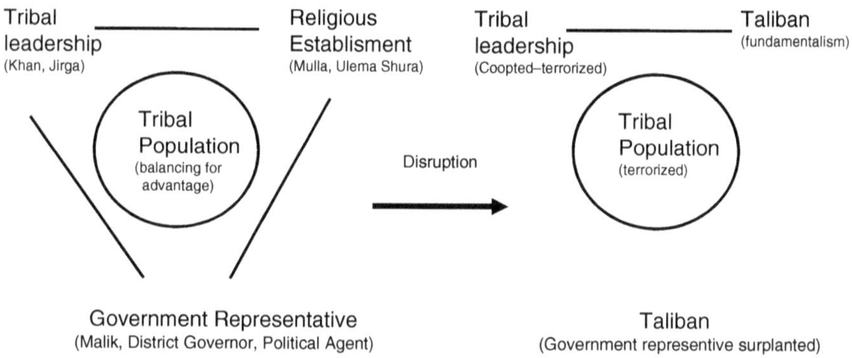

Fig. 12.3 Tribal governance triads (in balance and disrupted), adapted from Kilcullen 2009, pp. 80, 82

Netherlands 400 years to develop this particular form of governance and at first impression the figuration seems stable and balanced. But the tensions between stakeholders at times can be tremendously sharp and besides internal strife the triad can also be endangered by outside threats. European history is full of examples.

Outside the Western world other types of triads also provide functioning forms of governance. The triad might look differently, with different stakeholders, but it also provides governance and safety and security. Tribal societies can be just as stable as Western societies (or just as instable if you would prefer the analogy to the 'empty glass'). The actual local triad of a municipality or region might be a reversed triad as is the case in Afghan tribal society (Fig. 12.3, left image).[16] This is a governance triad upside down, because tribal leadership and religious establishment share the power and the government representative, representing the authority of Kabul, is the weakest party in the local power equation. It is the tribal population that balances out, meaning that they shift allegiance along the poles of the informal authority structure. The traditional tribal society is very much balanced, and it takes on the government form that one often sees in 'mountain democracies'. Whenever there is a problem an ad hoc council of elders will discuss and discuss until the problem is solved and agreement is established. The present local Afghan society is very much disrupted by war and conflict and therefore the traditional allegiances and negotiation structures do not function any more. It is very easy for 'spoilers', i.e. warlords and political entrepreneurs to try to disrupt the balance and to establish a shift in the axis of tensions that will effectively bring the spoilers in the position of the rejoicing third.[17] The result is of course that a disrupted triad for some time will have the characteristics of a fragile state until a new balance is struck. Tribal traditional leadership is co-opted or terrorized and

[16] Kilcullen 2009, pp. 80, 82.

[17] Swaan 2015.

likewise is the local population. The governance triad in conflict torn fragile states (Fig. 12.3, right image) is no longer functioning because one of the parties (the Taliban) has usurped leadership leaving no room for other countervailing parties to put forward justified claims for governance plans. Figure 12.3 illustrates graphically what happens when governance collapses.

The new balance may take a while to institutionalize, meanwhile the monopolies of violence and taxation are non-functioning, rule of law is absent and the moral order has broken down. When the governance triad in the Western world would be disrupted in a similar way, as it did in former Yugoslavia, the result would also show a rise in terror and violence.

12.3 The Governance Opportunity Structure and Its Dimensions

The actors who try to realize their goals within the triad, change the opportunity structure by the agency that they develop, but at the same time they are dependent on the same opportunity structure that has been laid down by actors before them and that has institutionalized and sedimented into organizational forms. The actors change the system, but the system also changes the actors because by internalization we deal not only with individuals in society but with society within individuals. The communal values and norms that arise from the interplay of individual and society constitute a *moral order* that cements people in such a way that the whole amounts to more than the sum of individuals (Fig. 12.4). A moral order

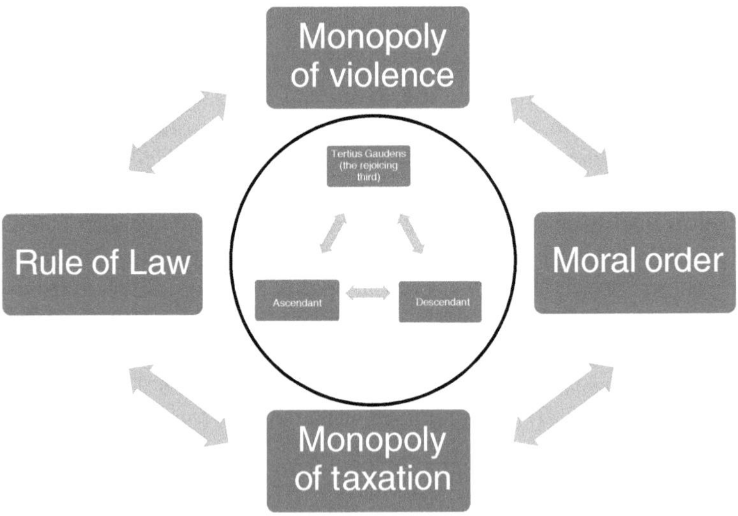

Fig. 12.4 The governance opportunity structure

brings some form of cohesion. A moral order can support strongly the value of 'individualism' and thus seemingly paradoxically 'individualism' can be a collectively shared value. A moral order can disintegrate or become very much segmented and even end in anomie.

Resulting from the moral order is the normative system that is codified into rules and regulations. When norms and values are broadly accepted they acquire legitimacy and within rationalized legal system they are written down and form a penal system that comprises law, penal institutions and policing. Once established the resulting *rule of law* guarantees safety and security to all whom live under the authority of this system, be it a tribal system, a state system or even a supranational system (Fig. 12.4).

Policing public order implies that the rule of law can be enforced. Coercion is always a possibility within the state system, since the state wields the *monopoly of violence* (Fig. 12.4). When a system enjoys legitimacy coercion is seldom an issue, but military and police can be deployed to defend the interest of the state and to defend national sovereignty. State violence can internationally be put to use to political ends. Violence in legitimate systems is normally used ultimo remedio. To use violence in the domestic realm (i.e., violence against the own population), is often regarded as a weakness of governance and a failure of democratic institutions. The monopoly of violence is in the political realm because governments decide on the use of force as an instrument for realizing policy objectives.

However, political decision-making about the use of force cannot function without financial means that enable government institutions, such as the armed forces, to exist. A band of robbers can live from the country and loot, steal, rob as a way of existence. A city guard system may follow the model of a militia army. Pre-modern merchant fleets could easily transform into naval forces, but modern technology requires communal funding as to withstand communal threats. Standing forces require a different financing model from forces that for example only expedite in summertime. The *monopoly of taxation* developed over time so that state institutions could deliver collective goods such as safety and security (Fig. 12.4).

To summarise, the tensions between the stakeholders in the governance triad lend the state building process its dynamic character. The stakeholders act according their own plan and logic within the given opportunity structure and by acting, whilst never knowing on forehand the intended or unintended outcomes, they change the structure. The way violence is organized, the way the finances are flowing, the legal and ethical regulations and the resulting moral order is changed because of all these stakeholders who try to attain their own goals by utilizing the possibilities in the opportunity structure. Groups on the ascendant may or may not acquire power and rise to the position of the rejoicing third. But if the rejoicing third plays his/her game well, he/she will favour the descendent and thus prevent the ascendant from claiming the 'king's' position.

12.4 Monopoly of Violence

War, what is it good for? Just as in the Edwin Starr song most people are emotionally seduced to answer 'absolutely nothing', but based on history and statistical analysis Ian Morris claims, "Leviathan raises the costs of force, making peace pay off better than violence, and the more peaceful that conditions become, the easier it is for commerce to flourish, increasing the payoffs to be won by conquering".[18] Pre-modern societies were extremely violent, and to experience conflict and war in one's lifetime was rather rule than exception. "Stone Age life was 10–20 times as violent as the tumultuous world of medieval Europe and 300–600 times as bad as mid-20th-century Europe". Morris ventures through history from hunter-gatherer societies to high tech killer robots and lards his evidence with irrefutable statistics that show that the decline of violence is correlated to the growth of destructive capacities of modern armed forces. Morris' hypothesis is provoking and it is reminiscent of Tilly's "War made the state, and the state made war".[19] However, Morris' argument would be sounder if he simply correlated state building with the decline of violence. It is not war that makes society safer. Thus 'more war' in Morris' book, is actually 'more state', and more governance, hence also the decline of violence. Other authors also notice the decline in the number of battle deaths coinciding with the growth of states.[20]

Max Weber defined the state as a "human community that successfully claims the monopoly of the legitimate use of physical force within a given territory".[21] The state is the only actor who uses legitimate force and when a state is successful it will logically lead to a decline of violence between non legitimate actors meaning that domestic safety and security will decline first. Civilians are not allowed to use violence other than in worst cases of self-defence. Internationally violence will also diminish because the chains of interdependence become longer and social webs become denser causing collective action to be profitable not for only those who enjoy less security but especially for those who are more fortunate.

"The dynamics of the collectivizing process [such as welfare and security, RM] stem largely from the conflicts among the elites over the creation of collective goods and the distribution of costs among them".[22] In other words, people worldwide are connected regarding safety and security, and the rich (the established) are less and less able to transfer risk to the poor (the outsiders) and be free riders themselves. Collective security (and goods) is in the own interest of the elites.

Pinker substantiates the theory and delivers the statistics.[23] He also refutes the argument that recent times have seen a rise of violence due to conflict in the

[18] Morris 2014.

[19] Tilly 1975, p. 42.

[20] Azar Gat 2006.

[21] Weber 1979.

[22] Swaan 1988, p. 3.

[23] Pinker 2011.

Middle East and specifically Syria. Despite these latest gruesome developments, the global rate of battle deaths per 100,000 people "does not come anywhere close to the rate of death in the past decades". "Conflicts claiming more than 1,000 lives, defined as wars, have declined by more than 50 percent, from 15 in the early 1990s to seven in 2013".[24] Regarding domestic violence Pinker points to ever declining homicide rates worldwide. For the United States of America the gap in homicide rates between the south and the east depends on differences in civilization, governance and rule of law (the famed second amendment).[25] The homicide rate for European countries is five times lower (circa 1 per 100,000) than the general rate for the United States. Contrary to popular intuition Pinker's data prove that the number of autocracies has fallen since 2009, and the number of democracies has increased.[26]

Governance does make the world a safer place, but at the same time it was democracies that were also responsible for the largest genocides of the past century.[27] These Killer States will be discussed in the conclusion. Political entrepreneurs were largely responsible for the genocides, but "extensive graphs on the history of genocide show that even the 1994 peak (from Rwanda) is a tiny fraction of the levels from the preceding decades".[28] One last governance issue to be discussed here in the section on the monopoly of violence is brought up by Goldstein and this relates to the importance of the United Nations and international peacekeeping.[29] The United Nations are not a supra national form of governance and thus not a super-leviathan resembling Godzilla, but their resolutions do bestow legitimacy onto the use of force and thus the decisions in this organization again prove that the chains of interdependence are lengthening. International peacekeeping is not the holy grail of conflict resolution, but it does fit the trend in the civilizing process.

12.5 Monopoly of Taxation

The monopoly of violence somehow has to be sustained by sponsors. Weapons, personnel and logistics are costly. Without funding military force cannot be deployed. An old Dutch truth goes as follows, *Geen geld, geen Zwitsers*, which translates to, *No money, no Swiss* [mercenaries].[30] In feudal times land was the

24 Pinker 2016, pp. 2–3.

25 Mennell 2007.

26 Pinker 2016, p. 13.

27 Mann 2005.

28 Pinker 2011, pp. 338–340.

29 Goldsteijn 2011.

30 Moelker et al. 2009.

most important factor of production and therefore serfs were coerced into working the property of the knight and/or aristocratic owner. The feudal landowner-knight lived of the land, exerted toll from travellers and fought his neighbours for gain. When the knight was successful in military expeditions his areal expanded beyond the span of control and he would have to lend land to a 'brother in arms'. He would raise himself to king and promote his vassal to nobility on condition of loyal assistance in his expeditions.[31] Empires rose and fell because during the Middle Ages no stable monopoly of taxation could be sustained that would uphold a standing army. Gradually the economy shifted from subsistence, land and barter to a monetary economy, lengthening the chains of interdependence by commerce and colonies.

Taxes were raised in antique Egypt, Greece, and Rome but never enjoyed popularity. The populace often tried to avoid taxation, and thus the promise of a tax reduction tempted Lady Godiva in eleventh century England to ride naked through the streets of her town. In the monetary economy the clergy was outside the governance triad as soon as the King asked the cities, which had grown rich beyond imagination from trade and colonial exploitation, for finances that were intended for strengthening naval and land forces. The monopoly of taxation begot its form when exchange between the political and the economic sector resulted in the transfer of power for money. During the American secession from Britain in 1768 the London Magazine headlined: *No taxation without representation.* In British parliamentary history and other Western states the power shifted from kings to the people who are represented in the *House of Commons*—or in the Netherlands in *de Tweede Kamer*. Non-Western states did not always follow a similar path, but they established other forms of representation albeit sometimes despotic in form (for the people, not by the people).

A breakdown of the monopoly of taxation is always a breakdown of governance that, when not handled well, can cause state failure. Cause and effect are often difficult to establish, but as is illustrated from history, the correlation is non-disputed. The great depression of the 1930s reflected on political systems that did not succeed at constructing coherent policies, and thus the haggling in Berlin eventually led to the rise of Hitler and his Nazi party. The succession of Gorbatjov by Jeltsin marked the transition to market systems, but almost destroyed the Russian Federation for not collecting taxes from large companies. Crude proto types of capitalism benefitted new oligarch companies like Yukos, but harmed state income that was necessary to pay the salary of the civil servants. Officers in the Russian army were selling weapons on the free market, and even sold their conscripts as hostage to the Chechen Rebels.[32] In the mid-nineties the Russian

[31] The clergy in the resulting governance triad was part of the figuration because religious men were literate and could write laws; Weber 1979 shows that the professional civil servants originated from this position as soon as the clergy was replaced by lawyers and other academics.

[32] Winslow et al. 2013.

Federation was on the brink of collapse and in dire need of reform from which Putin benefited from 2000 onwards. He did increase state revenue, but is criticized at the same time. “A state that is as corrupt as Russia is not strong but dysfunctional and thus weak… Russia is too rich, too educated, and too open to be so authoritarian”.[33] Without control over the monopoly of taxation the monopoly of violence would have eroded as well, handing over the power in the streets to organized crime.

Failing to collect taxes may cause state implosion. Reversely, a successful monopoly of taxation will contribute to state formation. The most recent example is derived from Islamic State. Loretta Napoleoni’s work on crime and jihadism is based on *Tracing the Dollars behind the Terrorist network* and her analysis of Islamic State (IS) departs from a similar methodology.[34] Islamic State benefited from start up capital from the Saudi’s, but only started growing when it succeeded at capturing natural resources (oil) and collecting taxes. How did they do it and what is the novelty in this phase of early statehood? According to Napoleoni IS is a *de facto* state and a *casco* state, meaning that all infrastructure is present (there are functioning monopolies of violence and taxation, a certain type of rule of law (Sharia)), except for self-determination and recognition by other states. The plan of course is to grow into statehood and gain self-determination and recognition by generating an even more solid military and financial foundation. The difference with the Palestine Liberation Organization (PLO), the Taliban or the Fuerzas Armadas Revolucionarias de Colombia (FARC), organizations who also generate wealth, is that IS has created a cohesive ideology, a common identity and a moral order by proclaiming the Caliphate. According to Napoleoni the Caliphate is as appealing to Muslims as is Israel to the Zionistic Jewish movement.[35] It is a strong statement, but the promise of this moral order is a promise of salvation and a better future and indeed this utopia is motivating many discontent people to join IS-forces.

Taxation is essential for state building. In reconstruction missions, where the central state’s authority is to be strengthened, the flow of finances is mission critical. Tax money is being used to pay police officers and armed forces in Afghanistan and therefore it is of outmost importance to fit the monetary system to local custom and culture. Sometimes the flow of finances is not as transparent as paymasters would like. What Westerners define as corruption, is in some parts of the world considered a fair share, but this does challenge the task of performance measurement and accountability.[36] The value of the currency in reconstructing a society is of the outmost importance. If for example the currency that is to be used in the payment system is debated in the political arena it will be difficult to

---

[33] Aslund 2008.

[34] Napoleoni 2003, 2015.

[35] Napoleoni 2015, p. 47.

[36] Davids 2011; Schut 2015; One may morally object to ‘corruption’, but on the other hand one might also object to ‘rent’ within the banking system, or ‘speculation’ in the stock market.

stabilize the currency. In Bosnia and Herzegovina and other former Yugoslavian states, the political arena was highly polarized along ethnic lines and as a result the outcome of these discussions did not bring financial stability.[37] Individuals were tempted to use stable foreign currencies, like the Euro or the Dollar, and by doing so it took long before the legitimacy of the financial authority was strengthened. In general, the economy, and specifically taxation, is one of the cornerstones of good governance and state building.

12.6 Rule of Law

"Civilization began the first time an angry person cast a word instead of a rock".[38] The use of violence within the state is a prerogative of police forces, and is (should be) regulated by law. Conflict resolution has become the field for lawyers and mediators. Violence outside of the safety and security container of the state neither has legitimate status since non-aggression pacts, the UN charter and international law prohibit violence. Ideally democratic states do not act violently against other democracies. Hence violence is most common where states are fragile and governance is low. We do not live in an ideal world, so some states do act aggressively (even when democratic), but overall violence and many indicators of governance and human development correlate with fragility. Corruption, rule of law, governmental effectiveness, voice and accountability and political stability are all correlated, and so are many other indicators, but statistics need careful interpretation since not all patterns are linear.[39] For example, with age of democracies and gross domestic product (GDP) in consideration, the correlation of governance (amongst others rule of law and corruption) with democracy follows an inverted U-curve.[40] What is required to make rule of law work? In this section the way rule of law works is illustrated by taking a closer look into the problem of conflict diamonds.

The objective of rule of law is to prevent that countries emerging from violent conflict will revert to conflict within 5 years. Currently half of countries relapse into violence in this manner.[41] Rule of law can prevent a relapse by building institutions and implementing basic human rights. The main elements of a complete rule-of-law system are: an independent judiciary; an independent human rights institutions; government powers that are determined by laws; free and fair elections; transparent and accountable access to political power; police and detention

[37] Lubberman-Schrotenboer 2014.

[38] Freud 2016.

[39] Davis 2014; Taylor 2014.

[40] Rock 2007, p. 32.

[41] Voorhoeve 2007, p. 11.

systems whose powers are defined precisely by laws; military and security systems that function under the law; access to justice through competent and affordable lawyers, and no prohibitive levies or delays which discourage seeking justice.[42] These elements work together and should be implemented to form a coherent system. The interplay between the elements can be put to use to end the logic behind warlord politics.[43] The warlord profits from the absence of the monopolies of violence and taxation simply because with no government above him, he is free to do as he pleases and to make money by all means, legal or illegal. The warlord obtains his objectives by disrupting the governance triad and by spoiling the balances in the triad.[44] The result is graphically illustrated in Fig. 12.3. This figure is from an Afghan context, but the mechanism of the spoiler is the same in all conflict areas.

For personal gain the warlord mobilises his troops and uses terror as an instrument to coerce the local population into forced labour or simply to scare them away from places were precious raw materials can be found. Thus the Revolutionary United Front (RUF) in the nineties obtained the diamonds from jungle rivers in Sierra Leone and then packed them on transport by human mules to Monrovia in Liberia where the Charles Taylor's presidential plane flew the raw diamonds to The Beers and other companies in London and Antwerp. In the nineties 90 per cent of market share was in the hands of this one distributer (nowadays 30 per cent). The presidential plane then returned to Monrovia stacked with small calibre weapons from East Europe, which then again were transported back to the jungle by human mules.[45] Thus a vicious circle was constituted.

It took military intervention to push back RUF, and it took some strange military bedfellows like *Executives Outcomes* and British troops to do it, simply because government forces were not up to it. But military intervention did not stop the trade in conflict diamonds. The vicious economic circle, gems for arms, could only be broken by instating rule of law.[46] In this case the *Kimberley Process* regulates the certification of diamonds and participants to this treaty can only trade with each other if they meet the requirements. Shipments of rough diamonds must have a certificate proving that they stem from areas that are conflict free. The idea is simple and efficient, but unfortunately not air tight because the certificates only cover batches of rough diamonds. But although the *Kimberley Process* does not provide for an individual track and trace system (such like laser inscription in the diamonds could provide) for cut and polished diamonds, the regulation was one of the policies that did end the gems for arms trade circle. It was not the only policy

[42] Voorhoeve 2007, p. 91.

[43] Reno 1999.

[44] Schleckener 2009.

[45] Campbell 2012.

[46] Campbell 2012.

that broke the circle, but it was a corner stone in the strategy of outlawing warlords and traders.

Lack of rule of law causes states to be fragile. Strengthening rule of law reinforces safety and security within societies.[47] Rule of law of course refers not only to laws and regulations but also to institutions, a penal system, police forces, and thus by improving rule of law one can close the security gap that arises shortly after a conflict zone gets rid of warlords, warring factions and other spoilers.[48] Whereas politics are capricious and civilisation is but a layer of varnish that is susceptible to erosion, rule of law and all the institutions that are built around it, assures the stability and longevity of safety and security systems.

12.7 The Moral Order

Foucault coined the concept of *governmentality* and others have developed it further. The concept was intended to add to a new understanding of power.[49] Governmentality is more all-encompassing than other concepts like sovereignty or discipline and that is what Foucault conceptually intended. Foucault does not only refer to the "ensemble of institutions and the technical apparatuses of security", but also to the process through which the state of justice of the Middle Ages during the fifteenth and sixteenth centuries, gradually becomes 'governmentalized'.[50] The concept gains clarity if one breaks it up into 'govern' and 'mentality', or mentalities of governing. Governmentality is more than the widening of the state, it is more than etatism, because with the lengthening of the chains of interdependence, also comes a mental disposition. In other words, the forms of governance that have developed also developed a collective mentality, or moral order, that fits the specific government of a certain time and place. The sociogenesis of governance is at the same time the psychogenesis of the moral order.[51] The safety and security institutions that historically grew into what they are now are also internalized into our minds and they control our conscious and unconscious behaviour, perception and emotions.

The dominant norm and value that is constitutive of the moral order in civilized societies is inhibition. Governmentality is the process whereby the objective norm also becomes subjectively internalized. So in civilized societies the objective and lawful norm is to refrain from violence, but emotionally we also may feel nausea when we are confronted with violence. We are even shocked when official police

[47] Friesendorf 2007; Friesendorf and Penska 2008.

[48] Neuteboom 2014.

[49] Foucault 1991.

[50] Foucault 1991, pp. 102–103.

[51] Elias 2000.

officers have to resort to physical violence even in situations where violence is appropriate and legitimated. The state as a safety and security container is successful because most people have internalized the norm of refraining from violence. Normally, we do not smack our children to teach them a lesson. Abusive language and conduct unbecoming is not only against the rules, but it is also outside the moral code of conduct. It makes us feel uneasy and uncomfortable. Violence is getting rare, and homicide in the Netherlands is at a low of 111 murders in 2015 (10 years ago 223 victims showed up in the statistics).[52] If we look closer at this number we see that it annually comprises five to fifteen per cent of liquidations within organized crime, there is another proportion that is crime related but half of incidences relate to sad and sorry stories in the category human tragedy (drugs, alcohol, relationships, mental disorders). In short, inhibition has become the dominant trait of civilized culture, which is beneficial to overall safety and security.

Since violence is outside the regular moral order, and violence normally automatically invokes a reaction of repulsion in people, police officers and military personnel have to train in order to be able to apply violence. Police and service members do not naturally 'like' violence, but they have to learn how to utilise it as an instrument of their profession.[53] They even have to learn how to kill and how to get over the basic inclination of aversion to death, that is associated with blood, stench, suffering, dirt and decaying bodies.[54] This means that those who are skilled in the profession of arms are also trained in dealing with professional risk and risk taking behaviours. Sookermany, Sand and Breivik present perhaps what is the best overview regarding risk taking behaviours of professional soldiers, but they miss one defining characteristics of similar professions.[55] Military service members, fire men, police men, all are *edge workers*.[56] The concept of edge work refers to professions that walk the thin line between risk propensity and self-control. Edge workers do not scare away from danger under condition that they can control the risky situation and themselves. In the end risk is also appealing to professional soldiers and they may even become adrenalin junkies because thrill is addictive.[57] When soldiers return home from mission they don't want less thrill, they want more! Professionals in violence are skilled at controlling their emotions, because they don't apply violence out of anger or frustration, but as instrument to realize

[52] Source is AD, http://www.nrc.nl/nieuws/2015/12/31/aantal-moorden-in-2015-in-nederland-afgenomen; Trends are downward disregarding the source; CBS reported 144 homicides in 2014 (AD reported 135 in 2014), http://www.cbs.nl/nl-nl/menu/themas/gezondheid-welzijn/publicaties/artikelen/archief/2015/ruim-helft-van-vermoorde-vrouwen-door-ex-of-partner-omgebracht.htm.

[53] Collins 2008.

[54] Grossman 1995.

[55] Sookermany et al. 2015.

[56] Lyng 1990; 2005.

[57] Breander 2015.

given political objectives.[58] Applying violence is (if you do a good job) the summit of self control, the summit of inhibition. It is no surprise that discipline still is a core value of the military because it helps soldiers to control their emotions.

12.8 Conclusion

In this chapter the relation of governance with safety and security was discussed. The most compendious conclusion is that governance and safety and security are positively correlated which leads to a decline of violence. The dimensions of the governance opportunity structure, the monopoly of violence and taxation, the rule of law and the moral order that instated inhibition as core value of civilized culture, are all positively correlated with safety and security. The monopolies of violence and taxation lay down the foundations of functioning states. The resulting political system is more inclusive, responsive and participatory when it is more democratic in form. The monopoly of taxation enhances efficiency and effectiveness in the distribution of collective goods. Rule of law can outlaw or side line the spoilers who have in interest in destabilizing the system. Rule of law also furthers transparency, accountability, fairness, and combats corruption and in this manner it safeguards governance from sliding into fragility. Governmentality is the process and inhibition is its culture; it is the moral order that originates from govermentality but that also strengthens it. Violence is simply outside the moral order and the attitude to refrain from violence is inculcated, whilst integrity and ethical behaviour are promoted. But despite this general conclusion serious challenges remain.

First of all the concept of *fragile states* deserves severe criticism. The fragility theme is indirectly derived from Thomas Hobbes because the implication of not being subdued to the Leviathan is the war of all against all. When studying conflict in a so-called fragile state like Congo the resulting governance triad proves not to be totally fragile after all. Verweijen shows that the regime in Congolese Kinshasa tries to balance ascendants and descendants in what geo politically is an archipelago.[59] Amidst tremendous fragmentation the balancing strategy for civilians comes down to a militarization of society. In order to preserve at least some safety and security civilians play along with this militarization strategy. Thus, although Congo scores low on all indicators of governance, there is a structure and there is a form of rule of law and there is a moral order, albeit by the norms of militarization, not by norms of inhibition and integrity. There is a governance structure, not anarchy, however when Kinshasa does not succeed at dealing with spoilers effectively the structure crumbles. We can label this 'fragile' as long as we realize that we are using a normative concept.

[58] Most interestingly and most complex, governmentality enables us to control the de-controlling of emotions. We can let go albeit in a controlled manner, Wouters 2007.

[59] Verweijen 2015.

A second challenge relates to intervention. Intervention by Western states often implies projecting Western ways of governance on post conflict areas as the panacea for Hobbesian chaos and anarchy. The governance triad "relies on agreement between the military, political elites and citizenry", but Schiff warns us that we are mistaken to mix two types of governance triads.[60] 'Our' governance triad is not universal. The Western governance triad normally departs from a separation between politics and the military. The governance triad in former conflict areas is mostly a disrupted one with intermingled political and military affairs. For intervention purposes Westerners should look for 'targetted partnership' and this means that alliances with unlikely but strategic partners should be part and parcel of the intervention strategy. Again, politics of inclusion, cultural awareness, diplomacy and negotiation are desirable and recommendable.

A third challenge hardly discussed previously relates to the Killer State. Abram de Swaan opens his book on the *The Killing Compartments* with the words, "these are peaceful times". Then he continues and sets the stage for his study on genocide. "Yet mass violence against unarmed civilians has claimed three to four times as many lives in the past century as war: one hundred million at least, and possibly many more. These large-scale killings have required the efforts of hundreds of thousands of perpetrators. Such men (almost all were males) were ready to kill, indiscriminately, for many hours a day, for days and weeks at a stretch, and sometimes for months or even years".[61]

In this chapter the focus was on governance contributing to safety and security, and indeed the correlates of governance point in this direction. However, Abram de Swaan remarks that in explaining the largest massacres of past century one should look into some the mechanisms unleashed by the state itself. Statehood does not automatically lead to good governance. The state was the largest killer of the 20th century and it mobilized willing accomplishes that cooperated in creating killing compartments that led to the extermination of Armenians, Jews, Chechens, Bosnian Muslims, Tutsi's, etceteras. The Islamic State is perhaps the latest example of a Killer State. And the collapse of Syria and simultaneous rise of Islamic State are serious threats. In a deliberate attempt the state and its political entrepreneurs singles out whole groups to scapegoat them with the one and only objective to gain or to stay in power. Politics of exclusion, in contrast to politics of inclusion, is 'bad governance' and leads to mobilization of discontented but willing executioners of compartmentalization and eventually to bloodshed. In trying to understand safety and security from a governance point of view it is worthwhile to study politics of exclusion more intensely. The utility of force still seems valid, since safety is not to be taken for granted and still needs the military for insurance policy. Threats from political, economic, ethnical, cultural and ecological instability are all around us. Perhaps Europeans are hesitant about applying military power, but they have no other option than to use it as one of the safeguards of good governance and a back up for diplomacy.

---

[60] Schiff 2012, p. 323.

[61] De Swaan 2015, p. 1.

References

Aslund A (2008) An assessment of Putin's economic policy. CESifo Forum 2, http://www.piie.com/publications/papers/paper.cfm?ResearchID=974. Accessed 6 March 2016

Bovens M, Thart P, van Twist MJW (2012) Openbaar bestuur. Kluwer, Deventer

Breander M (2015) Adrenalin junkies: why soldiers return from war wanting more. Armed Forces Soc 42:3–25

Bröckling U (2010) Gesellschaft beginnt mit Drei. Eine soziologische triadologie. In: Bedorf T, Fischer J, Lindemann G (eds) Theorien des Dritten. Innovationen in Soziologie und Sozialphilosophie. Wilhelm Fink, München, pp 189–211

Campbell G (2012) Blood diamonds. Tracing the deadly path of the world's most precious stones, revised edn. Basic Books, New York

Collins R (2008) Violence. A micro-sociological theory. Princeton University Press, Princeton

Davids C (2011) Performance measurement during military operations. Studies from Afghanistan. Ten Brink, Meppel

Davis K (2014) Getting to know the worldwide governance indicators. http://geovisualist.com/2014/04/. Accessed 7 March 2016

De Swaan A (1988) In care of the state. Health care, education and welfare in Europe and the USA in the Modern Era. Polity, Cambridge

De Swaan A (2015) The killing compartments. The mentality of mass murder. Yale University Press, New Haven

Elias N (2000) The civilizing process. Sociogenetic and psychogenetic investigations. Blackwell, Oxford

Elias N (2007) The genesis of the naval profession. University College Dublin Press, Dublin

Elias N (2012) What is sociology? University College Dublin Press, Dublin

Foucault M (1991) Governmentality. In: Burchell G, Gordon C, Miller P (eds) The Foucault effect. Studies in governmentality. University of Chicago Press, Geneva, pp 87–104

Freud S (2016) Civilization began the first time an angry person cast a word instead of a rock. http://izquotes.com/quote/65980. Accessed 5 February 2016

Friesendorf C (2007) The military and law enforcement in peace operations. Lessons from Bosnia-Herzegovina and Kosovo, DCAF, Geneva

Friesendorf C, Penksa S (2008) Militarized law enforcement in peace operations: EUFOR in Bosnia and Herzegovina. Int Peacekeep 15:677–694

Giddens A (1985) The nation-state and violence. Polity Press, Cambridge

Goldsteijn JS (2011) Winning the war on war. The decline of armed conflict worldwide. Dutton, New York

Grossman D (1995) On killing. The psychological costs of learning to kill in war and society. Little Brown, Boston

Hobbes T (1996) Leviathan. Oxford University Press, Oxford

Huizinga J (1997) Autumn of the middle ages. University of Chicago Press, Chicago

Kilcullen D (2009) The accidental guerrilla. Fighting small wars in the midst of a big one. Oxford University Press, Oxford

Lyng S (1990) Edgework: a social psychological analysis of voluntary risk-taking. Am J Soc 95:851–886

Lyng S (2005) Edgework: the sociology of risk taking. Routledge, New York

Lubberman-Schrotenboer IG (2014) Dynamics of payments, conflict and economic activity—case studies of Bosnia and Herzegovina and Serbia. Proefschrift Katholieke Universiteit Brabant, Tilburg

Mann M (2005) The dark side of democracy. Explaining ethnic cleansing. Cambridge University Press, Cambridge

Mennell S (2007) The American civilizing process. Polity, Cambridge

Moelker R, Noll J, de Weger M (2009) Krijgsmacht en samenleving. Boom, Amsterdam

Morris I (2014) War, what is it good for? The role of conflict in civilisation, from primates to robots. Profile Books, London

Napoleoni L (2003) Modern Jihad. Tracing the dollars behind the terrorist network. Pluto Press, Londen

Napoleoni L (2015) De terugkeer van het Kalifaat. De stormachtige opkomst van Islamitische Staat en de verwarring in het Westen. Uitgeverij Balans, Amsterdam

Neuteboom PCJ (2014) Beyond borders, the role of the Netherlands army in public security during crisis management operations. Wolf Legal Publishers, Oisterwijk

Petterson KA, Bjørnskau T (2015) Organizational contradictions between safety and security—perceived challenges and ways of integrating critical infrastructure protection in civil aviation. Saf Sci 71:167–177

Pinker S (2011) The Better Angels of Our Nature, the decline of violence in history and its causes. Allen Lane, London

Pinker S (2016) Has the decline of violence reversed since The Better Angels of Our Nature was written? http://stevenpinker.com/has-decline-violence-reversed-better-angels-our-nature-was-written. Accessed 5 Feb 2016

Reno W (1999) War lord politics and African states. Lynne Rienner Publishers, Boulder

Rock M (2007) Corruption and democracy. DESA Working Paper No. 55, http://www.un.org/esa/desa/papers/2007/wp55_2007.pdf. Accessed 7 March 2016

Schneckener U (2009) Spoilers or governance actors? Engaging armed non-state groups in areas of limited statehood. SFB-Governance Working Paper Series, Berlin

Schiff RL (2012) Concordance theory, targeted partnership, and counterinsurgency strategy. Armed Forces Soc 38:318–339

Schut M (2015) Soldiers as strangers. Morally and culturally critical situations. Radboud Universiteit Nijmegen, Nijmegen

Sheehan J (2006) The monopoly of violence. Why Europeans hate going to war. Faber and Faber, Berkeley

Simmel G (1908) Soziologie. Untersuchungen über die Formen der Vergesellschaftung. Duncker & Humblot, Berlin

Sookermany A, Sand TS, Breivik G (2015) Risk-taking attitudes and behaviors among military personnel in dangerous contexts. Moving Soldiers, 01. Norwegian School of Sport Sciences Defence Institute, Oslo

Taylor SA (2014) Fragile and conflict-affected states. Exploring the relationship between governance, instability and violence. Stability, Int J Secur Develop 3. doi: http://doi.org/10.5334/sta.dy

Tilly C (1975) Reflections on the history of European state-making. In: Tilly C (ed) The formation of national states in Western Europe. Princeton University Press, Princeton

Verweijen J (2015) The ambiguity of militarization. The complex interaction between the Congolese armed forces and civilians in the Kivu provinces, Eastern DR Congo. Utrecht University, Utrecht

Voorhoeve J (2007) From War to the Rule of Law. Peace building after violent conflict. Amsterdam University Press, Amsterdam

Weber M (1979 [1920/1968]) Economy and society. An outline of interpretive sociology. University of California Press, Berkeley

Winslow D, Moelker R, Companjen FJ (2013) Glocal Chechnya. From Russian Sovereignty to Pan-Islamic autonomy. Small Wars Insur 24:129–151

Wouters C (2007) Informalization. Manners and emotions since 1890. Sage Publications, Los Angeles

Chapter 13
Strategic Defence Supply Chain Security Management

Ton van Kampen, Paul C. van Fenema and Nynke Faber

Abstract Defence supply chains (SC) are increasingly geared towards expeditionary operations. Organized on a short notice, they support the theatre in a flexible and efficient manner, relying on limited resources and sourcing from multiple suppliers. Defence SC face risks as they are susceptible to disruptions. As a risk subcategory, SC *security* risks—which this chapter focuses on—concern intentional, man-made disruptions. Research so far has explored security as a generic concept and pertaining to SCs involving commercial firms. Less attention has been paid to defence SC and organizations. The objective of this chapter is to give insight into the management of SC security risks (as part of the planning and mission management process) within defence organizations. To this end, the role of risk management and adaptive capability are introduced and synthesized. Military logistic planning processes then embed these concepts in the defence context, leading to operational military SC security risk management. A short empirical study at the Dutch Directorate of Operations' Joint Staff J4 unit and long-term experiences in military logistics of the first author substantiate our conceptual findings. The chapter concludes with directions for future research: multiple-supplier strategy, creation of an adaptive operational SC network and information-based SC transparency. These network-level initiatives complement nation-based defence SC management, contributing to SC adaptivity and efficiency.

T. van Kampen (✉) · P.C. van Fenema · N. Faber
Faculty of Military Sciences, Netherlands Defence Academy, Breda, The Netherlands
e-mail: acm.v.kampen@mindef.nl

P.C. van Fenema
e-mail: pc.v.fenema@mindef.nl

N. Faber
e-mail: n.faber.01@mindef.nl

R. Beeres et al. (eds.), *NL ARMS Netherlands Annual Review of Military Studies 2016*, NL ARMS, DOI 10.1007/978-94-6265-135-7_13

Keywords Defence supply chains · Security risks · Supply chain management · Logistics · Value chain · Supply chain security management

Contents

13.1 Introduction

Major disruptions such as the 2001 terrorist attack in New York, the piracy attacks off-shore Somalia, global financial crisis, Iceland's ash-cloud, Japanese earthquake and Tsunami among others revealed a lack of preparedness of supply chain (SC) managers towards disruptive events.[1] From a SC perspective, such events represent various types of risks that may affect a supply chain. In this chapter, we focus on a specific category of risks pertaining to SCs: SC security risks. In the introductory chapter of this book, security is understood as protection against vital threats to society or community. Threats, interpreted in a dynamic and comprehensive sense and resulting from intentional behaviour, tend to originate outside the system being secured.[2] From a supply chain angle, security concerns protecting supply chain assets (i.e., product, facilities, equipment, information, and personnel) from intentional threats, whether from in or outside the chain. In this chapter, security is demarcated to physical logistical flows and associated information flow

[1] Sheffi and Rice 2005.

[2] DSyS 2016.

of relevance to military organizations. Security should be part of SC design and management processes, e.g. security of transportation hubs and partners involved in defence SCs. Research so far has explored security as a generic concept and pertaining to SCs involving commercial firms.[3] Such studies point for instance at objective and subjective dimensions of security and the possible tension between effectiveness and security.[4] But what does this mean for the military SC as security is inextricably linked to military functions?

Apart from measures anchored in their planning procedures, defence organizations seem to pay limited attention to SC security. From a research perspective, new research on risk-based security management has been applied to defence organizations in a limited sense (we call this Approach 1 to SC security management). Moreover, innovative approaches to SC security management stressing adaptation (Approach 2) can be useful to defence organizations given the unpredictability of missions and the broad international participation in missions. The objective of this chapter is to give insight into the management of SC security risks within defence organizations. We pursue this objective by explicitly positioning SC security as a research and professional domain and by exploring, synthesizing and applying current approaches to SC security management. Building on specialized literature on risk and security management and SC adaptation literatures, we examine how a military organization strategically manages SC security and faces current challenges. Empirical insight is provided by including a short empirical study at the Dutch Directorate of Operations' Joint Staff J4 unit as well as relying on long-term experiences of the first author, a military logistician.[5] The conceptual and empirical unit of analysis is Dutch Ministry of Defence (MoD) SC management, a level responsible for multiple missions; specific missions are not studied in this chapter, although the first author has ample first-hand experience in operational military logistics.

13.2 The (Generic) Military Supply Chain

Defence SCs, called logistics, support defence organizations' main value creation processes of (1) ensuring combat power elements, (2) preparing combat power and (3) enacting it (i.e., missions). Figure 13.1 shows a framework of Defence value creation and Defence logistics, offering a strategic concept for structuring activities of the Dutch MoD organization. The upper half depicts three main value creation processes constituting Defence value creation. The main value creation

[3] Hameri and Hintsa 2009; Natarajarathinam et al. 2009.

[4] Moustakis and German 2009; Russell and Saldanha 2003; Wolfe 2003.

[5] This unit takes care of logistics during military missions.

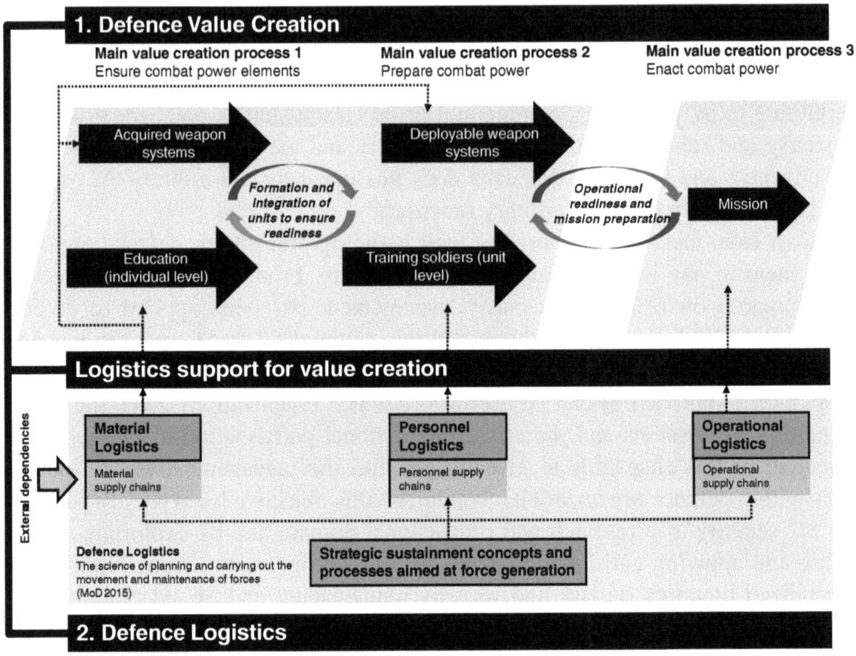

Fig. 13.1 Defence Value Creation and Defence Logistics Framework (The framework combines common Defence Value Chain and logistics concepts, de Bakker 2012, p. 552; MoD 2015a, b)

processes materialize the constitutional stipulations for the defence organization. Combat power consists of (trained) people and (deployable) weapon systems.[6]

The required logistical support—also called sustainment—focuses on personnel, material and operations; it is depicted as the bottom half of Fig. 13.1.[7] Supply chains operationalize logistical support such that logistical and value creation objectives can be met. Similar to the business world, defence organizations increasingly depend on external parties for providing logistical services including transportation, warehousing, service logistics and maintenance.[8] In the military context, logistics is the science of planning and carrying out the movement and maintenance of forces.[9] Operational logistics stretches across a network of nodes with multiple processes, through which personnel and material—equipment and supplies—flow and services are provided to a deployed force. See also Fig. 13.1: operational logistics supports missions, i.e. the process that enacts combat power.

---

[6] de Bakker 2012.

[7] Material logistics can be understood in a limited sense (focused on equipment) and in a broader sense (products and services required for force generation excluding personnel logistics).

[8] Davids et al. 2013.

[9] NATO 2014, p. 2-L-5.

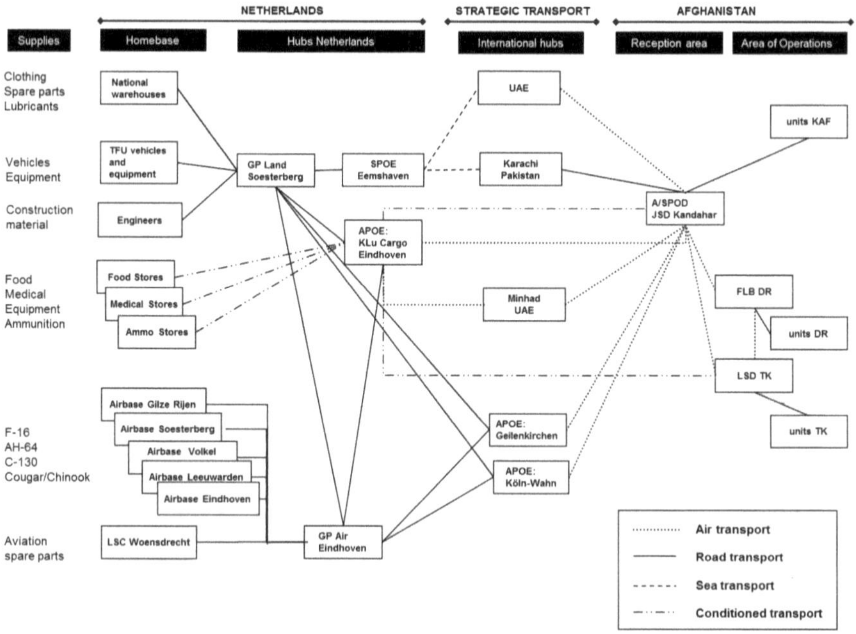

Fig. 13.2 (Dutch) Task Force Uruzgan (TFU) Logistics Supply Chain Network (Rietjens et al. 2010)

A military supply chain is designed as a flexible set of supply chains connecting points of production and use, ensuring the most appropriate and efficient use of resources across all its nodes, maximizing information and technology to assure logistic support to operational commanders.[10] A military supply chain is specifically tailored to the characteristics of the operation. By using different modes of transport—i.e. air, sea, rail, and road—the operational supply chain comes into action. As an example, Fig. 13.2 shows the tailored operational supply chain that supported the Dutch mission in Afghanistan. The networks shows how supplies are transported from the Home Base (Netherlands) via different hubs to the units in Afghanistan using different modes of transport.

Mainly because of the security risks and operational uncertainties this complex supply network was designed and needed a lot of logistic effort to manage it. Dutch MOD had no or only little experience to manage such a huge operation and a risk-based supply chain security management system did not exist.

[10] MoD 2015a, b, p. 9.

13.3 Supply Chain Security Management: Two Approaches

13.3.1 Approach 1: Risk-Based Supply Chain Security Management

In the literature, terminologies pertaining to either SC security or SC risk have been used somewhat interchangeably.[11] SC security entails the protection of supply chain assets (i.e., product, facilities, equipment, information, and personnel) from theft, damage, destruction, or terrorism, and to prevent the unauthorized introduction of contraband, people, or weapons of mass destruction into the supply chain.[12] SC risk is defined as the likelihood or chance of SC outcomes being susceptible to disruption, which would have detrimental effect on the firm.[13] Accordingly, SC security risks constitute a specific category of SC risks. SC security risks can be classified within the intentional SC disruptions category of Sheffi and Rice and Speier et al. or within the man-made attacks category of Markmann et al.[14]

The process for managing SC security is known as SC security management (SCSM). SCSM serves as a means to prevent and mitigate SC security risks. Closs and McGarrell define SCSM as "the application of policies, procedures, and technology to protect supply chain assets (i.e., product, facilities, equipment, information, and personnel) from theft, damage, or terrorism, and to prevent the introduction of unauthorized contraband, people, or weapons of mass destruction into the supply chain".[15] The process for managing SC risk is known as SC risk management (SCRM). SCRM refers to reducing SC vulnerability by ensuring business continuity via planning.[16] SCSM and SCRM are interrelated, as they are both focused on business continuity. SCSM is a specific interpretation of SCRM that seeks to prevent man-made attacks such as theft and damage to or destruction of products and assets (via planning or taking physical measures).[17] In the SCRM literature, consensus seems to exist on the SCRM processes: (1) risk identification; (2) risk assessment; (3) risk mitigation; and (4) response to risk incidents.[18] ISO14971 defines a risk R as the product of probability and impact of an event: $R = P_e \times S_e$, where P_e and S_e refer to the probability and impact (severity) of event e, respectively. The quality of identifying and assessing the probability and

---

[11] Autry and Bobbitt 2008.

[12] Closs and McGarrell 2004.

[13] Closs and McGarrell 2004.

[14] Sheffi and Rice 2005; Speier et al. 2011; Markmann et al. 2013.

[15] Closs and McGarrell 2004.

[16] Markmann et al. 2013.

[17] Markmann et al. 2013.

[18] Sodhi et al. 2012.

impact of risks (process 1 and 2) is strongly dependent on the availability and actuality of information, as well as on the experience of the risk assessor. Good estimates of the probability of the occurrence of any particular disruption and accurate measure of potential impact of each disruption appear difficult to obtain.[19] Therefore, many authors have stated that collaboration (i.e., information exchange) between SC partners is the key to security success.[20] An interesting phenomenon revealed by some researchers is that although companies state that their SCs are vulnerable to disruptions, many of them do not invest in programs that would reduce SC risk.[21] Tang speculates that in the absence of accurate measures of the probability of an occurrence of a major disruption, such as a terrorist attack, and the potential impact of the disruption, firms find it difficult to justify contingency plans.[22] In addition, firms have not invested in improving security beyond the minimum level due to difficulty in justifying security investments.[23] Thus, while the need for enhanced supply chain security is apparent, firms seem reluctant in developing contingency plans. Therefore, researchers have started to suggest that firms will be more willing to implement SC strategies that reduce risk and improve performance simultaneously.[24] That means that security and efficiency initiatives should not be a separated, but be a shared responsibility in firms.

13.3.2 Supply Chain Security Initiatives

Recent terrorist threats and security incidents have driven the introduction of new security initiatives or measures that transcend a single organization.[25] Governments, international organizations, and private sector are active in the design of SC security programs, regulations and standards. There is a great variety of SC security initiatives ranging from country-specific operational regulations to global security standards. For example:[26]

The *Customs-Trade Partnership Against Terrorism* (C-TPAT) program in the US. This program is a government-business initiative and is led by the U.S. Customs and Border Protection (CBP). Only importers and carriers based in the US are eligible to participate in the program. To join C-TPAT, a company promises to take responsibility for security throughout its entire supply chain. In return,

[19] Slovic 1987; Acedo and Florin 2007; Markmann et al. 2013; Rice and Caniato 2003; Zsidisin et al. 2004.

[20] Sheffi 2001; Rice and Caniato 2003; Kleindorfer and Saad 2005.

[21] Rice and Caniato 2003; Zsidisin et al. 2004.

[22] Tang 2006.

[23] Peleg-Gillai et al. 2006.

[24] Chopra and Sodhi 2004; Tang 2006.

[25] Hintsa et al. 2009.

[26] For more details see Hintsa et al. 2009.

CBP provides a great deal of benefits. The program focuses on improving the security of private companies' supply chains with respect to terrorism.

The *Authorized Economic Operator* (AEO) program presented by the European Commission. This program is comparable to C-TPAT in the US. The program designates the status that Customs authorities from European member states should grant to reliable traders established in the EU. AEO traders will be able to obtain one or both of the following certificates: Simplification for customs procedures and Facilitation for security and safety.

The *ISO/PAS 28000: 2005* standard "Specification for security management systems for the supply chain" by the International Standards Organization (ISO).

The *Business Alliance for Secured Commerce* (BASC). In this program companies operating in risky regions work together with national and international organizations to prevent drug smuggling in their supply chains.

The *Technology Asset Protection Association*, an initiative of high technology companies cooperating together against cargo theft.

Interestingly, with a few exceptions all security initiatives are voluntary. While these initiatives could improve security, some sceptics have doubts, because they require significant levels of investment.[27] This could also explain the rather limited adaptation and implementation of these SC security initiatives in businesses so far.

13.3.3 Approach 2: Supply Chain Security Management and Adaptive Capability

While a risk-based approach provides an organization with a framework for understanding SC security risks and taking measures, it seems too rigid for building an adaptive capability.[28] Risk-based thinking can become a logic that excludes a more entrepreneurial, pragmatic approach to security management. Strategic theorists stress a pluralistic approach to strategic challenges, including SC security as a strategic responsibility.[29] The actual necessity to invest in an adaptive capability for security management depends on the strategic urgency of SC.[30] Strategic urgency can be defined, first, as the extent to which items are strategic. This is derived from the level of supply risk and impact on organizational performance.[31] And second, the extra-organizational market conditions which contribute to the strategic urgency. Inspired by strategic analysis theory, strategic urgency for an organization like the MoD responsible for supply chains to mission theatre may increase when end-customers cannot adjust their demand or switch to alternative

[27] Tang 2006.

[28] Seifert and Langenberg 2011.

[29] Jean-Louis et al. 2007.

[30] Nilsson and Waidringer 2004.

[31] Caniels and Gelderman 2005.

sourcing, when no feasible substitutes are available, when alternative service provides are absent, and when the supplier base is limited.[32] Increasingly, as we expand on in the next section, defence organizations expand their supply options by enhancing network-level cooperation (inter-European countries, North Atlantic Treaty Organization (NATO), United Nations (UN), and military vis-à-vis non-governmental organizations).[33] Adaptive capability could contribute to strategic performance improvement, including security.[34] Literature on adaptive SCs and security remains scattered. Some authors use the notion of resilience as the interplay of vulnerabilities and capabilities.[35] Other scholars propose for instance Adaptive SC Management, or the 'Triple-A' (agile, adaptive, aligned) SC concept.[36] A number of approaches have been suggested to achieve these desirable properties of a SC, and to shape in a broader sense organizations and their networks responsible for SCs.

Strategic network adaptivity. First, an adaptive capability can refer to a multiple-supplier strategy, combining local and global sourcing.[37] A flexible supply base with 'safety nets' is called for when adaptation is required.[38] Next, given a resulting supply network, interorganizational governance contributes to understanding how organizations structure their interactions. Adaptive, collaborative governance facilitates adjustment of network participants' contributions and stabilization of the network.[39] Examples include service alliances and private-private or public-private partnerships.[40] Moreover, the SC security initiatives earlier mentioned introduce network governance innovations that enable a subset of suppliers to meet particular security standards.

Organizational and network learning. While the previous approach proposes strategic-structural measures, other scholars relate adaptation to interorganizational relationships and learning at organizational and interorganizational levels.[41] Such learning benefits from training; from involving diverse experts and managing their knowledge effectively; and from information sharing.[42]

Adaptive network tactics. Tactics as used in business literature refers to modes for (re)organizing operational actions. Adaptation improves when organizations develop a repertoire of tactics and use it effectively in a particular context. For SCs, organizations can vary the level redundancy, i.e. the locations and size of

32 Porter 2008.

33 Flavin 2007.

34 Ivanov et al. 2010.

35 Pettit et al. 2010.

36 Ivanov et al. 2010; Lee 2004.

37 Chopra and Sodhi 2004; Christopher 2011.

38 Tang 2006.

39 Folke et al. 2005; Provan et al. 2007.

40 van Fenema et al. 2014.

41 Kraatz 1998; Faust et al. 2015.

42 Newig et al. 2010; Jüttner and Maklan 2011.

(strategic) stocks.[43] Tactics can also imply versatile logistics conceptualization (instead of sticking to one particular concept), reliance on multiple scenarios, variation of lead times, lines of communications (LOC) or the point of product differentiation (postponement strategy).[44] This diversification reduces dependence on a particular modality of transportation (road, air, sea, and rail), service provider and logistical infrastructure. Scholars reinterpret these tactics from a complex science perspective. This theory postulates a number of principles fostering adaptivity and steers explicitly away from planning and centralized control.[45] Principles include decentralized self-organization/-healing/-adaptation of networks, emergence of order, autonomous cooperation and control, interactions between system actors and the environment, and operating on the 'edge of chaos'.[46] Applied to military logistics, 'sense and respond' concepts have been developed.[47]

Adaptive network operations. At the operational level, adaptation concerns changes to accommodate demand, as well as required SCs that are already structured in terms of sourcing, governance and tactics.[48] Given the resulting structural features, organizations can develop their planning, forecasting, assortment, and control processes to adjust parameters such as frequency and volume of transportation, security, safety, environmental impact, stock levels and fine-tuning SC business processes.[49] Operational adaptation may improve performance parameters such as security, capacity utilization, service levels and costs.

Network technology for adaptivity. Finally, technology is considered an important driver of supply organizations' adaptive capability. Technology plays a pervasive role as it impacts physical military technologies (complex and increasingly autonomous systems that enhance demand for intricate service logistics), physical transportation technologies (possible future logistical use of drones). Apart from physical technologies, information technology permeates SCs in the sense of enabling an organization's integrated planning and control processes. Scholars point at enhanced visibility of logistical flows. This adds to a shared recognized theatre logistic picture and hence opportunities for improving decision making.[50]

At the interorganizational level, platforms are developed of integrated information technologies to facilitate exchange. For instance, information architectures and a Networked Business Operating System (BOS) have been proposed to

---

[43] Staber and Sydow 2002; Tang 2006.

[44] Gartner and Blanken 2012; Dumke 2011; Tang 2006. LOC is a traditional logistics term, where communication refers to physical transportation, Scott et al. 2000.

[45] Hulsmann et al. 2008.

[46] Hulsmann et al. 2008; Bartholdi III et al. 2010.

[47] Hammond 2008.

[48] Kress 2002.

[49] Ivanov et al. 2010.

[50] 'In an operational environment, logistic information, combined with operational information and intelligence, provides full logistic situational awareness. This helps staff assess, plan and manage logistic resources in a coordinated manner... The recognised theatre logistic picture should provide a snapshot of the logistic situation', MoD 2015a, b, p. 30.

support transaction management of multiple organizations.[51] Technology may contribute to adaptation as it can support both centralized network control (e.g. control towers), and decentralized interactions (multi-agent systems and extended enterprise systems).[52]

How these approaches come together and relate to SC security requires insight in dependencies across approaches and relationships across SC structures.[53] For instance, explanatory reasoning across approaches argues that governance and integration contribute to information visibility, which in turn enables flexibility.[54] While commonly in logistics management, strategic business considerations are unilaterally translated into logistical concept development and planning, defence organizations' adaptation for security seems to be strongly influenced by theatre, strategic transportation, military partner availability and market features.[55] Such topics will be explored next.

13.3.4 Synthesis

One could stress differences between the two approaches just introduced. Security risk management starts with particular organizational preferences for security risks and security risk levels (i.e. to what extent is a negative impact on organizational goals and activities likely) and develops mitigation strategies to ensure performance. A focus on adaptive capability, on the other hand, concentrates on the extent to which preparing the organization to adapt to various circumstances is necessary and possible. Following research on scenario planning, synthesis of these approaches can be developed by letting the adaptive capability approach contribute to risk management (Fig. 13.3).[56]

Taking scenarios as a starting point, organizations can build adaptive capabilities and organize their risk management.[57] Adaptive capabilities can contribute in particular to reactive mitigation: the organization has already invested in its ability to switch sourcing partners for instance. Depending on an organization's context, the stability and variation of scenarios will differ. Consequently, the role and content of adaptive capabilities can be adjusted.

---

[51] Janssen 2007; van Heck and Vervest 2007.

[52] An example of decentralized optimization is calculation of routes at the actor level http://corporate.tomtom.com/releasedetail.cfm?ReleaseID=788391. Centralized optimization, on the other hand, strives for network level performance such as maximizing transportation flows (http://delta.tudelft.nl/article/reducing-congestion-with-artificial-intelligence/29203).

[53] Grover and Kohli 2012; Ivanov et al. 2010.

[54] Wang and Wei 2007.

[55] Rushton et al. 2014.

[56] Dani and Ranganathan 2008; http://scrmblog.com/review/agile-supply-chains-and-uncertainty.

[57] Scenarios may be used in a limited sense (considering alternative modes of transportation) or in a more extensive manner (covering alternative sourcing options).

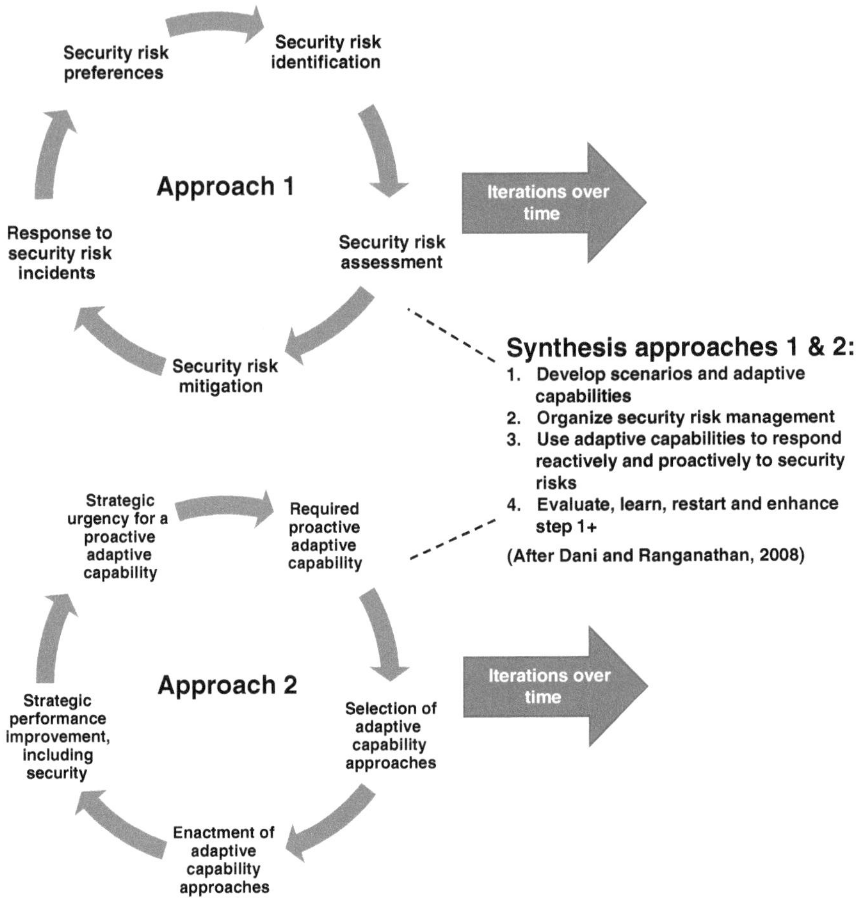

Fig. 13.3 Syntheses of approaches to SCSM

13.4 Empirical Insights from Dutch MoD

As stated in the introduction of this chapter we focus primarily on SCSM and build on security risk management and SC adaptation literature to examine how a defence organization strategically manages SC security and faces current challenges. The empirical part of this research is based upon national and international literature, an interview with logistic experts of the Directorate of Operations' Joint Staff J4 at the Dutch MoD, information from the Logistic Conference 2015 and personal experience as a subject matter expert on operational logistics. *Sentences in italics represent vignettes and refer to our empirical work (not citations unless noted otherwise).*

Because it takes a lot of resources and time to create the right conditions to conduct and sustain military operations and missions, much effort is put into the logistic planning process. Security is an important issue from the start of any military operation and therefore also one of the main topics in the logistic planning process. SCSM starts as part of a comprehensive and detailed logistic planning process.

In this section, we first present an overview of the generic military logistic planning process. As part of this planning process the (operational) SC planning is elaborated upon in Sect. 13.4.2. In Sect. 13.4.3, a shortlist of measures taken to reduce some of the security risks in order to assure logistic support is given.

13.4.1 The Generic Military Logistic Planning Process[58]

Effective operational logistics is vital to conducting and sustaining any military operation or mission. Regardless of the nature of the operation, the primary logistic aim should be to assure effective and efficient support and take all necessary measures to protect the logistic chain from theft, damage, destruction, and contraband.

Achieving the desired strategic coherence in the planning and conduct of operations requires building and fostering a shared comprehensive understanding of the factors central to the situation at all operational levels. This effort should commence from the very beginning of the planning process. Promoting this understanding needs to be accomplished continuously throughout the entire operational process.[59]

In the early stages of planning, the Logistic Operational Planning Group Team (LOPGT) may not have all of the required information to design the 'best' SC plan.[60] Initial estimations or assumptions can, however, be refined and agreed upon during the iterative stages of the planning process. To aid planning coherence, all logistics planners use a common set of assumptions.[61]

Vignette from empirical research

Within Dutch MoD a common set of generic (joint) logistic assumptions is not available. Logistic planners must be highly experienced and a subject matter expert in a specific logistic area.

Implication

MoD relies on logistics expertise rather than the use of a common set of generic assumptions.

---

[58] NATO 2010a, b, 2013a, b.

[59] NATO 2010a, b, p. 1.

[60] DOPS/J4 is in the lead of the LOPGT within Dutch MoD.

[61] Within Dutch MoD two types (sets) of assumptions are used. For Asset Management a set of specific factsheets—only for the main weapon systems—is used and for inventory management a framework of directives has been designed. A common set of generic (joint) logistic assumptions is currently not available.

As (operational and logistic) planning matures, more refined modelling provides decision support to the LOPGT. The analyses, and associated quantitative data, allow courses of action to be defined and enable assessment of the levels of logistic support that may be needed, or are available. Moreover, risks—both safety and security—of those courses of action become better understood.

Vignette from empirical research

"As we select our forces and plan our operations, ... we must understand how logistics can impact on our concepts of operations... Commanders must base all their concepts of operations on what they know they can do logistically".[62]

The information available at the beginning of an operation is inaccurate and highly uncertain because adversary activities could change rapidly, operational requirements are still unknown, and the overall security situation is unclear and perhaps even unstable. Contingency plans or mitigating actions must be in place to reduce the operational risks and to guarantee effective and efficient logistic support.

Implication

Versatility of operations require adaptive logistics planning and conversely, available resources and logistics impact operational affordance.

13.4.2 Operational Military SC Planning

The activities in the logistic planning process can be transformed into a generic SC planning model.[63] Although Dutch MoD does not have such a generic model the sequence of activities of the planning process is identical to those in the SC model descripted by the Director SC Support (SCS) of the British Defence Equipment and Supply (DE&S) Department.[64] This SC planning model is explained next and where appropriate a clarification will be given from Dutch MoD perspective. The (Joint) SC (JSC) planning model (Fig. 13.4) is explicit in stating the need for operational SC plans to ensure that the needs of the supported commander are met (i.e. to assure logistic support).[65]

The first activity in this model and the first step in the (JSC) planning process are the orientation on and analysis of the mission. The orientation in the field of

[62] Quote of Lieutenant General Alfred M. Gray, Jr., United States Marine Corps MoD 2015a, b.

[63] MoD 2015a, b, p. 7.

[64] MoD 2005.

[65] MoD 2005, p. A-23.

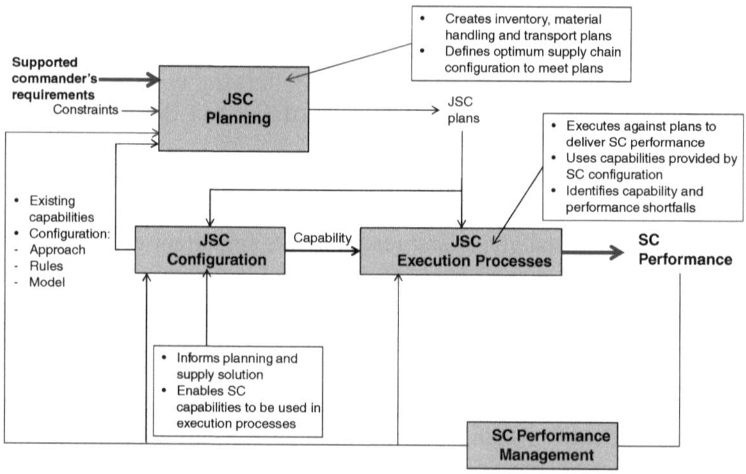

Fig. 13.4 Core activities essential to achieving a reliable and effective SC planning (MoD 2005, p. 15)

operational logistics focuses on the environment in which the unit must operate (i.e. constraints), and the expected action (i.e. commander's requirements). This first step creates clarity on how the logistic support to the mission and supply chain could be best designed (i.e. optimum supply chain configuration). Next step is to actually configure the support by bringing logistic capabilities and resources together. If there are shortfalls or capability gaps noticed this could mean that the first step of the planning process must be done again in order to adjust the initial plan. The third step in the process is the actual execution. During this phase again capability shortfalls could occur and also performance expectations could not be fulfilled as planned. This could lead to a second revision of the logistic plan. During the execution phase of the mission the performance of the supply chain is monitored (SC performance management).

Vignette from empirical research

Within Dutch MoD much effort is put in the decision-making and planning phase to create the right circumstances to provide effective logistic support to the deployed forces and in the design of an agile and resilient SC (as much as possible based on the information on hand). In practice, because of the pre-arrangements and contracts there is unfortunately little or no room left for changes during the execution phase. This lack of adaptiveness during execution makes logistics vulnerable. Small adjustments are communicated via additional Mission Specific Logistic Instructions (MSLI) or specific maintenance announcements.

Implication

MoD invests upfront in carefully deciding on logistic support while the resulting supply chain network is merely fine-tuned rather than adapted.

SC security risk management is an integral part of the model as shown in Fig. 13.4 and is done during all phases of the mission (i.e. planning, deployment, sustainment, redeployment and recuperation) by drawing up a list of constraints, identify capability gaps and performance shortfalls, and develop contingencies (i.e. what-if-scenarios).

In common with all levels of planning (strategic and operational or long-mid-short term), the quality of the higher level information, together with an understanding of available capabilities and resources are important determinants of the quality, and subsequent effectiveness of the lower level plans. The time available to put operational plans together—at the core dependent on the political process—will be a critical factor. A further requirement is to produce operational lessons identified. These provide a structured method to review SC operational plans and planning, configurations and execution processes, within the context of other operational factors to identify where performance improvements are needed.

The more accurately supported commanders state their logistic requirements, the easier it is for the SC to accurately interpret them, and prepare to provide the level of service required.[66] In the current state, the performance levels required are often not explicitly stated. Where required performance levels have not been decided previously, or indeed may still be unclear as an operation mounts, a SC is configured using the resources available in the hope that the level of performance it delivers will be acceptable. It reacts (adapts) as quickly as possible to improve performance if it is initially unacceptable. The SC has a responsibility to ensure that the type of information it requires is communicated to the supporting/supported commanders to assist in the provision of useful requirement statements and effective directives.

Vignette from empirical research
"*As J4 of the Directorate of Operations we act as the orchestrator of the SC. We are responsible, keep an overview, and communicate with other SC partners in case of shortfalls.*" *Unfortunately there is no performance management system and service parameters are not defined.*[67]

Implication
DOPS/J4 takes on an orchestrator rather than a performance management role.

[66] MoD 2005, p. 78.

[67] For example Readiness, Responsiveness, Reliability, Flexibility, Cost, Assets.

13.4.3 Operational Military SC Security Risk Management[68]

Ideally, the capabilities and capacity of the defence SC are matched to the levels of service required by its users (customers). In turn by understanding the limitations of the defence SC users are able to have more realistic expectations of its ability to support them, and of the (security) risks involved in not filling capability gaps. The importance of effective security risk management (i.e. approach 1 in Fig. 13.3) at every level of planning cannot be over-emphasized and is a constant message during the planning process.[69]

Vignette from empirical research
To assure logistic support means not only that one understands the limitations or the needs of the users, but also needs total (asset and information) visibility during the execution. Only by knowing the actual status of for instance our logistic means, assets and stocks, and goods in transit we are able to identity security risks and capability gaps and make contingencies or mitigate actions. By monitoring the SC and evaluating shortfalls and (security) risks, we are, hopefully on time, able to adapt to changing realities such as unpredictable events, enemy disruption, theft, sabotage.

Implication
Logistics visibility is required for adaptive user-oriented performance and security management.

Building proactive adaptive capabilities (i.e. approach 2 in Fig. 13.3) could contribute to strategic performance improvement including security. Within defence organizations options are limited due to the fact that supported commanders cannot simply adjust their demand or switch to alternative sourcing, no feasible substitutes are available, alternative service providers are absent, and the supplier base is limited. Still, this does not mean that it has no adaptive capabilities. Most of these options are however examples of (national orchestrated) reduction of security risk instead of building a proactive adaptive (multinational) network and are explained next.

Multinational logistics support. Nations are strongly encouraged to develop and agree to generic pre-arrangements for multinational logistics support to share the logistic 'burden' and more important to reduce (security) risks.[70] Multinational

---

[68] NATO 2013a, b, pp. 3–56.

[69] MoD 2005, p. 44.

[70] NATO 2013a, b, pp. 1–2.

logistics operations require harmonization and synchronization of responsibilities of all actors involved in the operational theatre. This is still a very viscous and lengthy process as nations still have the ultimate responsibility for the provision of required logistics resources to support their forces.

Vignette from empirical research

Opportunities for multinational cooperation, Host Nation Support and commercial cooperation opportunities need to be identified in the earliest stages of the planning process. For the inventory of commercial cooperation opportunities the NATO Support and Procurement Agency (NSPA) could be used as a contract integrator.

Implication

Logistics planning should start off at national and network levels.

Security stocks. To deal with operational uncertainty combined with long and complex LOCs security stocks are composed. In general the size of these security stocks is the compensation of 30 days 'consumption.'

Vignette from empirical research

The '30-day' concept was used in Iraq and Afghanistan and is currently used in Mali.

Implication

MoD sticks to a minimum-stock concept based on days of supply without inflow of goods, rather than for instance inbound performance capabilities of MoD logistics and suppliers.

The efficiency of these security stocks has, however, never been examined.

Differentiation. Military important and sensitive goods such as ammunition, crypto, medical supplies and private post etc. are transported by own means (preferred option) or a trusted contractor to reduce security risks. All other goods or supplies are transported via commercial couriers (as most cost effective option). In case of urgent shortfalls own means (i.e. airplanes) are also used.

Logistic command, control and information. The ability to deliver effective logistic command, control and information is essential for any deployment and must be considered at the earliest stage of the planning phase. The recognized (theatre) logistic picture is a means of delivering situational awareness across the deployed force. This information is unfortunately still immature and heavily caveated, but necessary to enable the planning process.[71] The more accurate that analysis is during the early planning stages, the more robust the operational sustainability baseline.

Vignette from empirical research
Information is vital to run contemporary and future operations and therefore sensitive to deliberate or unintentional disruptions. To secure logistic information should be one of the main topics within the security risk management system.

Implication
MoD needs to invest in capabilities to obtain and secure logistics information.

Although specialised academic research is done to define logistic security and methods are developed to qualify and quantify security risks (presented as approach 1), significant challenges still remain to improve logistic security especially during military operations. To be able to respond properly and rapidly to (possible) disruptions, additional research is needed to improve the security and adaptive capabilities of the military supply network in order to meet the operational support requirements of deployed forces (presented as the syntheses of approaches to SCSM, see also Fig. 13.3). How to make these networks less vulnerable for security risks and what is the subsequent impact on performance? Empirical data is also needed to enlarge insight in the two previous described approaches especially within a military context.

13.5 Reflection and Future Research

13.5.1 Reflection

The nature of warfare and how militaries prepare for it—along with their other strategic objectives,—has changed drastically over the last decade. Likewise the focus for military logisticians is now less on moving large volumes of equipment, such as vehicles, food, and fuel across thousands of miles from source to base; the focus is now on expeditionary operations, being prepared to rapidly deploy smaller

---

[71] Lessons Learned from recent operations in Iraq (SFIR), Afghanistan (ISAF) and Kosovo (KFOR); nations are not able or willing due to national regulations to share (operational) logistic information.

troop numbers and supplies to a wider range of theatres.[72] As the pace of change is speeding up and militaries are looking at more agile operations it is all about being able to supply deployed forces effectively (and cost efficient). Logistics operations must be smarter and smoother than ever. They will be stretched with fewer resources and required to perform at short notice.[73] As a result Supply Chain Security Management (SCSM) will gain importance to respond to these demands. To finalize this chapter, three examples for future research are elaborated upon in the next sections.

13.5.2 Future Research 1: Multiple-Supplier Strategy[74]

As stated before an adaptive capability can refer to a multiple-supplier strategy, combining local and global sourcing. Contractor Support to Operations (CSO) is a proven sourcing concept and an indispensable addition to military logistic capabilities and capacities.

Using CSO requires timely planning and exercising by both the MoD and industry.[75]

Operational experience, particularly during the early stages, highlighted the need to consider CSO (security) risks during the force planning process. The joint commander should ensure measures are in place to minimize the (security) risks to contractors in case of a withdrawal. Contingencies against CSO arrangements failing may include maintaining a military capability and using Reserve Forces.

Currently, CSO not only augments but is increasingly replacing military capability, once operations become established. Even while using contractors, planners should recognize operational (security) risk exists and continue to consider support from other resources such as Host Nation, international partners, multinational organizations or other government departments. One of the questions to be answered is: How to mitigate the subsequent security risks of CSO (to enlarge the supply base) in order to create a more adaptive supply chain? Or: to what amount can CSO be used as a substitute for military capabilities without creating additional operational security risks? To balance this process—i.e. seeking additional support from contractors or other resources versus limiting operational security risks—additional scientific research is needed.

---

[72] See http://www.defenceiq.com/air-land-and-sea-defence-services/articles/fujitsu-s-eric-bownes-discusses-the-future-of-defe/ and http://www.defenceiq.com/air-land-and-sea-defence-services/articles/why-equipment-and-supply-chain-management-is-centr/.

[73] See http://www.defenceiq.com/air-land-and-sea-defence-services/articles/why-equipment-and-supply-chain-management-is-centr/.

[74] MoD 2015a, b, p. 118–5.11.

[75] Together with the Netherlands Industries for Defence and Security Foundation (NIDV), the defence organization assesses which activities may be contracted out to the commercial sector, MoD 2012, p. 11.

13.5.3 Future Research 2: Reducing Security Risks by Creating an Adaptive Operational SC Network

Recent developments such as outsourcing of different activities to non-defence organizations, technological innovations, and various threats have made the defence SC more vulnerable for disruptions and mis-planning.[76] A (security) risk-based management system provides MoD with a framework for understanding SC security risks and taking timely measures. Building a proactive adaptive capability—e.g. by using a multi-supplier strategy—within the operational SC is needed because of strategic urgency due to the fact that supported commanders cannot simply adjust their demand or switch to alternative sourcing.

Vignette from empirical research
Although within Dutch MoD (security) risk management is considered essential it has not been elaborated in an operational management system. Security risks are constantly monitored and assessed but there is no framework for understanding these risks so that vital lessons can be learned from it. It is the personal ability of the logistic operator(s) to find adequate solutions that can be timely implemented to reduce the recognized (security) risks. This personal ability makes the system vulnerable.

Implication:
Implementation of results from the security risk monitoring process relies on logistics expertise rather than organizational routines.

To prepare operational SCs for the future they need to become more adaptive. Instead of working together as a set of national orientated SCs they need to operate more as a multinational operational SC network.

Vignette from empirical research
Although NATO has defined the overarching principle of collective responsibility, operational logistic support of today's missions is still, by and large, a national business.[77]

Implication
NATO principles at the network level are not yet enacted for operational logistics.

---

[76] Pijpers 2013; van Fenema et al. 2014; Xiao et al. 2007.

[77] Collective responsibility is a set of NATO's and nations' individual and largely complementary obligations to cooperatively organize and deliver the overall logistics support of NATO operations, taking into account one another's requirements and constraints, NATO 2013a, b, pp. 1–2.

Using a multiple-supplier strategy seems to be an effective way to make the operational SC more adaptive.[78] Contracting, as part of a multiple-supplier strategy, is a significant means by which a commander can introduce resources, services and capabilities to assist with generating, deploying, sustaining, and recovering the force. Using long-term partnership arrangements may provide additional risk mitigation. Such arrangements help to develop military-commercial relationships and encourage contractors to engage early in the planning cycle.

Additional scientific research is encouraged to investigate the right circumstances to implement a (security) risk management system and integrate them into current planning systems. Additional research is also needed to answer the question on how a multi-supplier strategy can transform currently national orchestrated SCs into a multinational adaptive operational SC network.

13.5.4 Future Research 3: Supply Chain Transparency and Security Implications

Complex supply chains require sophisticated, connected tools to monitor risks, predict disruptions, and support rapid recovery as part of an overall resilience strategy. Information is vital to run and control contemporary and future operations and therefore sensitive to deliberate or unintentional disruptions. To secure logistic information should therefore be one of the main topics within the security risk management system. At the same time, supply chain risks grow significantly as supply chains span more legal jurisdictions, different types of business practices, and widely varying cultural norms. In this context, supply chain transparency becomes the vital process of managing risks by accessing, learning from, and acting on supply chain information. By itself, transparency is an increasingly important capability for companies. But as part of a company's broader attempts to build supply chain resilience—the ability to recover from and reduce the impact of key risk events—transparency's role is pivotal.

The IT-world is facing disruptive innovations as we speak. These disruptions will certainly transform and change our understanding of logistics in the military as well. To name but a few of those "game changers" include 3D-printing; robotics; automation and the use of UAVs also for logistic purposes. These developments will affect our logistic processes and the way we design our defence support chain. As a result from these disruptions in the IT world, cyber security will become an urgent issue also for defence logistics. This becomes even more challenging as defence organizations are facing a more diverse and hybrid threat. So the challenge to secure data will be paramount, especially given the increasing

[78] Christopher 2011.

interconnectedness of command and control systems, weapon systems (both sensors and effectors) and our logistic information system.[79]

'How to mitigate subsequent security risks of IT innovations in order to enlarge supply chain transparency and create a more adaptive network?' is one of the questions that need to be answered. Additional scientific research is needed to search for the right circumstances to gain supply chain transparency and reduce its IT security implications. On the other hand additional research is also needed to explore IT innovations and how they affect the design of (military) supply chains.

Perhaps the most interesting and challenging research will be to combine all of these elaborated research subjects (i.e. increase adaptivity by using a multi-supplier strategy, enlarge supply chain transparency, implement a security (risk) management system and the use of IT innovations) in order to transform currently national orchestrated SCs into a multinational adaptive operational SC network (using Fig. 13.3 as a framework).

Acknowledgments The authors are grateful to MoD Directorate of Operations' DOPS/J4 and for feedback from NL ARMS editors and reviewers, Jan Willem Proper, and Jantine Verkaik. This research was supported by the Netherlands Defence Academy.

References

Acedo FJ, Florin J (2007) Understanding the risk perception of strategic opportunities: a tripartite model. Strateg Change 16:97–116

Autry CW, Bobbitt LM (2008) Supply chain security orientation: conceptual development and a proposed framework. Int J Logist Manag 19:42–64

Bartholdi JJ III, Eisenstein DD, Lim YF (2010) Self-organizing logistics systems. Annu Rev Control 34:111–117

Caniels MCJ, Gelderman CJ (2005) Purchasing strategies in the Kraljic matrix—a power and dependence perspective. J Purchasing Supply Manag 11:141–155

Chopra S, Sodhi MS (2004) Managing risk to avoid supply-chain breakdown. MIT Sloan Manag Rev 46:53–61

Christopher MG (2011) Logistics and supply chain management. Prentice Hall, Harlow

Closs DJ, McGarrell EF (2004) Enhancing security throughout the supply chain. IBM Center for the Business of Government, Washington, DC

Dani S, Ranganathan R (2008) Agility and supply chain uncertainty: a scenario planning perspective. Int J Agile Syst Manag. http://www.inderscienceonline.com/doi/abs/10.1504/IJASM.2008.021208

Davids C, Beeres R, van Fenema PC (2013) Operational defense sourcing: organizing military logistics in Afghanistan. Int J Phys Distrib Logist Manag 43:116–133

de Bakker E (2012) De toekomst van sourcing bij Defensie: Een beschouwing van de voor- en nadelen. Militaire Spectator 181:551–560

Dumke D (2011) Agile supply chains and uncertainty. http://scrmblog.com/review/agile-supply-chains-and-uncertainty

Faust V, Christens BD, Sparks SMA, Hilgendorf AE (2015) Exploring relationships among organizational capacity, collaboration, and network change. Psychosoc Interv 24:125–131

[79] http://www.defenceiq.com/air-land-and-sea-defence-services/articles/the-top-3-challenges-for-defence-logistics-experts/.

Flavin W (2007) Planning for conflict termination and post-conflict success. Parameters 33:95–112
Folke C, Hahn T, Olsson P (2005) Adaptive governance of social-ecological systems. Annu Rev Environ Resour 30:441–473
Gartner SS, Blanken L (2012) Beyond Victory and Defeat. In: Rothstein H et al (eds) Afghan Endgames: strategy and policy choices for America's longest war. Georgetown University Press, Washington, DC
Grover V, Kohli R (2012) Cocreating IT value: new capabilities and metrics for multifirm environments. MIS Q 36:225–232
Hameri A-P, Hintsa J (2009) Assessing the drivers of change for cross-border supply chains. Int J Phys Distrib Logist Manag 39:741–761
Hammond MF (2008) Sense and respond: military logistics in a global security environment. http://www.alu.army.mil/alog/issues/SepOct08/sense_response1.html. Army Logistician 40
Hintsa J, Wieser P, Gutierrez X, Hameri A-P (2009) Supply chain security management: an overview. Int J Logist Syst Manag 5:344–355
Hulsmann M, Grapp J, Li Y (2008) Strategic adaptivity in global supply chains—competitive advantage by autonomous cooperation. Int J Prod Econ 114:14–26
Ivanov D, Sokolov B, Kaeschel J (2010) A multi-structural framework for adaptive supply chain planning and operations control with structure dynamics considerations. Eur J Oper Res 200:409–420
Janssen MM (2007) Adaptability and accountability of information architectures in interorganizational networks. In: 1st International Conference on Theory and Practice of Electronic Governance, Macao
Jean-Louis D, Langley A, Rouleau L (2007) Strategizing in pluralistic contexts: rethinking theoretical frames. Hum Relat 60:179–215
Jüttner U, Maklan S (2011) Supply chain resilience in the global financial crisis: an empirical study. Supply Chain Manag: Int J 16:246–259
Kleindorfer PR, Saad GH (2005) Managing disruption risks in supply chains. Prod Oper Manag 14:53–68
Kraatz MS (1998) Learning by association? Interorganizational networks and adaptation to environmental change. Acad Manag J 41:621–643
Kress M (2002) Operational logistics: the art and science of sustaining military operations. Kluwer, Norwell, MA
Lee HL (2004) The Triple-A Supply Chain. Harvard Bus Rev 2–11
Markmann C, Darkow IL, von der Gracht H (2013) A Delphi-based risk analysis—identifying and assessing future challenges for supply chain security in a multi-stakeholder environment. Technol Forecast Soc Chang 80:1815–1833
MoD (2005) JSP 886 the defence logistics support chain manual, volume 1-part 2, DE&S SCS, Andover. https://www.gov.uk/government/uploads/system/uploads/attachment_data/file/48865/JSP886_Vol1_Pt2_BlueprintLevel3.pdf. UK Ministry of Defence
MoD (2012) In the interest of the Netherlands. https://www.defensie.nl/documenten/beleidsnotas/2013/10/11/in-the-interest-of-the-netherlands. Dutch Ministry of Defence, The Hague
MoD (2015a) CDS A-400 joint operational logistic instruction, Directorate of Operations. Dutch Ministry of Defence, The Hague
MoD (2015b) JDP 4-00 logistics for joint operations, DCDC, Swindon. UK Ministry of Defence
Moustakis F, German T (2009) Securing Europe: Western interventions towards a new security community. Tauris, London
Natarajarathinam M, Capar I, Narayanan A (2009) Managing supply chains in times of crisis: a review of literature and insights. Int J Phys Distrib Logist Manag 39:535–573
NATO (2010a) ACO comprehensive operative planning directive, ACO. https://info.publicintelligence.net/NATO-COPD.pdf. NATO, Brussels
NATO (2010b) ACO FPG LOG, ACO functional planning guidance logistics, ACO. NATO, Brussels

NATO (2013) AJP-5 Allied joint doctrine for operational Level Planning, NSA. http://www.google.nl/url?url=http://nso.nato.int/nso/zPublic/ap/AJP-5%2520E.pdf&rct=j&frm=1&q=&esrc=s&sa=U&ved=0ahUKEwj6gI_xrKHKAhWMPRQKHaG_BvAQFggUMAA&sig2=mfyyq437NNfF2G2YfM8KRA&usg=AFQjCNGVNKdnJAAYEltp_XzyoYbjiJ1jUw. NATO, Brussels

NATO (2013b) Bi-SC joint operational guidelines 13/01 LOGISTICS. ACT, NATO, Brussels

NATO (2014) AAP-06, glossary of terms and definitions. NATO, Brussels

Newig J, Günther D, Pahl-Wostl C (2010) Synapses in the network: learning in governance networks in the context of environmental management. Ecology and Society. http://www.ecologyandsociety.org/vol15/iss4/art24/

Nilsson F, Waidringer J (2004) Logistics management from a complexity perspective. ICFAI J Oper Manag 3:59–73

Peleg-Gillai B, Bhat G, Sept L (2006) Innovators in supply chain security: better security drives business value. http://www-148.ibm.com/tela/servlet/Asset/74686/Innovators

Pettit TJ, Fiksel J, Croxton KL (2010) Ensuring supply chain resilience: development of a conceptual framework. J Bus Logist 31:1–21

Pijpers PBMJ (2013) Outsourcing van militaire logistiek. Militaire Spectator 182:301–311

Porter ME (2008) The five competitive forces that shape strategy. Harvard Bus Rev 86–104

Provan KG, Fish A, Sydow J (2007) Interorganizational networks at the network level: a review of the empirical literature on whole networks. J Manag 33:479–516

Rice JB, Caniato F (2003) Building a secure and resilient supply network. Supply Chain Manag Rev 7:22–30

Rietjens SJH, Kampen T, Grant TJ (2010) Logistics planning and control: lessons learned in Afghanistan. In: Soeters JMML et al (eds) Managing military organizations: theory and practice. Routledge, London

Rushton A, Croucher P, Baker P (2014) The Handbook of logistics and distribution management. Kogan, London

Russell DM, Saldanha JP (2003) Five tenets of security-aware logistics and supply chain operation. Transp J 42:44–54

Scott BF, Rainey JC, Hunt AW (2000) The logistics of war. Air Force Logistics Management Agency. Maxwell AFB, ALA

Seifert RW, Langenberg KU (2011) Managing business dynamics with adaptive supply chain portfolios. Eur J Oper Res 215:551–562

Sheffi Y (2001) Supply chain management under the threat of international terrorism. Int J Logist Manag 12:1–11

Sheffi Y, Rice JB Jr (2005) A supply chain view of the resilient enterprise. MIT Sloan Manag Rev 47:41–48

Slovic P (1987) Perception of risk. Science 236:280–285

Sodhi MS, Son BG, Tang CS (2012) Researchers' perspectives on supply chain risk management. Prod Oper Manag 21:1–13

Speier C, Whipple JM, Closs DJ, Voss MD (2011) Global supply chain design considerations: mitigating product safety and security risks. J Oper Manag 29:721–736

Staber U, Sydow J (2002) Organizational adaptive capacity: a structuration perspective. J Manag Inq 11:408–424

Tang CS (2006) Robust strategies for mitigating supply chain disruptions. Int J Logist Res Appl 9:33–45

van Fenema PC, Keers BBM, Zijm WHM (2014) Interorganizational shared services: creating value across organizational boundaries. In: Bondarouk T (ed) Shared services as a new organizational form. Emerald, Bingley

van Heck E, Vervest PHM (2007) Smart business networks: how the network wins. Commun ACM 50:29–37

Wang ETG, Wei H-L (2007) Interorganizational governance value creation: coordinating for information visibility and flexibility in supply chains. Decis Sci 38:647–674

Wolfe M (2003) Supply chain security without tears. Supply Chain Manag Rev 7:12–20

Xiao Q, Boulet C, Gibbons T (2007) RFID security issues in military supply chains. In: The Second International Conference on Availability, Reliability and Security (ARES), Vienna

Zsidisin GA, Ellram LM, Carter JR, Cavinato JL (2004) An analysis of supply risk assessment techniques. Int J Phys Distrib Logist Manag 34:397–413

Chapter 14
Crew Resource Management as Shield and Spear for Safety and Security

Tom Bijlsma and Carla Broers

Abstract Crew Resource Management (CRM) is a vision and method to work safer by fostering social and communication competences like leadership, adaptability, and situational awareness of team members. By applying these non-technical skills professionally teams work more effective and are more robust as well. CRM then turns out to be an essential tool for save team work especially where the security of others is at stake. Some years ago CRM was introduced in a crisis service department of the Safety Region Noord-Holland-Noord. CRM trainings grew to integrated team exercises (i.e., technical and non-technical skills) and because of the propagated effects this ended in multidisciplinary team exercises. The Safety region is now working on embedding the CRM skills in relevant aspects, such as human resource management, education, training, and exercises, in an integrated and learning way.

Keywords Crew resource management · Team cooperation · Crisis management · Safety region · Soft skills

---

T. Bijlsma (✉)
Military Management and Organization Studies at the Faculty of Military Sciences of the Netherlands Defence Academy, Netherlands Defence Academy, Breda, The Netherlands
e-mail: t.bijlsma.01@mindef.nl

C. Broers
GHOR at Safety Region Noord-Holland Noord, Alkmaar, The Netherlands
e-mail: cbroers@vrnhn.nl

R. Beeres et al. (eds.), *NL ARMS Netherlands Annual Review of Military Studies 2016*, NL ARMS, DOI 10.1007/978-94-6265-135-7_14

Contents

14.1 Introduction

Teamwork is an essential ingredient for organizational success.[1] This is especially valid for organizations that operate within (potentially) hazardous environments such as the military. The domain of Human Factors studies this interaction between people, including thereby the study of their equipment and environment. An often-studied field within Human Factors is the aviation industry. Based on multiple studies into errors in cockpit teams, researchers and practitioners developed the concept of Cockpit Resource Management. Within this concept, individual competencies are indicated to be essential for successful cooperation and overall performance of the cockpit team. These competencies include amongst others leadership, adaptability and situational awareness. Nowadays, these competencies and their training and organizational implementation is often referred to as Crew Resource Management (CRM).

Research shows that CRM can be an effective and efficient tool to improve team cooperation. CRM has a proven track record in several industries such as off shoring, aviation, nuclear and process industry, as well as in within the military and crisis and disaster management.[2] The objectives of this chapter are to introduce CRM to the audience, to discuss its application within the Dutch crisis management, and to offer recommendations in this respect for further use.

To this end, section two provides some principles of CRM that can be found in the literature. In doing this, it also discusses its goals, history and seven main CRM-competencies. Section three discusses the application of CRM by presenting a case study of Dutch crisis management. Section four concludes the chapter, which discusses the crisis management case and, from there, the added value that CRM can have for other emergency providers and for the Dutch military.

[1] Jünger et al. 2007; Hoegl et al. 2004; Salas and Fiore 2004, p. 3.

[2] Flin 1995; Institute of Nuclear Power Operations 1993; Bijlsma 2015.

14.2 Crew Resource Management

In the aviation industry, from which CRM originates, the American Federal Aviation Administration (FAA) defines CRM as, "the utilization of all available human, informational, and equipment resources toward the goal of safe and efficient flight". They also write, "CRM is an active process by crewmembers to identify significant threats, to communicate them, and to develop, communicate, and carry out a plan and actions to avoid or mitigate each threat. CRM also deals directly with the avoidance of human errors and the management and mitigation of those errors that occur. CRM reflects the application of human factor knowledge to the special case of flight crews and their interactions with each other, with other groups and with the technology in the system".[3] This description shows that CRM contains many different elements. Especially it emphasizes the value of a team member's non-technical skills, among which his social and communication competences. The starting point of CRM is the individual team member. From a CRM perspective this member is assumed to be both technically and non-technically skilled, knowledgeable and experienced.

According to CRM principles, each team member should bring his professional value to the team, which is based on, among other things, skills, knowledge, experience, and attitudes. Of course there is a broad spectrum of competencies that relate to most tasks or jobs. Openness and vulnerability are specific important attitudes for working in a CRM-context. It is important that each individual has a profound knowledge at the least of his capabilities, and that team members know each other's proficiencies, or certain lacks in them.

As most people work in permanent teams in which team members know each other and know how to behave to increase their team's performance, CRM can be specifically helpful in cases of distress or crisis. Often ad hoc teams are composed to fight crises, whose members then still need to adapt, to each other, and the situation at hand while performing their jobs. CRM-competencies can then help these ad hoc teams, as one can imagine, to function quicker together and on a higher level than a team with not-CRM-equipped team members. In this chapter, an example of this has been given in case 3.

CRM requires more than training skills alone. Each team member has to master several competencies that must be present. Many of these competencies can only flourish, however, in a context where there is a just culture, sound leadership, and the right assets. When these elements are positively stimulating each other, organizations not only foster CRM, they also create cycles that foster learning, quality management, and change management as a whole. In this way, CRM forms a crucial catalyst for other constructive processes. And those processes will lead, among others, to more safety and security. The team-based view and the

[3] FAA 1989, p. 2.

appropriate CRM-behavior of each team member are the foundation. And that is a huge difference between CRM and approaches or trends like 'servant leadership' or 'lean six-sigma' which pretend to have similar output and outcome. First, however, the extrapolation of CRM to other sectors than the aviation sector will be discussed, as well as some of the key competencies of CRM.

14.3 Implementing Crew Resource Management Principles in Other Domains

As already addressed in the introduction, CRM started as Cockpit Resource Management. Over time, as CRM got implemented outside aviation also, the C in the abbreviation changed in the more neutral Crew. In the medical sector for example, the publication of the research report, *To err is human: building a safer health system*, boosted the implementation of CRM in this particular sector.[4] The report revealed striking figures of avoidable deaths and stressed the fallibility of healthcare professionals and teams. Although CRM has had a follow up in many other industries by now, there is hardly any scientific evidence of results related to safety or security when implementing or working with CRM. Still, there are some results to note. Meta-analyses show a positive effect on attitude, behaviour, and knowledge after CRM-training.[5] There are even some CRM-studies in healthcare that found positive effects on safety.[6] And CRM proves to be successful also for those teams that are not working 'at the edge' or 'the sharp end'.[7]

The primary processes and output of Defence forces are by definition related to security. To fulfil the operational task it is normal to endanger your own or another's safety. A slip in the safety mechanisms can lead to victims. The security part is in the actions against, and reactions of, the enemy (military, rebellion militias, or insurgents), and civil population (via stakeholder engagement) at the lower level of violence escalation. Here it is the professionalism of the military determining whether it is a success (mission accomplished or target deducted) or a defect (not accomplished, or worse: collateral damage with victims or blue on blue). During military operations safety and security are closely and dynamically intertwined, from showing the flag till delivering combat power.

As a Forward Air Controller (FAC) with operational experience in Uruzgan stated in an interview about 'killing': "You're always balancing speed and safety. Targets must be neutralized as soon as possible, but always with maximum safety

[4] Kohn et al. 2000.

[5] O'Connor et al. 2008.

[6] Powelll and Hill 2006; Jankouskas 2010; Haerkens et al. 2015.

[7] Marquardt et al. 2010.

for own troops. So you're constantly working to balance within those values while engaging targets. Safety of own troops is a key item and sometimes that conflicts with preventing any collateral damage. Ultimately the target must be destroyed, especially when friendlies are in danger."[8] Referring to the definition at the beginning of this section, CRM is an essential asset in this complex and dynamic environment to organize in a robust and reliable way.

Providing safety and security in "Netherlands Inc." on special occasions is for the Dutch Armed Forces their third task. Over the last years there has been a growing interest for CRM in the Armed Forces, the police force, fire departments, medical assistance organizations, and the Safety Regions. This national interest for CRM started because of several publications, seminars, and workshops initiated by the Netherlands Defence Academy, soon joined by the Police Academy, Fire Service Academy, and the Netherlands Institute for Physical Security (IFV), and a number of professionals working in the various crisis and emergency services in the diverse Safety Regions. The case on the Safety Region Noord-Holland Noord will illustrate this.

14.4 Competencies in Crew Resource Management

Communication and self-consciousness are key competence domains in CRM. The transformation of CRM from aviation to other industries yielded similar results regarding which competencies should be regarded important. The European Joint Aviation Authorities (JAA) has laid down four important categories of non-technical skills: Co-operation, Leadership or Managerial Skills, Situation Awareness, and Decision Making. Each category is split into elements and each element is concretized in behaviors. The Dutch Royal Air Force is working with a similar system: the Military Non-Technical Skills (MilNoTechS).[9]

In this section, we focus on seven competencies that originate from the US Naval Aviation Schools Command at Pensacola, Florida. These have been referred to as *the seven skills*, which have been adopted some 15 years ago by the Dutch Royal Navy. In the beginning this was used exclusively for the bridge (Bridge Resource Management). More recently, the Navy has implemented this system throughout the whole organization. In addition, some small units of the Royal Netherlands Army and the Military Police are also working with the seven skills. The seven skills can be memorized by the acronym DAMCLAS. They are discussed in this order below.

Decision making
Right and timely decisions are crucial, especially when teams have to cope with a threat, incident or disaster. There are roughly four methods of decision making: intuitive, rule-based, analytic, creative. These four methods differ in the amount of

[8] Jansen 2015, p. 45.

[9] MilNoTechS 2012.

cognitive effort they demand. How does the analytic *Rational Action Model* work, the *Bounded Rationality Model*, or a decision model like *Recognition-Primed Decision*, which is a mix of intuition and analytical thinking?[10] How and to what extent are these decision models affected by stress? Knowing about the backgrounds of these different decision models can help one in doing "the right thing". For instance, it turns out that intuition plays an important role in day-to-day decision making processes, especially with crisis responders. If that is the case, then it is necessary to get some knowledge at least on how this works. How, for instance, to foster and actualize your intuition? And what about the role of stress and fatigue? A lot of aspects to take into account.

Assertiveness
Assertiveness involves the willingness to actively participate and the ability to state and maintain your position. Essential in this is to demonstrate initiative and the courage to act and intervene. When this is not being done, there is a risk of the so-called by-stander-effect: seeing, hearing, knowing the negative effects, but not intervening, because the others are not moving either. A lack of assertiveness by most team members can lead to groupthink.[11] A more comprehensive definition is: "Assertiveness involves communicating one's feelings, concerns, ideas, and needs to others in a clear and direct manner, but without demeaning or infringing on the rights of others".[12]

Mission analysis
This involves the ability to make short-term, long-term, and contingency plans and to coordinate, allocate, and monitor crew resources. Aspects that are considered important to adequately carry out mission analyses include: the aim of the higher level, your aim, milestones, prioritization, delegation, and decentralization.

Communication
Both formal and informal communication structures in a team are important. The classical communication competency is often about formal structures, about clear and accurate sending and receiving of information, instructions, or commands, and about providing useful feedback. As we know now, there is more to it though. Non-verbal communication, for instance, can be influential also, as it is often impacting direct but sent implicit.[13] Non-verbally, each team member is thus always communicating content, procedure, interaction, and emotion, even if it is not his intent to communicate.

Leadership
Most teams have a hierarchical leader who can use the phases of team development (which lead to team learning and growth) to increase his team's performance.[14]

---

[10] Eisenhardt and Zbaracki 1992; Simon 1997; Klein 1998.

[11] Janis 1972.

[12] Salas et al. 2001, p. 76.

[13] Leary 1957.

[14] Tuckman and Jensen 1977.

According to CRM principles though, a CRM-minded team is based on distributed- or shared leadership. Because all team members are fully involved and committed to the team processes and outcome it is normal to make suggestions and ask questions. In some cases, one of the team members may naturally take or be given the lead because of his experience or expertise. So, apart from leadership, CRM particularly stresses followership and team play.

Adaptability
Working in the field of security and safety especially, not all scenarios are foreseen, let alone trained. Being adaptive is therefore an important attitude in such a context. At macro level Charles Darwin came to the same conclusion: It is not the strongest of species that survives, nor the most intelligent, but the one most adaptable to change. Adaptability might be seen as a psychological construct that is difficult to train or shape. Pulakos et al. though found after a theoretical and empirical study eight concrete dimensions of adaptability.[15] The American Institute for Defense Analyses (IDA), on the other hand, developed an adaptability model for training use.[16] Both studies conclude that adaptability is domain specific; it has to be studied and trained in the context of a particular job. Rosen et al. also developed a very interesting multi-dimensional model of team adaptability, with academically founded behavioural markers.[17] They include the CRM competencies and the model reflects the CRM vision and -method.

Situational Awareness
Situational Awareness (SA) is the degree of accuracy by which one's perception of the current environment mirrors reality so as to be able to make a projection of the situation in the near future. Technical limitations (because of (a lack of) the assets in use) and physical limits (such as fatigue, lack of sleep, or boredom), can muddle this reality. There are also, however, many psychological filters that can disturb this process (see prospect theory, the heuristics literature (e.g. Halo- and Horn Effect), and concepts such as priming or framing).[18] The SA-model of Endsley depicts a comprehensive picture.[19] In most situations it is preferred to have SA at team level: a Shared Mental Model. Especially in multidisciplinary teams this is a must.[20]

The seven CRM-competencies cannot be separated from each other. They are complementing and reinforcing each other. Training these skills is a first step but it is also essential to apply them in the daily context of the team. Training, discussing, coaching, evaluating, reviewing, these competencies in connection with the individual jobs, the technical skills, and the team goal and—processes do justice

[15] Pulakos et al. 2002.

[16] Freeman and Burns 2010.

[17] Rosen et al. 2011.

[18] Kahneman 2011.

[19] Endsley 1995.

[20] Van der Haar 2014.

to the bare existence of CRM. The next section explores the functioning of CRM in practice in the form of a case study in the context of crisis management in the Netherlands.

14.5 Crew Resource Management in Crisis Management in the Netherlands

14.5.1 Introduction

The emergency management structure in the Netherlands depends on the span of the crisis. Dependent on the effects of the incident, among which the size of the area that is impacted, the level of danger, or the impact on people, these levels are activated according to the so-called *Coordinated Regional Incident Management Procedure* (*Gecoördineerde Regionale Incidentenbestrijdings Procedure, GRIP*). The Netherlands has 25 different Safety Regions, each containing three separated coordination levels. The first level superseding the normal response arrangements is that of the *on-scene-command-team* (GRIP level 1), the second level that of the *operational team* (GRIP level 2). The *policy team* (GRIP level 3) makes up the third response level with a particular safety region. When a higher hierarchical response level is activated, the lower level coordinating teams remain intact. It is only the authority that shifts to that higher level.

In larger disasters or threats, the *on-scene-command-team* remains working around the hot spot, in 'here and now'. The *operational team* is responsible for the area that is affected by the incident and is looking forward in time: what can be expected in the next couple of hours? The *policy team* is concerned with the consequences of the incident that can occur in the next couple of days. The *policy team* is in this regard responsible for the strategic process and the mayor concerned is in charge. In case the effects of an incident or disaster transcends a mayor's responsibilities, a regionally acting *policy team* can be composed (GRIP level 4, or level 5 when more regions are involved).

The case studies below display the Dutch context and national organizational structure in which the crisis management organizations in the Netherlands have to cope with threats, incidents, and disasters. Case 1 illustrates the work of the on-scene-command-team. Case 2 illustrates that of the operational team. After the introduction, we will focus on CRM in the Safety Region Noord-Holland Noord (NHN). This safety region is responsible for managing incidents and disasters in the far north-western part of the Netherlands, which ranges roughly from Castricum to Texel.

Case 1: The work of an on-scene-command team[21]

On Friday February 24th 2014, the joint emergency room received an automatic burglar alarm from the Pettemerstraat 27 in Alkmaar at 00.37 am. On arriving at the scene, the police reported a fire in the building of a store. At 00.46 the Alkmaar centre fire fighters were alarmed, they rushed to the scene and ascertained that the building was considered lost. At 01:10 the fire department duty officer reported an escalation of the fire, which alarmed the on-scene-command team (GRIP level 1). All duty officers of the police, fire brigade, healthcare and municipality were called upon and the team rallied rapidly. Asbestos was released during the fire, contaminating the surrounding neighbourhood. At 01:48 the advisor toxic materials began measuring the levels of contamination and proclaimed to scale up to the second level of disaster management, the operational team (GRIP level 2). Transfer of fire to surrounding buildings was eventually prevented and at 03:17 the fire-under-control sign was given. The on-scene-command team scaled down to level GRIP 1 at 06:36 once the inventory of asbestos was obtained, and to GRIP 0 at 06:41.

Case 2: The work of the operational team[22]

As a result of maintenance work at a 380 kV high electricity plant at Diemen (nearby the city of Amsterdam), the region was hit by one of the biggest power failures in a decade on March 27th 2015. The plant was shut down due to safety reasons, resulting in a massive power failure, which affected most of the north-western part of the Netherlands: the province Noord-Holland. The joint emergency room of Safety Region NHN started receiving calls of power failure from 09:51 on. Elevators and traffic lights failed, calls of oxygen dependant patients at home came in, and also the railways suffered from a loss of power. At that point, no one had full situational awareness. The joint emergency room nevertheless assumed that a large part of Safety Region NHN experienced problems due to the power failure and activated GRIP level 2.

The operational team was complete within 45 min. According to procedures, all the emergency services involved were represented by one commander. For this particular situation, the police was represented by three

[21] Veiligheidsregio NHN 2014a.

[22] Veiligheidsregio NHN 2015b.

members. The operational team met five times during the 5 h of the incident. All meetings focussed on the developments of the incident:

1. Inventory of the most dangerous possible scenarios: there appeared to be none.
2. The arrangement of town halls as information points.
3. The preparation of scenarios for the recuperation phase.
4. Providing communication messages for the community.

The three response teams, the on-the-scene-command team, the operational team and the policy team, have several characteristics in common. First, all teams are multidisciplinary in nature, to include experts from all four main emergency response services: police, fire brigade, healthcare, and municipality. Second, many team members have not met each other before, or at least have not cooperated in this composition as a team as during normal business all members work for their parent organizations. Finally, frequently the teams have only limited opportunities, and often high interests at stake.

In 2012 the 'Law on Safety Regions' was evaluated, 2 years after implementation. The researchers drew several conclusions with respect to cooperation in and between the emergency response services.[23] They stated that the cooperation between the various emergency response services, as well as the cooperation with other emergency partners, had improved considerably. The cooperation between the various local authorities needed further improvement, however. In the next section we will focus on various aspects of cooperation in mono- and multidisciplinary teams in NHN.

14.5.2 Crew Resource Management in the Safety Region Noord-Holland-Noord

The Safety Region NHN covers the north-western part of the Dutch Noord-Holland province from the city of Castricum to the island of Texel. The approximately 640.00 inhabitants live in 17 municipalities. There are 416 professionals working at the Safety Region NHN, including 39 employees who work at the 24/7 emergency room. There are also 1200 volunteers, mainly firefighters. The Safety Region NHN has a rural character with its largest residential area situated near Alkmaar. This city has a population of 106,000 people.[24]

The most risky emergencies in NHN are considered to happen in companies that work with or store large quantities of dangerous goods. Such companies

[23] Van Veldhuisen et al. 2013.

[24] Veiligheidsregio NHN 2015a.

include the nuclear plant in Petten, the military airport ‘De Kooij’, the naval base at Den Helder, and the NAM plant at Den Helder, which processes natural gas obtained from the North Sea gas reserves. In addition, the region is surrounded by water from the North Sea, the Wadden Sea, and the IJsselmeer. Also, it features a lot of reclaimed land (polders) with many provincial and local roads.[25]

Different emergency response services such as the police, fire brigade, healthcare, joint emergency room, municipalities, and the department of risk and crisis management work closely together in the Safety Region to manage the emergencies in the best possible way, both mono- and multidisciplinary. Each emergency response service has a department that provides educational, training, and practice programs to improve the professional skills of their emergency response workers. An emergency response worker can either be a professional fire fighter, but also a mayor of one of the cities in the region who is being trained for his role during a major emergency. All the response services want to make sure that their people are well prepared and able to perform their duties to the best of their abilities in case of an emergency. Each emergency response service also has a department that evaluates the role of emergency responders during an emergency so as to improve future responses. Both sorts of departments (training and Lessons Learned) work in a monodisciplinary way but also in a multidisciplinary way by cooperating with the other departments.[26]

In 2012, the healthcare providers were the first emergency response service to implement Crew Resource Management tools into its competency training program. By evaluating the incidents and training programs two colleague-experts had concluded that the healthcare emergency response managers performed their core activities adequately. They, however, also concluded that there was room to improve human behaviour and that cooperating skills could be professionalized more. This related to the interaction within the healthcare-team as well as between the healthcare-team and teams of other emergency service providers. Accidentally both experts were invited during this period to participate in a 5-days CRM train-the-trainer programme, which was yearly carried out at the Royal Netherlands Institute of the Navy in Den Helder. CRM was seen as the coat rack to define the cooperation skills by which the healthcare-managers could be trained and which could be linked to their job-related skills as well.

Healthcare providers of the Safety Region NHN embraced the CRM-method and vision. In 2012, they started a new training program that integrated the seven CRM skills in their technical skills and expertise. Workload, stress and fatigue were also taken into consideration because these can influence those CRM competences severely. The emergency response workers were made familiar with CRM skills during the first 2 years of training. During trainings they got lessons about the seven skills and their factors of influence. Examples where shown and

[25] Veiligheidsregio NHN 2014b.

[26] Veiligheidsregio NHN 2014b.

discussed. After that they did team exercises as well, receiving personal feedback on their behaviour from an observer and co-participants (colleagues). Some even asked for a reflection on the behaviour that they demonstrated in other actions. Most team exercises were not work-related, which forced them to think out-of-the-box and to create a pleasant and safe learning environment. At the end of this first phase (the first 2 years) the CRM skills were more and more integrated with work related exercises.

An evaluation report on a fire emergency on the island of Texel illustrated in the meantime the need for the improvement of cooperation skills not only at the healthcare services but at all emergency services.

Case 3: Texel[27]

The on-the-scene-command team did not meet their job requirements:

- Deviating from procedures in general and specific from agreements accorded during the transit to Texel;
- Failing to communicate properly with a team member;
- No situational awareness due to lack of correct maps;
- Insufficient sharing of information with other teams and key functionaries;
- The OSC team was incomplete. Normally the team counted eight members; although mandatory one of the duty officers estimated he was not needed.

This case illustrates the need to cooperate and to acquire certain skills as an individual crisis and disaster manager working in a team. Managers from the other emergency services in the Safety Region NHN became infected by their healthcare colleagues and also showed interest in CRM. They were attracted by the almost simple look, the well-defined skills, the logic, and the results of CRM within the healthcare services. They also wanted to speak this CRM language and took over some of the initiatives.

The first multidisciplinary training started in 2014, scrutinizing operational teams in action in a realistic context. A striking example was the on-scene-command-team training in the beginning of 2015. In the morning two teams participated in a realistic exercise with the aid of virtual tools. During this exercise all on-the-scene-command-team meetings were video-taped. During the afternoon two professional trainer-observers evaluated the meetings with the complete team by analysing the important moments with the help of tapes. They did not focus on technical skills or on the incident itself. Team and individual behaviour, and its

[27] Veiligheidsregio NHN 2012.

outcome based on CRM skills were the most important topics at the review. So as to describe the commitment and eagerness of the team members involved, teams literally locked themselves up in a classroom, only to reappear a few hours later. Team members experienced this way first-hand the difficulties and value of properly analysing each other's behaviour, and of giving each other feedback on non-technical skills. They not only talked about improving one's behaviour but also about each other's personal qualities. The training received a positive response from the participants as appeared in the evaluation: "The OSCT-training team will set to work on continuing and customizing this new training method. The department of Risk and Emergency Management will further investigate extending the training method, possibly for other emergency teams too".

Besides the training in CRM skills and principles and the observation exercises, the Safety Region NHN started to implement the assessment of CRM skills. In 2015, the fire brigade and the healthcare providers introduced a 'profession check' for their duty officers in the field. A profession check is a quality check, assessing core skills, i.e. technical and non-technical skills. By introducing these checks the departments showed their responsibility to periodically assess the quality of their duty officers. Seventeen duty officers of the fire brigade and healthcare services participated during 4 days in a real life emergency scenario that embedded the qualification needs of the respective officers. External examiners assessed the operational skills of each individual officer. Also, a validated indication list based on the CRM skills was used to assess the non-technical skills of the participants. At the end a report was written for each individual participant. If the outcome of the assessment turned out unsatisfactory, the participant received an additional report with further personal advice for how to develop. Fifteen officers passed their test straight away. Two duty officers will be reassessed in the spring of 2016. The examiners also wrote a report that assessed each department in the safety region NHN for their performance. The report showed the results of all the assessments at departmental level, making it possible to see a trend where the duty officers excel or where they can improve. This report provided the fire brigade and healthcare services with valuable feedback on its training and practice programmes for duty officers.[28]

The Safety Region NHN keeps developing new ways to use CRM. This will be illustration with two examples. The first example concerns the recently erected *Multi Learning Agency*. The agency's motto is: Learning, Innovating and Quality. This agency is multidisciplinary in nature and meets every month to discuss and evaluate emergencies that have taken place in their own and other regions. For instance, at the request of the Multi Learning Agency the team leader of the OSCT emergency in Alphen aan den Rijn shared his experience. On August 3rd 2015 two building cranes carrying a part of a massive bridge fell down on top of several buildings. The team leader of the OSCT on the crash site joined the learning agency and shared his experiences. The agency members try to identify lessons

[28] Netwerkcentrum 2015.

from these situations so as to improve future responses. If possible these lessons are put in writing and implemented in the own organisation. The seven CRM skills are used as a valuable perspective to review and assess the emergencies.

A second example to illustrate that the Safety Region NHN continues to develop their CRM program concerns a new portfolio system that will be implemented in the Safety Region NHN in 2016. The aim of this Business Intelligence Tool (which is designed as a dashboard) is to keep the emergency response worker updated on his level of professional competencies. The Safety Region NHN is currently rewriting the behavioural competencies incorporated in this tool so as to adapt these to the seven CRM skills. This new system thus will enable the emergency response worker to use the seven CRM skills as a tool to professionalize cooperation in relation to the non-technical skills.

14.6 Conclusion and Discussion

The origin of CRM, and still the power of the vision, method and skills, lies in safety. That is why in the military the Dutch Airforce and Navy paired CRM with their core processes. So, growing safety by integrating CRM skills leads to more security, i.e. the output of Armed Forces (Diplomacy, Development, and Defence) is more robust, effective, and efficient. Apart from this, in the international operational context Armed Forces frequently meet obstacles in cooperation and coordination: functional organized services or departments that have to work together, diverse (expert-)languages and cultures, different protocols and procedures, a diversity in priorities and goals, restrictions from the parent organizations and/or governments that hinder cooperation, etc. Non-technical skills at all levels are essential assets to cope with these kinds of obstacles.

Over the last years there has been a growing interest for CRM in the Armed Forces, the police force, fire departments, medical assistance organizations, and the Safety Regions. The case on the Safety Region NHN illustrates the power of CRM itself: it was introduced and implemented bottom up by two committed crisis response managers.

Safety Region NHN has found in Crew Resource Management a well worked out method and vision for educating, training and exercising these soft skills. The seven skills have shown to integrate easily with the technical skills so that holistic team behaviour (technical and non-technical skills) can be analysed and trained at once. Other Safety Regions became acquainted with CRM in the last years also. This has led to training, workshops, and the implementation of CRM in several units in these regions. Most employees and managers of these organizations are convinced of the usefulness for their (part(s) of the) organizations. They consider CRM as a leverage to raise the professional cooperation between the emergency services who are otherwise destined to work in ad hoc teams that have no structural arrangements for working together amongst the different disciplines when an incident, disaster, or threat emerges. When working in such a dynamic and complex context and with high risks at stake one can consider CRM as a robust method for the team, as a shield and spear for providing safety and security respectively.

References

Bijlsma T (2015) Crew resource management; veilig en effectief samenwerken in teams. Vakmedianet, Alphen aan den Rijn

Eisenhardt KM, Zbaracki MJ (1992) Strategic decision making. Strateg Manag J 13:17–37

Endsley M (1995) Toward a theory of situation awareness in dynamic systems. J Hum Factors Ergon Soc 37:32–64

Federal Aviation Administration (1989) Cockpit resource management training (Advisory Circular 120-51A). Department of Transportation, Washington DC

Flin R (1995) Crew resource management for teams in the offshore oil industry. J Eur Ind Train 19:23–27

Freeman WD, Burns WR Jr (2010) Developing an adaptability training strategy and policy for the Department of Defense (DOD). Institute for Defense Analyses, Alexandria

Haerkens MHTM, Kox M, Lemson J, Houterman S, Hoeven JG, Pickkers P (2015) Crew resource management in the intensive care unit: a prospective 3-year cohort study. Acta Anaesthesiol Scand 59:1319–1329

Hoegl M, Weinkauf K, Gemuenden HG (2004) Interteam coordination, project commitment, and teamwork in multiteam R&D projects: a longitudinal study. Organ Sci 15:38–55

Institute of Nuclear Power Operations (1993) Control room teamwork development training: Course administration and facilitation guide. National Academy for Nuclear Training, Atlanta GA

Janis IL (1972) Victims of groupthink. Houghton Mifflin Company, Boston

Jankouskas TS (2010) Crisis resource management training: impact on team process and team effectiveness. Dissertation, The Pennsylvania State University

Jansen W (2015) Dutch FACs in Uruzgan; an exploration of cooperation, courage, responsibility, legitimacy and ... people getting killed. Master thesis, Faculty Military Sciences, Breda

Jünger S, Pestinger M, Elsner F, Krumm N, Radbruch L (2007) Criteria for successful multiprofessional cooperation in palliative care teams. Palliat Med 21:347–354

Kahneman D (2011) Thinking, fast and slow. Farrar, Straus, and Giroux, New York

Klein GA (1998) Sources of power: how people make decisions. MIT Press, Cambridge MA

Kohn LT, Corrigan JM, Donaldson MS (2000) To err is human. Building a safer health system. Committee on Quality of Health Care in America, National Academy Press, Washington DC

Leary T (1957) Interpersonal diagnosis of personality; A functional theory and methodology for personality evaluation. Ronald Press, Oxford

Marquardt N, Robelski S, Hoeger R (2010) Crew resource management training within the automotive industry: does it work? Hum Factors 52:308–315

MilNoTechS; handleiding voor het gebruik van Military NOTECHS. Ministerie van Defensie, Centrum voor Mens en Luchtvaart, 7 maart 2012, Soesterberg

Netwerkcentrum voor opgeschaalde zorg en crisisbeheersing (2015) Competentiemeting crisisfunctionarissen. Heukelum

O'Connor P, Campbell J, Newon J, Melton J, Salas E, Wilson K (2008) Crew resource management training effectiveness: a meta-analysis and some critical needs. Int J Aviat Psychol 18:353–368

Powell SM, Hill RK (2006) My copilot is a nurse; using crew resource management in the OR. AORN J 83:178–202

Pulakos ED, Schmitt N, Dorsey DW, Arad S, Hedge JW, Borman WC (2002) Predicting adaptive performance: further tests of a model of adaptability. Human Perform 15:299–323

Rosen MA, Bedwell WL, Wildman JL, Fritzsche BA, Salas E, Burke CS (2011) Managing adaptive performance in teams: guiding principles and behavioral markers for measurement. Human Resour Manage Rev 21:107–122

Salas E, Fiore SM (eds) (2004) Team cognition; understanding the factors that drive process and performance. American Psychology Association, Washington DC

Salas E, Bowers C, Edens E (2001) Improving teamwork in organizations: applications of resource management training. Lawrence Erlbaum Associates, Mahwah

Simon HA (1997) Models of bounded rationality. MIT Press

Tuckman BW, Jensen MC (1977) Stages of small group development revisited. Group and Organizational Studies December: 419–427

Van der Haar S (2014) Getting on the same page: team learning and team cognition in emergency management command-and-control teams. Doctoral thesis, Leiden University, Leiden

Van Veldhuisen A, Hagelstein R, Voskamp I, Van Genderen R (2013) Evaluatie Wet Veiligheidsregio's; GV188-3-27. Andersson Elffers Felix, Utrecht

Veiligheidsregio Noord-Holland Noord (2012) Evaluatierapport Grote Brand op Texel, 23 September 2012, Alkmaar

Veiligheidsregio Noord-Holland Noord (2014a) Multidisciplinair evaluatieverslag Asbestbrand Pettemerstraat Alkmaar 24 februari 2014. Incidentbestrijding en nafase, Alkmaar

Veiligheidsregio Noord-Holland Noord (2014b) Regionaal Crisisplan Noord-Holland Noord, Algemeen Bestuur VR NHN, versie 2.0 maart 2014. Alkmaar

Veiligheidsregio Noord Holland Noord (2015a) Begroting 2015, Alkmaar

Veiligheidsregio Noord Holland Noord (2015b) Thematische feitenrelaas, GRIP 2 Stroomstoring Noord-Holland Noord, 27 maart 2015, Alkmaar

Chapter 15
Improving the Management Control Mix for Safety and Security

Jacqueline Heeren-Bogers and Joseph Soeters

Abstract In this chapter we argue that management control with respect to financial and material resources is connected to issues of safety and security; the delivery of safety and security may be seriously hampered by improper management control. Starting from this connection we aim to decipher the dynamics that may improve current management control practices. Theoretically we endorse the distinction between so-called hard, formal and soft, informal controls. We performed an analysis of 17 interviews with financial specialists at the central staff units and 6 interviews with (deputy-) commanders of the services and support units of the Dutch defence organization; furthermore we analysed the answers to open questions in a survey study. These answers were given by employees with responsibilities in respectively financial and material resources management. We concluded that improvement in hard controls predominantly can be found in modernizing control procedures, which boils down to introducing less restrictive, simpler rules, auditing with the purpose to teach employees to improve their control practices and a smarter use of recording in the IT-systems. At the same time an improvement in soft controls—particularly feasibility, sanctionability, congruency and discussability—may be achieved if adequate attention is paid to these aspects of leadership, supervision and communication. Thus, management control is a matter of the right mix of both hard, formal instruments and soft, informal practices.

J. Heeren-Bogers (✉)
Faculty of Military Sciences, Netherlands Defence Academy, Breda, The Netherlands
e-mail: JJD.Heeren.Bogers@mindef.nl

J. Soeters
Faculty of Military Sciences, Netherlands Defence Academy, Breda;
Tilburg University, Tilburg, The Netherlands
e-mail: JMML.Soeters@mindef.nl

R. Beeres et al. (eds.), *NL ARMS Netherlands Annual Review of Military Studies 2016*, NL ARMS, DOI 10.1007/978-94-6265-135-7_15

Keywords Management control · Hard controls · Soft controls · Financial management · Material resources management · Military

Contents

15.1 Management Control

Management control includes all devices, systems and practices managers can use to ensure that behaviours and decisions of their employees are consistent with the organizations' objectives and strategies.[1] Military organizations' objectives relate to providing external security (i.e., security to people in society-at-large), which is based on internal safety (i.e., safety for the employees within the military organization). Hence, management control is a requisite to achieve both goals. There will be no safety or security without properly functioning management control. As it is a generic concept, management control can be seen as a package of tools, which consists of both *formal* and *informal* instruments and mechanisms.[2] Another way of labelling formal and informal control mechanisms is the distinction between so-called *hard*- and *soft*-controls. This distinction has become increasingly influential over the last few years and has recently been subjected to solid empirical research.[3]

Hard controls refer to the formal, often bureaucratic procedures such as rules, budgets, guidelines, job descriptions and other regulations that influence employees' behaviour into the direction that aligns with the organization's intentions. Hard controls are officially designed and implemented, and are often derived from international and national laws, sector agreements or legally binding contracts. Hard controls can be found in official documents, and their implications are built into computer software and programs. Soft controls, on the other hand, belong to informal, intangible organizational practices emerging from everyday lateral and vertical interactions among employees that are necessary "as a means of communication, of cohesion and of protecting the integrity of the individual", as Chester Barnard put it.[4]

[1] Merchant and van der Stede 2012.
[2] Malmi and Brown 2008.
[3] Kaptein 2008, 2011.
[4] Barnard 1982, p. 123.

Soft controls are of importance to enhance and sustain proper employee behaviour and organizational achievements.[5] These controls are often referred to as cultural and personnel control.[6]

Where bureaucracy and its legal implications evolved, the importance of hard controls is undisputed because non-compliance with rules and regulations can be sanctioned and in the end may even lead to prosecution by state or governmental agencies. Democratic nations cannot exist without bureaucracies and their procedural acts and justice.[7] Awareness of the importance of soft controls is more recent and goes in sync with the discovery of organizational culture as a main characteristic of organizations.[8] Over the last period the importance of soft controls has become acknowledged as a major factor in realizing organizational effectiveness and efficiency, or the lack thereof. It is said that the worldwide banking crisis of the last decade evolved because of lacking or inappropriate soft controls, of course next to failing hard controls: the organizational cultures in the banking sector—the banking employees' mind-sets, their values and norms—were not conducive to avoiding large risks that indeed led to the vaporization of incredible sums of money, i.e. other people's money. The demise of the giant Enron Company in the United States some 15 years ago had a similar background.[9]

Generally, it is assumed that an inappropriate management control mix of hard and soft controls can be related to the emergence of problems, such as overspending, or irregularities, such as purchasing or hiring practices that go against formal rules and procedures. It is also generally accepted that hard nor soft controls alone can do the reverse—i.e. secure a properly performing organization. Previous research shows that one needs both to realize organizational effectiveness (i.e., the attainment of organizational goals based on what the organization sees as proper employee behaviour) which in the military is the strive for safety and security. But what is the right mix of management controls in the sector of security and safety? In this study we aim to explore this question with qualitative data and attempt to decipher which specific management control factors influence financial and material resources management in the Dutch defence organization.[10] Specific aspects

---

[5] Kaptein 2011.

[6] Merchant and van der Stede 2012, pp. 83–92.

[7] Wilson 1989.

[8] For an overview see Alveson 2013.

[9] Sims and Brinkmann 2003.

[10] Public financial management may be defined as the system for generating and controlling public financial resources for effective and efficient public service delivery. It involves planning and budgeting, accounting and reporting, internal controls, audit and external oversight with a view to: availability of benefits to the greatest number of citizens, support of good governance and the attainment of the three budgetary goals of aggregate fiscal discipline, effective allocation of resources to priorities and efficient service delivery, Hamid 2013; Material management, according to Ghiani et al. 2004, deals with the planning and control of material flows and related information in organizations. Its goal is to get the right materials to the right place at the right time, while optimizing a given performance measure (e.g., minimizing total operating costs) and satisfying a given set of constraints (e.g., a budget constraint).

of management control in the military will be discussed in the next section, followed by a section on the design of our empirical qualitative research. In the next three sections the main findings of these analyses are presented. In the last section we discuss the main findings and formulate some general conclusions.

15.2 Management Control in the Military

The military can be seen as a sector that fulfils fundamental requirements of societies. Societies—communities of people—need to be protected from violent dangers and threats that may come from outside or from inside, and for that purpose they provide the military with the resources—budgets, material resources and manpower—to do that job. Hence, the military and its personnel can develop the unique skills that they need to have to conduct the task they are set to do. Because their skills and knowledge are so unique and cannot be compared to anything else, most military organisations steer and measure their own performance.[11] Traditionally they perform the evaluation of capacities in terms of quantities and qualities of the resources they have at their disposal.[12] Likewise, the military have developed a certain indifference to efficiency concerns, external judicial systems, and performance evaluations. Some would even say that performance evaluation and control needs adjustment given the fact that objectives are not always unambiguous and outputs are not always measurable.[13]

However, times are changing, "self-evident truths" are no longer accepted, and, as a consequence, there is a mounting pressure from society that urges the military to account for their actions and expenditures.[14] There is an increasing call for more accountability and transparency with respect to efficiency and effectiveness, and *evidence-based* operating is required to replace *eminence-based* decision-making.[15] Almost ceaseless budget cuts stimulate this development, but these are not the only reason for the growing political and societal pressure on the military to account for their performance and use of resources.[16]

However, given the traditional emphasis on self-measurement and self-steering in the military, the armed forces almost often display a tendency of not being good at cost control, particularly in operational—'hot'—conditions where for obvious reasons other considerations prevail.[17] Nor are they very good at time manage-

[11] Builder 1989; Soeters 2016.

[12] Builder 1989.

[13] Hofstede 1981; Mol and Beeres 2005.

[14] Catasús and Grönlund 2005.

[15] Soeters 2016.

[16] Catasús and Grönlund 2005; Rietjens and Soeters 2015.

[17] Builder 1989.

ment, particularly in non-operational—'cold'—conditions: overspending and failing time schedules, for instance in implementing new IT-systems, are well known in the military, in the Netherlands as much as in the armed forces of other nations, for instance the Bundeswehr in Germany.[18]

In the Netherlands the military has been criticized by the Court of Audit for inadequately managing their financial and material resources for many years in a row. The military was the only governmental agency in the Netherlands to receive such severe criticism—*yellow cards*—during such a long period. The reports of the Court of Audit (2005 till 2014) show that there has been no difference in this regard between the various military services from 2004 till 2008. After that year the Court of Audit announced their intention to intensify their audit activities regarding the Netherlands Defence organization; it urged the ministry explicitly to take action in order to improve their financial and material resources management. This resulted in an action plan for improvement, which turned out to be fairly successful at first, since as recent as 2012, financial management improved in all four military services. However, the improvement stagnated again in the year thereafter, particularly in the Navy and the Air Force. The Support Command and the Defence Materiel Organisation,—shared service centres that support the military services in delivering products and services—never showed an essential improvement in financial management. The improvement of the material resources management, on the other hand, proved to be more successful. Material resources management improved from 2011 on, and in 2013 virtually all inaccuracies were resolved.

Problems and solutions regarding managing resources do not only qualify as a concern for taxpayers. They also relate to safety and security concerns, since the material resources of a defence organization in the wrong hands can impact society in disastrous ways. Weapons and ammunition that disappear because of theft or loss during military exercises should not show up in bank robberies, hostages or terrorist attacks. For the soldiers themselves material resources in particular are especially important since in operational conditions their lives may depend on the availability of properly functioning gear, weapons and vehicles. When the heat is on, failing weapon systems, insufficiently available ammunition or vehicles that suddenly stop driving can cause serious harm to soldiers' lives, and can even bring an end to them. Failing instruments can cause collateral damage that could otherwise have been prevented.

Proper financial management is a precondition in this connection. Irregular advancing and spending, overspending or careless expenditures, procurement practices involving conflicts of interests, leaking liquid assets et cetera will harm all other aspects of organizational performance. Over the most recent years a number of exercises in the Dutch military has been cancelled because of insufficient budgets and material resources, such as ammunition. Thus failing efficiency in the organization may negatively impact on operational effectiveness. For sure, security

[18] Reich and Tillack 2014.

and safety are at stake if the control-mix of both financial and material resources management in the military is not adequate, which of course is not the same as saying that an appropriate management control mix makes all operational concerns disappear.

15.3 Methodology

In this article we present parts of the findings of a large-scale study on management control in the Dutch military.[19] This study finds it origin in the various reports of the Court of Audit we referred to above. Clearly, there was ample reason to dive into this aspect of the organization's performance. More precisely, we present two types of data:

(1) the results of 17 interviews with financial specialists at the higher level (central) staff units and 6 interviews with (deputy-)commanders of the different services and support units of the Dutch defence organization, and
(2) a qualitative analysis of the answers to open questions in a survey that were filled out by 238 employees with responsibilities in financial management and 197 employees with responsibilities in the field of material resources.[20] The questions pertained to the respondents' ideas on how to improve financial and material resources management by hard and soft controls.

The data for both analyses were gathered in 2010 and 2011. The interviews with the financial specialists were conducted by the first author and a student-assistant who worked on her Master thesis. The interviews with the deputy commanders and the survey were conducted by the first author. As such, this study adds to previous comparable studies aiming at assessing performance in the Dutch military.[21] While distinguishing between so-called hard and soft controls, we used further differentiated categories of both. As to hard controls, we discerned five types following the study of Vink and Kaptein. These five hard controls are derived from the original COSO report of 1992 and were made suitable for the Dutch government (Table 15.1).[22]

[19] Heeren-Bogers, Kaptein and Soeters 2013.

[20] Of the total of 111 selected units 571 employees with responsibilities in the area of finance and 436 employees with responsibilities in the area of material logistics were asked to fill out a hard copy questionnaire. We used pairwise deletion (Field 2009) to deal with missing values. This procedure led to two sub-samples of 238 respondents on financial management (=42 %) and 197 respondents on material resources management (=45 %) respectively for the analysis on the level of the individual respondent.

[21] Beeres et al. 2010.

[22] Vink and Kaptein 2008, p. 259.

Table 15.1 Types of hard controls

Code	Type	Definition
1	Risk assessment	Risk assessment involves a dynamic and iterative process for identifying and analysing risks to achieving the entity's objectives, forming a basis for determining how risks should be managed[a]
2	Internal auditing	Internal auditing is broadly defined as the process put in place by management to provide reasonable assurance regarding the achievement of effective and efficient operations, reliable financial reporting, and compliance with laws and regulations[b]
3	Segregation of duties	*Segregation of duties* is achieved when the functions of authorization (approving transactions and decisions), recording (preparing source documents, entering data into online systems, maintaining journals, ledgers, files or databases; preparing reconciliations and preparing performance reports) and custody (handling cash, tools, inventory or fixed assets; receiving incoming customer checks; writing checks on the organizations bank account) are separated[c]
4	Rules and procedures	The *rules and procedures* within an organization—often derived from, or aligned with external rules and regulations, such as governmental laws and contracts—are used to guide the execution of the process in the right way
5	Recording	Recording is preparing source documents; entering data into online systems; maintaining journals, ledgers, files or databases; preparing reconciliations and preparing performance reports[d]

[a]COSO 2013, p. 4
[b]Petrovits et al. 2011, p. 326
[c]Romney and Steinbart 2009, p. 243
[d]Romney and Steinbart 2009, p. 243

For soft controls, we relied on the seven types that were distinguished and empirically validated by Kaptein in the so-called Ethical Virtues Model (see Table 15.2).[23]

Based on these two sets of categories we conducted and analysed the interviews and the responses in the surveys following procedures of qualitative data analysis.[24] Because we explored the data with these sets of categories in mind and we were open to find new elements in the data at the same time, the analysis has an abductive character.[25] Quotations in italics are provided in the following sections to illustrate the general tendencies that could be found in the data.[26]

[23] Kaptein 2008.

[24] Rietjens 2014.

[25] See Richardson and Kramer 2006.

[26] [C] = commander; [FS] = financial specialist.

Table 15.2 Types of soft controls

Code	Type	Definition
1	Clarity	*Clarity* refers to the normative expectations in the organization regarding the conduct of employees; are the ethical standards clear, comprehensive and understandable?
2	Congruency	*Congruency* concerns the alignment between the expectations in the organization and concrete management behaviour
3	Feasibility	*Feasibility* refers to the extent to which the organization creates conditions enabling employees to comply with the expectations they are facing
4	Supportability	*Supportability* refers to the individual's identification with, involvement in and commitment to the normative expectations of the organization and the extent to which the organization stimulates this
5	Transparency	*Transparency* or visibility is important because employees can only be held responsible if they know, or could have known, the consequences of their actions and behaviour[a]
6	Discussability	*Discussability* relates to the opportunities employees see to raise and discuss current practices in the organization
7	Sanctionability	*Sanctionability* concerns the degree to which inappropriate employee behaviour will be punished or, on the contrary, condoned and tolerated by management, and the degree to which appropriate behaviour will be rewarded

[a]Bovens 1998

15.4 Specialists and Commanders on Management Control in the Military

The interviews were conducted to come to assess the perceived state of affairs and the improvement plan, as requested by the National Audit Agency, regarding management control practices in the Dutch military.

One of the salient issues that emerged from the interviews was the frequent reference to the so-called 'can-do' mentality in the military. This relates to a mind-set or aspect of organizational culture that stresses the willingness to take on the challenges that are set to do, without much hesitation, doubt or discussion.[27] This predominantly refers to the operational, 'hot' side of the organization. All six commanders stressed this point in varying words, as did six out of the 17 financial specialists.[28] Clearly, the on-going operations in Afghanistan during the time the interviews were conducted (2010, 2011), echo in these opinions. The following

[27] Soeters 2016.

[28] Five commanders express that the military culture is results-oriented, four describe the culture as military professional, two speak about the 'can-do-mentality in the military, two speak about the heavy focus on operations, and two other commanders believe that efficiency is of secondary importance.

two quotes illustrate how this mind-set suppresses considerations with respect to proper management control procedures.

> The culture is very results-oriented and there is a can-do mentality. During operations choices have to be made under strong pressure. The efficiency is of secondary importance [C].

> We need this equipment, so we order the items first and we arrange the authorization and finance later [FS].

Both quotes express the concern for employees' lives and the willingness to keep on going: they express a strong urge to continue thereby blending safety and security during operations. Rebuttals are not likely to emerge in these conditions; no one wants to see military women or men being wounded or killed because of resources that are too few in numbers or too low in quality. There may be other sides to this, though. A 'can-do' mentality implies acting without much ado. If this implies jumping to solutions and conclusions without getting to the root of the problem first, as one of the interviewees argued, a 'can-do' mentality may produce suboptimal results, both in peacetime and operational situations. Furthermore, no matter how important a 'can-do' mentality in matters of life and death may be, this mind-set becomes less acceptable if the threats would be exaggerated by commanders who have monopolized decision-making. Ceaseless referring to effectiveness may disarm those who want to know what effectiveness (or a results-orientation) in fact is supposed to be. In order to prevent effectiveness in operations from becoming "fighting for the sake of fighting",[29] a 'can-do' mentality should not become too pervasive. Nor should it lead to a weak cost awareness—which according to more than half of the 17 financial specialists is apparent in the organization—and suppress considerations of proper management control, because failing management control may have costly operational consequences, as argued before.

Another important finding that emerged from many interviews regards the complexity of the organization leading to fragmentation in the management control process, particularly with respect to hard controls. More than the previous finding this refers to the organization in peacetime conditions, the so-called 'cold' side of the organization. The following three quotes serve as an illustration of this phenomenon.

> If you are highly educated and you are overwhelmed with a bookcase full of regulations, you have a problem, that there might be an imbalance. I believe that when the capabilities of the individual increases, regulations should be minimized. [...] I'm allergic to regulation in extreme details [FS].

> The Defence Material Organization has the contract, the depot has the receipt document with a test report, and the invoice is at the Central Payment Office. These must be brought together [FS].[30]

---

[29] Brænder (2016) has shown that soldiers who have experienced combat often have come to enjoy it and as a result want more of it.

[30] The so-called 'Three Way Match'.

> In a management team meeting all sub-commanders were told to limit their expenditures. However, no one had insight into the extent to which his unit was responsible for the overruns so nobody felt the need to be more parsimonious [C].

Here, various problematic aspects of the traditional bureaucracy can be seen: extensive segregation of duties leading to administrative complexity combined with density of rules as well as a lack of oversight among the specialists and the commanders. "*Every auditor is looking through his own straw*", is a quote of a high-ranking financial specialist signifying the 'silo' or 'stovepipe'-character of the organization's various units. As a consequence, responsibilities are unclear, payments are late, budgets are not up-to-date, and those who are formally responsible tend to feel indifferent, as a number of respondents argue.

The answer to all this should be: serious rearrangement of the various elements of the hard controls-cycles, pursuing the idea of creating more simple procedures and more complex jobs.[31] The latter is even more relevant because many more of today's employees are better educated than in the past and can, hence, handle more complexities in their direct tasks.[32] This applies to the specialists in management control as well as to the commanders. Most likely the newly implemented IT-systems, especially ERP (Enterprise Resource Planning) software can play a useful role in this as well, as many interviewees believe.[33]

What about the role of hard and soft controls in the military? Is it possible to realize improvements in these categories of military management control? Is it possible to improve the management control-mix? Let's see what the respondents that participated in the survey-studies have to say about this.

15.5 Hard Controls to Improve Organizational Performance

Of 435 respondents in total, 182 respondents (42 %) have provided a useful response to the question "Which of the hard controls would you like to be improved and how do you think this can be realized"? In the subcategories of the 238 respondents with responsibilities in financial management, 98 respondents (41 %) and of the 197 respondents with responsibilities in material resources management, 84 respondents (43 %) provided a useful response.

Incidentally, per respondent multiple control measures are mentioned. The reactions of these 182 respondents can be on the one hand categorized into the

---

31 De Sitter, den Hertog and Dankbaar 1997; Interestingly the city of Amsterdam faced comparable problems in their financial management control: too many islands in the city's government running their own business, which made proper oversight of what was happening in the whole of the city impossible, Gualtherie van Weezel 2016.

32 Adler and Borys 1996.

33 Also see: Maas et al. 2014.

Table 15.3 Frequency hard controls

Code	Hard control/other factor	Frequency financial management	Frequency material resources management	Frequency total
1	HC Risk assessment	9	4	13
2	HC Internal auditing	15	16	31
3	HC Separation of duties	5	3	8
4	HC Rules and procedures	25	22	47
5	HC Recording	21	17	38
6	Budgetmanagement	14	0	14
7	Education/training	8	11	19
8	Sanctionability (soft control)	6	15	21
9	Awareness/responsibility	5	4	9
10	Capacity	2	6	8
11	Congruency (soft control)	1	5	6

five hard controls explained in the methodology section. On the other hand, six other elements (i.e., budget management, education/training, sanctionability, awareness/responsibility, capacity and congruency) come forward as can be seen in Table 15.3.

Interestingly, the employees responding to the questionnaire in general do not believe that intensifying hard controls, such as tighter rules and procedures and strict budget management, will lead to better management control practices; this is illustrated in the following response, "*Hard controls can be counter-productive and may raise aversion ... this regime would not work at home either, at least not in the long run*". They believe such policies would create indifference, aversion and possibly even cynicism among the employees.[34] That would be particularly worrisome because a number of respondents do not see that financial and material resources management is part of their task at all: "*My job is to train a brigade, nothing else*". Those latter respondents are few in numbers, though.

The majority of the respondents however believe that every employee is responsible for careful resources management and this can only be accomplished by using specific hard controls in a sophisticated way. The hard controls 'rules and procedures', 'recording' (in the IT-systems) and 'internal auditing' are mentioned most often. As said, this does not mean that respondents want these hard controls to be used more frequently and/or more intensively. Instead, the respondents call a different view on implementing hard controls meaning more flexibility in the obligation to adhere to strict budgetary rules and a decrease, clarification and/or simplification of rules and procedures: "*Avoid unnecessary duplications*". "*There is a need for more clarification and harmonization of rules and procedures throughout the whole organization.*"

[34] Naus et al. 2007.

The responses regarding recording all point towards a wider use of the IT-systems. They argue that more people need access to the IT-systems: "*The financial system must be removed from anonymity: every (budget)line in the system has an owner so that owner needs read access.*" Furthermore, managing material resources in particular will benefit considerably from a smarter use of the existing IT-systems: "*tracking and tracing, recording and control by using barcodes.*"

With regard to internal auditing respondents want this hard control to be used with the purpose to learn instead of being judged: "*Internal auditing is a snapshot and too much focused on finding errors [...], which is the main criterion the units are assessed on. Internal auditing should be more directed at giving advice and assistance to bring the material resources management of a unit to a higher level.*"

We already mentioned that next to the previously identified five categories of hard controls six other elements came forward in the many responses. Interestingly, a number of them refer to soft controls even though respondents were specifically asked what hard controls they would like to be improved. This may be an indication that respondents do not have a clear understanding of the differences between hard and soft controls. However, it may also be an indication of the need for the right mix of both categories of control. Apparently, also according to the respondents, there is no such thing as improving hard controls without paying attention to soft controls.

Respondents with responsibilities in financial management mention budget management as a way to improve the state of affairs, and they see value in more decentralization, i.e. giving more responsibilities to lower levels in the organization, including junior commanders and rank-and-file personnel at the company– and platoon-level: "*this helps to create cost awareness at a lower level in the organization.*" Additionally, the need for extra training and education emerged from the responses, which can be best categorized as the soft control 'feasibility': "*there is a need for mandatory courses for key employees with responsibilities in financial or material resources management.*" Another soft control—'sanctionability'—was mentioned as well, sometimes within the sense of punishment or rewarding but most of the time with the sense of calling each other to account for their conduct. Another element refers to awareness and taking responsibility in careful resources management. This seems to be especially important in material resources management: "*be aware of the usefulness and importance of materiel, (ask yourself...) do you need it in the performance of your task?*" A next element, capacity or actually the lack of capacity, can also be categorized as the soft control 'feasibility': "*provide personal capacity to regain insight, (then...) checks and corrections will follow automatically, like before.*" Finally, the last element can be categorized as another soft control, i.e. 'congruency'. Respondents attach great importance to role modelling of particularly commanders: "*compliance to existing measures regarding careful resources management, not so much by financial specialists but by commanders.*"

Table 15.4 Frequency soft controls

Code	Soft control/other factor		Frequency financial management	Frequency material resources management	Frequency total
1	SC Clarity		9	7	16
2	SC Congruency		13	20	33
3a	SC Feasibilty	Feasibility in general	6	10	16
3b		Feasibility education and training	10	13	23
3c		Feasibility IT	6	4	10
4	SC Supportability		4	1	5
5	SC Transparency		2	0	2
6	SC Discussability		14	10	24
7	SC Sanctionability	Sanctionability in general	1	7	8
7a		Addressing	7	4	11
7b		Rewarding	9	7	16
7c		Punishing	8	4	12
8	Awareness		14	6	20
9	Responsibility		11	7	18
10	Trust		2	1	3

15.6 Soft Controls to Improve Organizational Performance

Of 435 respondents in total, 161 respondents (37 %) have provided a useful response to the question "Which of the soft controls would you like to be improved and how do you think this can be realized"? In the subcategories of the 238 respondents having responsibilities in financial management, 87 respondents (37 %) and of the 197 respondents with responsibilities in material resources management, 74 respondents (38 %) provided a useful response.

Incidentally, per respondent multiple control measures are mentioned. The reactions of these 161 respondents can be categorized according to the seven soft controls of the Ethical Virtues Model. On the other hand, a number of other elements come forward, i.e. awareness, sense of responsibility and trust as can be seen in Table 15.4.

Following the various elements of soft controls that were distinguished and validated by Kaptein,[35] we first see the respondents' need for more 'clarity' of rules and procedures—among other things by means of better instruction –, which is in accordance with what we just saw: "*More uniformity, less fragmentation and simpler procedures and rules [...] leave some margin to manoeuvre within the rules.*"

[35] Kaptein 2008.

Most frequently mentioned (see Table 15.4), particularly with respect to material resources management, is the soft control 'congruency'. This refers to proper leadership entailing the need for commanders to set an example: "*Managers should always set a good example, be compliant with the rules and make adjustments where it is necessary.*" It is not surprising to see this emphasis in the respondents' reactions because the military organization is completely built around the idea of hierarchy.[36] Schaubroeck and others have convincingly demonstrated—with statistical data from U.S. soldiers deployed to Iraq—how ethical leadership not only impacts soldiers behaviour within the same hierarchical level, but also across levels, through trickle-down or bypassing effects.[37] This impact can hardly be overestimated. Schaubroeck et al.'s study showed that proper leadership behaviour at a lower level had a stronger positive influence when the higher level-commander was reported to exhibit stronger ethical leadership as well. Higher level-leadership can reinforce lower level-leadership. This study pertained to moral issues, such as transgressions against non-combatants, but issues like stealing stuff from the army—i.e. material resources management!—were also included in the study, hence making these results relevant for our discussion of soft controls as well.

The soft control 'feasibility' has been mentioned frequently as well, often in very specific ways (see Table. 15.2). In addition to the concept that was identified in Kaptein's previous research, the respondents discern general feasibility next to feasibility in training/education and feasibility in IT-facilities. These facilities could be improved considerably according to the answers of many respondents: "*More education or training of people on the shop floor (no weeks but days) about careful material resources management is needed.*" "*[...] It is hard to explain to employees that they need to manage the material resources more carefully whereas the IT is taking backward steps.*"

The soft controls 'supportability' and 'transparency' have not been referred to frequently. 'Discussability', however, was. The importance of clear communication as well as the possibility to discuss why certain rules and guidelines in some circumstances cannot be followed have been mentioned a number of times: "*Offer more opportunities for managers (platoon and company commanders) to explain why a regulation cannot be adhered to*". In general, the combination of collaborative talk, i.e. stressing shared interests and identities in the organization, and assertive talk, i.e. enabling the expression of differences and deviations, is likely to be conducive to the organization's achievements and results.[38] This applies to the military as much as it does elsewhere.[39]

Based on the answers of the respondents, the last soft control 'sanctionability' has been differentiated into four categories: 'sanctionability' in general, addressing,

[36] Resteigne and Soeters 2009; Soeters 2016.

[37] Schaubroeck et al. 2012.

[38] Hardy, Lawrence and Grant 2005.

[39] Resteigne and Soeters 2009.

rewarding and punishing employees. 'Addressing' refers to respondents who emphasize the need to make people fully responsible for management control issues and treating them as such: "*address people directly in regular performance evaluations if reports indicate failing practices.*" This comes along with the aspect of rewarding in 'sanctionability', the need to "*back-up those who take risks and reward those who suggest improvements*" and the aspect of punishing in 'sanctionability' "*to punish those who fail in this respect.*" The respondents' frequent references to aspects of 'sanctionability' align with the disciplinary character of organizational cultures in the military.[40]

As mentioned before, next to the soft controls of the Ethical Virtues Model, three other elements came forward i.e. 'awareness', 'responsibility' and 'trust'. Comparable to what financial specialists suggested in the interviews, (cost) awareness has been mentioned several times as an item that needs attention: "*personnel needs to become aware that everything costs money. Even after the many budgets cuts we have been facing in the last couple of years, it is still possible to economize on many things.*" The next step after awareness is being responsible, but this can only be accomplished when people are given this responsibility. Like said before: "*by decentralising budget responsibility, people will have better insight and a higher sense of responsibility.*" Finally, respondents mention trust as a precondition to transform from more hard control towards more soft control oriented.

Taking everything together, one can see that (the various forms of) 'feasibility', 'sanctionability', 'congruency' and 'discussability' are mentioned most often as soft controls to improve financial and material resources management. Fortunately, this fully aligns with general characteristics of organizational cultures in the military: the importance of discipline, communication and leadership. 'Congruency', i.e. leadership setting proper examples, is more important in material resources management, whereas cost awareness is more important in regards of financial management.

15.7 In Lieu of Elaborated Conclusions

In this study we have indicated how management control with respect to financial and material resources are connected to issues of safety and security. Management control is important for the military's peacetime and operational performance, and the consequences for both situations are mutually linked. Management control is also a matter of both hard, formal instruments and soft, informal dynamics. There is no way to improve management control without fixing the mixing of the two.

Hard controls, especially 'rules and procedures', 'internal auditing' and 'recording', were often mentioned by the respondents as instruments to improve financial and material resources management but they also relate these instruments to elements of soft controls. This result can be explained by the fact that

[40] Soeters 2016.

the impact of hard controls on financial and material resources management is mediated by soft controls. Only through soft controls do hard controls come to life. In modern societies and organizations, formal rules, regulations and procedures are indispensable, but the way they are applied and followed by managers and employees alike determines how and to what extent these formal instruments are effective in the organization's everyday life.

From our analysis we concluded that improvement in hard controls predominantly can be found in modernizing the control procedures in such a way that they align with new thoughts concerning the so-called 'enabling' bureaucracy.[41] At the same time improvement in soft control relates to the need of making the people in the organization more aware of the fact that everything needs to be paid for, that devices or gear should not disappear, that time is precious and that nothing is for free. Fortunately, attempts to guide this mind-set towards a more adequate management control direction can profit from essential features of militaries' organizational cultures, such as leadership and functional discipline.

Still there are a number of respondents who indicate that it is simply not their job to pay attention to such issues and that effectiveness in battle—without much pondering over what effectiveness—is more important than anything else. This is a remarkable point of view. All employees have taken an oath, which is connected to a code of conduct that makes perfectly clear to all employees what is expected from them when it comes to careful financial and material resources management.[42] Apparently those particular respondents do not see a direct relation between the code of conduct and careful financial and material resources management.

Opinions that indicate indifference towards the organization's resources seem like a relic of old times when indeed the military had almost unlimited resources available, and when military performance usually was not scrutinized, let alone by people from outside the own organization. Those times are gone.

Acknowledgments We are most grateful for the involvement of prof. dr. Muel Kaptein in this research project.

References

Adler PS, Borys B (1996) Two types of bureaucracy: enabling and coercive. Adm Sci Q 41:61–89

Alveson M (2013) Understanding organizational culture. Sage, Los Angeles, London

Barnard, CI (1982; originally 1938) The functions of the executive. Harvard University Press, Cambridge

Beeres R, de Waard E, Bollen M (2010) Ambitions and opportunities for assessing military performance in crisis response operations. Financ Account Manag 26:344–366

41 Adler and Borys 1996.

42 Ministry of Defence 2007 point 3, "I do not impair the interest of the Dutch defence organization and I set an example in attitude, appearance and behaviour. I deploy the resources entrusted to me in a responsible way and use them carefully and legitimately" (our translation).

Brænder M (2016) Adrenalin junkies; why soldiers return from war wanting more. Armed Forces Soc 42:3–25
Builder C (1989) The masks of war. American military styles in strategy and analysis. John Hopkins University Press, Baltimore
Catasús B, Grönlund A (2005) More peace for less money: measurement and accountability in the Armed Forces. Financ Account Manag 21:467–484
COSO (1994) Internal Control—Integrated Framework. Committee of Sponsoring Organizations of the Treadway Commission
COSO (2013) Internal Control—Integrated Framework. Executive Summary. The Committee of Sponsoring Organizations of the Treadway Commission
Court of Audit (2005 till 2014) Annual Reports on the Department of Defence, The Hague
De Sitter LU, den Hertog JF, Dankbaar B (1997) From complex organizations with simple jobs to simple organizations with complex jobs. Hum Relat 50:497–534
Ghiani G, Laporte G, Musmanno R (2004) Introduction to logistics systems planning and control. Wiley, Chichester
Gualtherie van Weezel T (2016) Een nulletje te veel kostte Amsterdam bijna 900 miljoen. Volkskrant, 23 februari
Hamid KT (2013) Good governance and new public sector financial management reform in Nigeria. A paper presented at the Executive Mandatory Professional Training Programme for Fellows of the Chartered Institute of Finance and Control of Nigeria (CIFCN), with the Theme "New Public Sector Financial Management Reform: A Panacea or placebo for transparency and accountability in Nigeria", 15th and 16th June, 2013. http://www.academia.edu
Hardy C, Lawrence ThB, Grant D (2005) Discourse and collaboration: the role of conversations and collective identity. Acad Manag Rev 30:58–77
Heeren-Bogers J, Kaptein M, Soeters J (2013) De harde noodzaak van soft-controls. Een onderzoek naar zorgvuldig financieel en materieel beheer bij defensie. Maandblad voor Accountancy and Bedrijfseconomie 87:185–197
Hofstede G (1981) Management control of public and not-for-profit activities. Acc Organ Soc 6:193–211
Kaptein M (2008) Developing and testing a measure for the ethical culture of organizations: the Corporate Ethical Virtues Model. J Organ Behav 29:923–947
Kaptein M (2011) Understanding unethical behavior by unraveling ethical culture. Hum Relat 64:843–869
Maas JB, van Fenema PC, Soeters J (2014) ERP system usage: the role of control and empowerment. New Technol Work Employ 29:88–103
Malmi T, Brown DA (2008) Management control systems as a package: opportunities, challenges and research directions. Manag Account Res 19:287–300
Merchant KA, van der Stede WA (2012) Management control systems: performance measurement, evaluation and incentives. Pearson Education, Harlow
Ministry of Defence (2007) Code of Conduct
Mol NP, Beeres RJ (2005) Performance management in a setting of deficient output controls. Int J Prod Perform Manag 54:533–550
Naus F, van Iterson A, Roe R (2007) Organizational cynicism: extending the exit, voice, loyalty and neglect model of employees' responses to adverse conditions in the workplace. Hum Relat 60:683–718
Petrovits C, Shakespeare C, Shih A (2011) The causes and consequences of internal control problems in nonprofit organizations. Account Rev 86:325–357
Reich F, Tillack HM (2014) Voll auf die Mütze. Die Stern 43:58–67
Resteigne D, Soeters J (2009) Managing militarily. Armed Forces Soc 35:307–332
Richardson R, Kramer EH (2006) Abduction as a type of inference that characterizes the development of a grounded theory. Qual Res 6:497–513
Rietjens S (2014) Qualitative data analysis: seeing the patterns in the fog of civil-military interaction. In: Soeters J, Shields P, Rietjens S (eds) The Routledge Handbook of Research Methods in Military Studies. Routledge, Abingdon, pp 129–141

Rietjens S, Soeters J (2015) Military management: effects-based approach. In: Bearfield D, Dubnick M (eds) Encyclopedia of public administration and public policy, vol 4. Taylor and Francis, New York, pp 2219–2226

Romney M, Steinbart P (2009) Accounting information systems. Pearson Education, New Jersey

Schaubroeck JM, Hannah ST, Avolio BL, Kozlowski SWJ, Lord RG, Trevino LK, Dimotakis N, Peng AC (2012) Embedding ethical leadership within and across organizational levels. Acad Manag J 55:1053–1078

Sims R, Brinkmann J (2003) Enron ethics (or: culture matters more than codes). J Bus Ethics 45:243–256

Soeters J (2016) Organizational cultures in the military. In: Caforio G, Nuciari M (eds) Handbook of the sociology of the military. Kluwer, New York

Vink HJ, Kaptein M (2008) Soft controls bij de rijksoverheid. De oorzaken van rechtmatigheidsfouten onderzocht. Maandblad voor Accountany en Bedrijfseconomie 6:256–262

Wilson JQ (1989) Bureaucracy. What government agencies do and why they do it. Basic Books, New York

Chapter 16
Cyber Threats to Position and Timing Data and Their Impact on Safety and Security

Erik Theunissen

Abstract Since the introduction of the Global Positioning System (GPS), many civil and military applications have become dependent on the continuous availability of GPS-derived position and timing information. Examples comprise financial transaction systems, electrical power grids and combat management systems. Both in the communication and navigation domain, security vulnerabilities exist that threaten the information continuity and integrity. This chapter starts with examples of applications of which safety depends on information security, in particular the integrity of the position and/or timing information provided by GPS or comparable satellite-based systems. Based on similarities in the proliferation of threats to information availability and integrity on the Internet, it is illustrated that legislation alone is not enough to mitigate the safety related risk. For the near term, solutions such as the use of existing dissimilar systems as a backup for applications that cannot afford a loss of position and timing information are proposed. For the long-term, potential solutions based on the use of encryption and authentication techniques are discussed.

Keywords Navigation · Cyber · Safety · Security · Risk · Threat · Hazard · Jamming · Spoofing

E. Theunissen (✉)
Faculty of Military Sciences, Netherlands Defence Academy, Den Helder, The Netherlands
e-mail: e.theunissen@mindef.nl

R. Beeres et al. (eds.), *NL ARMS Netherlands Annual Review of Military Studies 2016*, NL ARMS, DOI 10.1007/978-94-6265-135-7_16

Contents

16.1 Introduction

Constellations of satellites such as those of the Global Positioning System (GPS) transmit encoded, time-synchronized signals from which GPS time and the position of the receiver can be computed. Since the introduction of GPS, many civil and military applications have become dependent on the continuous availability of GPS-derived timing information. Examples comprise financial transaction systems, electrical power grids and combat management systems. The GPS anomaly on January 26, 2016, in which the coordinated universal time timing signal was off by 13 microseconds and caused alarms and resets for cell base stations, electrical grid synchrophasers, first responder radio systems, IT networks and science applications illustrated this dependency once more.[1]

GPS is an enabler for performance-based navigation. In the Required Navigation Performance (RNP) concept,[2] the target level of safety is achieved by specifying performance in terms of accuracy, integrity, availability and continuity.[3] Future Concepts of Operation (ConOps) developed in Europe under SESAR[4] and in the U.S. under the Nextgen[5] program, foresee an increased reliance both for the aircraft navigation function and for the surveillance function on Global Navigation Satellite System (GNSS) based position estimation.[6] Automatic Dependent Surveillance Broadcast (ADS-B) based surveillance, traffic management and conflict detection functions rely on position information computed from the time-referenced signals transmitted by the GPS satellites. In the nautical domain, the Automatic Identification System (AIS) relies heavily on the availability of GPS.[7]

[1] http://rntfnd.org/2016/01/28/gps-anomaly-official-usaf-statement/.

[2] ICAO 1995.

[3] RTCA 1997.

[4] SESAR Consortium 2009.

[5] JPDO 2010.

[6] GNSS is used as a container term for GPS, Galileo and other space-based positioning systems.

[7] AIS transceivers provide own ship and shore-based monitoring stations with information about the locations of other AIS equipped vessels.

For the types of GNNS dependent operations mentioned here, safety requires continuity and integrity of the position and timing information. Lack of awareness of the potential hazards, threats and vulnerabilities yields an (unjustified) illusion of safety. In chapter one, it was pointed out that in attempting to understand and provide meaning to security and safety, an all-encompassing framework offering clarity is not available. In this context, it is important to note that in the current chapter the use of the terms safety and security indeed slightly differs from the definitions used in chapter one. In that chapter, both safety and security are used to classify a situation, with the difference being dependent on whether the risk is accidental or not. In this chapter, the terms are defined from an engineering perspective. The term safety is used to classify the result of the control of recognized hazards designed to achieve an acceptable level of risk, independent of the fact whether the hazard is caused intentionally or not. The term security is used to indicate the degree of resistance to, or protection from, harm. In case of malicious intent, if the security of technical system is too low, this impacts the safety of the people that the system is designed to protect. If the appropriate measures to control the risk are not timely implemented, a gap during which vulnerability is higher than acceptable will occur. To minimize such gaps, measures to control the risk should be developed and implemented in anticipation of future threats.

Safe navigation relies on continuity in the accuracy and integrity of the position data. Thirty years ago, GPS was deemed rather invulnerable to a range of potential threats. However, today this is no longer the case. The proliferation of threats to information security[8] on the internet during the past 20 years shows a trend that also exists in the navigation-related information domain.

In the next section, similarities in the proliferation of threats to information availability and integrity on the Internet and with GPS are discussed. It is illustrated that the means to locally deny availability of the information (i.e., GPS jamming) have become commonly available. A far more dangerous vulnerability is one in which information integrity is compromised. In the third section, this vulnerability is exploited by so-called spoofing techniques which provide navigation and/or surveillance systems with falsified position information. With spoofing an attacker attempts to deceive the consumer of the information by sending falsified information which mimics the properties of truthful information to the extent that the falsification goes undetected. GPS and ADS-B spoofing are cyber-threats that are comparable to the so-called Man-in-the-Middle attack on the Internet and is the topic of Sect. 16.4. Given that jamming events have demonstrated that legislation alone is not sufficient to mitigate these threats, and spoofing threats are increasing, techniques to increase the resilience to these threats need to be designed and implemented. Various options to achieve this are discussed in Sect. 16.5.

[8] In the communication domain, information security aims to achieve confidentiality, integrity, and availability. A container term used for activities related to dealing with threats in this domain is Cybersecurity.

16.2 Vulnerabilities

Both in the communication and navigation domain security vulnerabilities exist that threaten the information continuity and integrity. On the Internet, so-called Distributed Denial of Service (DDoS) attacks can disrupt information availability, while Man-in-the-Middle (MitM) attacks threaten information integrity. In cryptography and computer security, a man-in-the-middle attack is an attack where the attacker secretly relays and possibly alters the communication between two parties who believe they are directly communicating with each other. The underlying causes of the vulnerabilities were known for a considerable time.

As early as 1989, vulnerability due to the possible sequence prediction in the transmission control protocol was discussed.[9] Although deemed unlikely by the experts at that time, years later this vulnerability was exploited by Kevin Mitnick to break into computers in San Diego. Due to several books and reports written about this break-in,[10] it serves as a useful warning that the barriers that need to be overcome to exploit vulnerabilities in a system are not cast in stone. Once vulnerability is known, more and different means to exploit it are likely to be developed. As a result, the original assessment of the likelihood that a particular vulnerability will be exploited may lose its validity. This applies equally well to GPS vulnerabilities, and should always be considered, especially in case safety depends on it. To prevent an unjustified perception of security, any (expert) assessment that a particular vulnerability does not pose a threat, should be accompanied with a well-supported rationale that both identifies the underlying assumptions and indicates how their validity may change in the future.

Whereas IP-spoofing as performed by Mitnick required considerable expertise, the proliferation of DDoS tools on the Internet (which started around 1997) provided anyone with an incentive the capability to harass a particular website by overloading it with requests. Although at the end of the Nineties of the previous century such events were still rather limited, their amount (and bandwidth) and their targets increased tremendously during the following decade. In the Netherlands alone, in 2014 the website of every major bank, most newspaper sites, websites from railways and airlines and several government websites suffered DDoS attacks. The timeline in Fig. 16.1 illustrates how the threats to information availability and integrity on the Internet evolved from 1994 to 2014.

In the navigation domain, the equivalent to a DDoS attack is jamming. Although in 1999 it was concluded that ‘there is no credible spoofing threat and jamming threats can be managed’,[11] the timeline in Fig. 16.2 illustrates how the jamming threat has evolved since that time.

---

[9] Bellovin 1989.

[10] Shimomura and Markoff 1996.

[11] GPS Risk Assessment Study Final Report, Jan. 1999.

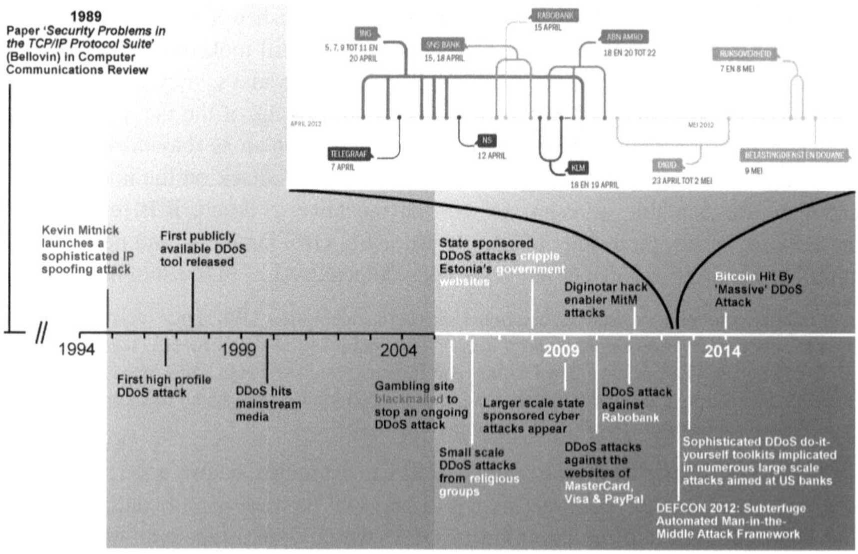

Fig. 16.1 Evolvement of DDoS and MitM threats from 1994 to 2014

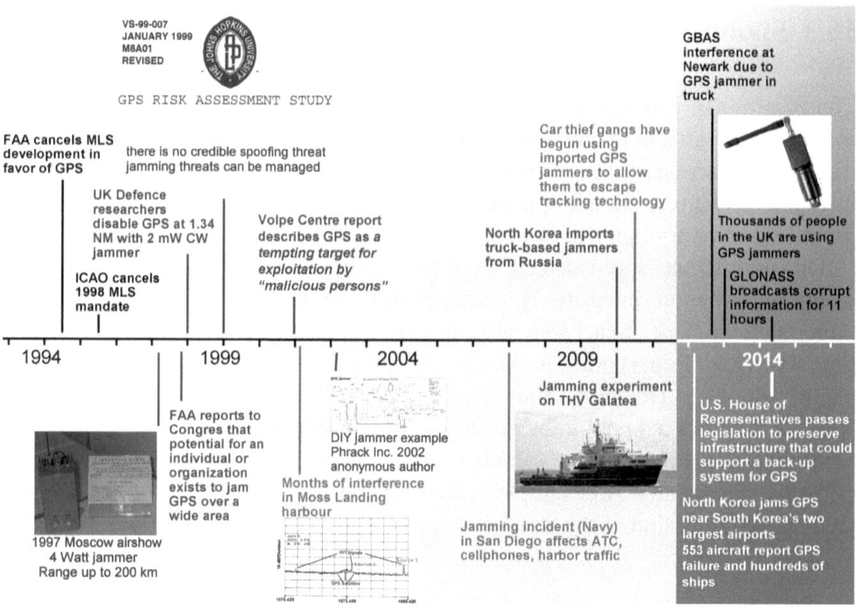

Fig. 16.2 Evolvement of GPS jamming threats from 1994 to 2014

Already in 2002 the hacker magazine Phrack published a schematic and software for a Do It Yourself (DIY) GPS jammer, but it still took some time for GPS jammers to reach a 'consumer electronics' level. Nowadays, they are offered on various websites, often with a 'privacy incentive'. In spite of the fact that sale, use or possession is forbidden in many countries, legislation alone may prove not to be enough. Similar to the tools needed to launch a DDoS attack on the internet, GPS jammers are available to everyone with an incentive to do so. It is reported that in the U.K. alone, thousands of people are using GPS jammers, and near airports multiple jamming events per day have been detected. Also, in the summer of 2015

> "multiple outbound vessels from a non-U.S. port suddenly lost GPS signal reception. The net effect was various alarms and a loss of GPS input to the ship's surface search radar, gyro units and Electronic Chart Display and Information System (ECDIS), resulting in no GPS data for position fixing, radar over ground speed inputs, gyro speed input and loss of collision avoidance capabilities on the radar display."[12]

Once the required effort to create a threat decreases below a certain threshold, the likelihood of the threat materializing will increase significantly. Both for the DDoS attacks and the jamming of GPS (which both affect availability of the required information) events have proven that, in spite of legislation, threats continue to increase. Hence, engineering remains the only option to control the risk.

16.3 Spoofing: Navigation Warfare Meets Cyber

The commonality between DDoS attacks and GPS jamming is that information availability is affected. The detection of the loss of availability can be used as a trigger for processes that are designed to maintain the target level of safety. If the information were to be manipulated *without* detection (i.e., the integrity is compromised), no warnings will be provided that falsified information is being used.

On the internet, sophisticated tools to 'explore' Man-in-the-Middle attacks in which information integrity is compromised on purpose have emerged. Two important techniques to achieve cybersecurity comprise encryption and authentication. The lack of encryption in the civil GPS signal makes it particularly vulnerable to spoofing. However, compared to a MitM attack on the internet, GPS spoofing requires a signal to be generated and synchronized with the actual signal before the spoofing can take effect. In research this is typically done by using a GPS signal simulator. An example is the research addressing questions concerning the required precision of the attacker's spoofing signals.[13]

---

[12] USCG Safety Alert 01–16, Jan. 19, 2016.

[13] Tippenhauer et al. 2011.

With typical prices for a GPS signal simulator above 100 k$, the spoofing threat may seem unlikely to happen. However, here too the barriers to be passed are reducing. Already in 2003, Logan Scott warned that 'rapid advances in computing power are making an all software implementation much more feasible', followed by the warning that at some time in the future, 'script kiddies using software downloaded from the Internet may mount a spoofing attack'.[14] It does not seem to have happened yet, and one might argue that this is unlikely to become a serious threat, but the same could be said about software to manufacture a gun. The latter will only become a hazard if the person planning mischief not only has Internet access but also a 3D-printer. Whereas in 2003 the 'all software implementation' was still a prediction, in 2009 it was demonstrated that such a spoofer can be realized using an existing software-defined receiver with some extensions.[15] Since that time, various demonstrations have proven technical feasibility of a portable, low-cost, software defined spoofer. To determine to what extent freely available components and systems can be used to impact accuracy, availability and integrity of GPS information, researchers at NLDA investigated the various spoofing attacker models.[16] In the Netherlands, TNO has provided several demonstrations in which the integrity of GPS information was affected. A high visibility demonstration occurred during the 2015 Future Force Conference in Soesterberg. Rather than reporting their true position, the Smartphones of the attendees at that conference reported the position specified in the TNO spoofing device instead of their true location.

Besides spoofing of the signals transmitted by the satellites, for surveillance functions based on ADS-B or AIS there is another threat on the horizon. Like the civil GPS signal, the ADS-B and AIS messages that are broadcast are unencrypted, which poses a significant security risk. The associated potential vulnerability did not go by unnoticed in the hacker community. In 2007, at the DefCon Hackers conference, it was suggested that '*one could easily fake an ADS-B transmission*'.[17] To prove the feasibility, an ADS-B out application was designed and implemented on GNU-radio,[18] and in 2012 it was indicated that the '*plan is to release the software*'. That same year, at the industry-sponsored Black Hat Security conference, another presentation about ADS-B spoofing using a software defined radio setup was presented. The paper[19] describes the hardware and software to generate ADS-B targets and concludes that the potential for Denial of Service on Air Traffic Surveillance Systems and aircraft using ADS-B information for the

[14] Scott 2003.

[15] Humpreys et al. 2009.

[16] Wevers 2015.

[17] Kunkel 2009.

[18] Haines 2012.

[19] Costin and Francillon 2012.

detection of other traffic exists. For IT specialists, the following assessment of ADS-B security made at the 2012 Black Hat security conference may be particularly insightful: ADS-B is almost like "ALL R/W with 'Guest as Admin' enabled".[20]

To stimulate discussions that lead to a better awareness of the potential security/safety implications an overview of and classification of possible attacks on ADS-B was provided.[21] In 2013, researchers from the University of Kaiserslautern in Germany, Armasuisse in Switzerland and the University of Oxford concluded that: 'attacks on ADS-B can be inexpensive and highly successful' followed by the conclusion that 'any safety-critical air traffic decision process should not rely exclusively on the ADS-B system'.[22] In follow-on research that analyzed current approaches to deal with this issue, it is concluded that 'solutions currently under consideration (and in use in practice such as multilateration) can only be a fill-in, providing a quick improvement to the security of the current system'.[23]

Using simulations, it has been illustrated how 'autonomous aircraft employing deterministic sense and avoid strategies can be forced into predetermined trajectories when their precise position and velocity are available to a potentially malicious craft'.[24] However, with the hybrid Traffic Alert and Collision Avoidance System (TCAS)/ADS-B surveillance, information from two independent sources is combined. Hence, a discrepancy that results from a mismatch between TCAS and ADS-B data can serve as a strong cue that the ADS-B target is not real. The timeline in Fig. 16.3 provides an overview of spoofing-related developments.

Interestingly enough, 2 years before experts concluded that there is no credible spoofing threat, in the 1997 James Bond Movie 'Tomorrow Never Dies' spoofing of GPS served as a major element in the plan of a villain to cause significant havoc. Perhaps the movie was so unrealistic that it strengthened the opinion that in reality spoofing of GPS would be impossible. It was very fitting that in 2013 researchers actually used an 80M$ super-yacht to demonstrate feasibility of the 3k$ software-defined spoofer. In 2015, the U.S. Department of Homeland Security reported that drug traffickers are putting money into spoofing and jamming of GPS with the intention of disrupting operations of the unmanned aircraft systems used by the Border Patrol.

---

[20] For non-IT specialists this translates to: "anyone using the default password will have full control over the system and can read, modify and add to all stored information".

[21] McCallie 2011.

[22] Schafer et al. 2013.

[23] Strohmeier et al. 2014.

[24] Pierpaoli et al. 2015.

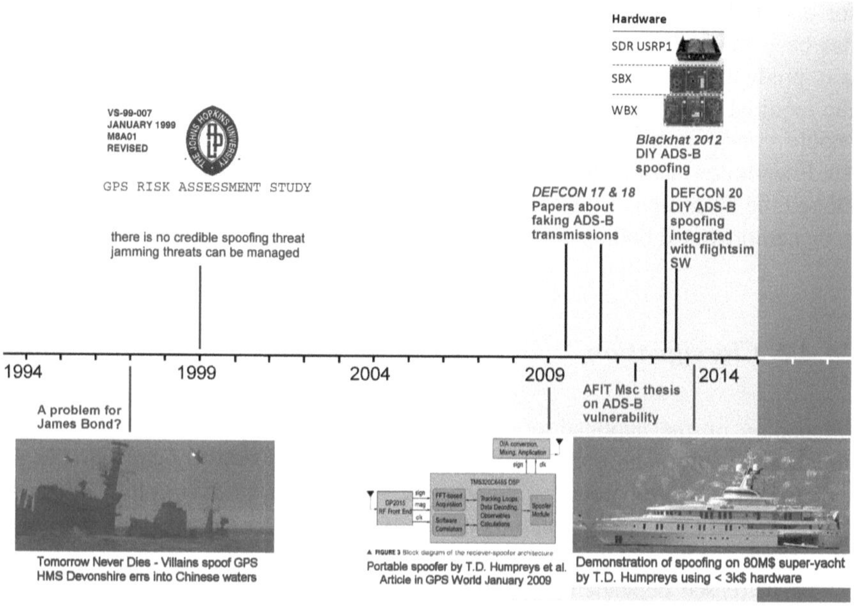

Fig. 16.3 Evolvement of GPS and ADS-B spoofing threats from 1994 to 2014

16.4 Dealing with the Threats

Safety results from risk mitigation, which can comprise both engineering responses and regulation to deal with threats. In order to make the associated trade-off in a responsible way, likelihood and consequence of sudden unavailability of information and of the undetected use of falsified information need to be established.

16.4.1 Recognition

Since 1999, society's dependency on the availability of accurate position and timing information has increased significantly. As a result, the consequence of a disruption will be far more severe than 15 years ago. Undeniably, the likelihood of occurrence of jamming and spoofing threats has increased in the past 15 years. Jamming and spoofing threats may have seemed unwarranted, impossible, unlikely, too difficult to realize or technically infeasible in 1999. Given that nowadays anyone can buy a GPS jammer for about 30$ through a webstore, such optimism is no longer justifiable nor affordable. Due to the developments in software defined radio and the increase in computing power, the barrier to be passed for both GPS and ADS-B spoofing in terms of investment, effort and experience has been lowered considerably. Nowadays, the type of GPS spoofing threat that was predicted in 2003 is possible. Fortunately the experts that have developed the required software did not (yet) release it to the general public. However, one should consider that the MP3 compression which was internally developed at the Fraunhofer laboratory was also not intended to be released. In the end, MP3 altered the landscape of the music industry. The possibility of ADS-B spoofing has been demonstrated both in Europe and the U.S.

16.4.2 Classification

Depending on the application, consequences from not having accurate position and/or time information can vary from a nuisance to catastrophic. For the latter category, the probability of occurrence should be extremely improbable. The matrix in Fig. 16.4 shows a method that is used to classify certain combinations of likelihood and consequence as unacceptable (blocks numbered 1–6). The impact of the increased dependency of GPS and the increased vulnerability due to the increased availability of jamming and spoofing devices is visualized by the two arrows in Fig. 16.4.

Compared to 1999, there are far more applications relying on continuous availability of truthful position and timing data that in case of jamming and/or spoofing will result in consequences of the categories major, hazardous or even catastrophic. The vertical arrow represents the effect that, due to the proliferation of jammers and spoofers, the likelihood that threats materialize has significantly increased. Hence, applications for which the consequence of GPS spoofing was deemed catastrophic but the likelihood of the spoofing occurring was estimated to be extremely remote (cell 7), may now have to deal with an unacceptable likelihood of this threat. The slanted arrow represents the effect of society's increased use of *and* dependency on accurate position and timing information, also in critical infrastructure.

		Consequence				
Prob. of occurrence		Catastrophic	Hazardous	Major	Minor	No effect
Frequent	$>10^{-2}$	1	3	6	10	21
Reasonably probable	10^{-2} to 10^{-5}	2	5	9	14	22
Remote	10^{-5} to 10^{-7}	4	8	13	17	23
Extremely remote	10^{-7} to 10^{-9}	7	12	16	19	24
Extremely improbable	$<10^{-9}$	11	15	18	20	25

Fig. 16.4 Impact of increased dependency on PNT and the increase in likelihood of threats

When looking how similar threats have increased on the internet, there is not a single reason to assume it will not get worse. Given today's vastly increased dependence on satellite based position and timing information, a periodic vulnerability assessment using a classification based on probability and consequence, combined with a rationale for the unacceptable combinations, should be part of any process in which systems rely on GPS or similar data and the consequence of failure is in the category 'major' or worse.

16.4.3 Mitigation

Jamming and spoofing are illegal. As indicated in the introduction, engineering and regulation are two of the most common options for risk mitigation. Regarding the latter option, an important question concerns what part of the threat can be 'legislated' away. In Sect. 16.3 it was pointed out that, in spite of legislation, events have proven that the likelihood of the threat materializing has increased significantly.

In his keynote address at the 2014 European Navigation Conference, Parkinson addressed the question what actions can/should be taken to reduce vulnerability and ensure Position, Navigation and Timing (PNT) availability.[25] His main recommendation was to, 'Protect the clear and truthful signal, Toughen user's receivers and Augment or substitute PNT sources'. An example of a local, alternative system that is being considered to guarantee PNT availability in the harbour of Rotterdam is eDLoran which has demonstrated accuracies in the order of 5 m.[26] Research performed at the Netherlands Defence Academy has addressed artillery positioning in a GNSS denied environment using enhanced Loran.[27] In spite of the very similar vulnerabilities of the yet uncompleted Galileo Navigation System, Europe has decided to not pursue a Loran-based backup capability. In fact, transmission of Loran signals was terminated on December 31, 2015. If the actual Loran stations will have been dismantled before a credible and proven backup system is in place, this will turn out to be a very costly cost-saving.

Solutions for the threat to integrity already have already been proposed over 10 years ago. A public key/private key authentication architecture for the low-rate data stream would enable receivers to detect spoofing attempts from data contents rather than from signal properties only.[28]

---

[25] Parkinson 2014.

[26] Van Willigen et al. 2014.

[27] Griffioen and Oonincx 2013.

[28] Scott 2003.

A comparable encryption/authentication approach could also solve the issues related to ADS-B spoofing. Encryption schemes and challenges associated with implementing confidentiality security protections for the ADS-B environment have been investigated.[29] Also, the continued development of so-called "mode 5 level 2 ADS-B"[30] broadcasts (using encrypted channels) has been suggested.[31] For the long term it is recommended that: 'for the creation of a long-term security solution in dependent air traffic surveillance it makes sense to consider the impact of both secure broadcast authentication approaches as well as of secure location verification'.[32]

For the near-term, detection of spoofed ADS-B reports will become crucial. Research has demonstrated that based on the use of an aircraft's received signal strength and message arrival times, simulated 'attackers' can be detected within a short time.[33] The same researchers have reported the existence of various distinct classes of the precise time periods between two subsequent messages (position, velocity, or call sign) which could be matched to aircraft transponder types by cross-referencing with open source data. This would allow for 'receiver finger-printing', and in turn to identify non-complying ones (i.e., likely malicious ADS-B transmission). Another potential verification method exploits the Doppler spread phenomenon and the short coherence time of the channel between a prover aircraft and verifier aircraft to check the velocity claims of the prover.[34] Finally, multi-lateration techniques can be applied to detect some types of malicious ADS-B transmissions.[35]

Regarding legislation, Parkinson recommended to increase current U.S. penalties for jamming (fines in the order of 12k$) to those enforced in Australia (up to 5 years imprisonment and/or fines approaching 1M$). Others propose a broader approach to the regulation and a range of required improvements to PNT governance.[36]

16.5 Discussion and Conclusion

Repeating the statement from chapter one, it seems safe to say, that countries, organizations and people that are not aware of—perceived—hazards or threats, cannot be expected to be aware of a lack of safety and security and, therefore, will

---

[29] Finke et al. 2013.

[30] Mode 5 is the most recent implementation of the Identification Friend or Foe system used by military aircraft. Level 2 refers to a class of messages.

[31] McCallie 2011.

[32] Strohmeier et al. 2014.

[33] Strohmeier et al. 2015.

[34] Ghose and Lazos 2015.

[35] Monteiro et al. 2015.

[36] Goward 2014.

not devote resources to invest in such assets. Cyber threats to position and timing data have increased significantly during the past 15 years. Similar to the proliferation of tools that threaten information confidentiality, integrity and availability on the internet, jamming or even spoofing satellite signals and manipulating data from surveillance systems such as ADS-B and AIS, no longer requires significant investments in hardware and software.

In the absence of a dissimilar backup system to today's satellite-based positioning systems, a disruption to the availability or continuity of the satellite signals used as the basis for accurate time and/or position will negatively impact safety. Legislation alone will not be sufficient to deal with these threats. Similar to the use of encryption and authentication techniques on the internet, the use of such techniques holds great promise to assure integrity of PNT information. However, engineering future-proof solutions and subsequently implementing them in the infrastructure will take time. More near-term solutions comprise the use of existing dissimilar systems as a backup for applications that cannot afford a loss of position and/or timing information. In the introduction it was pointed out that to minimize gaps during which vulnerability is higher than acceptable, measures to control the risk should be developed and implemented in *anticipation* of future threats. In the U.S. it has taken quite some time before the vulnerabilities were sufficiently acknowledged to warrant an independent backup system to be pursued. In August 2015, administration officials have identified GPS as a "single point of failure for critical infrastructure". U.S. government efforts showed that eLoran is the preferred, if not only reasonable, alternative. In December 2015, the Department of Defence Deputy Secretary and the Department of Transportation Deputy Secretary informed members of Congress that the administration is working on a "near-term solution" to address vulnerabilities of the GPS timing signal by establishing a complementary "timing-focused eLoran capability".[37] Following this, in February 2016 the U.S. National Institute of Standards and Technology (NIST) announced the Federal Funding Opportunity for the development and demonstration of reference designs for single-chip eLoran receivers.[38]

In Europe, the vulnerabilities seem to be outweighed by the confidence in its Galileo system. This may have been one of the reasons why, unlike the U.S., no backup system in the form of eLoran is being pursued. In fact, in Europe Loran was decommissioned in the same month that the U.S. indicated its existing Loran infrastructure would be upgraded to provide an eLoran capability as a backup for GPS. As pointed out earlier in this chapter, the barriers that need to be overcome to exploit vulnerabilities in a system are not cast in stone. Once vulnerability is known, more and different means to exploit it are likely to be developed.

---

[37] Mendez and Work 2015.

[38] Federal Funding Opportunity 2016.

Again, when looking at how threats to information security evolved on the internet and with GPS, it seems a bit naïve to believe that Galileo will remain as invulnerable as is currently claimed and/or believed. The fundamental weaknesses of a space-based system remain the same. To prevent an unjustified perception of security, any (expert) assessment that a particular vulnerability does not pose a threat, should be accompanied with a well-supported rationale. Such a rationale must both identify the underlying assumptions and indicate how their validity may change in the future. During a recent hearing into digital vulnerability and a secure society, the Norwegian Civil Aviation Authority has pointed out the relationship between eLoran and the risk of losing of timing for digital infrastructure. Furthermore, the British Government has approached Norway regarding cooperation on a new eLoran system designed to protect against the loss or malfunctioning of satellite systems, and in March 2016, Norway Minister of Transport Ketil Solvik-Olsen has suspended the demolition of the Norwegian Loran C stations. It would be most unfortunate if a too optimistic outlook on the yet to be proven robustness against jamming and spoofing, is the basis for an irreversible decision to destroy existing infrastructure that has the potential to provide a dissimilar backup system to GPS and Galileo in Europe.

References

Bellovin SM (1989) Security problems in the TCP/IP protocol suit. Comput Commun Rev 19:32–48

Costin A, Francillon A (2012) Ghost in the air (traffic): on insecurity of ADS-B protocol and practical attacks on ADS-B devices. In: Black Hat conference, July 21–26, Las Vegas, NV

Federal Funding Opportunity 2016-NIST-SBIR-01. U.S. Department of Commerce, National Institute of Standards and Technology

Finke C, Butts, J, Mills R (2013) ADS-B encryption. Confidentiality in friendly skies. In: Proceedings of the Eight Annual Cyber Security and Information Intelligence Research Workshop (CSIIRW), January 8–10, Oak Ridge, TN

Ghose N, Lazos L (2015) Verifying ADS-B navigation information through doppler shift measurements. In: Proceedings of the 34th Digital Avionics Systems Conference, 13–17 September, Prague

Goward DA (2014) Position, navigation, and timing (PNT) governance—required improvements. In: Proceedings of the European Navigation Conference, April 15–17, Rotterdam

GPS Risk Assessment Study Final Report, January 1999 M8A01 Revised. The John Hopkins University—Applied Physics Laboratory, Laurel, MD

Griffioen JW, Oonincx PJ (2013) Suitability of low-frequency navigation systems for artillery positioning in a GNSS denied environment. J Navig 66:35–48

Haines B (2012). Hackers + airplanes. No good can come of this. Defcon 20, July 26–29, Las Vegas, NV

Humpreys TE, Ledvina BA, Psiaki ML, O'Hanlon BW, Kitner Jr PM (2009) Assessing the spoofing threat. GPS World 20:28–38

ICAO (1995) Report of the special communications/operations divisional meeting, Document 9650

JPDO (2010) Concept of operations for the next generation air transportation system, Version 3.1

Kunkel R (2009) Air traffic control: insecurity and ADS-B. Defcon 17, July 30–August 2, Las Vegas, NV

McCallie DL (2011) Exploring potential ADS-B vulnerabilities in the FAA's NEXTGEN air transportation system. Air Force Institute of Technology, AFIT/IWC/ENG/11-09

Mendez VM, Work RO (2015) Letter to the Honorable John Garamendi, U.S. House of Representatives. http://rntfnd.org/wp-content/uploads/DSD-and-Dep-DOT-reply-to-Mr.-Garamendi.pdf

Monteiro M, Barreto A, Kacem T, Carvalho J, Wijesekera, D, Costa P (2015) Detecting malicious ADS-B broadcasts using wide multilateration. In: Proceedings of the 34th Digital Avionics Systems Conference, 13–17 September, Prague

Parkinson B (2014) Assured PNT—assured world economic benefits. Keynote address at the European Navigation Conference, 15–17 April, Rotterdam

Pierpaoli P, Egerstedt M, Rahmani A (2015) Altering UAV flight path by threatening collision. In: Proceedings of the 34th Digital Avionics Systems Conference, 13–17 September, Prague

RTCA (1997) Minimum aviation system performance standards: required navigation performance for area navigation

Schafer M, Lenders V, Martinovic I (2013) Experimental analysis of attacks on next generation air traffic communication. In: Applied cryptography and network security. Springer, pp 253–271

Scott L (2003) Anti-spoofing and authenticated signal architectures for civil navigation systems. In: Proceedings of the ION GPS/GNSS Conference, 9–12 September, Portland, OR

SESAR Consortium (2009) European air traffic management master plan, 1st edn

Shimomura T, Markoff J (1996) Takedown: the pursuit and capture of Kevin Mitnick. America's Most Wanted Computer Outlaw. Hyperion

Strohmeier M, Lenders V, Martinovic I (2014) On the Security of the Automatic Dependent Surveillance-Broadcast Protocol

Strohmeier M, Martinovic I, Fuchs M, Schäfer M, Lenders V (2015) Opensky: a Swiss army knife for Air Traffic Security. In: Proceedings of the 34th Digital Avionics Systems Conference, 13–17 September, Prague

Tippenhauer NO, Pöpper, C, Rasmussen KB, Čapkun S (2011) On the requirements for successful GPS spoofing attacks. In: Proceedings of the 18th ACM Conference on Computer Communications and Security, October 17–21, Chicago, Il

Van Willigen D, Kellenbach R, Dekker C, van Buuren W (2014) eDLoran—next generation of differential Loran. In: Proceedings of the European Navigation Conference, 15–17 April, Rotterdam

Vulnerability Assessment of the Transportation Infrastructure Relying on the Global Positioning System—Final Report, 29 August 2001. John A. Volpe National Transportation Systems Center

Wevers D (2015) GPS Spoofing—a systematic analysis of GPS spoofing: enablers, capabilities and requirements. BSc thesis

Chapter 17
Spanish Security Forces, Anti-terrorism and the Internal and External Security of Spain, 1959–1992

Michiel de Jong

Abstract There is a consensus in current literature and among Western European secret services that transnational organized crime, terrorism and human trafficking increased after 1989. These transnational threats make the distinction between internal and external security for European states increasingly difficult to maintain. These threats—especially transnational terrorism—are not new phenomena. Starting out from the beneficial advice to tackle terrorism on a case-by-case basis, this article analyzes the roles and transformation of the Spanish security forces in counterterrorism against *Euskadi Ta Askatasuna* (ETA) during the years 1959–1992. During these years of transformation from dictatorship to democracy and its subsequent consolidation, the Spanish governments were confronted with an internal security issue with important external security dimensions. From this tentative case study can be concluded that the Spanish governments and security forces became more effective once they comprehensively approached ETA as a transnational organization. The gradual demilitarization of the Spanish security forces formed an integral and important part of this process. This article also emphasizes that a state fighting transnational terrorism needs intensive international cooperation and can play a decisive role in its anti-terrorism policies and programs. Moreover, this study may demonstrate that the merger of internal and external security of Spain and the shifting roles of its security forces occurred in response to transnational terrorism already before 1989.

Keywords Anti-terrorism · Counterterrorism · ETA · Internal security · External security · Intelligence · Police · Security forces · Spain

---

M. de Jong (✉)
Faculty of Military Sciences, Netherlands Defence Academy, Breda, The Netherlands
e-mail: MAG.d.Jong.01@mindef.nl

R. Beeres et al. (eds.), *NL ARMS Netherlands Annual Review of Military Studies 2016*, NL ARMS, DOI 10.1007/978-94-6265-135-7_17

Contents

17.1 Introduction

A central security issue of European states is the increase of transnational organized crime, terrorism and human trafficking. Since the 1970s the Western European security services informally cooperate in the so-called TREVI-group, which focuses on *Terrorisme, Radicalisme, Extrémisme, et Violence Internationale.*[1] Among these services and in the current literature there is a consensus that the globalization after 1989 accelerates, and the corresponding challenges of organized crime, terrorism and human trafficking increase. Several authors argue that these transnational threats make the distinction between internal and external security increasingly difficult to maintain. They notice a blurring of internal and external security for military and police organizations of European states after 1989.

One of these authors is Derek Lutterbeck, who studies the changing functions and characteristics of internal and external security agencies in Western states. He identifies five major tendencies. First, police forces resort to military technology and hardware. Second, police forces increasingly orientate on inter- and transnational policing. Third, law enforcement and foreign intelligence converge. Fourth, military forces become involved in domestic security. And fifth, the importance of gendarmerie and paramilitary forces grows versus armed and police forces. As a result, boundaries and roles of the armed and police forces shift and lead to three paths of development: the militarization of the police or gendarmerie, the demilitarization of the police or gendarmerie, and the demilitarization or constabularization of the military.[2]

[1] The first meeting of the TREVI-group was held in Rome near the Trevi-fountain and initiated by the Dutch director-general of police A J Fonteijn (the Dutch word for 'fountain'), Monar 2008, p. 209; Bigo 2000, p. 320; Lutterbeck 2005, p. 232; Easton et al. 2010, p. 5.

[2] Lutterbeck 2005, p. 233; Other signals of militarization are the employment of the police on a 24-h basis, the military status of its personnel, its heavy military armament. Shifting roles are also reflected in a changing numerical balance between armed and police forces, Lutterbeck 2013, pp. 9–10.

Yet, the merging of internal and external security issues and the resulting, sometimes profound, reforms of the security forces are not a new phenomenon. Already since the nineteenth century terrorist movements, as the Anarchists in the 1880s or the Algerian nationalists in the 1950s, have been active on a transnational level and the question remains whether these did not have their impact on a state's security forces and their shifting roles in internal and external security. Surprisingly, however, the history of European terrorism as a transnational phenomenon remains understudied. A number of studies, either national cases or international overviews, exist, in which the political science studies outnumber historical studies and are focused on problem-solving counterterrorism. Nevertheless, a case study remains valuable. In his study on the police and gendarmerie in France, Malcolm Anderson cites the French magistrate and counter-terrorism expert Gilbert Thiel. Thiel stated that terrorisms existed in "many forms and moving contours" and he "sensibly recommended that terrorism be tackled on a case-by-case basis".[3]

This case study analyzes the roles and transformation of the Spanish security forces in counterterrorism against ETA during the years 1959–1992. During these years of transformation from dictatorship to democracy and its subsequent consolidation, the Spanish governments were confronted with an internal security issue with important external security dimensions. For analytical purposes, as José Olmeda does, it is important to define the nature of this security issue from the perspectives of the Spanish government and ETA. He regards ETA as a non-state terrorist group targeting its efforts against the Spanish government. He defines terrorism "as the deliberate creation of a sense of fear, or threat of use of symbolic acts of physical violence, to influence the political behaviour of a given target group". Thus, terrorism can be typified as a coercive military strategy, which aims "unlike conventional warfare … to break the spirit and create a sensation of fear within the target group, which will cause it to initiate political change". In these characteristics terrorism overlaps those of guerrilla warfare. It is not a coincidence that ETA aimed to achieve its ultimate goal, a future independent socialist Basque Country, through an insurgency and an armed struggle.[4] At the beginning of the period under scrutiny here, the Franco regime had regarded ETA as a group of opposition and had used indiscriminate force to repress it. After its echec, subsequent Spanish democratic governments repeatedly had to change their perception of ETA in order to fight it effectively.

Within this context, the focus of this article is on the anti-terrorism policies, programs and experiences of the Ministry of the Interior and the security forces. In particular, it examines to what extent these experiences led to changing roles, organizations and coordination of the Guardia Civil, national police and intelligence services. Historians and political scientists as Jaime Jimenez, Reinares and Dominguez Iribarren, and recently Van Dongen, have written extensively on these

---

[3] Gerwarth and Haupt 2007, p. 275; Anderson 2011, pp. 192–193.

[4] Citations and perspectives of Olmeda 2007, p. 161.

topics, and several of their studies form a starting point for this case study.[5] They repeatedly point out the strategic interplay or dialectics of strategic response between ETA and the subsequent Spanish governments.

This case study starts with an overview of the origins of the conflict during Franco's dictatorship (1939–1975). For the transition to democracy (1976–1982) and subsequent democratic governments (1982–present) it identifies the changes in strategy, operations and roles of the internal security forces and the judicial, political and international aspects. Since 1981 the Spanish anti-terrorism program gradually gained momentum in the second half of the 1980s and culminated in the capture of three ETA leaders in Bidart in 1992. At the end, the study shows the implications of the Spanish anti-terrorism program against ETA for period after 1992 and concludes that the Spanish governments and security forces became more effective once they comprehensively approached ETA as a transnational organization.

17.2 Prelude, 1939–1959

After Franco's victory in the civil war early 1939, his regime seemed to face an external security threat of the Allies and an internal security threat of Republican guerrillas. Yet, during the 1940s the external security environment gradually changed in Franco's favour. At first, Franco's regime had become isolated from the rest of Europe after the Second World War. But it managed to detach itself from Nazi-Germany in 1943, to run a more neutral course and to evade any confrontations with the Allies. Although supporters of the Second Republic hoped that the Allies would invade Fascist Spain, realist politics dominated, and the United States and Spain signed the bilateral Pacts of Madrid in 1953, as Spain was counted as one of the anticommunist countries. That same year Spain was admitted in the United Nations, after these had already allowed its members to re-establish diplomatic contacts in 1950.

A major form of internal resistance came from Republican fighters, who continued their struggle since 1939. But their guerrilla in several regions of Spain would end in total failure. The so-called *maquis*, assisted and commanded by a Republican government in exile and communist and anarchist opposition abroad, never managed to receive the help of the severely oppressed population. The Republican insurgency presented the Guardia Civil with a major task. The corps' experience with combating insurgencies descended from its long record of actions against social and political turmoil since its formation in 1844. The Guardia Civil fought a long and brutal war against the maquis, in which 2,216 maquis and 258 civil guards were killed. In the beginning of the 1950s organized resistance was

[5] Jaime Jimenez and Reinares 1998; Dominguez Iribarren 1998; Jaime Jimenez 2002; Van Dongen 2014; For a current overview of the literature on ETA, Buesa and Baumert 2013, p. 318, n. 3; See also the concise, but older historiographical overview of Dominguez Iribarren 1998, pp. 9–12.

broken, although trials of maquis by military tribunals and their executions continued sporadically into the second half of the 1950s.[6]

During and after the guerrilla Franco feverishly reformed his internal security forces. He thoroughly militarized the national police, the political police and the civil guard (*Policia Armada y de Trafico, Cuerpo General de Policia, Guardia Civil*). The complete internal security structure was intertwined with the army and imbued with a militarized ethos. Army officers held central commands and regional jurisdiction over the Guardia Civil and Policia Armada. They also took positions in the intelligence services of the Interior Ministry, the General Staff, and the governmental presidency and focused on oppositional forces to the regime. Furthermore, military courts could try civilians for any form of opposition to the armed and police forces.[7]

17.3 Franco Regime and ETA, 1959–1975

In the early 1950s, the authoritarian regime entered a period of relative calm. The regime liberalized the economy, which triggered a massive migration from the countryside to the cities and created new social and security problems. The internal security structures were adapted accordingly and the role of the Guardia Civil grew. In 1959, the Guardia Civil obtained the tasks of guarding prisons and traffic control from the Policia Armada. The corps's intelligence monitored political dissent throughout the national territory, with the exception of the major cities, that fell to the Cuerpo General de Policia. For this task the Guardia Civil relied on a dense network of barracks and its file-system.[8]

The major social changes and the regime's repression of dissent mentioned above met in the Basque Country between 1950 and 1970. Hundreds of thousands of non-Basque civilians migrated to the cities of the Basque Country. Franco repressed all fundamental elements of the Basque identity, because he envisioned Spain as a unitary state. His regime forbade the use of the Basque language in court, public organizations, schools and cultural life. Higher echelons within government organizations were off-limits for Basque citizens. Political nationalist parties were forbidden and labour unions were strictly monitored.[9]

Within these turbulent times, a group of students and a youth section of the *Partido Nacional Vasco* (PNV, Basque Nationalist Party) established the *Euskadi Ta Askatasuna* (ETA, Euskadi and Freedom) in 1959. Inspired by the contemporary decolonization and copying contemporary revolutionary movements, they

---

[6] During the years 1939–1943 200,000 Spaniards died in the regime's prisons and camps, Encarnacion 2007, p. 962; Jaime Jimenez 2002, pp. 78–79.

[7] Jaime Jimenez 2002, pp. 78, 81–82.

[8] Jaime Jimenez 2002, pp. 80–82.

[9] Van Dongen 2014, p. 178.

gathered in assemblies, annually or less than annually, in which they programmed their course for a completely independent Basque Country. The first decade of ETA's existence passed relatively unnoticed to the security forces. On its fourth assembly in 1965 ETA adopted a coercive strategy with an action-repression-action spiral. Their actions aimed to provoke state repression, which would generate more popular and active support for ETA that in turn would result in more repression and would end with a revolutionary rising of the Basque population. Three years later, ETA's first violent encounter with the Guardia Civil on 7 June 1968 left two dead, a guardsman and a leading member of ETA. On 2 August, ETA killed a commissary of the political police and more deadly attacks followed.[10]

In the operational execution of their coercive strategy ETA avoided collateral damage. Its attacks concentrated on the symbolic and armed representatives of the Spanish state: foremost the Guardia Civil, then the national police and, later, military personnel. The Etarras preferred to kill their victims by isolating and shooting them in public places or during patrols. The classic procedures for surveillance and patrolling in pairs of two policemen (*en parejas*) applied in the rest of Spain exposed the forces of the state in the Basque Country to clear risks.[11]

In response the Guardia Civil concentrated several command units in the Basque Country, among them a mobile command unit from Seville to nearby Logroño. Moreover, the civil guard, national and political police responded with mass arrests, which dismantled ETA in 1969. A military tribunal organized a public process of Burgos in 1970 around a number of Etarras and Marxist resistance workers. Instead of rallying support for the regime, the trials gained ETA media attention.[12] The security forces dismantled ETA again in 1972 after a new wave of ETA attacks, but their mass arrests, imprisonment and torture of suspects generated new members and widespread support among the Basque population. Moreover, at least since 1974 ETA reconstructed its organization in the interior of the Basque Country as well as in the French Basque Country or Iparralde where it founded command, logistical and operational bases.[13] It seemed that ETA's action-repression-action spiral began to work.

Meanwhile Franco started to prepare for his succession. In 1969 crown prince Juan Carlos of Bourbon was designated Franco's successor. In the following years Franco was increasingly suffering from Parkinson's disease. He withdrew from governmental affairs and appointed Prime Minister Admiral Luis Carrero Blanco, a staunch supporter of the regime, as president of the Spanish government in 1973. In the same year an ETA commando in Madrid started a complex operation,

---

[10] As ETA's first attacks Dominguez Iribarren counts several bombs in Bilbao, Vitoria and Santander in 1959 and a bomb attack in a stadium in 1960, Dominguez Iribarren 1998, p. 222; Other authors mark as ETA's first attack an attempt to derail a train of Franco supporters in 1961, All these attacks did not cause alarm, Tusell 2007, pp. 226–227; Van Dongen 2014, pp. 175–176.

[11] Van Dongen 2014, pp. 184, 202.

[12] Van Dongen 2014, p. 175.

[13] Dominguez Iribarren 1998, p. 93.

codenamed *Ogre*, which targeted Carrero Blanco. In a few months the commando members dug a tunnel under his daily route to mass in Madrid, blew up his car and killed Carrero Blanco and his bodyguards after their return from mass on December 1973. The assassination of Franco's successor gained widespread support among the Spanish and Basque population and many members of the left opposition silently approved. Meanwhile, between the Fall of 1973 and January 1975, and as the result of internal strife during a sixth assembly, ETA fell apart in a major group called ETA politico-military (ETA pm) and a minority group, ETA military (ETA m). Whereas ETA m concentrated itself on military activities and executed the majority of all attacks, ETA pm combined several attacks with the mobilization of the working masses.[14]

After the assassination of Carrero Blanco, General Carlos Arias Navarro replaced him as Prime Minister. He responded with the usual repressive methods as the security forces lacked a counterterrorist doctrine and the police forces acted according to their own discretion. From 1973 to 1975, the security agencies made more mass arrests in order to gather more information on ETA. The arrests bagged high numbers of militants and leading members but again provoked an increased inflow of members to ETA that committed new attacks. Until 1975, 100–250 Basques were arrested for nationalistic opposition, and during the last days of Franco's regime in November 1975 this number rose to 750. In order to operate on the required larger scale the Directorate General of Civil Guard reformed in April 1975 and created a *brigada de informacion*.[15]

The recent establishment of a safe haven in French Basque Country was a nasty surprise for the Spanish state. Following a plan of the late Carrero Blanco, Spanish police intelligence officers and the state's intelligence service, the *Servicio Central de Documentación* (SECED) cooperated with ultra right wing organizations, which operated against ETA members and supporters in Southwestern France and Spain since 1974. The core of these death squads consisted of extreme-right wing Italians. They operated under names as *Anti-terrorismo ETA*, *Battallón Vasco Español*, *Grupos Armadas Españoles*, and *Alianza Apostolica Anticommunista*. These squads continued to operate during the transition period and they killed more than thirty persons, Etarras and innocent civilians between 1974-1982. They formed one of the factors for escalated ETA violence.[16]

Regardless of the police forces or the ultra right wing death squads, the military intelligence service SECED booked the biggest results against ETA. It managed to infiltrate ETA pm through Miguel Lezarja, codenamed *El Lobo*, who rose to one of the leading positions within the organization in 1975. That same year, 158 members of ETA pm were arrested and ETA pm was practically dismantled.[17]

---

[14] Barton 2009, p. 257; Douglass and Zulaika 1990, p. 246; ETA m performed 743 attacks and killed 247 victims compared to 132 attacks and 13 victims by ETA pm between 1978 and 1981, Dominguez Iribarren 1998, p. 220.

[15] Jaime Jimenez 2002, pp. 25, 26, 82–84.

[16] Woodworth 2004, p. 171; Encarnacion 2007, pp. 954, 961.

[17] Cerdan and Rubio 2004, pp. 29–33, 110, 119.

17.4 Transicion, 1976–1982

When general Francisco Franco died in November 1975, king Juan Carlos took over as expected. In July 1976 Juan Carlos dismissed Arias Navarro as the last Prime Minister of Franco's regime, and installed Adolfo Suárez as the new Prime Minister. This marked the start of a period of transition towards general elections and complete democracy in October 1982. Within this *Transicion* the progressive Suárez government and Franco's conservative elite agreed upon the gradual legalization of political parties and trade unions, and the maintenance of the monarchy and the administration. Adolfo Suárez and the Unión de Centro Democrático (UCD, Democratic Central Union) led Spain and its population to its first general elections in June 1977. After the elections, the main political parties of the government and the opposition forged the Pact of Moncloa in order to challenge Spain's economic, fiscal, political and social problems.[18]

The Pact reflected, as Jaime Jimenez and Reinares note, the relative continuity of the political elite and the vaguely reformist mood among the legislators. Consequently, the transition government did not define a strategy and objectives for its police and armed forces until 1979, because it feared a military rebellion. More specifically, the government tried to enhance the antiterrorist means at various levels in an unconnected way, because a specific antiterrorist law was absent. The Ministry of the Interior, the former Ministry of Government, suffered numerous formal transformations, because of the absence of a precise police model. Interior Minister Rodolfo Martín Vila timidly tried to reduce the army's influence of the security forces. After a Police Act in 1978 his Ministry installed the Directorate General of State Security, which supervised the national police (*Cuerpo de Polica Nacional* and former *Policia Armada*), the *Cuerpo Superior de Policia* (CSP) including a *Comisaria General de Informacion* (CGI). The Police Act stripped the military courts of their former jurisdiction in antiterrorist matters, but could not immediately demilitarize the national police. The Guardia Civil held an awkward administrative position: it belonged to the Ministry of Interior, but in terms of internal organization, discipline and military service it depended on the Ministry of Defence. Moreover, the corps's status as a military or a civilian body became subject of furious debates. The Police Act and an organic law on Defence opened the way to demilitarization of the Policia Nacional and the Guardia Civil, but this process proved to be extremely sensitive and difficult to achieve.[19] Only in 1980 did the Directorate General of State Security supervise the Guardia Civil. The central problem was that military commanders still controlled two-thirds of the two police corps and they exerted their influence.

---

[18] Jaime Jimenez and Reinares 1998, pp. 175–176; Jaime Jimenez 2002, pp. 25–26; Barton 2009, pp. 260–262.

[19] Implementation of points of the organic law on defence was postponed until the Organic Law of Forces and Corps of Security (LOFCS) of 1986 paved the way under a PSOE civilian Luis Roldan that occupied the post of Director General, Jaime Jimenez and Reinares 1998, pp. 173, 176, 177; Jaime Jimenez 2002, pp. 84–88.

Thus, the security forces maintained a military operational approach, lacked clear political decisions on an antiterrorist police response and suffered from socio-political inertia and a lack of means. The result was temporary disorientation and disarray. Furthermore, with compliance of the police forces the ultra-right groups of the Franco era continued their uncontrolled actions against ETA in the Spanish and French Basque Country. Police effectiveness slackened because of the uncoordinated intelligence services of the police forces and a precarious network of trust. The collection and the analysis of information of the intelligence services of the security forces were uncoordinated and were manually maintained. In this setting the Basque citizens did not help the state's police forces.[20]

ETA welcomed the Spanish state's lack of focus and stepped up its terrorist attacks to the highest level in her existence so far: 210 claiming 62 victims in 1978. This provoked the government, under intense pressure of the military, to augment its antiterrorist means. In September 1978, before the terrorist offensive, Interior Minister Rodolfo Martin Villa visited Germany and England and returned to Spain with a fifteen-point program on anti-terrorism. He also created, in according with advice of foreign experts, several important units for special counterterrorist operations in 1978. The national police founded the *Grupo de Especial de Operaciones* (GEO). The Guardia Civil created the *Grupos Antiterroristas Rurales* (GAR) and the *Unidades Especiales de Intervencion* (UEI).[21]

Other countermeasures against ETA enhanced the state's intelligence. In September 1978, the *Grupo Especial de Policia Antiterrorista* was formed in Bilbao. A special police anti-terrorist group of 60 men led by the commissioner Roberto Conesa of the CSP arrived in the Basque Country. His main purpose was to update the available information on ETA. To assist him in this aim, two organic laws (21/1978 and 56/1978) dramatically increased police powers. Both laws allowed detaining suspects *incommunicado* for 3 days without charges and enabled phone taps, the opening of mail and house searches without warrants. Until 1979 Conesa's unit arrested, detained and interrogated 180 persons that were active in the nationalist political parties. Also the other units of the Guardia Civil and Policia Nacional acquitted themselves with searches, mass arrests, detention of suspects, and even torture. Yet, it resulted in more deadly attacks and the largest recruitment of ETA members ever recorded. In return, the Spanish security forces deployed 12,000 civil guards, 6,000 national policemen and 630 men of special police units (Conesa group, GEO and GAR).[22]

Meanwhile, Adolfo Suárez introduced a new constitution in 1978 and installed a bicameral parliamentary democracy in Spain. As the ban on anti-regime parties was also lifted in the Basque Country, various Basque nationalist parties were

[20] Jaime Jimenez 2002, pp. 25, 90, 91.

[21] The Corps also professionalized its expertise in explosive devices *Departamento Central de Desactivacion de Artefactos Explosivos* (DECEDEX) in 1979 and the *Escuela de Tecnicos Especialistas Desactivacion de Artefactos Explosivos Guardia Civil* (TEDAX-GC) in 1982, Dominguez Iribarren 1998, pp. 223, 259; Clavero 2015, pp. 155, 211; Jaime Jimenez 2002, p. 94.

[22] Jaime Jimenez 2002, pp. 26, 27, 92, 93; Van Dongen 2014, pp. 190, 192.

founded, as *Euskal Iraultzarako Alderdia* (EIA, Basque Revolutionary Party) in 1976, *Euskadiko Ezkerra* (EE, Basque Left) in 1977 and the *Herri Batasuna* (HB, Union of the Basque People) in 1978. Suárez granted amnesty to all political prisoners that were detained before 1977. In 1978 the majority of the Basque population voted for the Basque Autonomy Statute that gave the Basque Country a new parliament and a police force.[23]

ETA rejected the grant of Basque autonomy, although the majority of the Basque voters agreed. Nevertheless, ETA aligned with HB that entered the Basque parliament, and ETA presented the so-called *Koordinadora Abertzale Socialista* (KAS, Socialist Patriotic Coordinating Committee) alternative to the Spanish government. This KAS alternative was an Autonomy Statute and comprised a program of minimum demands: full self-determination of the Basque people; amnesty for ETA prisoners; the definition of the Basque Country including adjacent Navarre; the withdrawal of the Basque police and the Guardia Civil; democratic liberties and legalization of nationalist parties and improved conditions for the working class.[24] In turn, unsurprisingly to ETA, the Suárez government rejected the KAS alternative.

ETA still pursued its coercive strategy, although had shifted its ultimate aim. Instead of the creation of a revolution, it now continued to assassinate until the Spanish state accepted its KAS alternative. As Jaime Jimenez describes, the most radical Basque believed that the state was in an extremely weak position in which ETA could impose its terms without offering anything in return. Now, in its strategy ETA identified two phases. First, it aimed to achieve a truce before the approval of the constitution in 1978 through its execution of increasingly violent actions. Second, these initiated a subsequent phase that included the state's total acceptance of the KAS alternative, which would result in complete independence of the Basque Country.

ETA could pursue its strategy, as its headquarters of twelve commanders resided safely in the French Basque Country and it maintained a small structure of commandos. Each commander had one or two assistants and a staff, and was responsible for a zone in the Basque Country or a zone in the rest of Spain. Within their zones, the commanders conducted the operations of commandos of *illegales*. Each of these counted no more than five members, and was supported by commandos of *legales* (communication, intelligence, logistics, and finances). A broad supportive sector of sympathizers and cultural, political and social organizations existed in the Basque society. The attacks of ETA's commandos mainly targeted military officers and policemen and could even hit in Madrid, as an ETA commando did since 1978. ETA asserted this as the vulnerable spot of the Spanish

---

[23] After ETA pm had received a heavy blow in operation *Lobo* in 1975, it tried to pursue the mobilization of the Basque masses and it created in September 1976 a new party, the Euskal Iraultzarako Alderdia (EIA), Alonso 2011, pp. 698–699; Van Dongen 2014, p. 205; In 1977 the special commandos of ETA pm (Bereziak), that had survived Operation *Lobo* joined ETA m, Dominguez Iribarren 1998, p. 40.

[24] Clark 1984, p. 253; Douglass and Zulaika 1990, p. 247; Van Dongen 2014, p. 178.

government, where it could force it into an armistice leading to total independence. This also heightened the danger of unchaining a military coup.[25]

When the ETA attacks increased and killed several military officers, military criticism enhanced, and Interior Minister Martin Vila was replaced by General Ibáñez Freire in April 1979. ETA also attacked other symbols of state. Since 1977 the Etarras struck the construction site of the first Spanish nuclear power plant at Lemóniz for several years with arsons and outright attacks, killing four employees and wounding fifteen. The Spanish state scuttled the project in 1983, and the site remains abandoned to this day. The number of fatalities increased to 69 in 1979 and 85 in 1980, among these four civil guards in an ETA ambush of a Guardia Civil patrol near Ispaster in February 1980. General Ibáñez Freire was dismissed in May 1980.[26]

In the second half of 1980 Minister Juan José Rosón entered the Interior Ministry. Here the armed and police forces maintained close relations through a hierarchy of mainly military officers. The *franquista* resentment within the armed and police forces towards the political institutions of the transition fostered disaffection towards the emerging democratic state. Yet, this attitude did not imply an open rebellion. But, as Jaime Jimenez observes, Premier Suárez and the UCD aggravated the situation by its promotion of progressive officers, while bypassing the rigid system of promotion, and systematically neglecting any military insubordination towards the new political institutions.[27]

Meanwhile, the political environment deteriorated further as the Suárez government repeatedly found itself harassed by military pressure and terrorist acts. Suárez decided to step down. During the transfer of his government to Prime minister Leopoldo Calvo-Sotelo on 23 February 1981, Lieutenant-Colonel Antonio Tejero and 400 civil guards attempted a coup supported by parts of the armed forces. The coup failed through the quick condemnation of King Juan Carlos, who contacted all major military commanders, and due to acts of non-coordination and indecisiveness among the military plotters. The ensuing year the UCD government led by Calvo-Sotelo joined the NATO in December 1981, which helped to cleverly meet the army's professional demands of the armed forces. Furthermore, the terrorist attacks decreased. This all helped to ward off a new coup in later years.[28]

The Calvo-Sotelo government accomplished fundamental juridical reforms in the antiterrorist program in 1980 and 1981. First, an approved statute (organic laws 11/1980 1–12 and 2/1981) abandoned the laws by decree as a routine basis to

---

[25] Jaime Jimenez 2002, p. 91; Van Dongen 2014, pp. 180–181; Dominguez Iribarren 1998; pp. 197–200, 208–213; On the supporters and organizations around ETA see, Buesa and Baumert 2013; Heiberg 2007, pp. 30–36.

[26] Dominguez Iribarren 1998, pp. 223, 259.

[27] Jaime Jimenez 2002, pp. 88–89.

[28] Bernecker 1998, pp. 75–76, 80; The state's intelligence service *Centro Superior de Informacion de la Defensa* (CESID), which replaced the SECED in 1976, played an important role in disabling other plans for coups in 1982 and 1985, Tusell 2007, pp. 309–310; Jaime Jimenez 2002, p. 91.

legislate anti-terrorism. Second, exclusive jurisdiction over terrorist cases passed to the Central Courts and the High Court. Third, the detention periods of 72 h were extended to 10 days in order to win over repentant terrorists for their reintegration into society. The law of 1981 under Calvo-Sotelo broadened the definition of terrorism. It also restricted media that broadcasted supposedly separatist messages.[29]

In addition to this more ruthless legal base, the coordination of intelligence services for tracing and tracking terrorists urgently needed improvement. Minister of Interior Juan Jose Roson created a central command for the coordination of anti-terrorist logistics, operations and intelligence in March 1981. This *Mando Único para la Lucha Contraterrorista* (MULC) contained representatives of Interior Ministry, the CSP, the Guardia Civil and the *Centro Superior de Informacion de la Defensa* (CESID, Superior Centre of Defence Information, the former SECED). In addition to more narrowly coordinated decisions between these security forces and their intelligence components, the MULC focused on police analyses, the development of strategies and their operational implementation. However, already before its creation the number of fatalities had diminished due to the dismantling of numerous ETA commandos, which robbed the operational commandos of coverage and logistical support.

Another countermeasure was the temporary deployment of 2,000 soldiers of the Spanish Army along the French-Spanish border. They patrolled the Spanish Pyrenees in order to check ETA traffic of persons and goods, but these troops were withdrawn in the Fall of 1981. These troops included several *Compañías de Operaciones Especiales* (COE), the Spanish Special Forces.[30] But the hidden ETA bases behind the French-Spanish border remained beyond their reach.

France still did not cooperate with Spain according to its secret sanctuary policy that the Giscard d'Estaing government obtained. Its objective was to isolate France from the impact of foreign terrorist movements, and accordingly to make French soil as neutral as possible. Members of terrorist groups were neither arrested nor detained in France. The historical experiences of the French governments might have played an additional role. During the Independence War in Algeria 1954–1962, Spain had provided support and a safe haven for the *Organisation de l'Armée Sécrète* from its foundation in 1961 until 1966. Spain's supportive role was not forgotten, and as Spain's problems with ETA soared, the French premier Valéry Giscard d'Estaing might have given Spain the same treatment. The French were also wary of Spain as a state in a transition period that still had to prove itself on several policy terrains and the field of human rights.[31]

---

29 Laws by decree, examples see Jaime Jimenez 2002, pp. 231–237; The juridicial changes in 1980, see Jaime Jimenez 2002, pp. 237–239; Van Dongen 2014, p. 192.

30 The MULC was led by commissary Manuel Ballesteros of the CSP and former head of the Comisaría General de Información (CGI), Encarnacion 2007, p. 962; Jaime Jimenez 2002, pp. 27–28, 95–96; Clavero 2015, pp. 19, 31.

31 Van Dongen 2014, p. 199.

Although the French attitude hindered the Spanish antiterrorist policies, the Spanish government profited from the emerging hesitations within ETA pm. After tensions with a Basque nationalist party EIA, ETA pm wanted to pursue political action during ETA's attacks in 1979 and 1980. This resulted from the ongoing democratic development in Spain and the opportunities the Basque autonomy and its parliament offered to ETA pm. It declared a truce after the coup of 23 February 1981 and decided to disband in September 1982 after which its members reintegrated into Basque society and politics. The social reintegration plan for individual members of ETA pm resulted from an agreement between Interior Minister Rosón and the Basque nationalist party EE. The plan comprised the reduction of prison sentences, dropping of charges and lifting of exiles and led to the reintegration of 200 members of ETA pm into society and into the political party EE.[32]

17.5 Antiterrorist Policy in Spain, 1982–1986

In October 1982 the Partido Socialista Obrero Español (PSOE, Spanish Socialist Worker's Party) won an absolute majority in the general elections, but, as Woodworth observes, it immediately faced an important dilemma. The 1981 coup was only 18 months old. The former establishment of Franco's regime dominated the army, guardia civil and other security forces. It distrusted the democracy and the new allegedly 'marxist' government. A few days after the election of Prime Minister Felipe Gonzalez, ETA assassinated General Victor Lago Roman, commander of the Brunete Armoured Division. The new Minister of Interior, Jose Barrionuevo and deputy Rafael Vera attended his funeral, and so did numerous hard-line army officers who demanded harsh measures against ETA.[33]

After PSOE's victory in October 1982, the new team of the Ministry of the Interior under José Barrionuevo continued the policy line of minister Juan José Rosón. Pressure from the armed forces and the police unions still prevented the implementation of the *Ley de Fuerzas y Cuerpos de Seguridad del Estado* (Law of the forces and state's security forces) in 1982, which comprised the demilitarization of the Policia Nacional Police and its merge with the CSP. It was postponed until the second term of the socialists began in 1986, and implemented with the *Ley Organica de Fuerzas y Cuerpos de Seguridad* (LOFCS, Organic law of the forces and security organizations) the same year.[34]

During the persistent attacks of ETA in early 1983, José Barrionuevo and his team reorganized and developed a new coherent operational strategy, the *Plan Zona Especial Norte* (Plan ZEN, Plan Special Zone North). This plan embraced a multi-angled approach with the aim to isolate ETA from the Basque society.

---

[32] Douglass and Zulaika 1990, p. 247.

[33] Woodworth 2004, p. 171.

[34] Jaime Jimenez 2002, p. 99.

The plan encompassed coordination of policing; improvement of the police's public image and stimulation of the cooperation with Basque citizens; gathering political consensus on counterterrorism; rehabilitation and reinsertion of imprisoned Etarras; and the improvement of the security of police stations and barracks. These measures were not new, but were conferred in a unitary structure. The Plan ZEN reflected continuity and valued the expertise of the two previous Interior Ministers Rosón and Martin Villa who participated in its design.[35]

In order to achieve this plan, it was necessary to politically compromise with the moderate nationalist political parties in the Basque parliament. Initially, the Plan ZEN was badly received by all of them, but its implementation became the strategic axis of the state's coercive response to ETA during the 1980s. During this period various parties in the national parliament at Madrid and the Basque parliament at Vitoria succeeded in reaching an agreement against ETA's violence. These pacts were confirmed between the parties at a national level with the Pact of Madrid in 1987 on the one hand, and by almost all parties with the PSOE-PNV coalition in the Basque parliament in the Pact of Ajuria Enea in 1988 and the community of Navarre in the Pact of Navarre in 1988 on the other hand. The antiterrorist struggle was considered not a matter of dispute between the parties and all political parties would be informed about the antiterrorist struggle.[36]

Meanwhile, and in line with the Plan ZEN, Barrionuevo centralized the state's police actions in the *Secretaria de Estado para la Seguridad.* In this way Barrionuevo adopted the French organizational model for internal security. On a purely technical level, all bodies of information and commands of security agencies were decentralized. The socialist political leader Julen Elgorriaga directed the anti-terrorism program in the Basque Country in coordination with the new Secretary-General and security agencies. At the end of 1983 Barrionuevo further improved the coordination of information and analysis, and the planning and executing any major operation by all security forces and law enforcement bodies. To this end MULC was transformed into the *Gabinete de Informacion y Operaciones Especiales* (GAIOE, Cabinet of Information and Special Operations) and depended on the new chief of police in Bilbao and reduced the presence of the army and the CESID in it. In the GAIOE Barrionuevo gave prevalence to the Guardia Civil to the detriment of the Cuerpo de Policia Nacional as the military structured Corps was easier to control.[37]

In the wake of the Plan ZEN, the Spanish state followed a hardline policy for the next 2 years that held important changes in juridical sphere. In December 1984 Jose Barrionuevo implemented several laws (organic law 9/1984) in order to press charges against persons and organizations that publicly or privately supported radical nationalism. On the basis of these laws the Spanish government could even

[35] Jaime Jimenez 2002, pp. 109–110.

[36] Jaime Jimenez 2002, p. 30; Reinares 2003, p. 61.

[37] Jaime Jimenez 2002, pp. 103–104, 109–110; Reinares 2003, pp. 66–67.

ban political parties, organizations, newspapers and radio stations. These laws also enabled house searches without prior judicial authorization and preventive custody *incommunicado* until 10 days. However, Basque political parties undid all clauses of organic law 9/1984 via the Constitutional court and Spanish parliament in 1987 and *incommunicado* arrest (organic laws 3/1988 and 4/1988 25-5) was brought back from 10 to 5 days. Specialized courts focused on ETA's financial structures, social organizations and political branches.[38]

During the first two years of Barrionuevo's term, the previous policies on reintegration of Martin Vila and Roson began to work, which also formed an integral part of the Plan ZEN. The number of ETA prisoners in Spanish prisons diminished from 485 in October 1982 to 300 in January 1984, because of the state's compromises with old ETA pm members for the first time. However, the tough antiterrorist policy and the restrictive measures again led to a rise to 400 prisoners in December 1984. Meanwhile, Barrionuevo started another reintegration program in 1984: applicants could sign a statement in which they rejected the armed struggle. But ETA took countermeasures to control its imprisoned members and to neutralize Barrionuevo's efforts. Two leading members were killed that wanted to reintegrate, and ETA provided financial and social support to the family members of the prisoners through the organization Pro-Gestoria Amnestia.[39]

The implementation of the Plan ZEN weakened ETA. Two important leaders were arrested at the beginning of a series of successful police raids, which led to ETA's loss of operational expertise and accuracy in its attacks. The improved protection of surveillance vehicles and bases and other measures of the national police and the civil guard forced ETA to find other targets outside the Basque Country. This expansion of range was noticed by the Guardia Civil, which shifted from a territorial response to more central coordinated actions.[40] Terrorist activities significantly decreased during the years 1984-1986, from 180 to 128 attacks. However, starting in 1985, ETA conducted more indiscriminate attacks. Yet, the annual number of fatalities remained at high levels due to the use of car bombs by the ETA commandos. The absence of data on these car bomb attacks and their impact on public opinion prompted the Minister of Interior to order GAIOE to focus on the notorious ETA commando Madrid. Operation *Caza del Gato* achieved its partial dismantlement in 1986. Instead of a widespread use of force, the security forces now practiced discriminate actions in order to bring arrested

[38] In January 1987 a part of this antiterrorist Law became automatically outdated, and the remnant was withdrawn in November 1987. This relaxation might also have appeased the moderate nationalist Basque parties for the Pact of Ajuria-Enea, Jaime Jimenez 2002, pp. 28–30, 245–247, 253; Van Dongen 2014, pp. 197–198.

[39] Douglas and Zulaika 1990, p. 251; The dispersal policy led in 1989 to imprisoned Etarras spread over Spain far from the Basque Country and resulted in more reintegration under Gonzalez between 1989 and 1995; Aznar abandoned the reintegration program in 2002, Van Dongen 2014, pp. 211–214.

[40] Jaime Jimenez 2002, p. 97.

Etarras to trial. Relatively fewer people were arrested for gathering information and relatively more for terrorist related crimes.[41] It may be interpreted as a result of an improved and more closely coordinated antiterrorist intelligence.

17.6 The Subversive Campaign in the French Basque Country, 1983–1986

The safe haven of ETA in Southwestern France was a major problem that fell beyond the scope and means of Plan ZEN. Key to the problem was the French refusal to arrest ETA terrorists or to extradite them from French territory. This refusal was, as Wieviorka notes, related to a silent status quo between the French government and ETA. In it, the French sanctuary policy towards ETA was confirmed by a trade-off over *Iparretarak*, the minor counterpart of ETA that operated in the French Basque Country since 1973. After ETA and *Iparretarak* came into conflict in 1981, the first chose to maintain good relations with the French police. That same year ETA refrained from violent actions in France and in exchange for a continued refuge on French territory *Iparretarak* was sacrificed.[42]

The goals of the Gonzalez administration now became, as Woodworth clearly states: "first keeping the military and police on-side with democracy, striking ETA hard, and pressuring France to crack down on the terrorists in their safe haven".[43] The CESID hired mercenaries for a subversive counterterrorist campaign against ETA. French and Algerian veterans from the *Organisation de l'Armée Sécrète* formed the *Grupos Antiterroristas de Liberación* (GAL, Anti-terrorist Liberation Groups), which enjoyed the silent support of the Interior Ministry and the police forces. Undercover civil guards started the campaign by kidnapping and assassinating two supposedly Etarras. GAL

---

41 Since 1985 the commando Madrid placed car bombs on the routes of military personnel and civil guards. In 1986 it committed 22 assassinations. In July 1986, three members of the commando Madrid were detained, that led to more detentions, although three members succeeded to flee; In total ETA killed 37 victims in 1985 and 40 in 1986, which counted 148 and 128 attacks, Dominguez Iribarren 1998, pp. 223, 259; Jaime Jimenez 2002, pp. 91–92, 97, 108–109; Oneto 2014; Van Dongen 2014, p. 185, 195, 202.

42 French antiterrorist actions in the 1970s and the first half of the 1980s were led by two principles. First, the French government regarded domestic terrorism as subversive crime to be combated with law enforcement and preventive police infiltration, surveillance and research. Second, the French government regarded neutrality towards international terrorism, mainly of non-state actors and states in the Middle East, on the condition they did not aim at French interests or deviate French policy. This sanctuary doctrine required silent communication with terrorist movements, secrecy and refrained from international cooperation against terrorism. The doctrine became eroded in the 1980s by an increasing number of terrorist groups that targeted France, and by leaks to the press, which started to influence public opinion and judges. However, the French government did not fully abandon its doctrine and governed dealings with ETA. After series of counterraids by the French *Recherche Action Information Dissuassion* (RAID) and the arrest of its leader in 1988 Iparretarak seemed to be dismantled, Wieviorka 1991, pp. 158–161.

43 Woodworth 2004, p. 173.

continued with kidnappings, targeted killings, car bombs and shooting and bombing bars in the French Basque Country.[44] From its first action on 4 December 1983 until its last in July 1987 the GAL successively killed 27 persons and wounded 80 persons in the French Basque Country. These were ETA members and leaders, but also many civilians without any ties with ETA.

What were the results? On the one hand, the terrorist activity of the GAL strengthened ETA politically. ETA used GAL's assassinations to persuade the Basques that the new autonomy and institutions in democratic Spain were nothing but a continuation of the former *franquista* repression. Although its intention failed, ETA incited radical nationalist Basques to join its ranks. Woodworth concludes that GAL's campaign did not destroy ETA. Although ETA's losses to the GAL campaign were severe, it continued to kill 40 victims annually, and in 1987, when GAL ended its activities, ETA even killed 54 victims. On the other hand, the GAL activity pressured the French government to end the sanctuary policy towards ETA, whose existence was the cause of the attacks in the French Basque Country. It gained the Gonzalez government the cooperation of France that proved to be essential in the combat against ETA. The GAL stopped its brutal attacks once France shifted its policy towards ETA. Since 1984 the French first deported ETA members to countries as Gabon as they first refused to extradite them to Spain, but since 1988 honoured Spanish requests for immediate expulsion. In 1986 they started police actions, made arrests, and executed counter-raids against ETA's infrastructure.[45]

17.7 Anti-terrorism and the French Authorities 1986–1996

After PSOE's second victory in 1986, a first important reform was that the Policia Nacional, Guardia Civil and armed forces were brought under parliamentary control (organic law 2/1986) according to the Constitution of 1978. Second, minister Jose Barrionuevo outlined the internal security sector according French example in order to further improve antiterrorist coordination. A third change was the dissolution of the political police CSP, a silent wish of several Interior Ministers since the Police Act of 1978. Fourth, Barrionuevo also changed the top level within his ministry, very particularly within the area of counter-terrorism, by replacing military officers for civilian PSOE members. Fifth, he reformed police practices and the curricula of the police academies. Sixth, the CGI further specialized into four

---

[44] In the second half of the 1990s the leak of secret documents of the CESID led to court trials on the GAL operations. These became associated with Prime Minister Felipe Gonzalez, and especially Interior Minister Jose Barrionuevo and former Interior Minister Rafael Vera of the Suárez administration, Woodworth 2001, pp. 46–47, 76–77; Woodworth 2004, p. 173; Wieviorka 1991, p. 172; Encarnacion 2007, p. 964; Llera and Leonisio 2015, pp. 146–147; Van Dongen 2014, p. 191.

[45] A first sign of it came already in 1984: three ETA militants were handed over to Spain, Wieviorka 1991, pp. 163–164, 168–169; Cettina 2003, pp. 80, 82–83.

brigades. The first brigade analyzed and coordinated information for the other three brigades. The second brigade centred on operations against terrorist groups, primarily ETA. The third *Brigada de Interior* concentrated on far-right groups and liaisoned with the military intelligence and the fourth *Brigada de Exterior* liaisoned on an international level with other police corps preferably on antiterrorist matters.[46]

The number of fatalities rose in 1986 to 40 persons. The number of fatal victims of ETA was 50 in 1987, and among these were 34 civilians. Between 1988 and 1992 the number of killed stabilized at more than 26 annually, except for 1991 when it climbed to 45. After that ETA's armed activities substantially declined in the 1990s. During this phase, the antiterrorist policy continued the previous one.[47] In these years the Guardia Civil prevailed in the field compared to the national police. A new element, however, was that the Basque police or *Ertzaintza* started to combat ETA as well. According to Jaime Jimenez the effectiveness of the security agencies had raised to a high level since the early years of the PSOE.[48]

Various combined counter-raids of the French police and the Guardia Civil, providing intelligence, in Southwestern France in 1985 and 1986 resulted in the arrest of three ETA leaders. Financial support for ETA deteriorated after the capture in Sokoa in 1986 of important documentation in Sokoa on the organization of ETA and its members. This operation and its aftermath provided the Spanish and French security forces and Spanish judicial apparatus with in-depth information on the financial channels of ETA. Captured ETA members were deported and since 1988 extradited to France. In April 1986 an ETA leader was arrested. In November 1986 an ETA command centre in Hendaye was dismantled by a French police counter raid, which captured eleven Etarras, money and weapons. The French police arrested in September 1987 an ETA commander with documents that led to another 104 arrests. Logistical and propaganda chefs were arrested too.[49]

The loss of experienced leaders may have brought ETA to shift its focus in three ways: the option of car bomb attacks in the whole of Spain, cautious negotiations with the Spanish state and the quest for a political way out through cooperation with the moderate Basque political parties. In November 1986 ETA and the Spanish state started negotiations in Algiers. During these conversations the Spanish government aimed for an end to the conflict before 1992 as it hosted the

---

[46] Jaime Jimenez 2002, pp. 100, 103, 105–107; Van Dongen 2014, pp. 194–195.

[47] Dominguez Iribarren 1998, p. 223; Jaime Jimenez 2002, p. 32.

[48] Between 1982 and 1989 the part of CSP/CNP in arrests, and arrests leading to imprisonment, declined from 70 to 30 % and 70 to 9 % respectively. Guardia Civil in 1989 arrested more than 60 % of all suspected terrorists, and 58 % arrests that went to prison. Meanwhile, during this same year, the *Ertzaintza* arrested 8 people, of which 6 entered in prison. Thus, the role of the *Ertzaintza* increased as it became more involved in the fight against terrorism. This was also a result of the Interior Minister's decision to place a civilian of the Guardia Civil at the command of The *Secretaria de Estado para la Seguridad*, that diminished the CNP's competences, Jaime Jimenez 2002, p. 112.

[49] Van Dongen 2014, pp. 200–201.

Olympic games in Barcelona and the World Exhibition in Sevilla. ETA had reduced its five point KAS alternative to three points: self-determination of the Basque population, amnesty of all ETA prisoners and inclusion of Navarra into Basque Country. Whereas the state wanted ETA to stop its attacks before commencement of the talks, ETA first wanted the state's compliance to its KAS alternative before it would stop its attacks. The conversations failed in 1986, although contacts were maintained until April 1989. The results were mixed. The Gonzalez government hoped that a truce could create internal divisions between hardliners (Marxists) and moderates (Nationalists) within ETA, but in reality ETA concluded in these meetings that its attrition strategy was succeeding and raised the intensity of its actions in order to accumulate more bargaining power.[50]

ETA reopened its campaign with a car bomb, its weapon of choice, under the *Hipercor* supermarket in Barcelona in 1987, that killed 15 and wounded 38 people. In July 1987 ETA car bombed a *casa cuartel* in Zaragoza were families of the Guardia Civil lived and killed 11 people. Both attacks led to public outcries and massive public demonstrations. They formed one of the factors for all moderate Basque political parties, except the HB and EA, to sign the Pact of Madrid, and the Pact of Ajuria-Enea, that isolated ETA politically. Nevertheless, ETA's other commandos persevered and in 1990 and 1991 car bomb attacks followed against *casas cuartel* in Sabadell and in Vic and a special campaign targeted several Spanish embassies and consulates in Europe.[51]

During and after Algiers, the Spanish government pursued a determined anti-terrorism policy, not only in Spain but also in cooperation with France in Iparralde, where ETA had its main basis. It helped that the new Interior Minister José Luis Corcuera did not disturb the Spanish state's security sector with new reforms and maintained the French-Spanish anti-terrorism course of his predecessor Barrionuevo. Since 1987, the capture of hide-outs, command posts, and caches of finances and arms nearly completely destroyed ETA's organization. The regular finances of the ETA increasingly diminished. Its kidnappings, and significant contributions of the ransoms, disappeared, because they lacked popular support and ETA lacked skilled personnel to carry out these actions safely. ETA's revolutionary tax on Basque firms and organizations, a form of extortion, also dropped after the successful Operation *Easo* of the Basque police, the *Ertzaintza*, on 29 January 1992.[52]

Exactly 2 months later, on 29 March 1992 and after thorough preparatory intelligence of the Guardia Civil, the special French anti-terrorist force RAID (*Recherche Assistance Intervention Dissuasion*) successfully executed a counter-raid in Bidart. The RAID arrested the cupola of ETA, three important and experienced leaders. A chain of subsequent arrests followed, including two commanders responsible for finances and arms. To the dismay of imprisoned ETA leaders, four

[50] Dominguez Iribarren 1998, p. 259; Woodworth 2004, pp. 172–175; Van Dongen 2014, pp. 215–217.

[51] Van Dongen 2014, pp. 186, 217.

[52] ETA had already been encountering significant financial problems since 1985, Van Dongen 2014, p. 204; Jaime Jimenez 2002, pp. 110–111.

seconds-in-command were arrested too. The counter-raid thwarted the preparations of a terrorist offensive against the Olympic Games in Barcelona and the World Fair in Sevilla in 1992.[53]

The raid on Bidart had two long-term effects. First, it proved the success of intensive French-Spanish cooperation on anti-terrorism. In December 1993 premiers Felipe Gonzalez and François Mitterrand signed the first anti-terrorist agreement between France and Spain, whereby France promised to systematically extradite ETA members to Spain. In June 1994, agreements were signed to hinder ETA presence in the French Basque Country. Second, the raid diminished ETA's manpower, expertise, capabilities and disrupted logistics. Younger and less experienced members had to take over. ETA's operational capabilities continued to decrease during the 1990s. As a result of the actions of Spanish and French security forces, ETA became more detached from its supporters and its level of violence decreased.[54]

In the years 1989–1996 the Spanish government began to disperse imprisoned ETA members to prisons at a far distance from the Basque Country. This dispersal policy aimed to separate imprisoned Etarras and their families from ETA and its supporting collective, the Gestoras Pro-Amnestia, in order to facilitate a dialogue between the prisoners and the state. In this way, the state encouraged repentant or disgruntled Etarras to leave ETA and reintegrate into society. The dispersal policy reacted on ETA's earlier countermeasures to the reintegration programs. In turn, the ETA tried to counter this policy by attacking some of its former members, and also by attacking and kidnapping prison officers.[55]

17.8 After Bidart, 1992–Present

After Bidart, the security structure and police forces underwent several minor and major changes under Interior Ministers Antoni Asunción and Juan Alberto Belloch. Asunción's main decision was that he severed all contacts with ETA, since results were nil, and he clearly broke with the policy line of the late 1980s.[56] In 1995, the PSOE and Juan Alberto Belloch merged the Ministries of Interior and Justice into one ministry and separated the tasks of intelligence and operations. Belloch also dispensed with the GAIOE as during his term the GAIOE, CESID and the former Interior Minister Barrionuevo became discredited. A leak of CESID documents to the press revealed their involvement in the GAL campaign.

---

53 *El Pais*, 30 March 1992; Van Dongen 2014, p. 203.

54 Van Dongen 2014, pp. 181, 188, 201, 204.

55 Alonso 2011, p. 701.

56 It led to Rafael Vera's resignation, who had designed and implemented the governmental counterterrorism policy in the past decade, Jaime Jimenez 2002, pp. 32–33, 114–115.

In the ensuing scandal and juridical process the self-cleaning ability of the Spanish democratic state probably appealed to a larger group of moderate Basques.[57]

After the electoral victory of the *Partido Popular* (PP, Popular Party) in 1996, the Aznar government introduced a hard-line antiterrorist policy and corresponding reforms. He undid the merger of the Interior Ministry and the Ministry of Justice and almost all of Belloch's other changes. Excellent relations with France secured the continued extradition of ETA suspects and the combined operations against ETA hideouts in Southwestern France. The Interior Ministry, instead of the Ministry of Justice, supervised the prisons and the dispersal policy for ETA prisoners.[58]

Already a year before the 1996 elections, ETA launched high profile attacks on PSOE and PP politicians, including a failed bomb attack on Aznar in 1995. That same year, it also attempted to assassinate king Juan Carlos on Mallorca, and abducted and murdered the Basque PP politician Miguel Angel Blanco in 1997. Especially Blanco's assassination led to rallies of abhorred millions in order to end the conflict. But to the contrary, increasing tensions between the PP, PSOE and Basque nationalist parties broke the consensus of the Pact of Ajuria-Enea of 1988.[59] For its part, and realizing its isolated position, ETA and *Herri Batasuna* tempted and pressured the PNV and other Basque nationalist parties into joining the Pact of Lizarra.[60] Whereas these Basque nationalist parties hoped for ETA's pacification and reintegration, ETA tried to persuade the PNV to abandon the Basque and Spanish parliaments. When it failed in 1999, ETA left the Lizarra Pact and resumed hostilities.[61]

The Aznar government strengthened its hard-line course in two ways. First, in December 2000, the PP and PSOE agreed to lead the PNV back to the Ajuria-Enea

---

[57] The tasks of intelligence and operations were attached to the CGI and the CGPJ respectively, according to the renewed adaption of the French model for state security. At a regional level the *Unidad Territorial de Informacion* (UTI) and the *Unidad Territorial Antiterrorista* (UTA) clustered intelligence and operational tasks for both the Guardia Civil and national police. The GAIOE functions passed to the CGPJ, manned by national police and Guardia Civil, and the CGI became a general civilian intelligence service, Jaime Jimenez 2002, pp. 115–117; Woodworth 2001, pp. 186, 187; For information on the French model for state security, see Cettina 2003.

[58] The Interior Ministry installed the Secretary of State for Security as the main body for coordination and control of the anti-terrorism policy. It held two Directorates for the national police and the Guardia Civil and reunited intelligence and operations organizations under the secretary general's supervision. Again the Guardia Civil maintained its prominent role in Spain's anti-terrorism policy as the corps clearly benefited from its new commander, a prominent PP defense politician in the national parliament, to the detriment of the national police, whose commander was a security councilor in Valencia, Jaime Jimenez 2002, pp. 118–119.

[59] *El Pais*, 10 August 1995; Garza 1998, pp. 93, 97; One of the issues was that they diametrically disagreed over the question of amnesty and reintegration of imprisoned ETA assassins, Shepard 2002, p. 63; Jaime Jimenez 2002, p. 33; Van Dongen 2014, pp. 184–185.

[60] The Pacto de Lizarra is also called Pacto de Estella, see Reinares 2003, p. 61; Approximately 20 % of ETA actions now targeted journalists, politicians, academics and lawyers, Encarnacion 2007, p. 968; Van Dongen 2014, pp. 187–188, 204.

[61] The first move of ETA was a failed attack on the Torre Picasso in Madrid in 1999, 2 years in advance of 9/11, Celso 2006, pp. 130–133; Van Dongen 2014, pp. 216, 219–221.

Pact and to abstain from negotiations with ETA. Second, Aznar banned *Herri Batasuna* from the Basque Parliament in 2002 and declared it illegal. However, on 11 March 2004 Islamist radicals bombed several commuter trains and stations in Madrid, causing 191 deaths and 1755 wounded. Aznar wrongly accused ETA of this gravest terrorist attack in the nation's history, which contributed to a PSOE victory in the general elections a few days later. PSOE resumed talks with ETA, but further continued PP's hardline policy. During the talks ETA announced a ceasefire in March 2006, but when these conversations broke down, ETA bombed Madrid Airport Barrajas at the end of the same year. The Spanish government and ETA, unlike the belligerent parties in Northern Ireland, never reached consensus about a political solution to the conflict and always maintained two agendas.[62]

The last years show that the Spanish state has pursued to dismantle ETA commandos and the number of attacks has diminished. Several of these attacks, including a car bomb killing 11 young civil guards during their training on traffic control in Madrid, have met widespread disbelief and hostility among the population. Several political scientists and historians note a loss of the will to fight. Imprisoned ETA commanders wrote letters that it was time to acknowledge failure in 2004 and called to shift to political action in order to gain more popular support in 2010, acts that ETA considered as treason. Nevertheless, ETA publicly offered a ceasefire in September 2010, abandoned its arms on 10 January 2011 and again on October 2011, but the PP resolutely refused to negotiate. Yet, the Guardia Civil and national police in Spain and their counterparts in France have continued to cooperate intensively in their round-up of tens of Etarras, their hide-outs and arms caches.[63]

17.9 Conclusion

The result of this tentative case study indicates that the Spanish counterterrorism against ETA paralleled with a gradual demilitarization of the Guardia Civil and the national police. At first, Franco's militarized security forces were drawn into ETA's action-repression-action spiral. It resulted in a major crisis for the subsequent transition government that started this process in 1978, but it was not until 1986 before true demilitarization was realized. In this transition period the Suárez and Calvo-Sotelo governments introduced specialized antiterrorist units for its operations and specialized coordination bodies for its intelligence). The Gonzalez government started a comprehensive approach on anti-terrorism, which included the Plan ZEN addressing juridical means, repentance programs and coordination of intelligence and operations and started internal negotiations with the Basque parties and external negotiations with ETA. The government's dark page in the

62 Reinares 2003, p. 63; Van Dongen 2014, pp. 189–191; Barton 2009, p. 268; On the Madrid bombings and its aftermath focuses, Reinares 2009.

63 Alonso 2014, pp. 232–235; Harmon 2012, p. 590; Reinares 2009, pp. 369–370; Van Dongen 2014, pp. 222–223, 226.

contemporary history of Spain remains the subversive counterterrorist campaign of the GAL in Southwestern France, a true continuation of the subversive activities of ultra-right bands in the final years of Franco's era and during the *Transicion*. Nevertheless, its effect was an enduring French-Spanish cooperation of tracking down ETA's resources and extraditing their men and commanders.

Evidently, the Spanish security forces gradually evolved from using largely kinetic force during the Franco era against ETA to the use of more sophisticated and more non-kinetic weapons as intelligence, juridical measures, political pacts and international cooperation. As the Spanish state's use of force became more accurate and sophisticated, ETA's use of force became more inaccurate, less sophisticated and less effective. Against the security forces that liaisoned, gained more protection and took the initiative through counter-raids with specialized operative and intelligence units, ETA gradually has lost its ability to rebuild and replace its leadership, commandos and resources.

The gradual demilitarization of the Spanish security forces during the years 1976–1992 can also be compared with the current findings and theory of Lutterbeck for the European security forces. A comparison with his five tendencies can also reveal several lessons learned. First, the Spanish government steered their police forces to resort to unity of effort in intelligence and operations. Second, the role of Spanish law enforcement and that of foreign intelligence, for example of the Guardia Civil for operations in France, both gained in importance, but whether these converged remains a topic for further research. Both factors reveal that the antiterrorist programs of the Spanish state and security forces may have benefited from a comprehensive approach as described above. Third, the Spanish state and the Guardia Civil clearly orientated on inter- and transnational policies in their cooperation with the French state and police forces. It emphasizes that a state fighting transnational terrorism needs intensive international cooperation and can play a truly decisive role. Fourth, however, the Spanish military forces did not become involved into internal security, whereas, fifth, the role of the Guardia Civil, and later the *Ertzaintza*, in the Spanish anti-terrorism policies and programmes grew compared to other police forces. Consequently, the majority of these tendencies match with Lutterbeck's results. Thus, this case study may demonstrate that the merger of internal and external security of Spain and the shifting roles for its security forces already occurred in response to transnational terrorism before 1989.

Acknowledgments I would like to thank Floribert Baudet, Wim Klinkert and an anonymous reviewer for their valuable comments on earlier versions of this chapter.

References

Alonso R (2011) Why do terrorists stop? Analysing why ETA members abandon or continue with terrorism. Stud Conflict Terror 34:696–716

Alonso A (2014) La lucha contra el terrorismo en la estrategia de seguridad nacional 2013. UNISCI Discuss Pap 35:223–248

Anderson M (2011) In thrall to political change. Police and gendarmerie in France. Oxford University Press, Oxford
Barton S (2009) A history of Spain, 2nd edn. Palgrave MacMillan, Basingstoke
Bernecker WL (1998) Monarchy and democracy: the political role of king Juan Carlos in the Spanish transition. J Contemp Hist 33–1:65–84
Bigo D (2000) When two become one: internal and external securitisations in Europe. In: Kelstrup M, Williams M (eds) International relations theory and the politics of European integration. Power, security and community. Routledge, Londen, pp 171–204
Buesa M, Baumert T (2013) Untangling ETA's finance: an in-depth analysis of the Basque terrorist's economic network and the money it handles. Def Peace Econ 24:317–338
Celso AN (2006) Spain's dual security dilemma: strategic challenges of Basque and Islamist terror during the Aznar and Zapatero eras. Mediterr Q 17:121–141
Cerdán Alenda M, Rubio Campaña A (2004) Lobo: el topo que consiguió la caída de ETA. Debolsillo
Cettina N (2003) The French approach: vigour and vigilance. In: Van Leeuwen M (ed) Confronting terrorism. Kluwer Law International, Alphen aan de Rijn, pp 71–94
Clark RP (1984) The Basque insurgents. ETA, 1952–1980. University of Wisconscin Press, Madison
Clavero AG (2015) Unidades de élite españolas. Tropas de élite, Tikal Ediciones, Madrid
Dominguez Iribarren F (1998) ETA: estrategia organizativa y actuaciones 1978–1992. Universidad del País Vasco/Euskal Herriko Unibertsitateko Argitalpen Zerbitzua, Bilbao, Servicio Editorial
Douglass WA, Zulaika J (1990) On the interpretation of terrorist violence: ETA and the Basque political process. Comparative studies in society and history 32:238–257
Easton M, Den Boer M, Janssens J, Moelker R, Vanderbeken T (2010) Blurring military and police roles. Eleven International Publishing, The Hague
El Pais 30 March 1992, 10 August 1995
Encarnacion OG (2007) Democracy and dirty wars in Spain. Hum Rights Q 29:950–972
Garza C (1998) Spain's mobilization against terrorism: the death of Miguel Angel Blanco. Int J World Peace 15:91–99
Gerwarth R, Haupt H-G (2007) Internationalising historical research on terrorist movements in twentieth-century Europe. Eur Rev Hist: Revue europèene d'histoire 14:275–281
Harmon CC (2012) Spain's ETA terrorist group is dying. Orbis 56:588–607
Heiberg M (2007) ETA, redeeming an arcadia lost. In: Heiberg M, O'Leary B, Tirman J (eds) Terror, insurgency, and the state: ending protracted conflicts. University of Pennsylvania Press, Philadelphia, pp 19–49
Jaime Jimenez O (2002) Policía, terrorismo y cambio político en España, 1976–1996. Tirant lo blanch y Universidad de Burgos, Valencia
Jaime Jimenez O, Reinares F (1998) The policing of social protest in Spain: from dictatorship to democracy. In: Della Porta D, Reiter H (eds) Policing protest: the control of mass demonstrations in western democracies. University of Minnesota Press, Minneapolis, pp 166–187
Llcra FJ, Leonisio R (2015) Los secuestros de ETA y sus organizaciones afines, 1970–1997: una base de datos. Revista Española de Ciencia Política 37:141–160
Lutterbeck D (2005) Blurring the dividing line: the convergence of internal and external security in Western Europe. Eur Secur 14:231–253
Lutterbeck D (2013) The paradox of gendarmeries: between expansion, demilitarization and dissolution. SSR paper 8 DCAF
Monar J (2008) The European Union as a collective actor in the fight against post-9/11 terrorism: progress and problems of a primarily cooperative approach. In: Gani M, Mathew P (eds) Fresh perspectives on the 'war on terror'. ANU E Press, Canberra, pp 209–234
Olmeda JA (2007) War on terrorism: the Spanish experience, 1939-2006. In: Bowen WH, Alvarez JE (eds) A military history of modern Spain: from the Napoleonic era to the international war on terror. Praeger, Westport, pp 161–178
Oneto J (2014) Operación: Caza del Gato. Hacia el final de ETA, Leer-e/ibuku

Reinares F (2003) Democratization and state responses to protracted terrorism in Spain. In: Van den Leeuwen M (ed) Confronting terrorism: European experiences, threat perceptions, and policies. Brill Academic Publishers, Leiden, pp 57–70

Reinares F (2009) After Madrid bombings: internal security reforms and prevention of global terrorism in Spain. Stud Conflict Terror 32:367–388

Shepard WS (2002) The ETA: Spain fights Europe's last active terrorist group. Mediterr Quarter 13:54–68

Tusell J (2007) Spain: From Dictatorship to Democracy: 1939 to the Present. Blackwell Publishing, Malden

Van Dongen TW (2014) The science of fighting terrorism. The relation between terrorist actor type and counterterrorism effectiveness. Universiteit Leiden, Leiden

Wieviorka M (1991) France faced with terrorism. Terrorism 14:157–170

Woodworth P (2001) Dirty war, clean hands. ETA, the GAL and Spanish democracy. Cork University Press, Cork

Woodworth P (2004) The war against terrorism: the Spanish experience from ETA to al-Qaeda. I J Iber Stud 17:169–182

List of Contributors

H. van den As is Senior Lecturer in special operations, asymmetric warfare, and principles of resistance at the Joint Special Operations University, Tampa, USA. e-mail: h.vandenas@home.nl

Maj G.C.H. Bakx M.Sc. is Lecturer in Leadership and Behaviour at the Faculty of Military Sciences of the Netherlands Defence Academy, Netherlands Defence Academy, Breda, The Netherlands. e-mail: gch.bakx.02@mindef.nl

Prof. dr. R. Beeres is Professor of Defence Economics at the Faculty of Military Sciences of the Netherlands Defence Academy, Netherlands Defence Academy, Breda, The Netherlands. e-mail: rjm.beeres@mindef.nl

Dr. T. Bijlsma is Assistant Professor of Military Management and Organization Studies at the Faculty of Military Sciences of the Netherlands Defence Academy, Netherlands Defence Academy, Breda, The Netherlands. e-mail: t.bijlsma.01@mindef.nl

Prof. dr. M.T.I.B. Bollen is Professor of Civil-Military Interaction at the Faculty of Military Sciences of the Netherlands Defence Academy, Netherlands Defence Academy, Breda, The Netherlands. e-mail: mtib.bollen.01@mindef.nl

Dr. C.J.M. Broers is Senior Specialist Professional Skills GHOR at Safety Region Noord-Holland Noord, Safety Region Noord-Holland Noord, Alkmaar, The Netherlands. e-mail: cbroers@vrnhn.nl

Dr. T.P. op den Buijs is Assistant Professor of Human Resource Management and Military Leadership at the Faculty of Military Sciences of the Netherlands Defence Academy, Netherlands Defence Academy, Breda, The Netherlands. e-mail: tp.od.buijs@mindef.nl

R. Beeres et al. (eds.), *NL ARMS Netherlands Annual Review of Military Studies 2016*, NL ARMS, DOI 10.1007/978-94-6265-135-7

J.J.D. Heeren-Bogers M.Sc. is Assistant Professor of Defence Accounting Control and Economics at the Faculty of Military Sciences of the Netherlands Defence Academy, Netherlands Defence Academy, Breda, The Netherlands. e-mail: JJD.Heeren.Bogers@mindef.nl

Dr. P.J.M.D. Essens is Director of the Centre of Expertise Human Resource Management & Organizational Behaviour at the University of Groningen. University of Groningen, Groningen, The Netherlands. e-mail: p.j.m.d.essens@rug.nl

Dr. ir. N. Faber is Associate Professor of Military Logistics and Supply Chain Management at the Faculty of Military Sciences of the Netherlands Defence Academy. Netherlands Defence Academy, Breda, The Netherlands. e-mail: n.faber.01@mindef.nl

Prof. dr. P.C. van Fenema is Professor of Military Logistics at the Faculty of Military Sciences of the Netherlands Defence Academy, Netherlands Defence Academy, Breda, The Netherlands. e-mail: pc.v.fenema@mindef.nl

H. de Jong M.Sc. M.A. is Project Manager of EDUCEN, a European project on culture and disaster at the Faculty of Military Sciences of the Netherlands Defence Academy, Netherlands Defence Academy, Breda, The Netherlands. e-mail: h.d.jong.19@mindef.nl

Dr. M.A.G. de Jong is Lecturer in Military History and Strategy at the Faculty of Military Sciences of the Netherlands Defence Academy, Netherlands Defence Academy, Breda, The Netherlands. e-mail: MAG.d.Jong.01@mindef.nl

J.P. Kalkman M.Sc. is a Ph.D. Student of Civil-Military Collaboration at the Faculty of Military Sciences of the Netherlands Defence Academy, the Department of Organization Sciences at VU University and the department of Defence, Security and Safety of TNO, Netherlands Defence Academy, Breda, The Netherlands; Vrije Universiteit, Amsterdam, The Netherlands; TNO, Soesterberg, The Netherlands. e-mail: jp.kalkman@mindef.nl

LtCol A.C.M. van Kampen MTL is lecturer in military logistics at the Faculty of Military Sciences of the Netherlands Defence Academy, Netherlands Defence Academy, Breda, The Netherlands. e-mail: acm.v.kampen@mindef.nl

Dr. E.H. Kramer is Associate Professor Human Factors and Systems Safety at the Faculty of Military Sciences of the Netherlands Defence Academy, Netherlands Defence Academy, Breda, The Netherlands. e-mail: fj.kramer@mindef.nl

René Moelker is Associate Professor of Armed Forces and Society at the Faculty of Military Sciences of the Netherlands Defence Academy, Netherlands Defence Academy, Breda, The Netherlands. e-mail: r.moelker.01@mindef.nl

Prof. dr. E. Molleman is Professor of Human Resource Management & Organizational Behaviour at the Faculty of Economics and Business of the University of Groningen, University of Groningen, Groningen, The Netherlands. e-mail: h.b.m.molleman@rug.nl

M. Moorkamp, M.Sc. is Lecturer in Security Management at Saxion University of Applied Sciences in Apeldoorn, The Netherlands and Researcher at the University of Twente, Enschede, The Netherlands. e-mail: m.moorkamp@saxion.nl

Dr. P.C.J. Neuteboom is Research Fellow at the Faculty of Military Sciences of the Netherlands Defence Academy, Netherlands Defence Academy, Breda, The Netherlands. e-mail: peter.neuteboom@ziggo.nl

Prof. dr. J.M. Nyce is Professor in Cultural Anthropology at the Department of Anthropology of Ball State University. Ball State University, Muncie (IN), United States of America. e-mail: jnyce@bsu.edu

CDRE Prof. dr. F.P.B. Osinga is Professor of Military Operational Sciences at the Faculty of Military Sciences of the Netherlands Defence Academy, Netherlands Defence Academy, Breda, The Netherlands. e-mail: FPB.Osinga@mindef.nl

Dr. S.J.H. Rietjens is Associate Professor of Information Management at the Faculty of Military Sciences of the Netherlands Defence Academy, Netherlands Defence Academy, Breda, The Netherlands. e-mail: sjh.rietjens.01@mindef.nl

Prof. dr. Joseph Soeters is Professor of Management and Organization Studies at the Faculty of Military Sciences of the Netherlands Defence Academy and Tilburg University, Netherlands Defence Academy, Breda, The Netherlands. e-mail: JMML.Soeters@mindef.nl

Dr. S. Täuber is Associate Professor of Human Resource Management & Organizational Behaviour at the Faculty of Economics and Business of the University of Groningen. University of Groningen, Groningen, The Netherlands. e-mail: s.tauber@rug.nl

Prof. dr. ir. E. Theunissen is Professor of Avionics at the Faculty of Military Sciences of the Netherlands Defence Academy, Netherlands Defence Academy, Den Helder, The Netherlands. e-mail: e.theunissen@mindef.nl

Dr. E. de Waard is Associate Professor of Strategic Organizing and Change at the Faculty of Military Sciences of the Netherlands Defence Academy, Netherlands Defence Academy, Breda, The Netherlands. e-mail: ej.d.waard.01@mindef.nl

F.L. Wermser M.Sc. is a Ph.D. Candidate in Human Resource Management & Organizational Behaviour at the Faculty of Economics and Business of the University of Groningen. University of Groningen, Groningen, The Netherlands. e-mail: f.l.wermser@rug.nl

Dr. J.J. Wolbers is Postdoctoral Researcher on disaster governance at the Department of Organization Science at the Faculty of Social Sciences of the Vrije Universiteit Amsterdam, Vrije Universiteit Amsterdam, Amsterdam, The Netherlands. e-mail: j.j.wolbers@vu.nl

MIX
Papier aus verantwortungsvollen Quellen
Paper from responsible sources
FSC® C105338

If you have any concerns about our products,
you can contact us on
ProductSafety@springernature.com

In case Publisher is established outside the EU,
the EU authorized representative is:
Springer Nature Customer Service Center GmbH
Europaplatz 3, 69115 Heidelberg, Germany

Printed by Libri Plureos GmbH
in Hamburg, Germany